Modeling Longitudinal and Multilevel Data

Practical Issues, Applied Approaches and Specific Examples

Modeling Longitudinal and Multilevel Data

Practical Issues, Applied Approaches and Specific Examples

Edited by

Todd D. Little
Yale University

Kai U. Schnabel
Jürgen Baumert
Max Planck Institute for Human Development

LEA LAWRENCE ERLBAUM ASSOCIATES, PUBLISHERS
2000   Mahwah, New Jersey   London

Lawrence Erlbaum Associates, Inc., Publishers
10 Industrial Avenue
Mahwah, NJ 07430

Cover design by Kathryn Houghtaling Lacey

Library of Congress Cataloging-in-Publication Data

Modeling longitudinal and multilevel data : practical issues, applied approaches,
and specific examples / edited by Todd D. Little, Kai-Uwe Schnabel, Jürgen
Baumert.

p.   cm.

ISBN 0-8058-3054-5 (cloth : alk. paper)
1. Social sciences—Statistical methods   2. Longitudinal method. I. Little, Todd
D. II. Schnabel, Kai-Uwe. III. Baumert
QA76.76.E95S32   2000   006.3'31—dc21
97-5613   CIP

Books published by Lawrence Erlbaum Associates are printed on acid-free
paper, and their bindings are chosen for strength and durability.

The final camera copy for this book was prepared by the author and therefore the publisher takes no responsibility for consistency or correctness of
typographical style.

Printed in the United States of America
10   9   8   7   6   5   4   3   2

Contents

Preface

As with any undertaking of this magnitude, the list of persons to whom we are endebted is long and the degree of endebtedness is deep. At the beginning and throughout, the generous financial support by the Max Planck Institute for Human Development in Berlin made this project possible. The Institute funded the 1998 Berlin Summer School Conference on Multilevel and Longitudinal Modeling, supported the assembly of this volume, and helps to maintain the web page (http://www.mpib-berlin.mpg.de/research_resources/index.html). On the basis of the comments and enthusiasm of the participants as well as the presenters, we felt that a comprehensive volume on these issues was needed. We are particularly grateful to Dagmar Stenzel for editing and type-setting the contributions. We also appreciate the support and advice of Larry Erlbaum and his crack team at LEA throughout this process. Finally, the diligence and timeliness of all contributors can not be thanked enough. The efforts, patience, and expertise of all involved has brought a volume that we hope will become a standard reference for social sciences researchers.

Todd D. Little   Kai U. Schnabel   Jürgen Baumert
New Haven, CT, USA   Berlin, Germany   Berlin, Germany

We would like to dedicate this volume to the memory of our friend
and colleague Magret Baltes.

CHAPTER ONE

Modeling Longitudinal and Multilevel Data

Kai Uwe Schnabel
Max Planck Institute for Human Development, Berlin

Todd D. Little
Yale University

Jürgen Baumert
Max Planck Institute for Human Development, Berlin

Both longitudinal and multilevel designs can provide invaluable empirical evidence for many, if not most, of the central assertions made by theories in the social and behavioral sciences (Baltes & Nesselroade, 1979; Menard, 1991). However, because such designs often involve considerable investments of time and money, their use is only justifiable if the resulting data can be analyzed adequately and thereby represented clearly. More often than not, however, disillusionment is part of the researchers' experience after the longitudinal or multilevel data are collected. For example, the puzzling number of different ways to analyze longitudinal data is likely to frustrate many researchers who neither consider themselves experts in statistics nor intend to become one. And multilevel designs also offer a plethora of complexities when it comes to decomposing the various sources of variability in the participants' responses.

Although researchers in the behavioral and social sciences are quite sophisticated when it comes to methodological and statistical issues, keeping up with the rapid advances and understanding the inherent complexities in the various analytic techniques for addressing longitudinal and multilevel data can be daunting. Such frustrations are made even more salient because more and more research questions lead researchers to use increasingly sophisticated longitudinal or multilevel designs. This volume is targeted to those researchers who wish to understand the practical issues and to learn from actual applications to address such data.

Many practical and theoretical issues are involved when addressing longitudinal and multilevel data. Some of these issues include (a) what information should be evaluated, (b) what decision heuristics should be used, and (c) what procedures are most appropriate. In addressing these issues, a primary goal of each contribution is to highlight a specific set of issues and to demonstrate clear procedures for addressing those issues. Each contribution shares the theme that making strong tests of underlying theoretical models (i.e., bringing implicit assumptions into the explicit realm of model specification) is critical for drawing veridical conclusions from one's data. They also share the common theme that statistical procedures are not mechanistic ends in themselves (i.e., fixed and rule-bound), but rather are flexible tools that should be adjusted and adapted into an appropriate means for testing a given substantive theory.

Why Address Longitudinal and Multilevel Analysis Problems Simultaneously?

At first sight, our decision to integrate longitudinal and multilevel data analysis in this volume may seem surprising. However, when one goes beyond a "cookbook understanding" of statistical procedures and examines the basic rationale behind longitudinal and multilevel procedures, many linkages between both perspectives become clear. Hox (chap. 2, this volume), for instance, demonstrates a number of uses of the multiple-group option in structural equation programs to model hierarchically structured data. Similarly, MacCallum and Kim (chap. 4, this volume) show how both analytic perspectives can be integrated to investigate correlates of change. Little, Lindenberger, and Maier (chap. 10, this volume) also describe ways to integrate multilevel and longitudinal analyses to examine selectivity effects in longitudinal data.

Another reason for using multilevel comparisons in the context of longitudinal analysis is implicitly addressed in several chapters of this volume and is related to the common vagaries of most theories in the social sciences when it comes to precisely predicting change processes over time. It is common that a researcher is not able to derive an exact a priori hypothesis about the shape of the developmental function describing the nature of the changes over time. In this case, rules of parsimony then become an auxiliary guideline to help choose a developmental function that is mathematically feasible and is a reasonable approximation of the data (e.g., using simple models such as linear-growth functions, or polynomial functions of limited degrees such as quadratic and cubic trends; Schnabel, 1996). Although investigating interindividual differences in development is a fundamental issue in longitudinal research (Baltes & Nesselroade, 1979), many research questions that come up in this context often have an exploratory character to them. McArdle and Bell (chap. 5, this volume) offer clear recommendations when an analysis is more exploratory in nature, that is, to utilize a highly parameterized (i.e., saturated) time-to-time-change model (e.g., spline models; Meredith & Tisak, 1990), which does not fit a particular curve function across the sequence of measurements, in order to describe the degree of deviation between this solution and a less parameterized, more parsimonious, model. The crux of the problem with weakly justified decisions about the underlying change model is that they can have a strong influence on the estimation of the central parameters.

Checking the stability of the results across relevant subgroups is another heuristic to test the robustness of the model.

The merits of pragmatism is one lesson to learn across the chapters of this volume, including the realm of inferential statistics. For example, from the perspective of the general linear model, Widaman (chap. 9, this volume) emphasizes the idea of testing a hierarchically ordered sequence of alternative models that differ according to theoretically meaningful constraints (e.g., across time and/or groups) rather than relying on traditional hypothesis testing procedures when one is testing complex models. Such a shift in the empirical rationale is a well-known feature of structural equation modeling, but it is less common to traditional inferential approaches. Clearly, classical inferential statistics (e.g., ANOVA) have little or no ambiguity in the model when they are applied to fully experimental data (i.e., the adequacy of the implicit model underlying the data analysis is determined by the degree it correctly reflects the experimental design, with the only uncertainty being the assumptions about the distribution of the variable or variables in the population). However, as soon as one collects data using a nonexperimental design, the underlying statistical model needs to be used adaptively in order to test the assumptions about the processes generating the data. In other words, the shift from strict hypothesis testing to the logic of model testing is not made because one uses structural equation modeling procedures, but rather because one uses quasi-experimental data (Cook & Campbell, 1979).

Ambiguity in Longitudinal Research: Testing and Modeling

Analyzing longitudinal data sometimes renders the researcher with the uncomfortable feeling of ambiguity and relativity of the findings. However, such ambiguity can also be seen as a chance to investigate alternative uses of statistical analysis procedures; namely, to apply them in a creative (theory-driven) way. As mentioned, statistical procedures are only analytic tools that one uses to try to model the underlying dynamic of a set of variables—in this sense, there is no single best way for analyzing a given data set.

The long-standing debate about the epistemological value of structural equation models and the related debate about whether it is permissible to make causal inferences from cross-sectional data is not automatically solved by using longitudinal data. The problem may even be acerbated in a multiwave study when, for instance, the variance of a variable (or a latent construct) decreases over time, indicating a negative correlation between intercept and slope that is not easy to detect with fallible measures (Raykov, 1994b; Rogosa, Brandt, & Zimowski, 1982). Coleman (1968), for example, provided theoretical arguments why this is likely for many psychological variables that are embedded in a complex homeostatic system where the organism actively works to reduce extreme system states in order to regain equilibrium. It can easily be shown that any existing causal influence on the dependent variable from an independent variable measured on a prior occasion *(cross-lagged coefficient)* can only add variance to the dependent variable—irrespective of its sign. Thus, a shrinkage in variance does not indicate that other relevant explanatory variables were missing. This casts a slightly different light on the dichotomy of stability and change and the widely held belief that change needs to be explained because it is an active process whereas stability is considered the trivial nonactive behavior of the system. At least in the realm of psychological and educational research, understanding the processes related to stability should be given the same theoretical and empirical importance as understanding the processes related to change (Nesselroade, 1991).

Structural Equation Modeling and Hierarchical Linear Models —The Unequal Twins

The present volume focuses considerably on structural equation modeling (SEM) and hierarchical linear modeling (HLM) procedures to analyze longitudinal data. This emphasis is due primarily to the fact that both approaches are flexible tools for examining complicated data structures in a feasible way. In several chapters, the contributors show that both approaches yield exactly or approximately the same results. For example, Hox (chap. 2, this volume) shows that SEM can be used for nested data. Chou, Bentler, and Pentz (chap. 3, this volume) demonstrate their similarity in the context of latent growth modeling, showing that a less complex—although less efficient—two-step approach produces approximately the same point estimates. As MacCallum and Kim (chap. 4, this volume) demonstrate, it is possible to analyze simultaneously more than one dependent variable in the HLM framework, thus enabling the researcher, when the variables are combined in a latent growth model, to test hypotheses about correlations in change components. McArdle and Bell (chap. 5, this volume) similarly demonstrate the equivalence of both approaches, demonstrating that analysis based on raw data may be a robust alternative to classical SEM that analyzes covariance matrices when missing data have to be taken into account.

However, despite their similarities, particularly in the latent growth approach, SEM and HLM are not completely interchangeable from the viewpoint of practical data analysis because both have strengths and weaknesses. Although SEM has tremendous flexibility in modeling error structures (Steyer, Partchev, & Shanahan, chap. 6, this volume) and the possibility of modeling mutual influences over time, it is not very easy to analyze nested data structures with it (or it needs a fairly cumbersome setup). This is the domain of HLM, which, in turn, does not allow structuring error components according to a complex measurement structure (or it needs a fairly cumbersome setup). HLM is also more flexible when the repeated measurement occasions vary between individuals.

From a practical standpoint, another important difference between the SEM and HLM approaches is related to the handling of missing data—a feature where HLM was thought to be the more appropriate tool. However, as Wothke (chap. 12, this volume) demonstrates, SEM procedures have narrowed the gap by using full information maximum likelihood estimation of the covariance matrix (as implemented in the latest versions of Amos and Mx). Neale (chap. 14, this volume) extends these considerations to modeling the raw data, which may or may not contain patterns of missingness. Although further work must be done to demonstrate whether the results from these approaches can be generalized for all possible structures of missingness, these advances clearly broaden the scope of the ways in which such analyses can be adjusted to address different types of research designs.

On the basis of the considerations offered by Graham and Hofer (chap. 11, this volume) about new techniques for data imputation, one might speculate about future integration of imputation techniques in statistical software—not restricted to SEM or HLM programs, of course. In this regard, Arbuckle (chap. 13, this volume) describes some future directions for creating specific procedures that are tailored to handle the specific type of analysis problem of a given design, including issues of missingness. On the other hand, not all data structures can be handled in SEM or HLM procedures. In this respect, the latent transition analyses presented by Collins, Hyatt, and Graham (chap. 8, this volume) provide important alternative statistical procedures that do not assume interval scales—in particular for the latent variables.

As mentioned, a primary goal of this volume is to assist researchers in making decisions, such as what technique to use for what kind of question, when is one technique more appropriate than another, and how does one handle the numerous technical details involved in such procedures. Based on papers that were presented and discussed at a conference in conjunction with a summer school workshop held in Berlin, Germany, in June, 1997, all chapters in this volume address numerous practically relevant questions for empirical social scientists who desire to have an appropriate way to analyze their longitudinal and/or multilevel data. We are indebted to all the contributors to this volume for the tremendous work and gracious generosity that they have extended to this volume.

CHAPTER TWO

Multilevel Analyses of Grouped and Longitudinal Data

Joop J. Hox
University of Amsterdam
& Utrecht University

Social and behavioral research often concerns problems that have a hierarchical structure, such as, for example, when individuals are nested within groups. In multilevel analysis, data structures of this nature are viewed as a multistage sample from a hierarchical population. For example, in educational research there may be a sample of schools and within each school, a sample of pupils. This structure results in a data set consisting of pupil data (e.g., socioeconomic status [SES], intelligence, school career) and school data (e.g., school size, denomination, but also aggregated pupil variables such as mean SES). In this chapter, the generic term *multilevel* is used to refer to analysis models for hierarchically structured data, with variables defined at all levels of the hierarchy. Typically, such research problems include hypotheses of relationships between variables defined at different levels of the hierarchy.

A well-known multilevel model is the hierarchical linear regression model, which is essentially an extension of the familiar multiple regression model. It is known in the literature under a variety of names, such as "hierarchical-linear model" (Bryk & Raudenbush, 1992; Raudenbush & Bryk, 1986), "variance-component model" (Longford, 1989), and "random-coefficient model" (de Leeuw & Kreft, 1986; Longford, 1993). This model has become so popular that "multilevel modeling" has become almost synonymous with "applying a multilevel-regression model." However, because we also have multilevel extensions of other models, such as factor analysis or structural equation models (SEMs), I reserve the term *multilevel model* for the general case and refer to specific classes of models as "multilevel regression analysis" and "multilevel SEM," for example.

THE MULTILEVEL REGRESSION MODEL FOR GROUPED DATA

The *multilevel regression model* is a hierarchical linear regression model, with a dependent variable defined at the lowest (usually the individual) level and explanatory variables at all existing levels. Using dummy coding for categorical variables, the multilevel regression model can be used for analysis of variance (ANOVA), and it has been extended to include dependent variables that are binary, categorical, or otherwise non-normal data and generalized to include multivariate response models and cross-classified data (cf. Bryk & Raudenbush, 1992; Longford, 1993; and especially Goldstein, 1995).

The Basic Multilevel Regression Model

In most applications, the first (lowest) level consists of individuals, the second level of groups of individuals, and higher levels of sets of groups. Conceptually, the model can be viewed as a hierarchical system of regression equations. For example, assume that data has been collected in j schools, with a different number of pupils n_j in each school. On the pupil level, there are the dependent variable y_{ij} (e.g., school career) and the explanatory variable x_{ij} (e.g., pupil SES). One can set up a regression equation to predict the dependent variable y from the explanatory variable x:

$$y_{ij} = \beta_{0j} + \beta_{1j}x_{ij} + e_{ij} .$$ (1)

In Equation 1, x_{ij} and y_{ij} are the scores of pupil i in school j, β_{0j} is the regression intercept, β_{1j} the regression slope, and e_{ij} the residual error term. The multilevel regression model depicted in Equation 1 specifies that the different schools are characterized by different regression equations; each school has its own intercept β_{0j} and slope β_{1j}.

Because the regression coefficients β_{0j} and β_{1j} vary across the schools, this variation may be modeled with explanatory variables at the school level. Assume one school-level explanatory variable z_j (e.g., school size). Then, the model for the β's becomes:

$$\beta_{0j} = \gamma_{00} + \gamma_{01}z_j + u_{0j} ,$$ (2)

$$\beta_{1j} = \gamma_{10} + \gamma_{11}z_j + u_{1j} .$$ (3)

In Equation 2, γ_{00} and γ_{01} are the intercept and slope of the regression equation used to predict β_{0j} from z_j; u_{0j} is the residual error term in the equation for β_{0j}. Thus, if γ_{01} is positive and significant, one concludes that the school-career outcome is higher in large schools than in small schools. Similarly, in Equation 3, γ_{10} and γ_{11} are the intercept and slope to predict β_{1j} from z_j, and u_{1j} is the residual error term in the equation for β_{1j}. Thus, if γ_{11} is positive and significant, one concludes that the effect of x_{ij}, pupil SES in the example, is stronger in large schools. In this example, there can be an interaction effect of z_j (school size) and x_{ij} (pupil SES) on y_{ij} (school career). This possibility becomes clearer if the model is written as a single equation, by substituting Equations 2 and 3 into Equation 1:

$$y_{ij} = [\gamma_{00} + \gamma_{10}x_{ij} + \gamma_{01}z_j + \gamma_{11}z_jx_{ij}] + [u_{1j}x_{ij} + u_{0j} + e_{ij}]. \qquad (4)$$

In the multilevel regression model depicted in Equation 4, which is a special case of the general mixed-linear model (Harville, 1977), two parts can be distinguished. The fixed part contains the regression coefficients' gammas and their associated variables: $[\gamma_{00} + \gamma_{10}x_{ij} + \gamma_{01}z_j + \gamma_{11}z_jx_{ij}]$. The regression coefficients no longer carry a subscript j for schools because in the combined equation, they refer to the average value of the regression across all schools. The random part contains the residual error terms: $[u_{0j} + u_{1j}x_{ij} + e_{ij}]$. Note that these do carry subscripts for the schools because the residual error terms represent the deviation of the schools' regression coefficients from their overall mean. The interaction term z_jx_{ij} is sometimes referred to as a *cross-level interaction,* because it involves explanatory variables from different levels. The individual-level errors, e_{ij}, are assumed to be independent and to have a normal distribution with mean zero and variance σ_e^2. The school-level errors u_j are assumed to be independent and to have a multivariate normal distribution with mean vector zero and covariance matrix Σ. Because the school-level errors are the schools' deviations from the overall regression, this is equivalent to assuming that the regression coefficients, γ_j, follow a multivariate normal distribution.

Estimation and Significance Testing in the Multilevel Regression Model

The parameters (regression coefficients and variance components) of the multilevel regression model are commonly estimated using maximum likelihood (ML) methods. Asymptotic standard errors are available for hypothesis testing. The usual significance test in maximum likelihood estimation is the so-called Wald test: The parameter estimate is divided by its standard error, and the result is referred to the standard normal distribution. Bryk and Raudenbush (1992) argued that for fixed effects it is better to refer this ratio to a Student distribution with $J - q - 1$ degrees of freedom (J = number of groups; q = number of fixed parameters) and to use a chi-square test for the random effects. For a discussion of the issues involved in choosing between such tests, see Hox (1998).

The likelihood function can be used to test the significance of the difference between two nested models. Most multilevel programs output a value that is called the *deviance* (computed as: deviance = −2 the log likelihood). If a smaller model is a nested subset of a larger model, which means that it is obtained by either dropping parameters or imposing constraints on the larger model, the difference between the two deviances can be tested against a chi-square distribution. The degrees of freedom for this test is the difference in the number of parameters estimated. This test can be used instead of the Wald test for multivariate tests of groups of parameters and for tests of the variances in the random part where it is thought to be more accurate than the Wald test (Goldstein, 1995).

Two different maximum likelihood functions are used in the available software: Full ML (FML) and Restricted ML (RML). FML includes the fixed parameters in the likelihood function; RML does not. Most software offers a choice between the two methods. Because RML does not include the fixed parameters in the likelihood function, a deviance test based on RML can only be used to test for differences in the random part.

Example of Multilevel Regression Analysis of Grouped Data

The multilevel regression model is most appropriate for data structures that have many groups, because it is more flexible and more parsimonious than analysis-of-variance-type models. For instance, assume a study of school careers in 50 schools. In each school, take one class and measure the pupils' achievement scores, SES, gender, class size, and how experienced their teacher is. The study has a total of 979 pupils from 50 classes, with an average class size of just under 20. Note that by taking one class per school the school and the class level are collapsed: It is impossible to distinguish between school and class effects. Table 2.1 presents the results of a sequence of multilevel regression models with the achievement score as the dependent variable.

TABLE 2.1
Results of the Analysis of the School-Achievement Example

Parameter	Intercept only	+	Pupil variables	+	Teacher variables	+	Random slope	+	Cross-level interaction
Fixed part									
intercept	49.6 (.73)		16.7 (.91)		11.3 (4.70)		14.8 (4.52)		49.7 (.47)
pupil SES			9.0 (.17)		9.0 (.17)		9.0 (.35)		8.9 (.17)
pupil sex			−.8 (.31)		−.8 (.30)		−.6 (.28)		−.6 (.28)
class size					−.1 (.22)		−.1 (.20)		−.1 (.20)
teacher exp.					.5 (.07)		.2 (.07)		.5 (.07)
p.SES*t.exp.									.3 (.03)
Random part									
σ^2_e	88.8 (4.12)		21.9 (1.01)		21.9 (1.01)		17.9 (.85)		17.9 (.85)
$\sigma^2_{intercept}$	21.7 (5.27)		20.0 (4.01)		9.2 (2.07)		49.7 (13.64)		8.9 (1.96)
σ^2_{SES}							4.9 (1.24)		.3 (.30)
$\sigma_{intercept*SES}$							−14.4 (3.96)		.9 (.55)
Deviance	5,730		7,258		5,942		5,908		5,798

Note. Standard errors are listed parenthetically. The data and models used for this example are available at http://www.mpib-berlin.mpg.de/research_resources/index.html.

In Table 2.1, several different models are presented. The first model, the intercept-only model, serves as a baseline; it shows that the total variance is divided into two parts, 88.8 at the pupil level and 21.7 at the school level. This information gives the intraclass correlation, which is the proportion of variance accounted for at the group level. In the school data, in acchievement the intraclass correlation is 0.20 (i.e., 21.7/[88.8 + 21.7]). In other words, 20% of the variance is at the school level. Turning to the next model in Table 2.1, one sees that some of this variation is explained by pupil and school characteristics. Pupil SES turns out to have a regression coefficient with significant variance across schools, which is partly explained by the interaction with the teachers' experience. For a more detailed introduction to multilevel regression, see Bryk and Raudenbush (1992) and Hox (1995).

THE MULTILEVEL REGRESSION MODEL FOR LONGITUDINAL DATA

In the previous section, individuals are considered to be the lowest level of the hierarchy. In longitudinal research, one has a series of repeated measures for each individual. One way to model such data is to view the series of repeated measures as a separate level below the individual level. The individual level becomes the second level, and it is possible to add a third and higher levels for possible group structures. Multilevel models for longitudinal data are discussed by, among others, Bryk and Raudenbush (1987, 1992) and Goldstein (1987, 1995); for an introduction, see Snijders (1996).

The Basic Model for Longitudinal Data

The multilevel regression model for longitudinal data is a straightforward application of the multilevel regression model described earlier. It can also be written as a sequence of models for each level. At the lowest, repeated-measures level, one has:

$$y_{ti} = \pi_{0i} + \pi_{1i}c_{ti} + \pi_{2i}x_{ti} + e_{ti} . \tag{5}$$

In Equation 5, y_{ti} is the dependent variable of individual i measured at time point t, c is the time variable that indicates the time point, and x_{ti} is a time-varying covariate. For example, y_{ti} could be a reading score of a pupil, c_{ti} the age at the time the reading score is measured, and x_{ti} the experience of the teacher the pupil has at time t. Pupil characteristics, such as gender, are time-invariant covariates, which enter the equation at the second level:

$$\pi_{0i} = \beta_{00} + \beta_{01}z_i + r_{0i} , \tag{6}$$

$$\pi_{1i} = \beta_{10} + \beta_{11}z_i + r_{1i} , \tag{7}$$

$$\pi_{2i} = \beta_{20} + \beta_{21}z_i + r_{2i} . \tag{8}$$

By substitution, one gets the single equation:

$$y_{ti} = \beta_{00} + \beta_{10}c_{ti} + \beta_{20}x_{ti} + \beta_{01}z_i + \beta_{11}z_ic_{ti} + \beta_{21}z_ix_{ti} \tag{9}$$
$$+ r_{1i}c_{ti} + r_{2i}x_{ti} + r_{0i} + e_{ti}.$$

In longitudinal research, investigators sometimes have repeated measurements of individuals, who are all measured together on a small number of fixed occasions; this is typically the case with panel research. If they simply want to test the null hypothesis that the means are equal for all occasions, researchers can specify the repeated measures as observations on a multivariate response vector and use Multivariate Analysis of Variance (MANOVA). Multilevel regression offers an essentially equivalent analysis. One uses a multivariate response model (Goldstein, 1995) with dummy variables indicating the different occasions. The standard multilevel model in Equation 9 assumes that the residual errors, e_{ti}, are independent and have constant variance over time, whereas MANOVA assumes an unconstrained covariance matrix for the e_{ti}. Bryk and Raudenbush (1992, p. 132) argued that uncorrelated errors may be appropriate in short time series. However, the multilevel regression model can be extended to include an unconstrained covariance matrix at the lowest level (Goldstein, 1995; Maas & Snijders, 1997). Multilevel analysis is useful for fixed-occasion data when there are missing observations because of the absence of individuals at specific occasions or panel attrition. Because multilevel models do not assume equal numbers of identical occasions for all individuals, such missing data pose no special problems, whereas MANOVA handles missing data by deleting all individuals with incomplete data (see, however, Graham & Hofer, chap. 11, this volume).

The number of occasions and their spacing may also vary across individuals. This is often the case in growth-curve models, where an individual's development is a function of the time or age at the different occasions. The most important advantage of multilevel analysis for such research problems is its flexibility. In the multilevel regression model, the development over time is modeled by a linear regression equation, with possibly different regression coefficients for different individuals. Thus, each individual gets his or her own growth curve, specified by individual regression coefficients that may depend on individual attributes. Quadratic and higher functions can be used to model nonlinear dependencies on time, and both time-varying and person-level covariates can be added to the model. For a more detailed discussion of such models, see MacCallum and Kim (chap. 4, this volume).

As mentioned, multilevel regression models for growth curves commonly assume residual errors that are uncorrelated over time. Especially for growth curves with closely spaced observations, this assumption may be implausible. Models that are more complex are possible for the residual errors, e_{ti}. For instance, one can specify an autocorrelation structure for the residuals or model the variance of the residuals as a function of time or age. Some such models are discussed by Gibbons et al. (1993) and Goldstein (1995), and the program MixReg (Hedeker & Gibbons, 1996) has built-in options for correlated errors.

Example of Multilevel Analyses of Longitudinal Data

The example data have been generated by Rogosa and Saner (1995), with 200 individuals measured at five equidistant time-points and, at the person level, one time-invariant covariate. The model for these data is given by:

$$y_{ti} = \beta_{00} + \beta_{10}c_{ti} + \beta_{01}z_ic_{ti} + \beta_{11}z_ic_{ti} + r_{1i}c_{ti} + r_{0i} + e_{ti} \,. \tag{10}$$

The time points, c, are coded as $t = 0, 1, 2, 3, 4$, and the covariate, z, is centered around its overall mean. As a result, the intercept can be interpreted as the expected value at the first occasion for individuals with an average value of z. Although using time points $t = 1, 2, 3, 4, 5$ and raw scores for z would be completely equivalent, the estimates are slightly more difficult to interpret.

Table 2.2 presents the results of a multilevel analysis of these longitudinal data. Model 1 (intercept only) contains only an intercept term; this model serves as a null or baseline model. The intercept-only model estimates the repeated measures variance as 84.4 and the person level variance as 42.7. Thus, the intraclass correlation or the proportion of variance accounted for at the person level is estimated as 0.34 (i.e., 42.7/[84.4 + 42.7]). In other words, approximately two-thirds of the variance of the measures is variance over time and one-third is variance between individuals. In Model 2 (intercept + time), the time variable is added as a predictor with varying coefficients for different persons. The model predicts a value of 44.0 at the first occasion, which increases by 5.0 on each succeeding occasion. The variance components for the intercept and the regression slope for the time variable are both significant. The significant intercept variance means that individuals have different initial states, and the significant slope variance means that individuals also have different growth rates. There is a negative correlation between the initial status and the growth rate ($r = -.24$); individuals who start high tend to grow at a slower rate. In Model 3 (intercept + time + covariate) the covariate z is added to the model, both as a direct effect and as an interaction with the time variable. Part of the variation of the intercept and slope coefficients can be modeled by the covariate. Note that the type of correlation between the intercept and slope is different; in Model 2 it is an ordinary (zero-order) correlation, but in Model 3, it is a partial correlation, conditional on the covariate z.

One deficit of multilevel approaches is that they do not provide clear-cut values for the amount of variance explained by the various effects. Bryk and Raudenbush (1992) suggested using the residual error variance of the intercept-only model as a benchmark and examining how much this goes down when explanatory variables are added to the model. In Table 2.2, this strategy leads to inconsistencies, because in Model 2 the residual error variance for the intercept actually goes up when the time variable is added to the model. The reason is that in multilevel models with random coefficients the notion of amount of variance explained at a specific level is not a simple concept. As Snijders and Bosker (1994) explained in detail, the problem arises because the statistical model behind multilevel models is a hierarchical sampling model:

TABLE 2.2
Multilevel Results From the Rogosa-Saner Data

Parameter	Intercept only	+	Time	+	Covariate
Fixed part					
intercept	54.0 (.55)		44.0 (.56)		44.0 (.51)
time			5.0 (.17)		5.0 (.14)
z					1.5 (.14)
z*time					.6 (.07)
Random part					
σ^2_e	84.4 (4.22)		11.9 (.69)		11.9 (.69)
$\sigma^2_{intercept}$	42.7 (6.01)		54.8 (6.21)		45.3 (5.26)
σ^2_{time}			4.4 (.56)		2.7 (.40)
$\sigma_{intercept*time}$			−3.8 (1.39)		−7.7 (1.25)
r_{i^*t}			−.24		−.69
Deviance	7,525		6,251		6,032

Note. Standard errors are listed parenthetically.

Groups are sampled at the higher level and, at the lower level, individuals are sampled within groups. This sampling process creates some variability between the groups, even if there are in fact no real group differences. In time series, the lowest level is a series of measurements, which in many cases are (almost) the same for all individuals in the sample. Thus, the variability between persons in the time series variable is in fact much lower than the hierarchical sampling model assumes. Snijders and Bosker (1994) described procedures to correct the problem. A simple approximation is to use the occasion-level error variance from Model 1, and the person-level error variance of Model 2, which includes the time variable. Then, observe that the error variance at the repeated-measures level goes down from 84.4 to 11.9, which means that the time variable explains about 86% of the variance between the occasions. To see how much variance the person-level variable, z, explains, regard the intercept variance of 54.8 in Model 2 as the error variance and observe that in Model 3 this variance goes down to 45.3. Thus, at the person level, the covariate z explains about 17% of the initial variation among the persons. Likewise, one can calculate that z explains about 39% of the initial variance of the time slopes. These values are rough indications; however, more precise procedures are given by Snijders and Bosker (1994).

As the example makes clear, applying multilevel regression models to longitudinal data is straightforward, especially if investigators restrict themselves to a single dependent variable and to a linear or polynomial function of the time variable. More complicated models are possible, such as nonlinear models or multivariate models for several dependent variables; for illustrations, see MacCallum and Kim (chap. 4, this volume) and Goldstein (1995).

MULTILEVEL STRUCTURAL EQUATION MODELS

Structural equation models (SEMs) for multilevel data are described by, among others, Goldstein and McDonald (Goldstein & McDonald, 1988; McDonald & Goldstein, 1989), Muthén and Satorra (Muthén, 1989; Muthén & Satorra, 1989), Longford and Muthén (Longford, 1993; Longford & Muthén, 1992), and Lee and Poon (1992). Nontechnical introductions are given by Muthén (1994), McDonald (1994), and Hox (1995). This section describes an approximation proposed by Muthén (1989, 1994) that makes it possible to use standard SEM software to analyze multilevel structural equation models.

The Basic Multilevel Structural Equation Model

Multilevel structural equation models assume a population of individuals that can be divided into groups. Assume multivariate data from N individuals in G groups. For each individual, replace the observed total scores, y_i, by their components: the between-groups component, y_B, representing the disaggregated group means, and the within-groups component, y_W, representing the individual deviations from their respective group mean. These two components have the attractive property of being orthogonal and additive:

$$y = y_B + y_W .$$ (11)

If the population data is decomposed into between-groups variables and within-groups variables, three population covariance matrices are distinguished: the *total* covariance matrix, Σ_B; the *between-groups* covariance matrix, Σ_B; and the *within-groups* covariance matrix, Σ_W. Just as the group means and the individual deviation scores themselves, the covariance matrices, Σ_B and Σ_W, are orthogonal and sum to the total covariance matrix, Σ:

$$\Sigma = \Sigma_B + \Sigma_W .$$ (12)

Muthén (1989) showed that an unbiased estimate of the population within-groups covariance matrix, Σ_W, is given by the pooled within-groups covariance matrix, S_{PW}:

$$S_{PW} = \frac{\sum_{1}^{G}\sum_{1}^{n_g}(y_{ig} - \bar{y}_g)(y_{ig} - \bar{y}_{ig})'}{N - G}.$$ (13)

Equation 13 corresponds to the conventional equation for the covariance matrix of the individual deviation scores, with $N - G$ in the denominator instead of the usual $N - 1$. Thus, one can model the population within-group structure by constructing and testing a structural model for S_{PW}.

The between-groups covariance matrix for the disaggregated group means, S_B, calculated in the sample, is given by:

$$S_B = \frac{\sum_{1}^{G} n_g (\bar{\mathbf{y}}_g - \bar{\mathbf{y}})(\bar{\mathbf{y}}_g - \bar{\mathbf{y}})'}{G}. \qquad (14)$$

Equation 14 corresponds to the conventional equation for the covariance matrix of the disaggregated group means, with G in the denominator instead of the usual N – 1. Unfortunately, S_B is not a simple estimator of the population between-groups covariance matrix, S_B. Instead, S_B is an estimator of the sum of two matrices:

$$S_B = \Sigma_W + d\Sigma_B \qquad (15)$$

where d is a scaling factor equal to the common group size (Muthén, 1989, 1994). Thus, to model the between-groups structure, specify two models for S_B: one for the within-groups structure and one for the between-groups structure. Muthén (1989, 1994) proposed using the multigroup option of standard SEM software to analyze these models. There are two groups, with covariance matrices, S_{PW} and S_B, based on N – G and G observations. The model for Σ_W must be specified for both S_{PW} and S_B, with equality restrictions between both groups. The model for Σ_B is added to the model for S_B, with the scale factor, d, built into the model.

The reasoning underlying this approach assumes balanced data, where all groups have the same group size n (with $nG = N$). For unbalanced data, proceed as if the group sizes were equal, and calculate the scaling factor as a combination of the observed group sizes given by:

$$d = \frac{N^2 - \sum_{1}^{G} n_g^2}{N(G-1)}. \qquad (16)$$

This pseudobalanced solution (McDonald, 1994), which Muthén (1989, 1994) called the MUML estimator, is not a full maximum likelihood solution. However, if the samples are reasonably large and the group sizes are not extremely different, the pseudobalanced estimates are close enough to the full maximum likelihood estimates to be useful in their own right. Comparisons of pseudobalanced estimates with full maximum likelihood estimates or with known population values have been made by Muthén (1991b, 1994), Hox (1993), and McDonald (1994). They all conclude that the pseudobalanced estimates are generally accurate.

The multilevel part of the covariance structure model outlined is simpler than that of the multilevel regression model. It is comparable to the multilevel regression model with random variation of the intercepts. There is no provision for randomly varying slopes (factor loadings and path coefficients). Chou, Bentler, and Pentz (chap. 3, this volume) showed that, provided that the sample sizes of the groups are large, it is possible to analyze more general models by employing a two-step approach.

Multilevel covariance structure analyses model the population covariance matrices, Σ_B and Σ_W, by specifying separate structural models for the between-groups and within-groups covariances. To apply structural equation models to multilevel data, it is helpful to have a program that calculates the required matrices and the scaling factor. Public domain programs for this are available from Muthén (BW) and Hox (SPLIT2). Gustafsson has developed a program called STREAMS (Gustafsson & Stahl, 1997), which not only calculates the required matrices, but also writes the required program setups for a variety of SEM packages.

Example of Multilevel Factor Analysis

The example data are taken from van Peet (1992). They are the scores on six intelligence tests of 269 children from 49 families. The six intelligence tests are word lists, cards, matrices, figures, animals, and occupations. The data have a multilevel structure, with children nested within families. Assuming that intelligence is strongly influenced by shared genetic and environmental influences, one expects strong between-family effects.

The individual scores on the six measures are decomposed into the disaggregated group means and the individual deviations from these group means. The intraclass correlations (the proportion of variance at the family level) of the six tests vary from 0.18 to 0.36, which suggests considerable family-level variance. The model specification strategy starts with seeking a within-level model, and then goes on with the between-level model (for details see Hox, 1995). The principle of utilizing the simplest model that fits well leads to a model with two factors on the individual level and one general factor on the family level. The path diagram is given in Figure 2.1.

The model fits fairly well (χ^2 = 28.0, df = 17, p = .05; GFI = 0.97; TLI = 0.93). Figure 2.1 actually shows the model for the between-groups matrix, which contains a model for both Σ_B and Σ_W. The lower half is the model for Σ_W, and the upper half is the model for Σ_B. The model for Σ_W is also specified for the pooled within-groups matrix, with equality restrictions for all corresponding parameters. The fixed regression coefficients of 2.34 for the between-group variables, which are represented by the factors *wlb* to *anb*, are the scaling constants, which are equal to the square root of *d*. The one-factor model for the between-groups variables looks quite ordinary, until one realizes that the factor loadings are actually regression coefficients going from one latent variable to another. Although this does not affect their interpretation as factor loadings, it does complicate the setups.

Table 2.3 presents the standardized parameter estimates for the multilevel factor model. The model in Table 2.3 suggests that on the family level, where the effects of the shared genetic and environmental influences are visible, one general factor, *g*, is

FIGURE 2.1
Multilevel Model of Person and Family Contributions
to Cognitive Performance

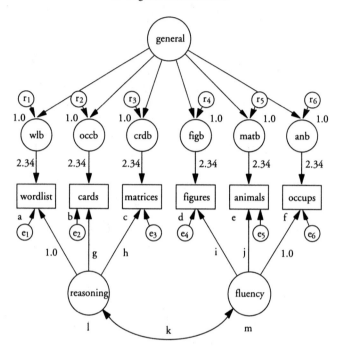

Note. Letters indicate estimated parameters; numbers are fixed coefficients.

TABLE 2.3
Individual and Family Model, Standardized Factor Loadings

| | Individual | | Family |
	I	II	I
Word list	.19*	-	.86*
Cards	.33	-	.62
Matrices	.49	-	.95
Figures	-	.29	.51
Animals	-	.45	.91
Occupations	-	.31*	.45

Note. Correlation between individual factors: 0.38. * = fixed.

sufficient to explain the covariances between the intelligence measures. On the individual level, where the effects of individual idiosyncratic influences are visible, two factors are needed. The first factor could be interpreted as reasoning, and the second as perceptual fluency.

Specifying multilevel path models follows the general approach outlined, but complications may arise because, in multilevel path models, it is not unusual to have variables that are only defined at the group level, such as group size, or that have virtually no variance at the group level, such as gender. In these cases, the number of variables in the between-groups and the within-groups matrix are not the same. This is not a fundamental problem, and standard SEM software can still be used. Although some SEM software (e.g., Amos, EQS) handle this with ease, other programs (e.g., LISREL, LISCOMP) require a more involved setup to solve this problem.

LATENT CURVE AND MULTILEVEL REGRESSION MODELS

An interesting model for longitudinal data with fixed occasions is the latent curve model, also known as the latent growth model. In the latent curve model, the time dimension is incorporated into the specification of the latent variables in the structural model. Consecutive measurements are modeled by a latent variable for the intercept of the growth curve and a second latent variable for the slope of the curve (see MacCallum & Kim, chap. 4, this volume; Meredith & Tisak, 1990; Muthén, 1991a; Willet & Sayer, 1994).

Figure 2.2 shows the path diagram of a simple latent curve model for the panel data, with five time points and one explanatory variable, W. In Figure 2.2, $Y_{t=0}$, $Y_{t=1}$, $Y_{t=2}$, $Y_{t=3}$, and $Y_{t=4}$ are the observations at the five time points. In the latent curve model, the expected score at time point zero is modeled by an intercept factor. The intercept is constant over time, which is modeled by fixing the loadings of all time points on this factor to one. The slope factor is the slope of a linear curve, modeled by fixing the loadings of the five time points on this factor to 0, 1, 2, 3, and 4, respectively. A quadratic trend would be specified by a third latent variable, with loadings fixed at 0, 1, 4, 9, and 16. The latent curve model also includes the means of the variables and factors in the model. All the intercepts of the time points are fixed at zero, which makes the mean of the intercept factor an estimate of the common intercept. The mean of the slope factor is an estimate of the common slope. Individual deviations from the common intercept are modeled by the variance of the intercept factor, and individual deviations in the slope of the curve are modeled by the variance of the slope factor. The intercept and slope factors can both be predicted in a model including explanatory variables. In the example, the one explanatory variable, W, is used to predict the variability in the intercepts and slopes at the same individuals.

The latent growth model is a random coefficient model, which is equivalent to the multilevel regression model with a random component for both the intercept and the slope of the time variable. To make the latent growth model equivalent to the usual

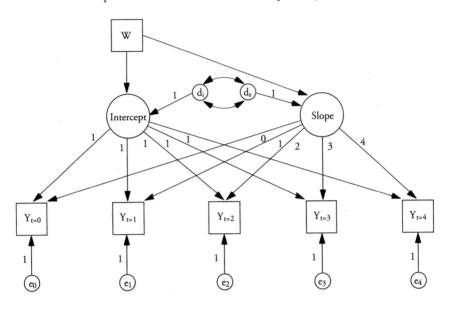

FIGURE 2.2
Simple Latent Curve Model With One Explanatory Variable

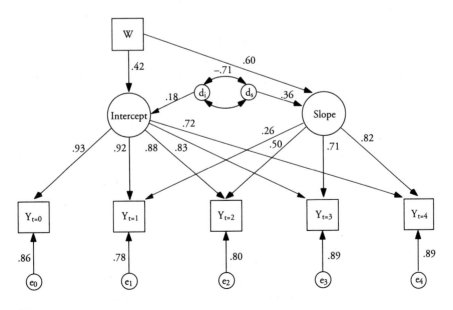

FIGURE 2.3
Standardized Estimates From the Latent Curve Model of the Simulated Data

TABLE 2.4
Compensor of the Results From the Latent Curve and Multilevel Regression Models

Model	Latent curve		Multilevel		Population value
Fixed part					
intercept	44.1	(.51)	44.0	(.51)	44
time	4.9	(.14)	5.0	(.14)	5
W	1.5	(.24)	1.5	(.14)	1.4
W*time	.61	(.07)	.62	(.07)	.67
Random part					
σ^2	12.4		11.9	(.69)	12
σ^2_{int}	45.1	(5.26)	45.3	(5.26)	47
σ^2_{time}	2.9	(.41)	2.7	(.40)	3.2
$\sigma_{int*time}$	−8.0	(1.28)	−7.7	(1.25)	9.0
r_{i*t}	−.71		−.70		−.73

Note. Standard erors are listed parenthetically. For the latent-curve model, $\chi^2_{(8)} = 33.8$; and for the multilevel regression model, deviance = 6,032.

multilevel regression model, one must restrict the error terms, e_0 to e_4, to have the same variance and allow the residuals, d_i and d_s, to correlate. Figure 2.3 shows the standardized estimates for the data, and Table 2.4 shows the unstandardized estimates along with the estimates obtained previously from the multilevel regression model. Both sets of parameter estimates and standard errors are very close, about as close as one would expect if comparing estimates produced by two different multilevel or SEM packages (cf. Hox, 1995; Kreft, de Leeuw, & van der Leeden, 1994). Because these data are simulated, the population values are known. The last column in Table 2.4 presents the known population values. All estimates are close to the known population values, and none are significantly different.

HANDLING MISSING DATA

An often-cited advantage of multilevel analysis of longitudinal data is its ability to handle missing data (Bryk & Raudenbush, 1992; Maas & Snijders, 1997; Snijders, 1996). More accurately, this advantage refers to the ability to handle models with varying time points. In a fixed occasions model, observations may be missing because, at some time points, respondents were not measured. In MANOVA, the usual treatment of missing time points is to remove the case from the analysis. Multilevel regression models do not assume equal numbers of observations, or even fixed time points, so respondents with missing observations pose no special problems. However, this advantage of multilevel modeling does not extend to missing observations on the explanatory variables. If explanatory variables are missing, the usual treatment is again to remove the case from the analysis. In structural equations modeling, missing observations can best be handled by direct estimation, where the algorithm estimates the model using all available data on all cases (Arbuckle, 1996; Graham & Hofer, chap. 11, this volume; Wothke, chap. 12, this volume). At least two SEM programs include direct estimation with missing values: Amos (Arbuckle, 1995) and Mx (Neale, 1997).

Little and Rubin (1987, 1989) distinguished between data that are missing completely at random (MCAR) and data that are missing at random (MAR). In both cases, the failure to observe a certain data point is assumed to be independent of the unobserved (missing) value. With MCAR data, the missingness is completely independent of all other variables as well, whereas with MAR data, the missingness may depend on other variables. For a more detailed treatment of missing data problems, see Graham and Hofer (chap. 11, this volume). By way of example, two data sets with missing data are analyzed. The first data set is the longitudinal Rogosa-Saner data, which was presented earlier, but this time is presented with 7% of the values randomly deleted. These data represent an MCAR data set. In the second data set, an MAR process of panel attrition has been added to this MCAR process. Dependent on the value of the explanatory variable W, about 5% of the data points T0 to T1 were made missing (i.e., deleted). Next, if a datum point was missing, all following time points were also deleted in order to simulate panel attrition. Both data sets are analyzed using standard multivariate MANOVA, multilevel regression analysis, and direct estimation of a latent curve model. The MANOVA results are discussed in the text; the results of the multilevel regression and the latent curve models are in Table 2.5.

Table 2.5 shows that if the data are MCAR, all models lead to estimates that are very close to each other and to the known population values that are given in Table 2.4. This outcome is as expected, because when data are missing completely at random, all three methods used are unbiased; however, they are not equally efficient.

TABLE 2.5

Multilevel Regression (MR) and Latent Curve Modeling (LCM) on MCAR and MAR Data Sets

Data model	MCAR				MAR			
	MR		LCM		MR		LCM	
Fixed part								
intercept	44.2	(.52)	44.2	(.50)	43.7	(.53)	44.1	(.52)
time	4.9	(.14)	4.9	(.14)	4.6	(.15)	4.8	(.15)
W	1.4	(.24)	1.5	(.24)	2.5	(.20)	1.5	(.25)
W*time	.61	(.07)	.58	(.07)	.58	(.08)	.55	(.07)
Random part								
σ^2_e	12.4	(.79)	12.4	(.69)	12.5	(.85)	12.0	
$\sigma^2_{intercept}$	40.8	(5.16)	42.0	(5.19)	40.9	(5.32)	42.4	(5.4)
σ^2_{time}	2.5	(.41)	2.6	(.42)	2.5	(.44)	2.7	(.46)
$\sigma^2_{int*time}$	−6.6	(1.24)	−7.1	(1.27)	−8.8	(1.32)	−7.4	
r_{i*t}	−.66		−.68		−.67		−.6	
% data	73%		93%		64%		84%	

The last line in Table 2.5 shows the percentage of data points that are used in the analysis. In the full data set, six observations are used for each case, making a total of 1,200 data points. In MANOVA, all incomplete cases are removed, which leaves 126 cases (out of 200) or 63% of the original observations. In the multilevel analysis, all cases with a missing observation on the explanatory variable, W, are removed. For cases with a missing observation on one of the time points, only that specific time point is removed from the data set. This removal leaves a data set with 866 observations for 186 persons, or 73% of the original number of observations. Finally, the direct-estimation method for the latent curve model uses all available data points, or 93% of the original number of cases. However, with these sample sizes and these strong effects, all estimates and standard errors are very similar, and one would draw the same conclusion, irrespective of the method used.

This similarity across the estimation methods is not true for the MAR data set. The MANOVA uses 116 or 58% of the original data; multilevel regression, 64%; and direct estimation of the latent curve model, 84%. The effects for measurement occasion and the covariate, W, are again significant in all analyses, including MANOVA. The multilevel regression model estimates the slope for time as 4.63, and the latent curve model estimates the slope as 4.83, both reasonably close to the population value of 5.0. In this example, the multilevel regression does not perform quite as well as the latent curve approach, probably because cases with the predictor W missing had to be deleted. Simple MANOVA on the observed means does not perform well at all. It is instructive to compare the means presented in Table 2.6. These are the means at the five time points. In the first column, the means under the casewise-deletion scheme that MANOVA uses are presented; in the second column, the means as predicted by the full multilevel regression model are listed. Finally, in the third column, the means as predicted by the latent curve model are listed. Again, the latent curve model performs the best, the multilevel-regression somewhat worse, and the MANOVA procedure worst. This pattern is as expected because the data are missing at random (MAR). The MANOVA method, which assumes that data are missing completely at random (MCAR), shows a clear bias. The other two methods, which both assume only MAR, produce very acceptable estimates.

TABLE 2.6
Means for Different Treatments of Missing Observations, MAR Data

Time point	Population	Observed (full deletion)	Predicted (multilevel)	Predicted (latent curve)
0	44	43.5	43.7	44.1
1	49	46.9	48.4	48.9
2	54	52.5	53.0	53.7
3	59	57.6	57.6	58.5
4	64	62.1	62.2	63.3

CONCLUDING COMMENTS

For grouped data, both MANOVA and multilevel regression models lead to similar estimates. However, multilevel modeling is much more flexible than MANOVA if there are a large number of groups, more than two nested levels of grouping, or explanatory variables are estimated at various levels. This benefit also holds when the grouping factors are not nested but crossed period; Goldstein (1995) described extensions of the multilevel model to cross-classified data, which can be modeled using standard multilevel software.

For longitudinal data with fixed occasions, both multilevel regression and latent curve analyses produce very similar estimates. There are, however, differences in the range of applications. In latent curve modeling, each time point is represented by an additional observed variable, whereas in multilevel regression each time point is an additional observation on the same dependent variable. Multilevel regression analysis is clearly more elegant with a large number of varying measurements. In multilevel regression, it is also simple to add additional levels to the model. On the other hand, latent growth curves can be used in applications where the rate of growth (the slope) is used as a predictor in a more complicated path model. In multilevel regression, this flexibility is not possible. The last example also suggests that handling missing observations using the direct-estimation method is more accurate than the simple multilevel approach.

Multilevel structural equation modeling is mainly an alternative when one has a complex factor or path model and a large number of groups. Although more than three levels are possible, this is not really attractive; even with two levels, the setups can become quite complicated (cf. Hox, 1995; Kaplan & Elliott, 1997). An interesting option is to combine latent growth models with multilevel structural equation models, as in Muthén (1997). The result is a very powerful modeling tool; unfortunately again, with complicated setups.

CHAPTER THREE

A Two-Stage Approach to Multilevel Structural Equation Models: Application to Longitudinal Data

Chih-Ping Chou
University of Southern California

Peter M. Bentler
University of California, Los Angeles

Mary Ann Pentz
University of Southern California

The multilevel analytical approach has become widely adopted in social science research, especially since software programs such as HLM (Bryk, Raudenbush, & Congdon, 1996), MLn (Rasbash, Yang, Woodhouse, & Goldstein, 1995), and VARCL (Longford, 1990) have become available. The *multilevel concept* refers to a data structure that is hierarchical; that is, the data are usually collected from units that are nested within another larger social context. This chapter applies a classical multilevel analytical approach to a longitudinal data set from a study of substance abuse prevention. Data were collected both from schools and from students who are nested within schools. Considering students as the first-level (or microlevel) units, and schools as the second-level (or the macrolevel) units, the data structure contains two levels of hierarchy. Analysis can proceed at either level alone or with both levels considered in some optimal way as implemented via multilevel modeling. Although there have been a number of applications of this methodology to student and school-level data (e.g., Li, Duncan, Duncan, Harmer, & Acock, 1997), our approach may be novel because we resurrect an old methodology that uses both levels in a practical way. And we extend this methodology from ordinary multilevel regression models to more general structural equation models. In this chapter, the term *multilevel analytical approach* refers to all the statistical techniques developed to analyze multilevel structured data (also see Hox, 1998; Hox, chap. 2, this volume).

Using the individual as the unit of analysis while ignoring the higher level is certainly the simplest thing to do in many situations. This approach is common in prevention research. Most prevention interventions for adolescents are developed as school-based programs, with the school being the unit assigned to experiment conditions and students within the school receiving the intervention. Data are usually collected from both levels. The data structure, therefore, is hierarchical with students (the microlevel) nested within schools (the macrolevel), which is exactly the situation for which there is common agreement that analysis at the individual level alone poses some problems. In particular, a major concern is that the observations are no longer independent because students in the same school resemble each other more than they resemble students in different schools. Consider the multiple regression model, which is generally based on the four basic assumptions of linearity, normality, homoscedasticity, and independence. For hierarchically structured data, the last two assumptions are obviously violated, especially the assumption of independent observations. In the case of regression analyses that are based on an incorrect assumption about the error distribution, it is quite likely that parameter estimates remain consistent, but that computed standard errors, based on an inappropriate information matrix, are incorrect (and typically underestimated). Thus, hierarchical structure could be ignored if the estimates were of sole interest, but this is rarely the case given that evaluating the significance of effects requires an appropriate standard error estimate. As a result, it would be inappropriate to apply regression models with the individual as the unit of analysis to evaluate intervention effects while ignoring the hierarchical structure of the data. Typically, when interdependence is ignored, there is an inflation of Type I error rate (Addelman, 1970; Hopkins, 1982). An inflation of Type I error indicates that a true null hypothesis is more likely to be rejected. In prevention research, where the experimental effect is of primary interest, an inflation of Type I error may lead researchers to erroneously conclude that there is a program effect.

An alternative approach is to base the analysis on the higher level, or larger social unit. Because schools are commonly treated as the unit of assignment for intervention in prevention research (e.g., through cluster sampling), it is more appropriate to use the unit of assignment as the unit of analysis (see Cook & Campbell, 1979). Unfortunately, severe problems can also arise when using school as the analysis unit, one of the most serious being the small number of schools sometimes included in a prevention study. All the statistical problems associated with small sample size, therefore, also apply to the situation in which only a small number of schools are involved in the analyses—estimates can be inaccurate and unreliable, statistical power can be very poor, and statistical inference can be misleading. In addition, using the school as the unit of analysis usually involves aggregating students' data, which may lead to other problems. For example, a great deal of information on within-school or between-students variation is lost due to aggregation. And finally, the meaning of a variable at the aggregated level can be different from that at the individual level (Blalock, 1979), and relationships among the aggregated data are usually inflated relative to the individual level. The conceptual issues associated with interpreting variation and correlations among aggregated components, such as schools, remain when considering a multilevel model that has a between-school component. However, some of the statistical inefficiencies can be improved by considering both levels simultaneously, even though having a small number of second-level units will always pose a challenge to correct inference no matter what the methodology.

The multilevel analytical approach that takes interdependence into account in the analytical process ideally weds the best features of the individual and higher order levels of analysis. As reviewed by Bryk and Raudenbush (1992), Goldstein (1995), Kaplan (1996), and others, specification of appropriate within- and between-school error structures for a simultaneous estimation of all effects allows a more precise, and perhaps optimal, estimation of effects at both individual and school levels. In the context of structural equation models, such an approach was developed by Lee and Poon (in press). Nonetheless, even a theoretically optimal approach may not always perform best in practical situations. For example, the generalized least squares approach to estimating multilevel regression models that may be optimal in theory, may not perform as well as simpler approaches when its basic assumptions, such as multivariate normality of errors, are not met. Violations of assumptions can occur in many different ways. Kennedy (1992), for example, stated that the generalized least squares estimator may have higher variance than the presumably less optimal ordinary least squares estimator if the weight matrix is poorly estimated. The breakdown of generalized least squares can also be illustrated with covariance structure models. Although there is an asymptotically optimal methodology for such models when the observations are independent (i.e., Browne's, 1984, asymptotically distribution-free methodology), in practice standard errors and tests based on this methodology are highly unreliable unless the sample size is extremely large (e.g., Bentler & Dudgeon, 1996; Yuan & Bentler, 1997).

We found no empirical evidence in the multilevel literature on the extent to which, and the conditions under which, the technically optimal estimator, with its standard errors and test statistics, actually performs better in a variety of practical data analysis contexts than do alternative, simpler, and theoretically less optimal approaches. Older and less sophisticated approaches may outperform the optimal approaches in some contexts, for example, with a not too large number of second-level units. With this in mind, we resurrect an older regression approach and apply it to the newer context of structural equation modeling. We propose a two-stage estimation approach to multilevel data, appropriate for situations in which the number of observations at the first level may vary and the number of observations at the highest level is sufficiently large to allow application of standard large-sample theory.

The impetus for this two-stage approach comes from the 20-year-old "slopes-as-outcomes" analysis used by Burstein and his colleagues (Burstein, 1980; Burstein, Linn, & Cappel, 1978; Burstein & Miller, 1981). Conceptually, a slope reflects the impact of a covariate on an outcome variable. A slope is computed within a school based on the independent observations within the school, thus, the steepness of a slope can vary from school to school. Furthermore, variation in the size of each slope is associated with differences in school-level variables, such as school policies, orientation, and so forth. We extend this approach to structural equation models, where the outcome for a given school may be not only a slope but also, in fact, any parameter of a structural equation model obtained from that school. Variation in such parameters across schools can then be studied.

Two-Stage Estimation Approach

With the two-stage estimation approach to multilevel structural equation modeling, a mean and/or covariance structure model is estimated at the first level for each unit at the next level. In a two-level situation, there are as many such models as there are units at the second level, that is, there are as many models as there are schools. These models do not need to be constrained to be equal across observations at the second level (i.e., across schools), although some parameters could be constrained in principle. The estimated parameters for each unit (school), along with other variables that may be available only at this (school) level, provide a new data matrix that can be analyzed by any structural equation model. Such a model would summarize the low-level model and explain the variability at the second level. A structured means model of the data at the second level provides model-based means that reflect a meta-analytic summary of the parameters of the average within-school structural model. The mean and covariance structure parameters can also be used to describe differences between schools.

In practice, it is convenient to estimate within-school models without worrying about equality of any parameters across schools. As a result, a homogeneous random effect in the Level 1 model, sometimes called σ_e^2, cannot be adequately estimated with this two-stage approach. One possibility to obtain this estimate is through an equality constraint on the Level 1 residual variances across the higher level units, which can be done in multiple group structural equation modeling (McArdle & Hamagami, 1996). However, this technique can become very complex and quite inefficient if the number of Level 2 units is large. We do not pursue such an illustration in this chapter.

In their discussion on various estimation methods based on two-stage approaches, de Leeuw and Kreft (1986) concluded that different estimation methods do not seem to affect the size of regression coefficients. Similar conclusions were also reached by Tate and Wongbundhit (1983), who compared single-equation, separate-equations, and mixed-estimation procedures. However, de Leeuw and Kreft found that estimates of disturbances in the second stage of analysis (i.e., a between-school model) can be different (1986, p. 79). Comparing the single-stage and two-stage approaches using ordinary least squares estimation, they showed that estimates of fixed effects were very similar between the two approaches. However, standard errors obtained from the single-stage approach were consistently smaller than those from the two-stage approach. Thus, although the two-stage approach may not be the most efficient statistically, generality is obtained because both regression and latent-variable models can be accommodated equally well at any level, and any appropriate statistical estimation and testing machinery can be used at any level.

To better understand the statistical properties of the two-stage approach, we first compare it with the one-stage, or simultaneous, estimation approach utilized in HLM

(Bryk et al., 1996). In these comparisons, we use a regression model and a latent curve model (Meredith & Tisak, 1990), which can be considered as a special case of both multilevel regression and structural equation models, and a multilevel structural equation model. All these models are developed using longitudinal data obtained from a substance use prevention program for adolescents (Pentz et al., 1989).

In summary, based on earlier research, we take advantage of the SEM on multilevel data using a two-stage estimation approach. The application of multilevel SEM would yield more information in understanding school-level variability. In practical terms, the multilevel SEM approach would enable more comprehensive estimation of school effects on student behaviors, in this case, adolescent drug use in a prevention study, and would more adequately account for the variance in drug use than has been possible in previous prevention research.

STATISTICAL BACKGROUND

The proposed two-stage approach to multilevel structural equation modeling is a new attempt to resurrect a useful old approach to dealing with hierarchically structured data and then to apply it to structural equation models. To understand this approach, we begin with an introduction to the most commonly used multilevel analytical approach with a regression model. The latent curve model, which can be considered to be a special case of both the multilevel regression model and the structural equation model, is discussed next. Finally, we discuss the multilevel structural equation model.

Multilevel Regression Model

The multilevel regression model consists of at least two levels. The Level 1 (also known as the microlevel, within-unit, or within-group) model is shown in Equation 1:

$$y_{ij} = x_{ij}\beta_j + e_{ij}, \tag{1}$$

where y_{ij} stands for the outcome variable of subject i in group j, x_{ij} is a vector containing p covariates for participant i in group j, β_j is a $p \times 1$ vector of regression weights in group j, and e_{ij} is normally distributed with mean 0 and variance σ_e^2, or $e_{ij} \sim N(0, \sigma_e^2)$. It should be noted that the intercept is also included in the β_j vector, that is, it is a common practice to insert a constant 1 as the first covariate in x_{ij} and thus, the first element in the β_j vector is interpreted as the intercept.

The Level 2 (also known as the macrolevel, between-unit, or between-group) model is developed using the regression weights, β, as outcomes:

$$\beta_j = z_j\gamma + u_j. \tag{2}$$

Treating the regression weights as the dependent variable, Equation 2 models the impacts of macrolevel variables z_j on β_j. Again, the γ-vector contains both the relevant intercept term and the regression weights to demonstrate the strength of the influence of variables z_j on β_j. The u_j is a vector of random errors, assumed to be normally distributed with mean 0 and variance σ_u^2. The Level 2 model investigates the influence of the covariates z_j at macrolevel on the intercepts and regression weights obtained from the microlevel model. One of the most important statistical advantages of this analytical approach is that β_j parameters are treated as stochastic, or random, and thus, they are "slopes as outcomes."

Latent Curve Model

Next consider the latent curve model (LCM) as a special case of the multilevel regression model setup. This model, also referred to as the latent growth curve model, was developed as a generalized method of representing development (Meredith & Tisak, 1990). It can also be considered as a special case of the structural equation model (Bentler & Weeks, 1980; Jöreskog, 1973, 1977b; McDonald, 1978; Sörbom, 1974). The LCM includes repeated measures of individual behavior as a function of chronological development in the Level 1 model such that change in substance use behavior among students is explicitly modeled as a function of age/grade. Thus, considering the profile of within-unit growth across time in the Level 1 model, the between-unit variation in growth is summarized in the Level 2 model. The intercept and regression slope associated with age/grade, obtained from the within-individual model, are treated as outcome measures in the Level 2 model. The intercept represents the initial status of substance use, whereas the regression slope reflects the developmental trajectory of substance use as the individuals get older.

This application of the LCM uses only schools as units of analysis and considers the school-level variable, prevalence rate of monthly cigarette use, as the outcome variable at the lowest level of analysis. This outcome variable is modeled as a function of time. Subsequently, in the higher order model, the coefficients of the time trend are regressed on independent variables of school type and experimental condition. The Level 1 model with a linear growth assumption for the outcome measure can therefore be expressed as:

$$y_{tj} = \pi_{0j} + c_{tj}\pi_{1j} + e_{tj}, \tag{3}$$

where y_{tj} represents the prevalence rate of monthly cigarette use for school j at time t; c_{tj} represents the time of measurement (e.g., $c_{tj} = 0, 1, 2$, etc.); π_{0j} and π_{1j} stand for the growth parameters of interest, that is, the initial status and growth trajectory of monthly cigarette use prevalence for each respective school; and e_{tj} is a normally distributed residual with mean 0 and variance σ_e^2. In addition to the distributional assumption on e_{tj}, typically one also hypothesizes that e_{tj} is homoscedastic over time. Compared with Equation 1, the Level 1 LCM model uses c_{tj}, or the time variable, as the only covariate for repeated measures of outcome. Time is usually coded to reflect the actual time interval in months or years between observations. In practice, other covariates besides time could be used in Equation 3, but we do not do so.

At the next level, the coefficients on time are explained by higher order variables. Using two explanatory variables, say z_{1j} and z_{2j}, for the outcome measures π_{0j} and π_{1j}, the Level 2 equations can be specified as:

$$\pi_{0j} = \beta_{00} + \beta_{01}z_{1j} + \beta_{02}z_{2j} + r_{0j}, \tag{4}$$

$$\pi_{1j} = \beta_{10} + \beta_{11}z_{1j} + \beta_{12}z_{2j} + r_{1j}, \tag{5}$$

where β_{00} and β_{10} stand for the adjusted means, or intercepts, of π_{0j} and π_{1j}, respectively. The β_{01} and β_{11} are the regression weights for the impacts of z_1 on initial status (π_0) and growth rate (π_1), respectively, whereas β_{02} and β_{12} represent the impacts of the z_2 explanatory variable.

The parameters of this model can also be considered as either fixed or random effects. In each of Equations 4 and 5, the β coefficients are fixed effects. The variances and covariances of the residual r variables in Equations 4 and 5 and the variance of the e_{tj} in Equation 3 are considered random effects. The Level 1 model in Equation 3 can also include other time-varying covariates (see Equation 5 in Hox, chap. 2, this volume). Other extensions of the LCM are discussed in MacCallum and Kim (chap. 4, this volume).

Structural Equation Model

As is well known, structural equation modeling (SEM) is used to evaluate a substantive theory with empirical data through a hypothesized model. Good introductions to SEM can be found, for example, in Byrne (1994), Dunn, Everitt, and Pickles (1993), Hoyle (1995), Mueller (1996), and Schumacker and Lomax (1996). SEM models represent hypothesized relations among variables, including latent or unmeasured variables, in the form of sets of equations. A simple way to think about SEM modeling applied to the multilevel context is to consider a generalized set of SEM equations as a substitute for the basic regression model given in Equation 1 at the lowest level and simultaneously as a substitute for the regression model at the next level, Equation 2. Consequently, the multilevel regression and latent curve models can be considered as a special case of the multilevel structural equation model.

In principle, any set of SEM equations could be used, but we use the Bentler-Weeks (1980) model as implemented in the computer program we use to exemplify our ideas (EQS; Bentler, 1995). Consider a vector of p observed variables x selected from a larger set of variables V that may include latent variables, errors of measurement, and so forth. Thus $x = GV$, where G is a known selection matrix. Furthermore, let the variables V contain variables predicted from other variables—so-called dependent variables—arranged in the vector η, and the remaining variables—so-called independent variables—arranged in the vector ξ. Any variable at the receiving end of a one-way arrow in the path diagram of a model is a dependent variable; otherwise, it is an independent variable. In the Bentler-Weeks model, factors, measured variables, measurement errors for measured variables, and disturbances associated with factors can be defined as either independent variables or dependent variables, depending on the model specification. Let $V = (\eta', \xi')'$. The Bentler-Weeks model can be expressed as the matrix equation

$$v = Bv + \Gamma\xi, \tag{6}$$

where the coefficient matrices B and Γ contain the unknown path coefficients or regression weights. In addition to B and Γ, the parameters of the model also include the covariance matrix of the independent variables ξ, namely Φ. Standard covariance structure algebra gives

$$\Sigma = G(I - B)^{-1}\Gamma\Phi\Gamma'(I - B)^{-1}{}'G' \tag{7}$$

as the covariance matrix of the x variables and, when there is also a structure on the means, μ, of the measured variables,

$$\mu = G(I - B)^{-1}\Gamma\mu_\xi, \tag{8}$$

where the means of the independent variables μ_ξ are also parameters. When applied to multilevel modeling, Equation 6 and its associated covariance in Equation 7 and mean structure parameters in Equation 8 can be considered at any level of the hierarchy.

To be specific to multilevel structural equation modeling, a model is constructed for each higher level unit, say school, based on the students within that school:

$$v_j = B_j v_j + \Gamma_j \xi_j, \tag{9}$$

where subscript j represents the jth school in the data. Thus, this equation is consistent with the conceptualization given in Equation 1 as the Level 1, or within-school, model. Further, let us consider the mean and covariance matrix of the x variables within the jth school to be given by μ_j and Σ_j, which depend on the parameters given by B_j, Γ_j, Φ_j, and $\mu_{\xi j}$. For convenience, now assemble all the free parameters in a vector θ_j, that is, θ_j consists of all the free parameters specified in B_j, Γ_j, Φ_j, $\mu_{\xi j}$. Then write, in a compact and general way, $\mu_j = \mu(\theta_j)$ and $\Sigma_j = \Sigma(\theta_j)$, which may be considered the SEM null hypothesis. Note that the form of the specific model determines the type of parameters in a given model. For example, a confirmatory factor analysis model has factor loadings and factor and unique variances and covariances as parameters. See Bollen (1989) for a further description of various types of SEM models.

Different schools may have different estimates of parameters θ_j. The variations in the estimates of the θ_j parameters at the school level are of interest in the multilevel structural equation model. In general terms, one can equate the θ_j for each school with the random variables v defined in Equation 6, and develop a complete Bentler-Weeks parameterization of these variables at the next level using an equation such as Equation 6, with its consequent mean and covariance structure. Here, we are more narrow and consider the special case that we used in our example. That is, following the Level 2 model commonly adopted in the multilevel approach, a regression model is developed with θ_j as the outcome measures and other school-level variables, z_j, as the predictors. Then, the between-school model can be expressed as:

$$\theta_j = z_j \beta + r_j . \tag{10}$$

Equation 10 models the impacts of school-level variables z_j on θ_j. The β vector contains both the intercept term and the regression weights to demonstrate the strength of the influence of z_j on θ_j. The r_j is a vector of random errors that are assumed to be normally distributed with mean 0 and variances $\sigma_{r_j}^2$ as is commonly defined in the multilevel approach. Clearly, the Level 2 model concentrates on the influence of the covariates at the macrolevel on the intercepts, regression coefficients, and covariances of the structural model that describes the microlevel data.

In principle, it is possible to simultaneously estimate all the parameters of a SEM model that has specifications at multiple levels. For example, Muthén and colleagues (see Longford & Muthén, 1992; Muthén, 1989; Muthén & Satorra, 1989) proposed a single-stage approach for a multilevel factor analytical model (see also Hox, chap. 2, this volume). This approach requires the sample covariance matrix to be decomposed into a between-unit covariance matrix and a within-unit covariance matrix before data can be adequately analyzed. Statistics associated with such an approach can be approximately optimal (e.g., Muthén, 1994) or optimal under appropriate assumptions (e.g., Lee & Poon, in press). These types of approaches are widely known. In this chapter, we use only the proposed two-stage SEM approach, in which a model based on Equation 9 is estimated first, and the results are used in a model based on Equation 10 at the higher level.

METHODOLOGY

The data used in this chapter to investigate the two-stage estimation approach for a multilevel structural equation model are obtained from a longitudinal substance use prevention study of adolescents (Pentz et al., 1989). These data are used to compare the proposed two-stage estimation approach with single-stage estimation, using the same statistical model. The similarities and differences between the results observed may provide a better understanding of the proposed two-stage approach and its feasibility.

Subjects

The data contain a total of 57 middle- or junior-high schools in Indianapolis, which were randomly assigned to a health education program that contained a control group or a substance use prevention intervention program group. For simplicity of comparisons between the single-stage and two-stage approaches, we concentrate only on the 50 junior-high schools (23 control and 27 program schools) where seventh grade was the baseline data collection year. A total of 2,779 students were surveyed at the baseline wave.

Measures

Four follow-ups were conducted: the first one was 6 months after baseline; and the other three follow-ups were at 1-year intervals. At each assessment, students completed a self-report questionnaire consisting of about 100 items that measured demographic characteristics, behaviors, attitudes, and social influences related to adolescent drug use. To clearly reflect the variables selected for comparisons, variables starting with the letter "I" indicate that it is selected at the individual level and those starting with the letter "S" that it is from the school level. The individual-level variables are monthly cigarette use (ICIGUSE) and three social-norm (NORM) variables: perceived percentage of cigarettes (ICIGPP), alcohol (IALCPP), and marijuana (IMARPP) used among students of the same age. Three school-level covariates were selected to investigate their impact on the intercept and slope parameters obtained from the within-school model. These three covariates are group membership (SGROUP = 0 for control group and 1 for program group), school type (STYPE = 0 for private school and 1 for public school), and the prevalence of monthly cigarette use (SCIGUSE = percentage of students reporting any monthly cigarette use) within each school. A numerical value is attached to the end of the variable name, if necessary, to reflect the wave on which the variable was obtained, with 0 for baseline and 1 for the first follow-up, and so forth. These variables were used as either covariates or outcome variables in the comparisons below.

Analysis Plan

To investigate the properties of the two-stage estimation approach as opposed to the single-stage approach in most multilevel analytical techniques, we use the multilevel regression and latent curve models. In the multilevel regression model, the Level 1, or student-level model, was developed using monthly cigarette use at the first follow-up as the dependent variable (ICIGUSE1). In addition to an intercept, monthly cigarette use (ICIGUSE0) and perceived percentage of students of the same age using cigarettes (ICIGPP0) at the baseline were used as covariates in Equation 1. The Level 2, or school-level model, used intercept, β_{0j}, and slopes, β_j(ICIGUSE0) and β_j(ICIGPP0), as the outcomes and group membership (SGROUP), school type (STYPE), and the prevalence of monthly cigarette use (SCIGUSE) as the covariates in Equation 2. The single-stage multilevel regression approach was implemented using the HLM program (Bryk et al., 1996), whereas the two-stage approach was computed at each of the two stages using the maximum likelihood option of EQS (Bentler, 1995).

In the second comparison with a latent curve model, schools were used as the units of analysis. The prevalence of monthly cigarette use in each school (SCIGUSE) was computed across all five waves and was used as the outcome measure in the Level 1 model of Equation 3. In this model, time of measurement relative to the baseline was used as the only covariate for the repeated measures of SCIGUSE. To more accurately represent this spacing of the measurements, time was defined at 0 for baseline and 1, 3, 5, and 7 for the four follow-ups, respectively, because the first follow-up was only 6 months after baseline and the subsequent three follow-ups were 1 year apart. The Level 2 model of Equations 4 and 5 used an intercept plus SGROUP and STYPE as predictors. In this setup, the HLM program was used to obtain the standard multilevel effects, whereas EQS was used in two different ways. First, following the approach described by Chou, Bentler, and Pentz (1998), a standard one-level growth curve SEM model was set up. Second, the two-stage approach described previously was used.

Finally, a multilevel structural equation model was developed and evaluated using the two-stage estimation approach. The Level 1 model based on Equation 9 (see Figure 3.1) consists of two factors, NORM0 and NORM1. There is a path from NORM0 to NORM1 and an intercept for NORM1 based on its regression on the constant, τ_1. Three intercepts for the six measured variables, held equal as shown in Figure 3.1, were also estimated. Each factor contains three indicators, which are perceived percentage of cigarette, alcohol, and marijuana use among students of the same age, respectively. Indicators for NORM0 were observed at the baseline, whereas those for NORM1 were observed at the first follow-up. The Level 2 model based on Equation 10 was a path model with four factor loadings (λ_{21}, λ_{31}, λ_{52}, and λ_{62}), one factor

FIGURE 3.1
Level 1 Model of a Multilevel Structural Equation Model

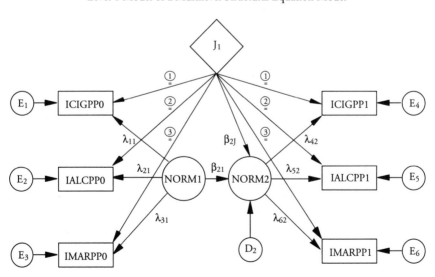

Note. Three pairs of parameters are constrained equal as indicated by the "=" sign.

intercept (β_{2j}), and the stability coefficient (β_{21}) for the NORM factor as the outcomes, whereas SGROUP and STYPE are the covariates. The intercepts of the measured variables, estimated at the first stage, were not considered of interest and are not studied at the second stage. The two-stage approach is performed using EQS to analyze this model, which cannot be estimated with HLM due to the presence of the latent variables.

RESULTS

Multilevel Regression Model

Because 9 schools did not have sufficient statistics and were excluded from the estimation procedure by the HLM program, comparisons between the HLM and the two-stage (T-S) approaches were made only on the remaining 41 schools. Comparisons of the HLM and the T-S approaches are summarized in Table 3.1, which is organized so that results for the fixed effects are given in the top part of the table and results for the random effects are given in the bottom part. There are three coefficients, β_j, from Equation 1, associated with the intercept, ICIGUSE0, and ICIGPP0. For each, there is a Level 2 equation (see Equation 2), and therefore each has four fixed γ coefficients. These coefficients are associated with intercept, SGROUP, STYPE, and SCIGUSE, respectively, at the school level. The estimates for these coefficients and their standard errors are given in Table 3.1. The bottom part of the table contains the results for the random effects. These represent the variances and covariances of the u_j at Level 2, based on Equation 2, and variance of the e_{ij} at Level 1, based on Equation 1. The estimates and standard errors for the random effects are also given in Table 3.1. Note that HLM does not produce standard errors for the random effects unless the full maximum likelihood estimates are requested, whereas the T-S approach does not produce variance estimate for the e_{ij}.

The estimates from the two approaches are quite similar for several parameters. For the fixed effects, the significance tests are very consistent, except for the impact of group membership (SGROUP) on the slope of baseline monthly cigarette use (ICIGUSE0). Results from HLM showed a significant effect, whereas the two-stage approach showed a nonsignificant effect. This discrepancy is due mainly to the larger estimate of the standard error of the parameter in the T-S approach. In fact, the two-stage approach consistently yielded larger standard errors than did the HLM approach. This finding is consistent with similar results using ordinary least squares estimation as demonstrated by de Leeuw and Kreft (1986).

Latent Curve Model

Results obtained from the HLM, single-stage EQS, and two-stage EQS approaches are reported in Table 3.2. As in Table 3.1, the top part of the table gives results for the

TABLE 3.1
TABLE 3.1
Parameter Estimates From HLM and the Two-Stage (T-S) Approach
on a Multilevel Regression Model

Parameter	HLM		T-S	
Fixed effects				
For β_{0j} or intercept				
Intercept	1.42	(0.36)**	1.49	(0.64)**
SGROUP	−0.16	(0.07)*	−0.20	(0.08)*
STYPE	0.13	(0.08)	0.13	(0.08)
SCIGUSE	2.74	(0.50)**	3.44	(0.54)**
For β_j (ICIGUSE0)				
Intercept	0.42	(0.06)**	0.39	(0.09)**
SGROUP	−0.33	(0.09)**	−0.20	(0.17)
STYPE	0.12	(0.10)	0.26	(0.17)
SCIGUSE	1.09	(0.62)	0.88	(1.12)
For β_j (ICIGPP0)				
Intercept	−0.15	(0.04)**	−0.18	(0.07)**
SGROUP	−0.15	(0.08)	−0.16	(0.15)
STYPE	−0.07	(0.09)	0.03	(0.15)
SCIGUSE	0.70	(0.58)	−0.91	(0.95)
Random effects				
Intercept, σ^2_{u0}	0.03	(0.01)**	0.07	(0.02)**
β_j(ICIGUSE0), σ^2_{u1}	0.03	(0.01)**	0.29	(0.06)**
β_j(ICIGPP0), σ^2_{u2}	0.02	(0.01)	0.21	(0.05)**
$cov(u_0, u_1)$	0.02	(0.01)	0.02	(0.02)
$cov(u_0, u_2)$	−0.02	(0.01)	−0.04	(0.02)*
$cov(u_1, u_2)$	−0.01	(0.01)	0.12	(0.04)*
σ^2_e	1.01	(0.04)**	−	−

Note. Standard errors are listed parenthetically. * Significant at .05 level. ** Significant at .01 level.
− Estimate not computed.

fixed effects; these are the β coefficients of Equations 4 and 5 associated with the intercept, SGROUP, and STYPE used in predicting the π_{0j} and π_{1j} coefficients. The bottom part of the table gives results for the random effects, that is, the variances and covariances of the residuals in the equations.

The first columns of Table 3.2 were obtained from Chou et al. (1998), who discussed the similarities and differences that result from the application of HLM and a single-group SEM as applied to a latent curve model. The two-stage approach yields results of the fixed effects that are virtually the same as those obtained from HLM and the LCM model in the middle column, with equivalent significance levels. For the

TABLE 3.2
Parameter Estimates from the HLM, EQS, and Two-Stage (T-S) Approaches
Using a Linear Latent Curve Model

Parameter	HLM		EQS		T-S	
Fixed effects						
For π_{0j} or intercept						
Intercept	12.02	(1.22)**	12.02	(1.38)**	12.03	(1.38)**
SGROUP	−1.13	(2.45)	−1.13	(2.40)	−1.12	(2.40)
STYPE	9.11	(2.46)**	9.11	(2.41)**	9.11	(2.41)**
For π_{1j} (TIME)						
Intercept	2.19	(0.22)**	2.19	(0.25)**	2.19	(0.25)**
SGROUP	−0.57	(0.44)	−0.57	(0.43)	−0.57	(0.43)
STYPE	−1.60	(0.44)**	−1.60	(0.43)**	−1.60	(0.43)**
Random effects						
Intercept [$\sigma^2(r_0)$]	53.79	(14.16)**	50.35	(14.59)**	71.22	(14.39)**
π_{1j}(TIME) [$\sigma^2(r_1)$]	1.17	(0.47)**	1.05	(0.48)+	2.29	(0.46)**
$\sigma(r_0,r_1)$	−2.41	(2.01)	−2.08	(2.07)	−6.05	(2.02)**
σ^2_e	39.94	(4.61)**	40.74	(4.75)**	–	–

Note. Standard errors are listed parenthetically. * Significant at .05 level. ** Significant at .01 level.
– Estimate not available. (First column adapted from Chou et al., 1998.)

random effects, the estimates obtained with the T-S approach consistently show an upward bias.

As mentioned earlier, the T-S approach does not allow the estimation of the random effect in the Level 1 model (i.e., the variance of e_{ij} in Equation 3); this can be considered as a major drawback of this approach. An estimate of this random effect can be obtained by setting an equality constraint on Level 1 error variances using multiple group SEM approach (see McArdle & Hamagami, 1996). This approach was more complicated in the first example with a multilevel regression model because the sample sizes within each school were different, so we did not apply it there. Applying this approach to the LCM example of Table 3.2, we obtained a value of 39.93, which is very comparable to the 39.94 and 40.74 obtained from the HLM and EQS programs, respectively.

Multilevel Structural Equation Model

The Level 1 SEM was evaluated for each of the 50 schools in the first stage of estimation. Of the 50 schools analyzed, only 45 yielded acceptable results. Five schools were excluded from the second-stage analysis because data from these schools did not yield a convergent solution or had multiple problems, such as Heywood cases or linear dependencies in the estimation procedure (see Bentler & Chou, 1987, for a discussion of estimation problems in SEM). The impact of SGROUP and STYPE on the parameters in the first-stage structural model are investigated in the second stage.

The results are summarized in Table 3.3, where, as before, the fixed effects are given in the top of the table and the random effects are given in the bottom. There are six second-level equations, corresponding to each coefficient from the first stage. The results for each equation are shown as a column in the top part of the table. The coefficients in each equation are the fixed coefficients for intercept, SGROUP, and STYPE, which are used as predictors in each equation. Finally, the variance and covariances among the estimates yielded from the first stage are given in the bottom part of the table.

Results of the fixed effects indicate that the means of the parameters obtained from the Level 1 model are significant. Another significant impact of the school-level variables on these parameters is the experimental condition (SGROUP) on the stability of

TABLE 3.3
Results From a Multilevel Structural Equation Model

Parameter	λ_{21}	λ_{31}	λ_{52}	λ_{62}	γ_{2j}	β_{21}
Fixed effects						
Intercept	1.15**	0.89**	1.22**	0.97**	0.65**	0.51**
	(0.05)	(0.05)	(0.11)	(0.12)	(0.10)	(0.04)
SGROUP	0.01	−0.06	−0.18	−0.42	0.02	−0.16*
	(0.11)	(0.11)	(0.21)	(0.24)	(0.20)	(0.08)
STYPE	0.06	−0.07	−0.06	0.03	−0.03	−0.05
	(0.11)	(0.11)	(0.21)	(0.24)	(0.20)	(0.08)
Random effects						
λ_{21}	0.13**					
	(0.03)					
λ_{31}	0.08**	0.13**				
	(0.02)	(0.03)				
λ_{52}	0.04	0.13**	0.48**			
	(0.04)	(0.04)	(0.10)			
λ_{62}	0.04	0.16**	0.51**	0.62**		
	(0.04)	(0.05)	(0.11)	(0.12)		
β_{2j}	0.06	0.01	−0.07	−0.09	0.45**	
	(0.04)	(0.04)	(0.07)	(0.08)	(0.10)	
β_{21}	0.02	0.02	−0.06*	−0.06	0.01	0.06**
	(0.01)	(0.01)	(0.03)	(0.03)	(0.03)	(0.01)

Note. Standard errors are listed parenthetically. * Significant at .05 level. ** Significant at .01 level. λ_{21}, λ_{31}, λ_{52}, and λ_{62} indicate factor loadings of V2 and V3 on factor NORM0, and V5 and V6 on factor NORM1, respectively. β_{2j} is the factor mean of NORM1, and β_{21} is the regression weight of NORM1 on NORM0. Variance of the parameters are along the diagonal and covariances are below the diagonal.

48   CHOU, BENTLER, PENTZ

the NORM factor. The negative regression coefficient indicates that the strength of the relationship between the NORM factors at the baseline and first follow-up has been significantly weakened by the prevention program. In other words, the control group demonstrates a more stable perception of the norm of substance use among students of the same age across time, whereas the prevention program disrupts what is otherwise the normal developmental sequence of the perceived social norm for drug use. Information on random effects is not particularly informative, except that estimates of some coefficients significantly covaried across the schools.

CONCLUSION

Muthén and Satorra (1995) pointed out that with multilevel data, one could do aggregated and disaggregated modeling. In the former, the total variation in variables is analyzed, recognizing that it can be represented as a sum of between-level (here, school) and pooled within-level (here, individual) variation, although there is no special interest in isolating these sources of variance. In the approach presented here, based on disaggregated modeling, there is a specific interest in both levels of variation because under the null hypothesis each part represents an integral part of the data generation method whose parameters are of interest. The ability to isolate these sources of variance is, of course, the promise of multilevel modeling.

A two-stage approach was proposed in this chapter to provide parameter estimates for multilevel structural equation models. The multilevel structural equation model can be considered as a more general model than either the multilevel regression model or the latent curve model because the latter two can be estimated using standard hierarchical modeling computer software. Comparisons were made between the two-stage and HLM approaches to get a better understanding of the properties associated with a two-stage approach. Although the results yielded by these two approaches were not identical, the significance tests and, thus, the statistical inferences, were quite consistent. Comparisons with the latent curve model offered almost the same results among the HLM, one-stage EQS, and the two-stage (T-S) approach on the parameter estimates of the fixed effects. Although the corresponding standard errors were the same between the EQS and two-stage approach, they were slightly different with HLM. For the Level 2 random effects, the T-S approach yielded much larger estimates than did the HLM and one-stage EQS approaches. The Level 1 random effect, however, is not directly available in the T-S approach.

In general, the T-S approach, which is computationally cumbersome, offered quite acceptable results compared to stand-alone software programs, such as HLM and one-stage EQS. In a general multilevel SEM context with latent variables, these alternatives are not available, and either the T-S approach or a more optimal approach such as that of Lee and Poon (in press) must be used. Although the statistics that result from the T-S approach may not be the most efficient asymptotically, lack of asymptotic optimality has not prevented other approaches to multilevel modeling from becoming popular. For example, Muthén's (1994) MUML estimator is, in the case of unbalanced data, not optimal, and the actual behavior of the associated test statistics and standard errors are not really known. Nonetheless, informal opinion holds that the MUML approach seems to provide acceptable statistical results. Clearly the T-S approach, as the MUML approach, needs further extensive empirical evaluation to determine when it could be reliably used and when caution would be clearly indicated.

With all the limitations of the two-stage approach in mind, it nonetheless seems promising in its application to multilevel analysis. The two-stage approach allows more general specification for both Level 1 and Level 2 models than do regression-based multilevel models. Whereas the multilevel structural equation model developed in this chapter constructed a latent variable SEM for the Level 1 units and only a regression model for the Level 2 units, this is not an inherent limitation. Another SEM can, in fact, be specified for the Level 2 units also. Other issues relevant to SEM awaiting further investigation may also be considered in the context of multilevel structural equation modeling. For example, a structural equation model allowing finite mixtures of different types of units can be used at any stage. For example, in the context of students nested within schools, a mixture of several population models—in which population membership is not known or changes across time (e.g., students who change schools during the course of a study)—could be used at the student level or at the school level (Yung, 1997). Also, multiple group or multiple population models can be used, such as at the school level, when it is known that there are different types of schools, (e.g., private and public). Finally, advanced estimation techniques, such as those for nonnormal data (e.g., Yuan & Bentler, 1997), could be utilized when they become available.

CHAPTER FOUR

Modeling Multivariate Change

Robert C. MacCallum
Cheongtag Kim
Ohio State University

In longitudinal research, investigators are often interested in studying individual differences in patterns of change on measured variables over time. Conventional approaches to this problem, along with the vast majority of published applications, have focused on analysis of change in one variable at a time. However, there often exist interesting and important questions involving relationships between patterns of change on different variables. For instance, what is the association between the rate of increase on different measures of physical growth or of psychological development? What is the association between patterns of learning in different domains or on different kinds of tasks? In this chapter, we consider methods for the analysis of multivariate change so as to obtain information about relationships between patterns of change on different variables. This is essentially an expository presentation wherein we review existing methods, illustrate their use, and discuss relationships among them.

Our primary focus is on the use of multilevel models for studying change on multiple outcome variables simultaneously. We first consider the data structure to which such an approach is applicable. We then review the use of multilevel models for the analysis of univariate change and the extension of such models to the multivariate case, and we present an empirical illustration of this technique. Finally, we briefly describe and illustrate the close relationship of these models to latent curve models. More detailed coverage of these topics is provided by MacCallum, Kim, Malarkey, and Kiecolt-Glaser (1997).

DATA STRUCTURES

The data structure of interest consists of measures on multiple variables (to be called outcome variables or response variables in this chapter) for the same group of subjects at multiple points in time. It is not necessary that all subjects be measured at the same time points, nor at the same number of time points. Also, the various response variables may be measured at different time points, or different numbers of time points. For either method, it is most desirable that the sample size, N, be large relative to the number of variables and number of time points, although little information is available to establish minimum levels of N. The methods we describe involve fitting models to observational data and thus require reasonably large N to yield precise parameter estimates and for asymptotic properties to hold adequately. We do not consider the case where data are available for a small number of subjects at a very large number of occasions. Such data are typically analyzed using time series methods. It is desirable, however, that the number of measurement occasions not be small. We consider models representing patterns of change over time, and it is obvious that more complex models require the availability of data at more time points. There is no reliable rule of thumb, but we suggest that linear change models probably require at least four to five occasions of measurement, and more complex models involving parameters indicating such aspects as acceleration and asymptote require substantially more than that. The critical point is that the number of time points minus the number of parameters estimated per individual not be too small. For instance, for a linear model fit to data from five occasions, we are estimating two parameters (slope and intercept) per person, resulting in a difference of three. From another perspective, difficulties may also arise if the number of measurement occasions is large relative to the complexity of the model of change. For instance, the ability of a model of linear change to explain data will likely deteriorate as the number of time points increases well beyond five or six. Real complexities and random influences may tend to make it difficult to fit a parsimonious model to data from a large number of time points. Thus, it is not necessarily advisable to design studies such that measures are obtained at a maximum number of occasions. Rather, one must obtain measures at a sufficient number of occasions to provide adequate data for fitting the most complex model under consideration.

MULTILEVEL MODELS FOR LONGITUDINAL DATA

Multilevel Models for Univariate Change

In general, multilevel models are used for studying the structure in hierarchically organized data, where units of observation at one level are nested in units of observation at a higher level. A common example is students nested within classes nested within schools. Hierarchical data structures may have any number of levels, and there may be variables measured on the units at any or all levels. Multilevel models (also called mixed models, random coefficient models, hierarchical linear models) provide a framework for representing the structure of such data within and between levels, thus eliminating the need to aggregate data or to analyze different levels separately. Longitudinal data can be considered to have a hierarchical structure, where occasions of measurement are nested within subjects. In the univariate case, we are interested in a single response variable measured at each occasion for each individual. The variable measured at the lowest level, occasion of measurement, is time of measurement. There may also be individual differences variables measured at the individual level and not varying over time.

Bryk and Raudenbush (1987, 1992), Goldstein (1995), and others describe the use of multilevel models to analyze change on a single response variable. This approach is also described by Hox (chap. 2, this volume). For simplicity of presentation, we use the model of linear change to illustrate this framework. Let y_{it} represent the measure of the response variable y for individual i at occasion t, where there are N individuals and m occasions of measurement. Let x_{it} represent the measure of time for individual i at occasion t. This measure may indicate real time (e.g., elapsed minutes or years since some baseline time point) or may just indicate ordinal position of the occasions (e.g., 0, 1, 2, etc.). In the model of linear change, the outcome variable y is represented as a linear function of time:

$$y_{it} = \beta_{0i} + \beta_{1i}x_{it} + e_{it} \tag{1}$$

where β_{0i} is the intercept for individual i, β_{1i} is the slope for individual i, and e_{it} is the residual for individual i at occasion t. The intercept and slope are random variables, with their variation across individuals modeled as follows:

$$\beta_{0i} = \beta_0 + u_{0i} \tag{2}$$

$$\beta_{1i} = \beta_1 + u_{1i}. \tag{3}$$

Here β_0 and β_1 represent the fixed effects for the intercept and slope, or the mean of those values, and u_{0i} and u_{1i} represent random variation of individuals around the mean intercept and slope, respectively. According to this model, the pattern of change for a given individual i is approximated by a straight line with intercept β_{0i}, representing initial level of the outcome variable, and slope β_{1i}, representing rate of change of the outcome variable. Furthermore, these parameters vary across individuals.

Substitution of Equations 2 and 3 into Equation 1 yields the combined model:

$$y_{it} = \beta_0 + \beta_1 x_{it} + u_{0i} + u_{1i}x_{it} + e_{it}. \tag{4}$$

In fitting this model to data, we estimate two fixed effects, the mean intercept β_0 and the mean slope β_1. We also estimate four variance/covariance parameters: the residual variance $\sigma_e^2 = var(e_{it})$, the intercept variance $\sigma_{u0}^2 = var(u_{0i})$, the slope variance $\sigma_{u1}^2 =$

$var(u_{1i})$, and the covariance between the intercept and slope $\sigma_{u01} = cov(u_{0i}, u_{1i})$. In practice, it is most common to obtain maximum likelihood (ML) estimates of these fixed effects and variance/covariance parameters. Approximate standard errors are available, which allows calculation of confidence intervals and significance tests. One can also obtain estimates of the individual intercepts and slopes if desired. Under normality and ML estimation, a likelihood ratio statistic is available and is widely used in the multilevel literature for testing differences between nested models (Bryk & Raudenbush, 1992; Goldstein, 1995). Methods of estimation are discussed by Bryk and Raudenbush and by Goldstein and others.

It is straightforward to extend the model just described in a number of ways that are useful in practice. Most obvious is the generalization to a nonlinear representation of change. Change over multiple occasions of measurement is usually not linear, so the use of nonlinear change functions would be valuable in many applications. This can be achieved in a number of ways. One approach is to introduce nonlinear transformations of x_{it} into the model in Equation 1. For instance, a polynomial change function could be constructed by introducing quadratic, cubic, and so forth, functions of x_{it}, that is, x_{it}^2, x_{it}^3, etc. Such a model would still be linear with respect to the parameters, that is, the model would represent y as a linear combination of x and its transformed values. Another approach would involve constructing models that are nonlinear with respect to the parameters. For instance, for learning or growth data, one might employ a Gompertz function (e.g., Browne, 1993; Browne & DuToit, 1991), which includes three parameters defining the pattern of change in y as a function of x. Browne (1993) employed the following parameterization of the Gompertz function:

$$y_{it} = a_i \exp\left[ln\left(\frac{b_i}{a_i}\right) \exp(-(x_{it}-1)p_i) \right] + e_{it}. \tag{5}$$

Given this parameterization, a_i is the asymptote for individual i, representing potential or maximum level of the response variable; b_i is the predicted value of y_{it} at the first measurement occasion; and p_i represents the predicted rate of change for individual i. As in the linear model given in Equations 1 to 4, these parameters can be represented as random coefficients varying across individuals around some fixed mean. In this model, each individual's pattern of change is modeled using a Gompertz curve. Note, however, that the mean of all of these curves may not be a Gompertz curve. Browne and DuToit (1991) described this model and provided an illustration of fitting it to data from a learning experiment.

A wide variety of other nonlinear models of change could be specified. For any such extension in the multilevel model framework, one is simply defining Equation 1 as a more complex function of time. Regardless of the nature of that function, one can define each of its parameters as random variables, analogous to Equations 2 and 3, meaning that the pattern of change for a given individual is approximated by a curve whose parameters represent that individual. Then the estimation process would yield an estimate of a fixed (mean) coefficient for each parameter, along with estimates of the variances and covariances of the parameters designated as random, and a residual variance. As indicated earlier, there are two classes of such models. One class, exemplified by simple polynomials, employs the linear model structure to represent nonlinear relationships between the response variable and time. In such models, the response variable is a linear function of time and of other nonlinear (e.g., polynomial) functions of time. All such models are linear with respect to their parameters; they yield the same simple moment structure and can be estimated using widely available commercial software. The second class of models is that which is nonlinear with respect to the parameters, such as in Equation 5. Such models introduce substantial complications into the model specification and estimation process, in that the corresponding moment structure is not simple and conventional methods of estimation for linear models are not applicable. Cudeck (1996) described several such models along with methods of estimation. (Note that the fitting of such models cannot be achieved using conventional commercial software. Browne and DuToit, 1991, used a program called AUFIT, in Browne & DuToit, 1992, for fitting nonstandard models.) Despite these complications, the notion of random parameters in such models is potentially valuable in representing individual differences in patterns of nonlinear change.

Another useful extension of the multilevel model of univariate change is to introduce predictors of the parameters designated as random variables. For instance, Equations 2 and 3 define intercepts and slopes as varying randomly across individuals. Selected variables measured on the individuals might be useful as predictors of the variation in intercepts and slopes. These predictors could include a wide range of measures such as gender, socioeconomic status, psychosocial measures, and so forth. Such variables may be useful in explaining individual differences in parameters representing change. The mechanism for this procedure is simply to introduce these predictors as independent variables in the equations that represent random variation in the parameters, such as Equations 2 and 3. Suppose there are two such predictors, such as gender and a measure of SES, and they are denoted as w_1 and w_2. The model for intercepts and slopes given in Equations 2 and 3 would be modified as follows:

$$\beta_{0i} = \beta_0 + \gamma_{01} w_{i1} + \gamma_{02} w_{i2} + u_{0i} \tag{6}$$

$$\beta_{1i} = \beta_1 + \gamma_{11} w_{i1} + \gamma_{12} w_{i2} + u_{1i}. \tag{7}$$

According to these equations, individual intercepts and slopes are predicted by gender and SES. Equations 6 and 7 could be substituted into Equation 1 to yield an extended combined model analogous to Equation 4:

$$y_{it} = \beta_0 + \gamma_{01} w_{i1} + \gamma_{02} w_{i2} + \beta_1 x_{it} + \gamma_{11} w_{i1} x_{it} + \gamma_{12} w_{i2} x_{it} + u_{0i} + u_{1i} x_{it} + e_{it}. \tag{8}$$

Fitting this extended model to data would yield estimates of the same parameters as the fitting of the model in Equation 4, with the addition of estimates of the fixed coefficients represented by the γ's in Equations 6 and 7. In addition, the interpretation of the variances and covariances of the u's would change. Prior to introducing the w predictors, the variances and covariances of the u's were interpreted as variances and covariances of the random intercepts and slopes. After introduction of the w's, those terms would be interpreted as variances and covariances of residual intercepts and slopes, after partialling out the w variables. In practice, it is common to fit a sequence of models. At the first step a model could be fit as in Equation 4 to determine intercept and slope variances. At a subsequent step, a model such as Equation 8 could be fit; the reduction in the variances of the u's would provide an estimate of variance in intercepts and slopes accounted for by the w predictors.

The various extensions of multilevel models that have been described do not nearly exhaust the possibilities. Numerous other extensions have been described in the literature. For example, it is possible to model residual variance as a function of time (Browne & DuToit, 1991; Goldstein, 1995) or to introduce additional variables measured at the individual level that vary over time. Such extensions, although interesting and useful, are beyond the scope of the present chapter. We encourage readers to investigate standard references, such as Bryk and Raudenbush (1992) and Goldstein (1995).

In this section, we have described the use of multilevel models for investigating individual differences in patterns of change on a single outcome variable. Although individuals are viewed as changing in different ways, it is assumed that the pattern of change for each individual follows the same functional form (e.g., linear) and that individual differences are represented by variation in parameters (e.g., intercepts and slopes). Those individual differences might be predicted by individual level variables, such as gender. Next, we consider the extension of this approach to the situation in which more than one variable changes over time and in which we wish to study how individual differences in patterns of change on one variable might be related to individual differences in patterns of change on another variable.

Multilevel Models for Multivariate Change

We now consider the case where we have measured p response variables, $y_1, y_2, \ldots, y_p$, each measured on multiple occasions. The response variables need not be measured at the same time points, nor at the same number of time points. Different response variables could be based on the study of the same individuals in different experiments or over different sets of measurement occasions. To extend the univariate multilevel model to the multivariate case, we use a mechanism suggested by Goldstein (1995) and others. In specifying a multivariate multilevel model, the data are treated as if only a single outcome variable is measured. Let y_{itk*} be a score for individual i at occasion t on outcome variable k^*, but consider y as if it were a single variable with aspects of its measurement defined by its subscripts. We then define dummy variables $\delta_1, \delta_2, \ldots, \delta_p$, one for each outcome variable, where $\delta_k = 1$ if a given measure is on y_k and $\delta_k = 0$ otherwise. That is, considering a particular score y_{itk*}, then $\delta_k = 1$ if $k = k^*$ and $\delta_k = 0$ if $k \neq k^*$.

TABLE 4.1
Data Array Form for an Individual, Two Variables, and Five Measurements

Outcome variable y_{itk*}	Dummy δ_1	Dummy δ_2	Time x_{itk*}
y_{i11} (Variable 1, Time 0)	1	0	0
y_{i21} (Variable 1, Time 1)	1	0	1
y_{i31} (Variable 1, Time 2)	1	0	2
y_{i41} (Variable 1, Time 3)	1	0	3
y_{i51} (Variable 1, Time 4)	1	0	4
y_{i12} (Variable 2, Time 0)	0	1	0
y_{i22} (Variable 2, Time 1)	0	1	1
y_{i32} (Variable 2, Time 2)	0	1	2
y_{i42} (Variable 2, Time 3)	0	1	3
y_{i52} (Variable 2, Time 4)	0	1	4

To illustrate, the data array for measures of a single individual on two outcome variables at five measurement occasions would have the form shown in Table 4.1. Dummy variable δ_1 indicates measures on the first outcome variable, dummy variable δ_2 indicates measures on the second outcome variable, and x_{itk*} represents occasion of measurement coded as 0, 1, 2, 3, and 4. Data for N individuals would be stacked to form a complete data array.

In defining a multilevel model for multivariate change in such a data structure, let us first consider the case where the same model of change is used for all response variables (e.g., a linear model for all response variables). A general representation of the multivariate multilevel model for change could then be given as

$$y_{itk*} = \sum_k \delta_k \text{ (univariate model expression)} \qquad (9)$$

where "univariate model expression" refers to the univariate change model employed for all response variables, with a subscript k added to all variables, parameters, and residual terms to index the response variables. Following this framework, the model of linear change given in Equations 1 to 4 could be extended as follows:

$$y_{itk*} = \sum_k \delta_k (\beta_{0ik} + \beta_{1ik} x_{itk} + e_{itk}) \qquad (10)$$

where β_{0ik} is the intercept for individual i on outcome variable k, β_{1ik} is the slope for individual i on outcome variable k, x_{itk} is the measure of time for individual i on occasion t for outcome variable k (note that these x values do not have to be the same for each individual and each outcome variable), and e_{itk} is the residual for individual

i at occasion t for outcome variable k. The intercepts and slopes for the p outcome variables are themselves random variables, with their variation across individuals modeled as follows:

$$\beta_{0ik} = \beta_{0k} + u_{0ik} \tag{11}$$

$$\beta_{1ik} = \beta_{1k} + u_{1ik}. \tag{12}$$

Here β_{0k} and β_{1k} represent the fixed effects for the intercept and slope on outcome k, or the mean of those values, and u_{0ik} and u_{1ik} represent random variation of individuals around the mean intercept and slope, respectively, for outcome k. Substitution of Equations 11 and 12 into Equation 10 yields the combined model:

$$y_{itk*} = \sum_k \delta_k (\beta_{0k} + \beta_{1k}x_{itk} + u_{0ik} + u_{1ik}x_{itk} + e_{itk}) \tag{13}$$

$$= \sum_k (\beta_{0k}\delta_k + \beta_{1k}\delta_k x_{itk} + \delta_k u_{0ik} + u_{1ik}\delta_k x_{itk} + \delta_k e_{itk}).$$

Note that the fixed intercept terms for the k response variables are actually regression coefficients for the dummy variables and that the fixed slope terms are regression coefficients for product variables each a product of one dummy variable and the time measure, x. This model could be fit to data in the same manner as the model in Equation 4. The logistical key to conducting such analyses is that the data are treated as if there is only one outcome variable. Estimation yields estimates of a fixed intercept β_{0k} and a fixed slope β_{1k} for each outcome variable k. Random effects estimates are as follows for each outcome variable: $\sigma^2_{ek} = var(e_{itk})$, the residual variance; $\sigma^2_{u0k} = var(u_{0ik})$, the intercept variance; $\sigma^2_{u1k} = var(u_{1ik})$, the slope variance; and $\sigma_{u01k} = cov(u_{0ik}, u_{1ik})$, covariance of intercepts and slopes. In addition, random effects are estimated for covariances of intercepts and slopes for each pair of outcomes, j and k: $\sigma_{u0j1k} = cov(u_{0ij}, u_{1ik})$, the covariance of intercepts on outcome j with slopes on outcome k; $\sigma_{u0j0k} = cov(u_{0ij}, u_{0ik})$, the covariance of intercepts on outcome j with intercepts on outcome k; and $\sigma_{u1j1k} = cov(u_{1ij}, u_{1ik})$, the covariance of slopes on outcome j with slopes on outcome k. In sum, with respect to random effects, the fitting process would yield estimates of a residual variance for each outcome as well as estimates of variances and covariances for random change parameters both within and between outcome variables. It is these last random effects that make this approach potentially valuable. In the linear case, for instance, we obtain estimates of covariances of slopes on different outcome variables, indicating degree of association between rates of linear change on different variables. As in the univariate case, one could also obtain estimates of the individual coefficients. In addition, a likelihood ratio statistic is available for model tests and comparisons.

As with the univariate case, there are a variety of extensions and generalizations of this multivariate change model that are potentially useful. Most obvious is the generalization to allow nonlinear models of change. Representing such a model is straightforward. The nonlinear functional form of the change model would be specified and substituted in place of the "univariate model expression" in Equation 9. The estimation process would then yield estimates of fixed effects, residual variances, and random parameter variances and covariances for each outcome, as well as random parameter covariances for random parameters representing different outcomes. This approach assumes that the same model for change is used for all outcomes. It is straightforward to make use of different change models for different outcomes. For instance, one may use a linear model for one outcome and a Gompertz model for another. In such cases, one could not use the summation representation in Equation 9, but would instead specify the entire model, with a separate expression of the change model for each outcome, each such expression weighted by a dummy variable, and the various expressions summed. Fitting such models would yield estimates of the usual fixed, residual, and random effects for each outcome and covariances between random parameters for different outcomes. This latter set of estimates might include such things as estimates of covariance between linear slope on one outcome and acceleration on another. We do not argue that all such estimates would be meaningful in all cases, but in our own research we are routinely interested in covariances between random parameters representing corresponding aspects of change on different outcome variables.

Other extensions of the univariate multilevel model discussed could be adapted easily into the multivariate framework. These include the use of more complex models of residual variance and the introduction of individual-level variables to predict individual differences in coefficients representing aspects of change.

To summarize the developments in this section, we have described how multilevel models can be used to study change on more than one variable simultaneously. In this framework, change on each variable is represented using a specified functional form, and individual differences in patterns of change are represented by variation in parameters of those functions. Relationships between patterns of change on different variables are represented in terms of covariances between parameters of the change functions for different variables. Next, we provide an illustration of this approach to studying multivariate change.

ILLUSTRATION

Design of Study

We illustrate the multivariate multilevel linear model of change using data from a study of physiological response to marital conflict in older couples. We present basic information about the study here (for additional detail, refer to Malarkey, Kiecolt-Glaser, Pearl, & Glaser, 1994). Thirty-one married couples between the ages of 55 and 75 participated in this study. The average length of marriage for this sample was approximately 42 years. The analyses reported here are based on 53 subjects, 27 wives and 26 husbands. Eight diabetic subjects were excluded because diabetes would confound the hormonal response examined here, and 1 additional subject was excluded because of missing data. The couples were admitted to the Ohio State University Clinical Research Center at 7 a.m. and remained there for an 8-hour period during which a variety of activities occurred. Upon admission, a heparin well was inserted in each subject's arm to allow for easy and unobtrusive drawing of blood during subsequent activities. Early in the day the subjects were interviewed to identify specific topics for a later discussion of problems. Subsequently, couples were seated at a table, facing each other, and were asked to spend 30 minutes talking in an effort to resolve two or three of the issues identified in the earlier interview. The experimenter selected issues that were deemed most likely to produce conflict. During the subsequent discussion, blood was drawn through the heparin well at regular intervals via a long plastic tube leading behind a screen. The present analyses make use of data from five blood samples. The first is a baseline sample taken prior to discussion; the second is taken at the start of the discussion; the third after 15 minutes of discussion; the fourth after 30 minutes of discussion; and the fifth 15 minutes after completion of the discussion. From each blood sample, endocrine assays were conducted to measure levels of various hormones. For the current illustration we use measures on two hormones: cortisol and adrenocorticotropic hormone (ACTH). For details on the nature of the assays and the scales of measurement for representing hormone levels, the reader is referred to Malarkey et al. (1994). Prior research has shown these hormones to be related to stress in various degrees and contexts. For each of these hormones, we would expect changes in levels across the five time points, with individuals exhibiting different patterns of change reflecting differential physiological responses to the conflict inherent in the discussion. The current focus involves assessment of the relationship between patterns of change on different hormones.

Data from this study can be organized into a data array as described in the previous section. A single individual provides a total of 10 data values (two hormones at five occasions) and thus provides 10 rows in a data matrix. The first five rows would contain measures of ACTH at the five occasions, and the next five rows would contain measures of cortisol at the five occasions. Dummy variables δ_{ACTH} and δ_{cort} are defined to indicate which hormone is represented by each outcome measure, and the time measure x_{it} is coded 0, 1, 2, 3, and 4, to indicate measurement occasion. The data array for the full sample, $N = 53$, thus contains 530 rows.

Models and Analyses

In the multilevel model for representing change on the two outcome variables (hormone levels), the hormone levels are predicted as a linear function of time. The regression of each hormone on time is assumed to have a random slope varying across individuals around a mean slope, and a random intercept varying across individuals around a mean intercept. The intercept for a given individual represents the predicted initial level of the hormone, and the slope represents the predicted rate of linear change in that hormone over time. The mean slopes and the mean intercepts are estimated as fixed parameters, and variances and covariances among the two intercepts and two slopes are estimated as random parameters. In addition to these parameters, residual variances for the two hormones are also estimated. The model is specified as follows:

$$y_{itk*} = \delta_{\text{ACTH}}(\beta_{0i(\text{ACTH})} + \beta_{1i(\text{ACTH})}x_{it} + e_{it(\text{ACTH})}) \tag{14}$$
$$+ \delta_{\text{cort}}(\beta_{0i(\text{cort})} + \beta_{1i(\text{cort})}x_{it} + e_{it(\text{cort})}).$$

This equation has the same form as Equation 10 which represented the general form of a multivariate multilevel model for linear change. Here y_{itk*} is the measure for individual i at time t on hormone $k*$; δ_{ACTH} and δ_{cort} are dummy variables for ACTH and cortisol, respectively. The variable x_{it} is the measure of time for individual i at occasion t. In the present example, because all individuals are measured at the same five occasions, x_{it} is the same for all i, and is set equal to the occasion number, 0, 1, 2, 3, and 4. The baseline occasion number is set to 0 so that the intercepts in the model may be interpreted as the predicted level of the corresponding hormone at baseline. (Note that standard references on multilevel models, e.g., Bryk & Raudenbush, 1992; Goldstein, 1995, often recommend centering x prior to model fitting. Such centering alters the interpretation of the intercept. In the present example, centering x so that occasion numbers were transformed to values of $-2, -1, 0, 1, 2$ would result in intercepts being interpreted as predicted hormone levels at the third measurement occasion. Because we desired to retain the interpretation of intercepts relative to the baseline occasion, we did not center x in our analyses.) The terms $\beta_{0i(\text{ACTH})}$ and $\beta_{0i(\text{cort})}$ are the random intercepts of ACTH and cortisol, respectively; $\beta_{1i(\text{ACTH})}$ and $\beta_{1i(\text{cort})}$ represent the random slopes of ACTH and cortisol, respectively; and $e_{it(\text{ACTH})}$ and $e_{it(\text{cort})}$ are random residuals of the two outcome variables, respectively. More specifically, each random coefficient is defined as a fixed mean plus a random effect term that has a mean of zero. The model is rewritten by decomposing each parameter into a fixed effect and a random effect as follows:

$$\beta_{0i(\text{ACTH})} = \beta_{0(\text{ACTH})} + u_{0i(\text{ACTH})} \tag{15}$$

$$\beta_{0i(\text{cort})} = \beta_{0(\text{cort})} + u_{0i(\text{cort})} \tag{16}$$

$$\beta_{1i(\text{ACTH})} = \beta_{1(\text{ACTH})} + u_{1i(\text{ACTH})} \tag{17}$$

$$\beta_{1i(\text{cort})} = \beta_{1(\text{cort})} + u_{1i(\text{cort})}. \tag{18}$$

Substitution of Equations 15 through 18 into Equation 14 yields the combined model, which has the same general form as Equation 13:

$$y_{itk*} = \delta_{\text{ACTH}}(\beta_{0(\text{ACTH})} + \beta_{1(\text{ACTH})}x_{it} + u_{0i(\text{ACTH})} + u_{1i(\text{ACTH})}x_{it} + e_{it(\text{ACTH})}) \tag{19}$$
$$+ \delta_{\text{cort}}(\beta_{0(\text{cort})} + \beta_{1(\text{cort})}x_{it} + u_{0i(\text{cort})} + u_{1i(\text{cort})}x_{it} + e_{it(\text{cort})}).$$

Because expected values for all u's and e's are zero, average trajectories for the two hormones are estimated using fixed effects estimates β's:

$$E(y_{it(\text{ACTH})}) = \beta_{0(\text{ACTH})} + \beta_{1(\text{ACTH})}x_{it} \tag{20}$$

$$E(y_{it(\text{cort})}) = \beta_{0(\text{cort})} + \beta_{1(\text{cort})}x_{it}$$

In addition to the fixed effects estimates, we can also estimate 12 variance and covariance parameters: 10 variances and covariances among four random intercepts and slopes (u's), which vary across individuals; and variances of residuals (e's) for two hormones, which vary across time and individuals. Residual variance is assumed to be the same at each occasion. Finally, estimates of the individual intercepts and slopes represented in Equations 15 through 18 can also be obtained.

This model was fit to the sample data using the multilevel modeling software package MLn (Woodhouse, 1995).

Results

The fixed effects in this model include mean slopes and intercepts for the three outcome variables as shown in Table 4.2 and as represented in the following equations:

$$E(y_{it(\text{ACTH})}) = 15.08 - 0.20x_{it} \tag{21}$$

$$E(y_{it(\text{cort})}) = 13.98 - 0.15x_{it}. \tag{22}$$

The intercepts in Equations 21 and 22 represent the predicted mean level of the respective hormones at the beginning of the conflict discussion, and the slopes represent mean rate of change in each hormone. For both hormones, the mean slope was not significantly different from zero.

Our primary interest, however, is in the variation and covariation among individuals around these mean intercepts and slopes. The absence of a significant fixed effect of time on ACTH and cortisol is not indicative of the potential degree of individual variation in rate of linear change. Therefore, we considered the random effects representing variance and covariance of random intercepts and slopes, as shown in Table 4.3. Note that all variances were significant, as seen by noting that each variance was at least several times the magnitude of its approximate standard error. Thus, individuals showed statistically significant variance in their rates of linear change on both hormones. The covariance between the slope of cortisol and ACTH was significant: $cov(u_{1i(\text{cort})}, u_{1i(\text{ACTH})}) = 1.54$; $z = 4.150$; $r = .873$. This result suggests that rate of linear change on ACTH and cortisol were highly correlated across individuals, even though no significant linear trends were found from estimates of fixed effects. To further illustrate this high correlation between random slopes, estimated random slopes of cortisol, $\hat{\beta}_{1i(\text{cort})}$, are plotted against estimated random slopes of ACTH, $\hat{\beta}_{1i(\text{ACTH})}$ in Figure 4.1. This plot clearly shows the high correlation between change patterns on the two hormones. Note that the plotted slope estimates are not ordinary least squares (OLS) slopes computed from standard regression analyses, but rather are consistent estimates of the true slopes; these estimates are more precise than the OLS es-

TABLE 4.2
Estimates of Fixed Effects for Multilevel Model of Change in Two Hormones

Coefficient	Estimate	Standard error	z ratio
ACTH intercept $\beta_{0(ACTH)}$	15.08	1.05	14.42
Cortisol intercept $\beta_{0(cort)}$	13.98	0.71	19.59
ACTH slope $\beta_{1(ACTH)}$	−0.20	0.28	−0.71
Cortisol slope $\beta_{1(cort)}$	−0.15	0.15	−0.96

timates. The correlation between the individual OLS slopes for ACTH and cortisol is only .67. This value represents a sample correlation between estimated slopes, which are subject to error. The estimated slope correlation of .87 produced by the multilevel analysis of the same data is an estimate of the correlation between true slopes, in effect correcting for error that would be present in the OLS slopes. The difference between these values and their meaning exemplifies a major advantage of the multilevel approach to such data over OLS regression analysis of each individual.

Table 4.3 shows three other high correlations (covariances) between random coefficients: −.63 between the slope and the intercept of ACTH; −.70 between the slope and the intercept of cortisol; and −.81 between the ACTH slope and the cortisol intercept. The negative correlations between slopes and intercepts imply that subjects

TABLE 4.3
Estimates of Variances, Covariances, and Intercorrelations of Random Intercept and Slope
for Multilevel Model of Change in Two Hormones

	ACTH intercept	Cortisol intercept	ACTH slope	Cortisol slope
ACTH intercept	50.90	10.34	−7.87	−1.78
$u_{0i(ACTH)}$	(11.30)	(5.62)	(2.59)	(1.20)
Cortisol intercept	.29	25.58	−7.16	−3.54
$u_{0i(cort)}$		(5.25)	(1.77)	(.97)
ACTH slope	−.63	−.81	3.08	1.54
$u_{1i(ACTH)}$			(.84)	(.38)
Cortisol slope	−.25	−.70	.87	1.01
$u_{1i(cort)}$				(.24)
Residual variance of ACTH $Var(e_{ij(ACTH)})$			11.90	
			(1.34)	
Residual variance of Cortisol $Var(e_{ij(cort)})$			2.36	
			(.26)	

Note. The numbers in the upper right triangle and the diagonal are covariances and their standard errors (parentheses), and the lower triangle contain correlations.

FIGURE 4.1
Scatterplot of Estimated Slopes for Cortisol and ACTH

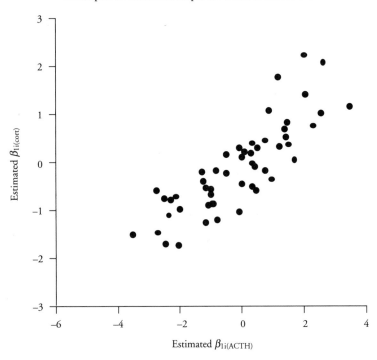

who had high levels of ACTH and cortisol hormones at baseline had lower slopes than those who had low hormone levels at baseline. These negative correlations are consistent with the negative correlation between the ACTH slope and the cortisol intercept, and in turn with the high positive correlation between ACTH and cortisol slopes. (As would be expected, these high negative correlations between intercept and slope for ACTH and cortisol were greatly reduced when the time measure was centered. In that case the correlations were as follows: for ACTH, .12; for cortisol, .46. The high negative correlation between slopes for ACTH and cortisol was unaffected by this centering.)

This example could be extended in a variety of ways. One generalization involves the model for the residual variances. As presented, the model specifies that residual variance for a given hormone is the same at every occasion. One simple alternative model would allow for estimation of a different residual variance at each occasion. Another alternative would specify residual variance as some function of time. Models for residual variance are discussed by Goldstein (1995). Another variation on the example would specify hormone level as a nonlinear, rather than linear, function of time. For example, a hypothesis that hormone levels would rise and then fall during the conflict discussion could be evaluated by fitting a quadratic change model to these data. Parameter estimates and fit relative to the linear model could then be evaluated for support of the hypothesis. Parameter estimates would also provide estimates of the association between quadratic trends on the two hormones. One further extension of the model would be to introduce predictors of individual differences in rates of change on the hormones. For instance, marital satisfaction might be negatively related to slopes on cortisol and ACTH. That is, individuals less satisfied with their marriage might show higher rates of increase in these hormones under the stress induced by the conflict discussion. Such a model could be evaluated by introducing a measure of marital satisfaction as a predictor, as represented in Equations 6 and 7. The proportion of variance in slopes accounted for by marital satisfaction could be estimated by comparing estimates of (residual) slope variances from models with and without the marital satisfaction predictor.

This example illustrates a procedure for using multilevel models to study change on more than one variable simultaneously and also shows the type of information that is obtained by such an approach. In this case, there is a strong association between rate of linear change on two variables. Such information would not be available if each variable was studied separately.

LATENT CURVE MODELS

The multilevel modeling approach described above is closely related to another class of models called *latent curve* models, or often latent growth curve models. Latent curve models for univariate change are described by Meredith and Tisak (1990), Willett and Sayer (1994), and others. The extension of these latent curve models to the multiple outcome case is discussed by Tisak and Meredith (1990), Willett and Sayer (1996), and others. MacCallum et al. (1997) discussed relationships among multilevel and latent curve models for both the univariate and multivariate cases. For present purposes, we show how the multilevel model used in the illustration can be expressed in equivalent form as a latent curve model.

In this context, a latent curve model can be viewed as a restricted factor analysis model containing nonzero factor means. This model can be fit easily to means and covariances of the outcome variables using commercial software such as LISREL 8 (Jöreskog & Sörbom, 1994). To illustrate, a linear latent curve model for the example presented earlier is shown in Figure 4.2 as a path diagram. The 10 measured variables are the two hormones each measured at five occasions. The model is intended to account for the means, variances, and covariances of these 10 measures. Two factors are specified for each hormone, an intercept factor and a slope factor. The loadings for the intercept factor are all fixed to 1.0, indicating that this factor has a fixed and equal influence on all measures of a given hormone. The loadings for the slope factor are fixed at the known values of the time measure (in this case, the occasion indicator 0, 1, 2, 3, and 4). This pattern of loadings implies that the slope factor has an increasing

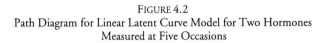

FIGURE 4.2
Path Diagram for Linear Latent Curve Model for Two Hormones
Measured at Five Occasions

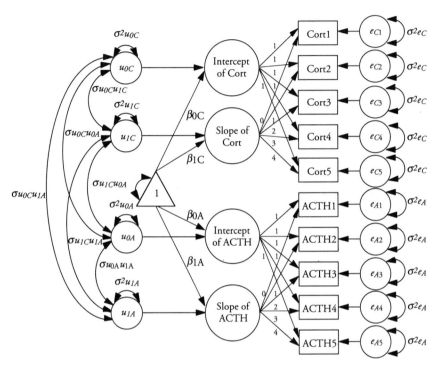

effect on the successive measures of a given hormone. To illustrate, consider an individual whose score on the slope factor for cortisol is zero. According to the model, that individual would exhibit a flat pattern of cortisol measures across the five occasions, with the level of those scores determined by the individual's score on the intercept factor. On the other hand, an individual with a high positive score on the cortisol slope factor would, according to the model, exhibit rapidly increasing measures of cortisol. Mean levels on these factors are represented in this diagram using a device suggested by McArdle (1988) and used subsequently by others. A constant value of unity is shown in a triangle, with influences on each of the factors. The weights corresponding to those influences are factor means. Individual differences on the intercept and slope factors are represented by the random portion of each factor, shown for each factor as a separate latent variable with a variance parameter. Finally, the residual variance of each measured variable is shown by a corresponding residual term with a variance parameter. The diagram shows those variances specified to have the same value across occasions for each hormone, although that constraint is easily dropped.

The model shown in Figure 4.2 is logically and mathematically equivalent to the multilevel model used in the illustration. The parameters of the multilevel model correspond in a one-to-one fashion with the parameters of the latent curve model. The fixed effects in the multilevel model correspond to factor means in the latent curve model, and the random effects in the multilevel model correspond to factor variances and covariances and residual variances in the latent curve model. The latent curve model in Figure 4.2 was fit to the hormone data from the illustration using LISREL 8, and resulting parameter estimates matched within rounding error those obtained in the multilevel analysis using MLn. These relationships are discussed in more detail by MacCallum et al. (1997).

As was the case with the multilevel model, the latent curve model for multiple outcomes can be extended in a variety of ways. These include specification of nonlinear models for change, complex models of residual variance, and introduction of additional variables representing predictors, correlates, or consequences of aspects of change. Many of these extensions are described in detail by MacCallum et al. (1997). Latent curve models for analyzing change on multiple outcomes have been used in the literature by Stoolmiller (1994), Curran, Harford, and Muthén (1997), Curran, Stice, and Chassin (1997), and others.

COMMENTS ON STRATEGIES FOR MODEL SPECIFICATION

In any given circumstance where multivariate change is of interest, investigators are urged to consider the potential value of multilevel models or latent curve models and to make use of the approach that is most appropriate for their data structure and that best answers their research questions. Both approaches have the potential to provide valuable information about associations between patterns of change in different variables. Regardless of which approach is used, an investigator will be faced with a variety of alternative models and strategies. For instance, one might consider (a) various linear and nonlinear models for representing change on each outcome, (b) the analysis of multiple outcomes separately versus simultaneously, and (c) the potential inclusion of additional variables that might be related to the random parameters representing individual differences in patterns of change on the outcome variables. Rather than begin by fitting a complete model including all outcomes and other variables, we recommend a sequential strategy. The first step is to develop an appropriate model of univariate change for each outcome separately. This process involves consideration of linear versus nonlinear models for change, as well as appropriate models for residual variance. The second step is to combine these separate models into a multiple-outcome model, thus obtaining information about relationships between aspects of change on different outcomes. The third step is to introduce any additional variables serving as prospective predictors or correlates or consequences of aspects of change. Such an approach should provide an opportunity to understand individual differences in patterns of change on each variable separately, as well as associations in patterns of change on different variables.

SUMMARY

Researchers are often interested in questions about how individual differences in patterns of change on one variable might be related to individual differences in patterns of change on another variable. The present chapter shows how methods of multilevel modeling can be easily extended to investigate such questions and that such analyses can be carried out using conventional software. The illustration provided shows the implementation of this procedure as well as the gain in information achieved by considering multiple outcome variables simultaneously. We have also described briefly the close relationship between this approach and latent curve models. Taken together, multilevel models and latent curve models provide a set of useful tools for investigating questions about multivariate change.

CHAPTER FIVE

An Introduction to Latent Growth Models for Developmental Data Analysis

John J. McArdle
Richard Q. Bell
University of Virginia

Since the 1970s a wide range of behavioral scientists have engaged in the collection and analysis of longitudinal data (e.g., Nesselroade & Baltes, 1979). There is no doubt that the collection of longitudinal data has become frequent and often necessary. Longitudinal data have become an important ingredient in the research of individual developmental investigators and in the portfolio of national and international funding agencies (e.g., Chase-Lansdale, Mott, Brooks-Gunn, & Phillips, 1991; Young, Savola, & Phelps, 1991).

Given this increasing emphasis for longitudinal data collection, it seems worthwhile to examine some of the goals of this seemingly "new" emphasis. Many researchers have defined these issues in great detail (e.g., Harris, 1963; Horn & Little, 1966; Wohwill, 1973). One brief but comprehensive statement of these issues can be found in Baltes and Nesselroade (1979, pp. 21–27) where the authors outlined some key "objectives for longitudinal research" as:

- Direct identification of *intra*individual change;
- Direct identification of *inter*individual differences in intraindividual change;
- Analysis of *interrelationships* in change;
- Analysis of *causes* (determinants) of intraindividual change;
- Analysis of causes (determinants) of interindividual differences in intraindividual change.

These objectives are of obvious importance in any research study, so it is not surprising that methodological techniques focusing on these issues have also become highly valued. During the 1990s, many methodologists have added to the knowledge base, and longitudinal methods have enjoyed a remarkable period of growth—hardly a day goes by without "new and improved" methods sprouting up. Several attempts have been made to organize these new approaches and have shown how they represent new solutions to some classical data analysis problems. In the last section here, we return to these five points.

Although these overviews are critically important, this chapter has more modest goals. Here, we introduce one class of longitudinal data analysis models—*latent growth curve model* (LGM) analysis using *structural equation modeling* (SEM) techniques. We limit our discussion to a set of longitudinal data selected from the publicly available archives of the National Longitudinal Study of Youth (NLSY), and we analyze these data using widely available SEM software (i.e., LISREL, Mx, RAMONA). This chapter is intended to provide some basic foundations of the LGM methods used, some more advanced but natural extensions, and references to further technical details.

This chapter is intended as an introduction to the use of some contemporary developmental methods. Numerical examples are used to convey the main assumptions and procedures used, and all analyses are carried out using readily available computer programs. In the next section, some longitudinal data from the NLSY are described and summarized. After this, some basic alternative structural models based on concepts of latent growth are defined and fitted to the available data. In a third section, some advanced extensions to the latent growth models are added. These include the use of external predictors of the underlying growth components using demographic variables and multiple groups. A final section includes some efforts to examine the inclusion of all available data based on some consideration among patterns of available data at specific ages-at-testing. In the final section, we discuss future analyses based on using this approach. (A set of technical notes is also included for further clarity.) Our broad goal is to introduce the reader to this kind of data analysis methodology and to relate these methods to some key issues in developmental research.

Perspectives on Structural Equation Modeling

As stated earlier, the search for the best methods to address longitudinal data analysis issues has been a major concern of much developmental research (e.g., Bayley, 1956; Bell, 1953; Collins & Horn, 1991; Harris, 1963; Horn & Little, 1966; Nesselroade & Baltes, 1979; Tanner, 1960; Wohwill, 1973). There has been an increasing interest in the possibility of using concepts derived from linear structural equation modeling (Bollen, 1989; Jöreskog & Sörbom, 1979, 1993; Loehlin, 1992; McDonald, 1985), and the associated computer programs (e.g., LISREL, Mx, RAMONA, etc.) to deal with these kinds of problems.

In this general way, these SEM techniques provide mathematical and statistical devices that permit researchers to focus on the construct validation of theoretical propositions. In our view, these modern SEM techniques can be useful in a number of ways:

- To organize concepts about data analysis into scientific models;
- To provide tools for the estimation of the mathematical components of models;

FIGURE 5.1
SEM and Construct Validation (adapted from McArdle, 1994)

"Single Factor"

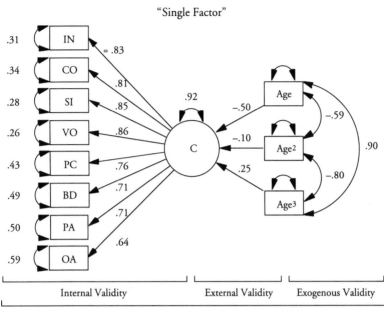

- To provide tools for the evaluation of statistical features of these models;
- To include flexible provisions for models with unobserved or latent variables;
- To permit a flexible approach for dealing with incomplete data patterns.

An initial example of our perspective is illustrated by the two path diagrams in Figures 5.1 and 5.2 (from McArdle, 1994). These figures include two path diagrams representing two alternative theoretical models for the same data set. In both figures, the eight squares on the left-hand side of each figure represent a set of intellectual ability variables (from the Wechsler Adult Intelligence Scale-Revised, WAIS-R) and the three squares on the right represent functions of chronological age (age, age², and age³). However, these two figures differ in the model for the connections among these variables. In the first model, a single circle is used to represent the concept of a single latent common factor ("g"). In the second model, two connected circles are used to convey a theory of two correlated factors ("g_f-g_c"). The resulting SEM analysis of these alternatives suggested that the second model fits the data far better than the first. Thus, the one-factor model of age-ability relationships was not as useful a construct or organizing principle as the two-factor model of age-ability relations (for more details, see McArdle, 1994; McArdle & Prescott, 1992).

It is well-known that the term *structure* in a structural equation model refers to the precise way a model prescribes a pattern for the statistical expectations about the data.

FIGURE 5.2
SEM and Construct Validation (adapted from McArdle, 1994)

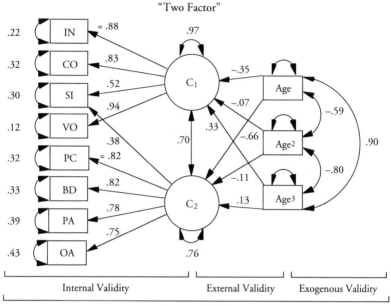

"Two Factor"

Internal Validity   External Validity   Exogenous Validity

Construct Validity

The algebraic approach to generating model expectations used here is based on a simplified SEM approach termed *Reticular Analytic Modeling (RAM) notation* (see Horn & McArdle, 1980; McArdle & Aber, 1990; McArdle & Boker, 1990; McArdle & McDonald, 1984). This notation for structural algebra and graphics permits models with covariances and means, including latent growth models, and has made these models easier to understand and analyze. In most applications, the choice of algebraic representation is arbitrary but, because of the complexity of the longitudinal models, this simplified algebraic approach is useful (for examples, see McArdle & Hamagami, 1996; McArdle, Prescott, Hamagami, & Horn, 1998; McArdle & Woodcock, 1997).

Longitudinal Structural Equation Models

There are many models for the analysis of longitudinal data (e.g., Collins & Horn, 1991; Diggle, Liang & Zeger, 1994; Dwyer, Feinleib, Lippert, & Hoffmeister, 1992; Jones, 1993; Lindsey, 1993). There is also an extensive history on the use of SEM with longitudinal data (see Alwin, 1988; Collins & Horn, 1991; Horn & McArdle, 1980; Jöreskog & Sörbom, 1979; McArdle, 1988, 1991b).

FIGURE 5.3
Equivalent Structural Path Models for Longitudinal Data (a) Current Path Diagram;
(b) Complete RAM Diagram; (c) Compact but Equivalent Diagram
(adapted from McArdle & Aber, 1990)

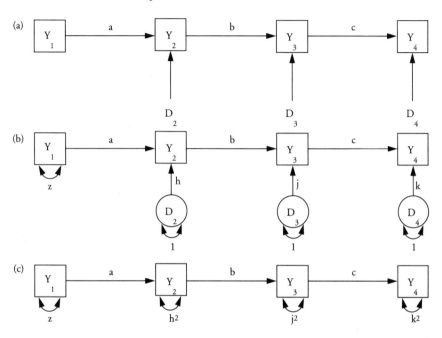

Some popular structural equation models for longitudinal data have emerged from the extensive literature on regression modeling approaches to time-series analysis (e.g., Pankratz, 1991). One popular structural equation model is based on a stationary autoregressive change model (see Jöreskog & Sörbom, 1979; McArdle & Aber, 1990). In a typical application of this model, one first "de-trends" a time-series by removing the mean score at each time point. Then, one writes a model for these deviation scores as a proportional function of the individual's previous score at time $t - 1$ (plus some new unique error at each time). The simplicity of this model is described in detail by many others, and some important details can also be seen in the path diagrams of Figure 5.3.

This kind of autoregressive change model also makes a different kind of explicit prediction—the pattern or "structure" of the expected covariances for any pair of specific time points is determined only by the distance between points and the coefficients between these points. This covariance pattern is taken as a statistical hypothesis that is restrictive and rejectable with observed data, and these features make this (or any other) model scientifically valuable. One theoretical limitation of this model is noteworthy—the standard autoregressive representation does not explicitly provide parameters for representing changes in the means over time.

FIGURE 5.4
A Latent Growth Model (adapted from McArdle & Hamagami, 1992)

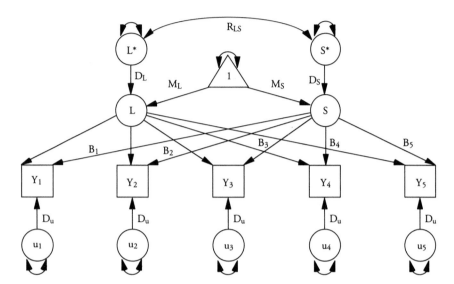

The specific longitudinal models examined here are termed *latent growth models* (*LGMs*). These models are slightly different because they are based on organizing trends around group and individual differences in growth and change functions. The LGMs were originally developed in early work by both Tucker (1958) and Rao (1958), and first related to SEM in 1985 by William Meredith (see Meredith & Tisak, 1990). Some basic aspects of these LGMs are displayed in Figure 5.4, including:

- The relationships among the observed scores (Y[t]) are thought to exist due to three underlying latent variables, termed a level score (L), a slope score (S), and a unique score (U).
- The relationships between the latent slope, S, and the observed scores is defined by the value of another set of basis parameters, (B [t]), which may take on a range of values.
- These basis parameters and the latent means, (M_l and M_s), are used to describe group characteristics, such as the shape of the growth curve.
- The latent deviations, (D_l, D_s and D_u), and correlations, (R_{ls}), are used to describe individual differences within each group.
- This organization of the longitudinal data makes explicit predictions about the means and covariances of a set of data, so the LGM organization may be rejected on a statistical basis.

These original models have been expanded by many others (Browne & Du Toit, 1991; Duncan & Duncan, 1995; McArdle, 1986, 1988, 1989, 1991b, 1998; McArdle &

Aber, 1990; McArdle & Anderson, 1990; McArdle & Epstein, 1987; McArdle & Hamagami, 1991, 1992, 1996, 1998; McArdle & Woodcock, 1997; Willett & Sayer, 1994). Some of this work has lead to a wider range of possibilities for analyses of longitudinal data. For example, these LGMs are related to other models in the current literature—for example, two-stage growth models, multilevel models, and factorial invariance models. Other aspects of this approach are also seen as direct descendents of earlier work by the second author (Bell, 1953, 1954) on combining longitudinal and cross-sectional information—the "convergence" analysis of the "accelerated longitudinal design." These kind of LGM extensions may be needed to deal with the complexities of real data collections, and these advances are described in our last section.

ILLUSTRATIVE LONGITUDINAL DATA

Participants and Variables

All of the following illustrations are based on a selected set of raw longitudinal data from the National Longitudinal Study of Youth (NLSY; Baker, Keck, Mott, & Quinlan, 1993; Chase-Lansdale et al., 1991; see Technical Note [1]). The NLSY data set used here includes repeated measurements of up to $N = 405$ children in various locations in the United States. These children and other family members were initially measured as part of NLSY in 1986. At this initial testing, the children were about ages 6 to 8, and they were measured on a wide variety of individual and group variables. Many of these same children ($N = 233$) were then measured up to four times over 8 years as part of the NLSY follow-ups.

A variety of cognitive and noncognitive variables are available, but only a selected few of these variables are used in these illustrations. The key variables examined are the reading scores from the NLSY administration of the Peabody Individual Achievement Test (NLSY-PIAT-R). The original NLSY-PIAT-R reading scores ranged from 0 to 80 but, in order to simplify the scaling and interpretation here, we have converted these raw scores into a "percent-correct" metric from 0 to 100 by dividing by 80 (Cohen, 1996; McArdle, 1988, 1994). This simple re-scaling does not enhance or alter any of the psychometric or statistical comparisons we make, but it does facilitate presentation and interpretation.

A wide variety of additional NLSY data is available, including a wide variety of demographic and family characteristics (for details, see Baker et al., 1993). To illustrate the use of these models, four additional variables were selected: (a) *Sex* is initially coded here as 0 for female and 1 for male, (b) *Kids-Age* is age in years at the initial testing occasion, (c) *HOME-Emotional* is a subscale created from the primary caregiver's (e.g., mother's) rating of the "emotional support" in the child's home, and is based on an abbreviated form of the HOME scale, and (d) *HOME-Cognitive* is a similar subscale created from the primary caregiver's (e.g., mother's) rating of the "cognitive support" in the child's home.

FIGURE 5.5
Within-Occasion Histograms of the NLSY-PIAT-R Scores (*N* = 405)

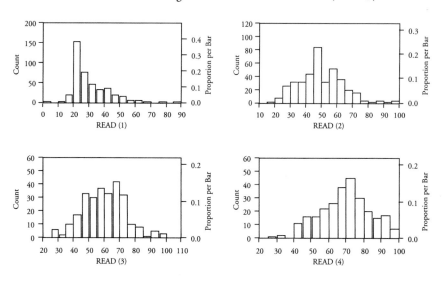

FIGURE 5.6
Within-Occasion Histograms of the NLSY-PIAT-R Demographic Data (*N* = 405)

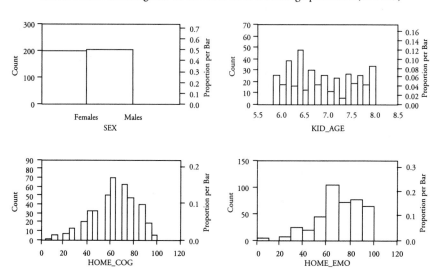

Raw Data Displays

A plot of all available data on these longitudinal scores is initially presented in Figure 5.5. In this plot, the data for each of the four time points for the NLSY-PIAT-R variable are plotted in a separate histogram (the frequency of the score on the y-axis against the numerical score on the x-axis). Over the four occasions of measurement there are some shifts in these distributions toward higher scores. Figure 5.6 presents a similar kind of histogram for each of the 4 additional demographic and family variables.

In Figure 5.7 we represent the same longitudinal information in a different way. Here the NLSY-PIAT-R data for each individual is drawn as a connected line—that is, these are individual growth curves. This plot includes data on all subjects, even if a subject missed one or more occasions of measurement. Because of the relatively large number of lines, this plot is a bit hard to understand. To clarify some of these features, we include Figure 5.8; this is the same kind of individual growth curve plot, but now only for the first 30 subjects. The different patterns of growth and incomplete data are more obvious here.

Statistical Summaries

An initial statistical summary of some of this information is presented in Table 5.1 (see Technical Note [2]).

FIGURE 5.7
NLSY-PIAT-R Data Over Four Occasions (N = 405)

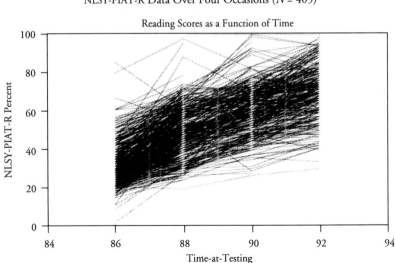

FIGURE 5.8
NLSY-PIAT-R Scores Over Four Occasions (N = 30)

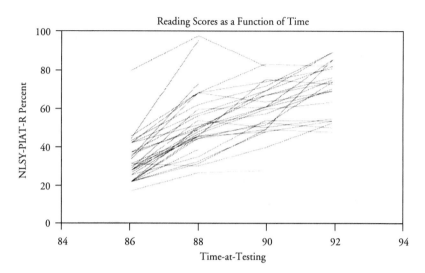

These summary statistics are based on the N = 233 children who had complete data on all four occasions of measurement. Here, for example, the mean of NLSY-PIAT-R at the first occasion is about 29% (i.e., $M[1]$ = 28.8) whereas the same statistic at the fourth occasion is about 69% ($M[4]$ = 69.3). This indicates that on average for the NLSY-PIAT-R, these children answered 29% of the items correctly at the first occasion and 69% of the same items correctly about 8 years later. The standard deviations of these measures also increase (from $D[1]$ = 10.5 to $D[4]$ = 14.5), and the correlation between the first and fourth occasions is positive ($R[1, 4]$ = .45). Further interpretation of these statistics will depend upon the model guiding the analyses.

The last two matrices in Table 5.1 provide a different summary of this same information. First is a covariance matrix formed from the deviations and correlations. This matrix is used in analyses to retain the information in the changes in both the correlations and the variances over time. The final matrix in Table 5.1 is an average of sums of squares and cross-products *(SSCP)* or central moments matrix. This constant-augmented matrix is used in analyses to retain the information in the changes in the correlations, variances, and the mean over time (for further details, see Browne & Arminger, 1995; McArdle & Aber, 1990; see Technical Note [3]).

Table 5.2 is a statistical summary of the additional relationships with these demographic and family data. The first part includes the means and standard deviations for these four variables at the initial time of testing (for N = 233, NLSY participants with complete data). The second matrix includes the internal correlations among the four variables themselves. The third matrix includes the external correlations among the

TABLE 5.1
Summary Statistics From the NLSY-PIAT-R Scores With Longitudinal Data
at Four Time Points (*N* = 233)

	Read [1]	Read [2]	Read [3]	Read [4]	
a: Means (M) Standard Deviations (D)					
	29.80	48.08	59.93	69.33	
	(10.45)	(11.94)	(13.15)	(14.50)	
b: Correlation Matrix (R)					
Read [1]	1.000				
Read [2]	0.625	1.000			
Read [3]	0.532	0.809	1.000		
Read [4]	0.451	0.752	0.813	1.000	
c: Covariance Matrix (C = DRD')					
Read [1]	109.20				
Read [2]	77.98	142.56			
Read [3]	73.11	127.02	172.92		
Read [4]	68.34	130.19	155.02	210.25	
d: Moment Matrix (W = C + MM')					
Read [1]	997.24				
Read [2]	1,510.77	2,454.25			
Read [3]	1,859.02	3,008.46	3,764.53		
Read [4]	2,134.37	3,463.58	4,309.97	5,016.90	
Constant	29.80	48.08	59.93	69.33	1.00

four variables at Time 1 and the NLSY-PIAT-R scores at all four occasions. These matrices are combined with those in Table 5.1 in some of the following analyses.

These NLSY-PIAT-R data can also be subdivided in different ways. In Table 5.3, we present the means, deviations, and correlation matrices separately for the female (N_f = 113) and male (N_m = 120) participants with complete longitudinal data. Although there are striking similarities between the comparable statistics in the females and males, differences between these groups are explored in more detail using some of the models to follow.

TABLE 5.2

Additional Summary Statistics From the NLSY-PIAT-R Scores With Longitudinal Data at Four Time Points (N = 233)

a: Means (and Standard Deviations)	SexDiff	KidsAge	HomeEmo	HomeCog
	.515	6.90	71.90	64.93
	(.50)	(.62)	(17.2)	(17.6)
b: Internal Correlations				
SexDiff	1.00			
KidsAge	−0.07	1.00		
HomeEmo	0.08	−0.11	1.00	
HomeCog	−0.02	0.64	0.32	1.00
c: External Correlations	Read [1]	Read [2]	Read [3]	Read [4]
SexDiff	−0.05	−0.09	−0.05	−0.04
KidsAge	0.58	0.28	0.19	0.09
HomeEmo	−0.01	0.15	0.18	0.27
HomeCog	0.07	0.19	0.17	0.20

TABLE 5.3

Summary Statistics for Females and Males on the NLSY-PIAT-R With Longitudinal Data at Four Points

	Read [1]	Read [2]	Read [3]	Read [4]
a: Female Means (and Standard Deviations [N_f = 113])				
	30.61	49.20	60.32	69.64
	(9.47)	(11.39)	(12.43)	(13.72)
b: Male Means (and Standard Deviations [N_m = 120])				
	29.36	47.13	59.28	69.59
	(11.30)	(12.41)	(13.77)	(15.18)
c: Female Correlation Matrix (N_f = 113)				
Read [1]	1.000			
Read [2]	0.676	1.000		
Read [3]	0.540	0.811	1.000	
Read [4]	0.424	0.739	0.820	1.000
d: Male Correlation Matrix (N_m = 120)				
Read [1]	1.000			
Read [2]	0.579	1.000		
Read [3]	0.528	0.805	1.000	
Read [4]	0.483	0.762	0.813	1.000

LATENT GROWTH STRUCTURAL EQUATION MODELS

Basic Features of Latent Growth Models

There are many alternative models that can be termed latent growth models (e.g., Browne & DuToit, 1991; McArdle, 1988; McArdle & Epstein, 1987; Meredith & Tisak, 1990). Most of these models use the following approach. First, write a *latent growth curve model* for longitudinal data as

$$Y[t]_n = L_n + (S_n \times B[t]) + U[t]_n, \tag{1}$$

where the individual scores at a particular time are a linear and additive function of the individual's intercept or level, (L_n); a slope, (S_n), multiplied by a group-level age basis $(B[t])$; and a unique or random error, $(U[t]_n)$, within each time. One can also write the change over time as

$$\Delta Y[t]_n / \Delta B[t] = S_n, \tag{2}$$

where changes in the score (ΔY_n) as a function of changes in time $(\Delta B[t])$ are constant S_n for each person (see Technical Note [4]). Thus, interpret this factor as an individual slope for each person (Bayley, 1956; McArdle, 1986; Nesselroade & Baltes, 1979; Rogosa & Willett, 1985b). This also means that the trajectory over time implies that any change in the observed score is based on the individual slope but is also directly proportional to the basis coefficients or saturation coefficients $(B[t])$.

A path diagram portraying this longitudinal growth model was presented earlier in Figure 5.4, and we return to this diagram because it illustrates a few additional assumptions about the unobserved scores. The relationships between the latent level, L, and observed scores, $Y[t]$, are fixed at a value of one. In contrast, the relationships between the latent slope, S, and observed scores, $Y[t]$, are assigned a value of parameter $B[t]$ which, depending on the application, may be fixed or free. The random components $(U[t])$ have mean zero, constant deviation (D_u), and are uncorrelated with all other components.

The latent variable means are an important feature of LGMs. In order to include the means in the path model, we have added a new graphic device: A triangle is used in this picture to represent the constant ($K = 1$; see Table 5.1, section d), and this new variable allows the means and intercepts to be written as regression coefficients (i.e., one-headed arrows from the constant to the variable). Using this device, one can see that other latent components (L and S) have means (M_l and M_s), deviations (D_l and D_s) and some correlation (R_{ls}).

After writing these as formal expressions, statistical expectations for the means, variances, and covariances of the longitudinal data are used to obtain optimal estimates from the available data. If this model leads to restrictive hypotheses about both the means and the covariances, then one can also evaluate the goodness of fit of the model to the data (see Technical Note [5]). These expectations differ from those of the traditional autoregressive model (in Figure 5.4) because these expectations (a) include the means, (b) have additive components for the covariance, and (c) include the same B [t] coefficients for both the means and the covariances. Because the observed moments do not necessarily follow this simple pattern, these expectations are restrictive and rejectable, so the model is scientifically useful. Most important here is that, at least in theory, this model can be fitted to the same longitudinal data as the previous autoregressive models.

The basis coefficients B [t] are not fixed, but they can be, and this permits the formation of a variety of alternative models. To start, assume there is no second component (i.e., B [t] = 0, M_s = 0, D_s = 0) and this leads to what is termed a *no-growth* or *level-only* model. As before, this model is often used as a baseline against which to judge the size of the growth components. In an alternative model, one can write a time basis (B [t]), where the values are fixed at "years since initial testing" (e.g., here B [t] = [0, 2, 4, 6]). This linear time basis is used to define the equal interval for changes over time, and this can be defined on an a priori basis.

A variety of more complex models are possible. The B [t] coefficients can be estimated from the data to yield an overall group shape (as in McArdle, 1986; McArdle & Hamagami, 1991, 1992, 1996; Meredith & Tisak, 1990). Although this "latent basis" approach is not used by many other researchers (e.g., Duncan & Duncan, 1995; Walker, Acock, Bowman, & Li, 1996; Willett & Sayer, 1994), it was the original basis of the LGM (e.g., Rao, 1958; Tucker, 1958), and it is certainly a viable option in LGMs. In more advanced models, options for curvature (e.g., quadratic, exponential) can be prespecified in a number of ways. Additional components can be used to represent an individual practice or "test-wiseness" effect that may be further specified in any of several ways (for details, see McArdle & Woodcock, 1997).

Model Fitting Computer Programs

There are in the late 1990s many different SEM computer programs that can carry out such analyses, including some with friendly and colorful names (see Hamagami, 1997; Technical Note [6]). All such computer programs have common technical features, and many of these programs can be used for analysis of the present set of data. The longitudinal analyses presented here were initially carried out using the LISREL 8 computer program by Jöreskog and Sörbom (1993). These analyses were also carried out using the Mx computer program by Neale (1993).

Within each of these SEM programs there exist a wide variety of ways to use this general approach, and this flexibility can create unnecessary confusion. Among many algebraic approaches to generating model expectations, we use RAM notation (see McArdle & Boker, 1990; Technical Note [7]). The computer programs were set up using this notation and the previous diagram (Figure 5.4) as a guide. Four alternative latent growth models were first fitted to the moment matrix (Table 5.1, section 1d) using LISREL 8 and Mx programs. These input scripts include the RAM algebra needed for the automatic generation of mean and covariance expectations.

This numerical technique is used because it allows one to simultaneously evaluate hypotheses about both the covariances and the mean structures (for further details, see Browne & Arminger, 1995; McArdle, 1988; Meredith & Tisak, 1990; Sörbom, 1974). All analyses to follow are based on maximum likelihood estimation (MLE). In many cases, these MLE can be obtained from an augmented moments matrix such as the one in Table 5.1, section d. Finally, there are many statistical approaches for dealing with the question of goodness of fit with longitudinal data. We report an approximate likelihood ratio test statistic *(LRT),* and the differences *(dLRT)* with the associated degrees of freedom *(df)* and a root mean square error of approximation (RMSEA) statistic. This minimal statistical information permits the calculation of several alternative indices of goodness of fit (Technical Note [8]).

Initial Latent Growth Results

The initial LGM results are given in Table 5.4. The first model fitted is a no-growth model. This model assumes that individual differences over time are a function of the individual's unique starting point, plus random error at each time of evaluation. This model results in estimates for both means ($M_l = 51.8$) and deviations ($D_l = 5.7$, and $D_u = 18.5$). When these optimal parameters are placed into the LGM expectations

TABLE 5.4
Numerical Results From Latent Growth Models Fitted
to the Complete Longitudinal NLSY-PIAT-R Scores

Parameter and fit index	ξ_0 Level	ξ_1 Linear	ξ_2 Latent	ξ_3 Re-scaled
Loading B[1]	1, 0	1, 0	1, 0	1, 0
Loading B[2]	1, 0	1, 2	1, 2.8 (.07)	1, 0.47 (.01)
Loading B[3]	1, 0	1, 4	1, 4.6 (.07)	1, 0.76 (.01)
Loading B[4]	1, 0	1, 6	1, 6	1, 1
Unique D_u	18.5 (.5)	6.6 (.2)	5.6 (.2)	5.6 (.2)
Level M_l	51.8 (.7)	32.2 (.7)	29.7 (.7)	29.7 (.7)
Level D_l	5.7 (1)	8.6 (.6)	9.0 (.6)	9.0 (.6)
Slope M_s	—	6.5 (.1)	6.6 (.2)	39.6 (.9)
Slope D_s	—	1.6 (.1)	1.8 (.1)	10.8 (.8)
Correl. R_{ls}	—	.13 (.1)	−.06 (.1)	−.06 (.1)
Num. Para.	3	6	8	8
Deg. Freedom	11	8	6	6
Likel. Ratio	1,452	150	9.1	9.1
RMSEA	0.75	.28	.047	.047
Probability			$p < .46$	
RMSEA < .05	$p < .001$			

Note. All scores rescaled into 0–100 Percent Correct form; *B* [Time 1] = 0, *B* [Time 4] = 8. Moments-based MLE (and SE) from RAMONA, LISREL 8, and Mx-96/1.04 for $N_s = 233$.

(Technical Note [4]), they lead to a relatively large likelihood ratio (LRT = 1,452 on df = 11, $RMSEA$ = .75). This result indicates that this highly restrictive model does not fit these data very well.

The second model evaluated is a linear basis model which, in addition to the initial level and unique error, includes a linear age-based slope for each person. This basis is fixed at values indicating the time difference between the first and current testing (i.e., $B[t]$ = [0, 2, 4, 6]). This second model results in revised estimates for the initial level (M_l = 32.2, D_l = 8.6, and D_u = 6.6), as well as additional estimates for the slopes (M_s = 6.5, D_s = 1.6, and R_{ls} = .13). These new estimates imply there is a strong positive linear change per year in the overall reading score (M_s = 6.5), but they also suggest a small but potentially systematic set of individual differences in these changes (D_s = 1.6, so the variance V_s = D_s^2 = 2.56). When placed back into the estimation Equations 3 and 4, introduced later, these new estimates show this linear model still does not fit these data very well (LRT = 150 on df = 8, and $RMSEA$ = .28). However, this is an important improvement in fit over the previous no-growth model ($dLRT$ = 1,302 on ddf = 3).

The third model evaluated in Table 5.4 includes a latent basis model where the change in the group over time is based on a linear slope with an unknown but more flexible functional form. This model results in similar estimates for most model parameters, but key differences in the parameters here are the two estimated basis coefficients (i.e., $B[t]$ = [0.0, 2.8, 4.6, 6.0]). By comparison to the linear basis (where $B[t]$ = [0.0, 2.0, 4.0, 6.0]), one can interpret the single optimal curve as one where the NLSY-PIAT-R changes are largest between the first and second years of testing: 2.8 latent years versus 2.0 manifest years. After this initial jump, the curves are relatively flat from second to third to fourth occasions. These new LGM estimates also lead to a good-fitting model (LRT = 9.1 on df = 6), and this is an improvement in fit over the previous model (with $dLRT$ = 139.9 on ddf = 2). In contrast to the linear basis model, this kind of flexible latent growth model does fit these data very well (with $RMSEA$ = .047).

The previous model illustrates how, by estimating the $B[t]$ coefficients from the data, one can obtain group growth curves that are not necessarily linear (and not even monotone). However, in order to properly interpret the latent basis, one needs to recognize at least one additional limitation in the model—the $B[t]$ values cannot all be estimated uniquely. As in any latent variable model, at least some of the model parameters need to be fixed to obtain a unique solution. In all cases here, we fixed the first occasion ($B[1]$ = 0) to allow a separation of the level and slope components, and we fixed the last occasion ($B[4]$ = 6) to provide a scale of measurement for the slopes (i.e., in "years"). This representation of the basis is somewhat arbitrary, and it often leads to some parameters that are arbitrarily scaled.

To illustrate these scaling issues, the model of Table 5.4 includes an alternative scaling of this model (where the $B[4]$ = 1.0). This results in a different set of $B[t]$ coefficients (i.e., $B[t]$ = [.00, .47, .76, 1.00]), but the overall fit is identical (LRT = 9.1 on df = 6). Although these new values are still arbitrary, this scaling permits substantive interpretations in terms of percentages of growth, and a plot with the same shape is drawn from the growth estimates obtained under any rescaling (see Technical Note [9]).

Latent Growth Model Predictions

The previous models each make different kinds of predictions about the means and covariances. The goodness of fit suggested that the choice of the latent growth model (either 3 or 4) is a distinct improvement over the no-growth or linear basis options. This choice of alternative models can be more clearly demonstrated by a more thorough examination of the structural model expectations.

In Figure 5.9 we show the expected mean trajectory from the first three models. These are the expected means formed from the model parameters of Table 5.4 (see Technical Note [5] for calculation details). The no-growth mean starts at an initial value (of $M_l = 52$) at the first time point and remains at this value over all occasions. In contrast, the linear basis model starts at an initial level ($M_l = 32$) at the first occasion and increases the same amount (by $M_s = 6.5$) each year (e.g., after 2 years, the second occasion increase is 13 points). In the final model, the latent basis model starts at the initial level ($M_l = 30$) on the first occasion and increases by the mean slope ($M_s = 6.6$) each year. Here the amount of increase is this slope multiplied by the basis coefficient ($B[t] = [0.0, 2.8, 4.6, 6.0]$). Both curves eventually end up at close to the same point on occasion 4. So, except for the notable differences between occasions 1

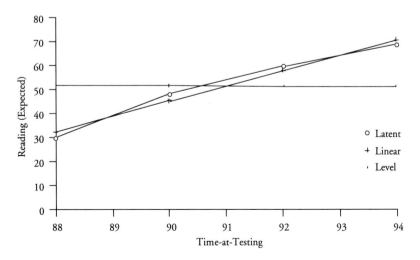

FIGURE 5.9
Growth Model Predictions for Reading From the First Three Growth Models

FIGURE 5.10
NLSY-PIAT-R Score Expectations From the Latent Growth Model

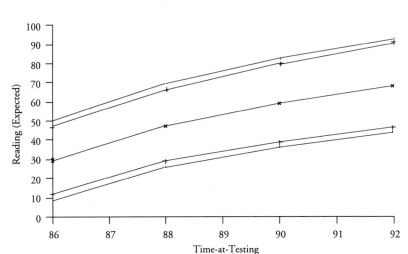

and 2, the best-fitting latent basis group trends are only slightly different from the linear basis group trends.

These group curves in Figure 5.9 are based only on mean changes, and these do not completely display the covariance model expectations. In Figure 5.10, a more complete set of expectations are drawn for the third model of Table 5.4. Here, we re-display the expected means in the central part of the plot. To these we calculate the expected variance ($V_f[t]$) of the function at each time point and use this to plot a 95% confidence boundary around the predicted scores. Finally, we calculate the unique variance (V_u) and add this to the 95% confidence boundary.

Although the scores are latent, the model parameters can be used to describe all of these fundamental features of the underlying growth curves. These curves show how the estimated model parameters can be used to draw a growth curve representation of the model expectations, and how it is also possible to calculate the explained variance due to growth sources at age (or occasion) t. In some cases, these estimates can also be used to calculate a curve of the reliability of factor growth ($r_f[t]$, as in McArdle, 1986; McArdle & Woodcock, 1997).

It may now be obvious, but a variety of more complex latent growth models are possible using this general logic, including options for more complex curvature (e.g., quadratic, exponential, etc.), and for other general restrictions (e.g., monotonicity). Comments are made about more advanced basis models in the discussion here (but see McArdle & Hamagami, 1992, 1996; Meredith & Tisak, 1990). We turn to a selected set of these applications in the next section.

EXTENDING LATENT GROWTH MODEL ANALYSES

Models Including Extension Variables

In most longitudinal analyses, it will be important to deal with a variety of additional variables. There are several potential models described elsewhere (e.g. McArdle & Epstein, 1987; Rogosa & Willett, 1985b), but we only deal with a few of these here.

Let us start by writing the latent growth model shown in Equation 1, but now add a set of additional variables, X and Z, measured at the first time only. One way to include these in this model is to write an additional model for the prediction of the latent scores as

$$L_n = I_l + (X_n \times G_{lx}) + (Z_n \times G_{lz}) + E_{ln}, \text{ and} \qquad (3)$$
$$S_n = I_s + (X_n \times G_{sx}) + (Z_n \times G_{sz}) + E_{ln},$$

where the coefficients G are regressions for the prediction of individual differences in the level and slope scores from the variables, X and Z. In this way the latent scores can now be considered as the outcome variables in another prediction system.

This simple modeling strategy is not novel, and it is fairly widely used. For example, exactly the same logic of correlating factor scores with external variables was the

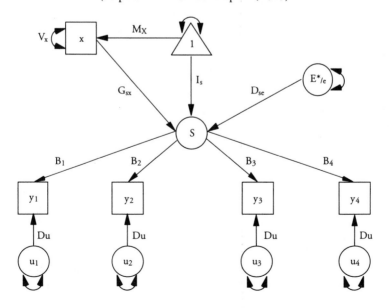

FIGURE 5.11
Extension Variable Models for Slope Prediction
(adapted from McArdle & Epstein, 1987)

basis of extension factor analysis (see Horn, 1976). In the context of growth models, this strategy has often been proposed in two stages and has been used to examine correlates of change (e.g., Rogosa & Willett, 1985b). Likewise, exactly the same logic was used in what are popularly termed multilevel models, hierarchical or random coefficients models (see Bryk & Raudenbush, 1992; Goldstein & McDonald, 1988; Longford, 1993; McArdle & Hamagami, 1996).

An example of this model is illustrated in Figure 5.11. This is a path diagram taken from McArdle and Epstein (1987), where the common factor of the time series is a slope variable. In this chapter, the scores were repeated measures on the Wechsler Intelligence Scale for Children (WISC) between ages 6 and 11, the component model included a single curve score (termed "s" in Figure 5.11 and drawn as a circle), the external variable was mother's education at the initial age (termed "x" in Figure 5.11 and drawn in a square), and the regression results showed a positive impact of mother's education on the slope of intellectual ability. Although we may be interested in a different set of outcomes and we have a different set of predictors, the basic structural questions are the same.

Extension Variable Results

A selected set of numerical results are presented in Table 5.5. These models were fitted with a program that included the summary statistics in Tables 5.1 and 5.2. All four external variables (Sex, Kids-Age, Home-Emotional, and Home-Cognitive) were used in the prediction of the latent variables of level (L) and slope (S) scores. For comparative purposes, results for the model with a linear basis (columns 1 and 2) and results for the model with a latent basis (columns 3 and 4) are presented.

In the first column, we report the latent variable regression for the linear level. This includes a significant prediction for Kids-Age ($G_{la} = 9.0$), but the other three variables add little. By comparing the level variance from Table 5.4 ($D_l = 8.6$, so $V_l = 74.0$) with the residual variance in this model ($D_x = 6.5$, so $V_x = 42.3$), we can calculate an estimated explained variance ($R^2 = 1 - [V_x/V_l]$), and this equals $R_l^2 = .43$ here. The third column shows virtually the same pattern of prediction for the latent basis model ($G_{la} = 9.5$, $R_l^2 = .43$). Thus, the finding here seems to be that the initial level differs as a function of the age of the child at the initial testing. This is not surprising because the kids range in age between 6 and 8 years at the first occasion, and this relationship may need to be considered in more detail in additional models.

The second column shows that the prediction of the linear slope includes a negative regression coefficient for Kids-Age (−1.1), a significant positive contribution from Home-Emotional scores (.03), and an $R_s^2 = .38$ for the prediction of latent slope scores. This pattern of results is also found in the latent basis model of the fourth column. This result suggests that the children who were older at the initial time point are not changing as much in reading scores, and this may need to be studied in more detail in further analyses. This result also suggests that children with higher Home-

TABLE 5.5
Numerical Results From Latent Growth Models of NLSY-PIAT-R Scores
Fitted With Four Extension Variables

Parameter	E {Linear} level	E {Linear} slope	E {Latent} level	E {Latent} slope
Intercept I_x	−33.6 (7)	11.9 (.2)	−38.7 (7)	12.2 (1.6)
Regression from SexDiff G_s	−.8 (1)	−.17 (.3)	−.64(1)	−.20 (.3)
Regression KidsAge G_a	9.0 (.9)*	−1.1 (.2)*	9.5 (.9)*	−1.2 (.2)*
Regression HomeEmo G_e	.03 (.03)	.03 (.01)*	.02 (.03)	.03 (.01)*
Regression HomeCog G_c	.03 (.03)	.01 (.01)	.02 (.03)	.01 (.01)
Residual D_x	6.5 (.5)	1.3 (.2)	6.8 (.5)	1.5 (.12)
Initial D_x	8.60	1.60	9.0	1.8
Estimated R^2	.43	.38	.43	.44
Num. Para.	14		16	
Deg. Freedom	16		14	
Likel. Ratio	162		16.8	
RMSEA	.20		.03	
Probability RMSEA < .05	p < .001		p < .73	

Note. Model N_s = 233; Linear with zero predictors yields LRT = 289 on df = 24; Latent with zero predictors yields LRT = 148 on df = 22.

Emotional scores also have higher reading slopes and, possibly of more consequence, the reading slopes are not directly related to the Home-Cognitive scores.

In making this kind of substantive interpretation, one needs to keep in mind that these regression coefficients (G) separate the unique contributions of each variable to the prediction of the latent scores. In this case, the two Home variables are positively correlated (.32), and the Kids-Age and the Home-Cognitive are also positively correlated (.64), so it is possible that some of the positive impacts of the Home-Cognitive scores are masked by the other variables in the equations. Also, it may be appropriate to consider the measurement characteristics of the Home scales before further inferences are put forward.

The linear basis model yields a poor fit (of LRT = 162 on df = 16, so $RMSEA$ = .20), and the latent basis model yields an excellent fit (of LRT = 16.8 on df = 14, so $RMSEA$ = .03). So, although the two models both yield approximately the same results, the latent basis model is preferred. It is important to note that in both cases, the inclusion of the extension variable at the latent level leads to only a small loss of fit from the previous growth models (Table 5.4; $dLRT$ = 12, $dLRT$ = 7.7). These small differences imply that a model with these external predictors having direct effects on these latent scores rather than on the manifest scores at each time point is a reasonable organization of these data.

Multiple Group Invariance Models

There are many more NLSY variables that are possible to study in this way. However, there are also a slightly different set of theoretical questions that need to be addressed. The previous extension analyses seemed to show that there were no significant differences between the males and females on these reading scores. The latent variable regression approach used here addresses questions about mean differences between the males and females (on the latent level and slope scores). However, it may be appropriate to ask whether other aspects of the growth functions were the same for males and females.

These kind of questions can be answered by examining a model of multiple group factorial invariance (see Horn & McArdle, 1980, 1992; Jöreskog, 1971; Little, 1997; Meredith, 1964, 1993; Sörbom, 1974). These kinds of multiple group structural invariance models have a long history in psychometrics and educational research, often in the form of questions about factorial invariance, measurement invariance, or test-bias. In contemporary work, a sequence of alternative models may be fitted to better understand the most salient differences between the groups.

An overview of these models has been presented by McArdle and Cattell (1994), and the path diagram of Figure 5.12 is taken from this work. In this two-group growth model, one initially writes a separate growth model for the separate groups. In the notation developed earlier, one can write

$$Y[t]_n^{(m)} = L_n^{(m)} + (S_n^{(m)} \times B[t]^{(m)}) + U[t]_n^{(m)}, \text{ and} \qquad (4)$$
$$Y[t]_n^{(f)} = L_n^{(f)} + (S_n^{(f)} \times B[t]^{(f)}) + U[t]_n^{(f)},$$

so there is one growth model for the males (with superscript m) and a possibly different growth model for the females (with superscript f). One key question now is: Are the growth functions the same for males and females? This can be answered by fitting a series of models starting with the restriction of loading invariance (i.e., $B[t]^{(m)} = B[t]^{(f)}$). If this model fits the data, then one might pursue a more complex set of constraints, including the equality of the basis ($B[t]^{(m)} = B[t]^{(f)}$) and the equality of the latent means ($M_s^{(m)} = M_s^{(f)}$).

Multiple Group Invariance Results

A selected set of results for a multiple group analysis of the longitudinal NLSY-PIAT-R scores for each Sex are presented in Table 5.6. These models were fitted to the separate group means, deviation, and correlations of Table 5.3 using a computer program for two groups.

The first two columns of Table 5.6 show results from a model of configural invariance. Here the same overall diagram is fitted (Figure 5.4) but no between-groups constraints are used. The first column is a list of results for a latent growth model fitted to the Females (based on Table 5.3, section a and section c). The second column gives

FIGURE 5.12
A Two Common Factor Model With CONFACTOR INVARIANCE Over Multiple Groups
(adapted from McArdle & Cattell, 1994)

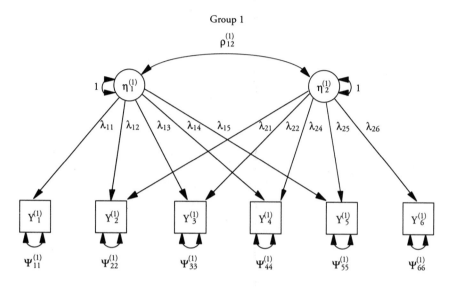

Group 1

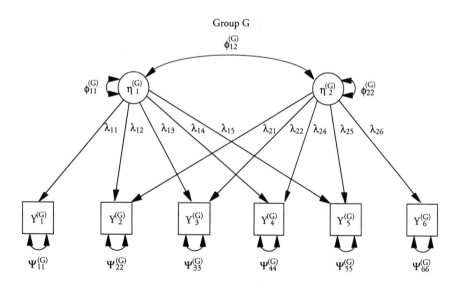

Group G

results for the same model fitted to the Males (based on Table 5.3, section b and section d). Because of the independence of the matrices and estimates, one can add the parameters for each separate model (8 + 8 = 16), the likelihoods for each model (*LRT*

= 7.8 + 6.5 = 14.3), and the degrees of freedom (df = 6 + 6 = 12). This model of configural invariance fits these statistics very well.

The third column of Table 5.6 gives results from a model of metric invariance. Here one uses the same LGM but all parameters are required to be identical or invariant over groups. The *MLE* turns out to be identical to results obtained before any group split was made (i.e., the third model of Table 5.4), but the goodness of fit here (LRT = 27.1 on df = 20) indicates the adequacy of this underlying assumption. In this case, the difference between this model of metric invariance and the previous model of configural invariance is relatively small ($dLRT$ = 13.2 on ddf = 8). The assumption of an equivalent growth process for males and females seems appropriate.

The overall results obtained here are relatively simple—there are no differences between male and female groups in the growth process. This kind of simple result is not often found in real data, and other differences in growth functions are likely in some groups. The differences between metric and configural invariance may be an important consideration. For example, McArdle and Epstein (1987) found that the basis loadings, (B [t]), were different for different groups of children separated on mothers' education—these growth parameters were highest for children whose mothers had the lowest formal education. Many different kinds of groups can be defined by the previous extension variables, and all models applied to such group data have this possibility of this form of a structural interaction.

TABLE 5.6
Numerical Results From Latent Growth Models
Fitted to Multiple Group Male-Female NLSY-PIAT-R

Growth model parameter	E {Latent} growth for FEMALES	E {Latent} growth for MALES	E {Invariant} growth for both groups
Loading *B[1]*	1, 0.0 =	1, 0.0 =	1, 0.0 =
Loading *B[2]*	1, 2.86	1, 2.76	1, 2.81
Loading *B[3]*	1, 4.56	1, 4.59	1, 4.58
Loading *B[4]*	1, 6.0 =	1, 6.0 =	1, 6.0 =
Unique D_u	5.1	6.2	5.6
Level M_l	30.6	29.3	29.7
Level D_l	8.6	9.3	9.0
Slope M_s	6.5	6.5	6.6
Slope D_s	1.8	1.8	1.8
Correl. R_{ls}	−.10	.00	−.05
Num. Para.	16 = 8 + 8		8
Likel. Ratio	14.3 = 7.8 + 6.5		27.1 = 15.1 + 12.0
Deg. Freedom	12 = 6 + 6		20
RMSEA	.041		.055
Probability *RMSEA* < .05	$p < .72$		$p < .66$

Note. All scores rescaled into 0–100 Percent Correct form; Fixed *B* [Time 1] = 0, *B* [Time 4] = 6. MLE from RAMONA, LISREL-8, and Mx-96/1.04 for each data group. The sum of the likelihood for the first two models is L = 14.3, so the difference due to invariance is a likelihood ratio of dLR = 12.8 on ddf = 8.

Models for Incomplete and Missing Longitudinal Data

Up to this point we have examined the data from participants with complete data at all occasions of measurement. But practical problems of missing data occur in any longitudinal study, including initial subject self-selection and subject dropout (attrition). In this case, the sample was reduced to 57% (from $N = 405$ to $N = 233$). We also found that some features of the model (levels and slopes) were related to the age of the subject at the initial occasion of measurement. In this regard, the main problem with the previous analyses is that we fit the function X over time-of-measurement ($t = 1$ to $t = 4$) rather than over age-at-measurement (age = 6 to 16 years), and in developmental analyses one is often interested in both functions (e.g., McArdle & Anderson, 1990). In the following models we make some effort to account for missing data and to consider a model for a more complete range of age-based functions.

The patterns of available and incomplete data in the NLSY can be displayed in several ways. These common problems of longitudinal data are displayed for the NLSY-PIAT-R variables in Figure 5.13. This plot gives individual growths on reading data for all participants ($N = 405$) as a function of age. The plot of Figure 5.14 includes only the first $n = 30$ participants, and here a few individual patterns are clearer. One can again see that not everyone has four time points of measurement. More notably, one also sees that, even for those that are measured on 4 occasions, the participants are measured at different ages.

In Table 5.7 we present the same data using a simple incomplete data display technique originally devised by J.-B. Lohmöller (1989; for programming details, see Rovine & Delany, 1991). In this display, a variable is created to define the pattern of complete data for each subject across an array of other variables, and the frequency counts on this new variable yield the size of each pattern. Among the four reading scores, the number of people measured only at the first occasion (the pattern of 0001)

TABLE 5.7
Initial Patterns of Incomplete Data in the NLSY Longitudinal PIAT-R Scores (Using Lohmöller's Method)

Pattern of retesting (4321)	Frequency	Percent
0001	16	4.0
0021	83	20.5
0301	5	1.2
0321	31	7.7
4001	3	0.7
4021	28	6.9
4301	6	1.5
4321	233	57.5
Totals	405	100.0

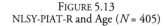

FIGURE 5.13
NLSY-PIAT-R and Age (*N* = 405)

Reading Scores as a Function of Age

FIGURE 5.14
NLSY-PIAT-R and Age (*N* = 30)

Reading Scores as a Function of Age

included 16 people (4.0% of the total). Next, the number of people measured at the first and second occasions (0021) is large, including 83 people (20.5%). In contrast, the number of people measured only at the first and third occasion (the pattern of 0301) is small, including only 5 people (1.2%). This approach shows there are only eight distinct patterns of incompleteness in these data. These subjects were selected for having complete data at the first occasion, otherwise there would probably be many more patterns (e.g., 4020).

The multiple group path diagram presented in Figure 5.15 from McArdle and Hamagami (1991) can be used to describe this model. Here, subject vectors are assigned to groups by having a common pattern of complete and incomplete data. The identical latent growth model is assumed to account for these data, but the number of manifest variables in the Y vector is across groups—the eight groups in Figure 5.15 have different patterns of circles and squares.

As long as there is enough information within each group, this model can be fitted using standard SEM programs allowing multiple groups. Each group is specified with one invariant A regression matrix and one invariant S moment matrix, but the observed variables are "filtered" using different F matrices. A simple algebraic expression for this kind of latent growth model can be written for each group as

$$Y[t]_{g,n} = F_g \times Y[t]_n \qquad (5)$$
$$= F_g \times \{L_n + (S_n \times B[t]) + U[t]_n\},$$

where the F_g is a matrix of ones and zeros defining the pattern of observed data within each group. In this approach, one does not attempt to impute the scores that are missing, but does attempt to compute the model parameters using all available data. Usually this estimation requires some untestable assumptions about the data, such as the blocks of data are missing at random (Little & Rubin, 1987) and there is metric factorial invariance (Meredith, 1993) across all groups. More details on this approach are presented in related research (e.g., Allison, 1987; Horn & McArdle, 1980; McArdle, 1994; McArdle & Hamagami, 1992).

On a conceptual basis, the previous multiple-group approach is appealing and requires no new SEM software. One technical problem that emerges here is that there are very small sample sizes in some of the groups (e.g., 4001 has $n = 3$), and this is likely to lead to a singular moment matrix (and full MLE is not possible). This kind of problem is even more severe if one wishes to estimate a model about the age-at-testing. If one uses the same technique but makes a slot for each age (in, say, one-half-year increments), there are 16 possible ages-at-measurement, from 6.0 to 13.5. Because any individual can fill a maximum of four of these age slots (i.e., the ages at which they were measured), one can end up with a large number of age patterns. The 405 subjects measured here have over 50 different patterns of ages-at-measurement, and many of these patterns have very small sample sizes.

The complexity of this problem suggests one consider a nonstandard approach to model fitting—estimating the parameters using all individual raw data. This raw data procedure, described earlier, has been implemented in the Mx program (Neale, 1993) using a *pedigree analysis* technique (originally used by Lange, Westlake, & Spence, 1976). In this approach, a structural model is defined and a likelihood (L) is formed from the raw data matrix (Y). This statistical approach guarantees that, if the data are

FIGURE 5.15
A Multiple Group Latent Path Model Used for Incomplete Latent Growth Curves
(adapted from McArdle & Hamagami, 1991)

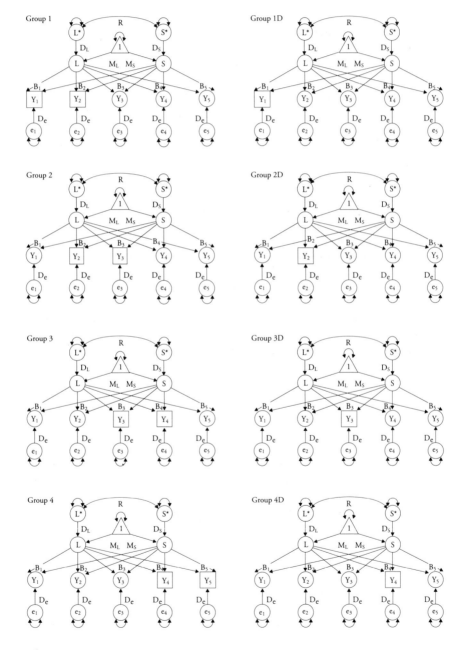

96

complete for all variables, the same maximum likelihood estimates are obtained as would emerge from fitting the model to the augmented moment matrix (W). However, in other cases the available information for any subject on any data point (i.e., any variable measured at any occasion) is used to build up the likelihood function and optimize the model parameters with respect to the available data.

There are at least two limitations to this raw data approach: (a) the raw data approach is computationally slower than the standard matrix approach, and (b) an individual baseline model must also be fit to obtain a baseline likelihood (L_0), so that the *LRT* can be formed ($LRT = L_0 - L$). But there are also two distinct advantages of this raw data approach: (a) the overall likelihood function can also be decomposed into individual components and the contribution to the overall likelihood can be evaluated (i.e., outliers can be examined; see McArdle, 1998), and (b) the raw data approach does not require complete data on all subjects, nor does it require the data to be completely blocked into patterns (as in Figure 5.15).

Results From Raw Data Latent Growth Models

In all analyses here we have fit the LGM using the (405 by 4) raw data matrix as input to the Mx program (using the RAW data option). This matrix includes 1,620 possible data points, but only 1,325 of these data points are complete (81.2%; see Table 5.6). These data were set up to include only 16 possible ages-at-testing (i.e., Age[t] = [6.0, 6.5, 7.0, 7.5, ..., 13.5]). This grouping by one-half-year ages was not completely necessary, but it was easy to implement.

In Table 5.8 we present results from four models fitted to the raw data. The first model is a no-growth model, including three parameters, and a fit to the raw data (with a likelihood of $L_0 = 11,616$). No further test of fit is made here but this likelihood is used as our null baseline.

The linear model includes a linear basis for 16 possible ages-at-testing (i.e., $B[t] =$ Age[t]) and two parameters ($B[6] = 0$ and $B[7] = 1$) were fixed to identify the latent scale. This model includes six parameters including an initial level ($M_l = 25.6$) and deviation ($D_l = 4.7$) at age 6, a mean slope ($M_s = 6.7$) and deviation ($D_s = 1.6$) for one year of age, a unique deviation ($D_u = 7.2$), and a latent correlation ($R_{ls} = .95$). The expected mean values of this model are presented as the straight increasing line in Figure 5.16. This linear age basis fits the raw data ($L = 9,790$) and, by comparison with the baseline model ($L_0 = 11,616$), obtains a significantly better overall fit ($L_0 - L = LRT = 1,826$ on $df = 3$). This linear model is a large improvement over the no-growth model (see Technical Note [10]).

The next model fitted is a classical quadratic polynomial trend model. This was fitted by starting with the linear model and then adding a second basis for the acceleration $A[t] = B[t]^2$. To fit this standard model completely, we also added a mean M_q, deviation D_q, and correlations R_{lq} and R_{sq}. In these results several of the correlations among the components are very high for the reasons described earlier. Nevertheless, this 10-parameter model fits the data with $L = 9,541$, and this is a clear improve-

TABLE 5.8
Numerical Results From Latent Growth Convergence Models
Fitted to the NLSY-PIAT-R Scores

Parameter and fit index	ξ_0 Level	ξ_1 Linear	ξ_2 Quadratic	ξ_3 Latent
Unique D_u	18.4	7.2	5.9	6.3
Level M_l	49.0	25.6	20.6	20.4
Level D_l	6.5	4.7	3.0	3.7
Slope M_s	–	6.7	109	9.2
Slope D_s	–	1.6	3.7	2.2
Accel. M_q	–	–	–.57	–
Accel. D_q	–	–	.34	–
Correl. R_{ls}	–	.95	.93	.80
Correl. R_{lq}	–	–	.99	–
Correl. R_{sq}	–	–	.92	–
Num. para.	3	6	10	20
Likelihood ($-2lnL$) model	11,616	9,790	9,541	9,544
Likel. ratio	–	1,826	249	246
Deg. freedom	–	3	4	14

Note. All scores rescaled into 0–100 Percent Correct form; B [Age 6] = 0, B [Age 7] = 1. Raw data based MLE from Mx-96/1.04 for full model N_s = 405, N_o = 1,325.

FIGURE 5.16
Reading Expectations for Four Latent Growth Models

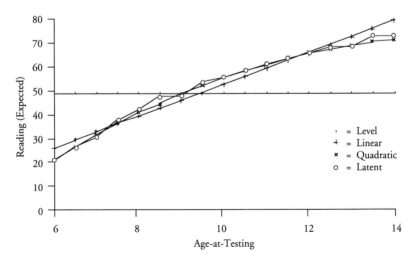

ment in fit over the linear model (LRT = 249 with df = 4). As before, the expected mean values can be formed from the model expectations, and the quadratic expectations are seen as one of the curved lines in Figure 5.16.

The last model fitted is a latent basis model where 14 of the 16 loadings (B [t]) are estimated from the data. The resulting basis loadings are presented in Table 5.9, and the resulting mean curve is drawn in Figure 5.16. The second column of Table 5.9 includes the linear age basis and the fourth column includes the ratios of the corresponding latent age to the observed age. In the early ages, the latent basis is fixed to be identical to chronological age, but from age 7 to age 9.5, one sees that the latent basis is proportionally larger than the corresponding linear age. We interpret this to mean that there is proportionally more latent growth during this period of age. This changes after age 10, and the growth flattens out (the ratios are lower than 1).

As it turns out, these latent loadings produce a set of expected means that are very close to those obtained from the previous quadratic model. The difference in fit is also trivial—this latent age basis yields a fit (L = 9,544 with 20 parameters) that, in contrast to the linear model, yields an improved fit (LRT = 246 on df = 14). In this case, the quadratic model yields the same fit but uses less parameters. However, the quadratic model should not generally be assumed to be best—the quadratic model is much more rigid (requiring the same form at all ages), and it includes a vector of la-

TABLE 5.9
Numerical Results From Latent Growth Convergence Models
for Alternative Latent Curve Models

Loading B[t] parameters	ξ {Linear} age	ξ {Latent} age	$\frac{\xi\{Latent\}}{\xi\{Linear\}}$
B[1]	6.0	6.0	1.00
B[2]	6.5	6.6*	1.02
B[3]	7.0	7.0	1.00
B[4]	7.5	7.8*	1.04
B[5]	8.0	8.3*	1.17
B[6]	8.5	8.9*	1.05
B[7]	9.0	8.9*	0.98
B[8]	9.5	9.6*	1.01
B[9]	10.0	9.8*	0.98
B[10]	10.5	10.1*	0.96
B[11]	11.0	10.3*	0.93
B[12]	11.5	10.6*	0.92
B[13]	12.0	10.9*	0.91
B[14]	12.5	11.2*	0.90
B[15]	13.0	11.2*	0.86
B[16]	13.5	11.7*	0.87

Note. All scores rescaled into 0–100 Percent Correct form; B [Age6] = 0, B [Age7] = 1. MLE from Mx-96/1.04 for full convergence models.
* Free parameter.

tent score components (Q), which may complicate further uses of the model (e.g., in extension analysis, etc.). The choice among these models is not clear and may be determined by later use.

Table 5.10 presents a direct comparison of some of the model fits when using the complete and incomplete data sets. An important issue here is the individual analysis of the misfit. The individual likelihood indices were calculated for all 405 subjects on all models (by Mx and saved using a standard OUTPUT option). This procedure allows the numerical results from the latent growth model to be plotted sequentially for each of the subjects. Although there are no notable outliers here, these are reasonable problems that can be taken care of in a number of ways. This analysis of individual misfits certainly provides some useful information about these outliers.

All previous extension analyses and multiple-group models can be fitted using the same raw data approach. For example, the complete comparison of males versus females can now use all the available reading data. As presented in Table 5.11, there are N_f = 203 females with 654 observed scores, and there are N_m = 202 males with 671 observed scores. The fit of a linear model using all available data yields reasonable fit in each case (L_f = 4,766 and L_m = 5,017) and the sum of the likelihoods (L_{f+m} = 9,797) is not much different from the fit of the overall linear model (L = 9,790, so LRT = 7 on df = 6). So, even when all available data are used, there are still no notable differences in the growth patterns of reading for males and females.

TABLE 5.10

Likelihood (L) and Likelihood Ratio (LR) Tests of Selection Effects From Latent Growth Convergence Models Fitted to the NLSY-PIAT-R Scores

Data set	ξ_0 Level	ξ_1 Linear	ξ_2 Quadratic	ξ_3 Latent
All data (N_s = 405, N_o = 1325)	11,116	9,790	9,541	9,544
Complete data T = 4 (N_s = 233, N_o = 932)	8,161	6,779	6,593	6,593
LR Difference vs. complete (df = 393)	2,955	3,014	2,948	2,951
LR Difference from incompl. Baseline	0	1,326	1,575	1,572
LR Difference from compl. Baseline	0	1,382	1,568	1,568
LR Difference in baselines		−56	8	6

Note. Likelihood (L) and Likelihood Ratios (LR) from Mx-96/1.04 using different data selections.

TABLE 5.11
Numerical Results From LINEAR Latent Growth Convergence
Models Fitted to Multiple Groups From the NLSY-PIAT-R Data

Growth model parameter	Reading for females	Reading for males	Readings for both
Unique D_u	6.8	7.5	7.2
Level M_l	26.2	25.1	25.6
Level D_l	4.5	4.9	4.7
Slope M_s	6.7	6.7	6.7
Slope D_s	1.5	1.6	1.6
Correl. R_{ls}	.85	.99	.95
Sizes of subjects and	$N_s = 203$	$N_s = 202$	$N_s = 405$
observations	$N_o = 654$	$N_o = 671$	$N_o = 1,325$
Likelihood			
($-2lnL$) model	4,766	5,017	9,790
Deg. freedom	6	6	6

Note. All scores rescaled into 0–100 Percent Correct form; $B[Age6] = 0$, $B[Age7] = 1$. MLE from Mx-96/1.04 for each data group. The sum of the likelihoods for the first two models is $L = 9,797$, so the difference due to invariance is a Likelihood Ratio of $LR = 7$ on $df = 6$.

CURRENT AND FUTURE GOALS

The latent growth models just described serve some, but not all, of the goals of longitudinal data analysis proposed by Baltes and Nesselroade (1979). In this last section, we use these five goals to discuss some benefits and limitations of these models and to emphasize future possibilities.

Direct Identification of Intraindividual Change

The LGMs used here allowed us to reorganize the longitudinal time-series data into common factors representing components of change. Group changes were represented in the shape of the slope (B [t]) and the average slope (M_s), and individual differences in change were represented in the slope deviations (D_s). In some LGMs here, the basis loadings were estimated as free parameters and compared to fixed loadings (i.e., linear, quadratic). These latent basis models are not widely used (cf. Duncan & Duncan, 1995; Walker et al., 1996; Willett & Sayer, 1994) and may be too sensitive to outliers (McArdle, 1998). However, these kind of "rubber rulers" can be mathematically simpler than some other a priori alternatives (e.g., quadratic), and these latent curves may be useful as exploratory devices for further theory generation.

The careful reader will notice that the scores for the level (L) and slope (S) were not actually calculated using these SEM (or multilevel) procedures. Because of the well-known problems of factor score estimation, this is a clear benefit (see Horn & Miller, 1966; Saris, Pijper, & Mulder, 1978; Wackwitz & Horn, 1971). However, factor score indeterminacy creates an important limitation on current SEM. In many practical situations, estimation of such scores would be a useful thing to be able to do, especially if one wanted to get a clearer understanding of the distribution of factor scores, to look for outliers, or to explore the characteristics of the latent variable regression models (McArdle, 1998; Meehl, 1995).

Long time series are not always possible in behavioral data collections, so other alternative data collection designs need to be considered. The techniques used here to model incomplete data can be used in reverse fashion. McArdle and Woodcock (1997) estimated an LGM based on an essentially random set of only two scores for each person. The pattern of the time of measurement was kept intact, however, so the same models could, at least in theory, be fitted to the sparse test-retest data set. It is also possible that, after losing so much of the longitudinal data, one might not estimate easily the model parameters or standard errors, and it may no longer be possible to distinguish between the fit of the alternative models. However, the numerical results from this kind of sparse data analysis can be used in data collection designs to optimize plans for gathering less data over time (as in McArdle, 1994; McArdle & Hamagami, 1992).

Direct Identification of Interindividual Differences in Intraindividual Change

The LGM analyses presented here permitted a direct look at the interindividual differences in change in several ways: (a) by estimating the size of the variance of the latent levels and slopes, (b) by calculating regression coefficients related to external variables, (c) by re-examining the entire growth model for different groups, and (d) by including between-age variance into the within-time growth functions. These approaches represent a variety of contemporary models being used to investigate behaviors that have both between-person and within-person components.

There are a variety of innovative analyses for these general problems that one can use here, including multiple imputation and Gibbs sampling (e.g., Little & Rubin, 1987). There are also a number of computer programs for carrying out similar analyses. For example, the first three age-based growth models of Table 5.9 can be fitted with computer programs for multilevel random coefficients models (e.g., HLM, ML3, VARCL; see Longford, 1993) with identical results. We are not aware of any practical way to fit the latent basis model except using these kind of SEM raw data programs (i.e., Mx, as in McArdle & Hamagami, 1996), but these options may be available in the future programs.

One key problem for future work involves the appropriate measurement and assessment of the key between-person variables. The overall assumption of homogeneity of the growth processes is not ideal theoretically or empirically (e.g., Tanner, 1960). Models with latent groups are still very hard to identify (e.g., Meehl, 1995;

Yung, 1997). So, until these key variables are measured, the resulting growth models may not provide adequate representations of invariant processes (Nesselroade, 1983).

Analysis of Interrelationships in Change

The LGM illustrations presented here did not go very far toward dealing with problems of interrelationships among different growth variables. In previous work, McArdle (1989, 1991) outlined some of these issues and fit a model where the levels and slopes (L_y, S_y) of one series ($Y[t]$) was correlated with, or regressed on, the levels and slopes (L_x, S_x) of a different series ($X[t]$). A similar kind of LGM analysis has been presented by Walker et al. (1996) and Raykov (1997c).

Of most importance in these kinds of analyses is the idea that the correlation among the slopes of two different variables may reflect something about the common changes (McArdle & Nesselroade, 1993). In this sense, these LGM results follow the lead of multivariate analyses in biological sciences (Griffiths & Sandland, 1984). However, it is also important to recognize that models of individual differences with relationships among dynamic variables (L_x and L_y) do not necessarily reflect dynamic processes for the group. The latter requires more focus on time-based models (as shown by Gollob & Reichardt, 1987). These are complex questions, so it is not surprising that the LGM presented earlier do not answer these questions directly.

Analysis of Causes (Determinants) of Intraindividual Change

One of the clear reasons researchers collect longitudinal data is to better understand the time-course of multiple behaviors within an individual. Some aspects of these questions are based on concepts derived from autoregressive models, and combinations of both concepts are identifiable with longer time series. Arminger (1986) developed a way to reinterpret standard LISREL results from panel data using differential equations (dY/dt). Gollob and Reichardt (1987) also considered the importance of inferences about the specific time-lag in longitudinal data.

McArdle and Hamagami (1995, 1998) used models from linear dynamics combined with SEM based on first differences $\Delta Y / \Delta t$ and considered a model written as

$$\frac{\Delta y[t]_n}{\Delta[t]} = a \times Y[t-1]_n + b \times S_n, \qquad (6)$$

where changes in the score (ΔY_n) as a function of changes in time ($\Delta B[t]$) are both proportional to the previous score ($a \times Y[t-1]$) and related to the constant ($b \times S_n$) change. This trajectory over time is determined by the means ($M_y[t-1]$ and M_s) and the coefficients (a and b). This approach also permits models for effectively dealing with more than one dynamic variable. For example, one may write

$$\frac{\Delta Y[t]_n}{\Delta[t]} = a_y \times Y[t{-}1]_n + b_y \times S_{yn'} + c_y \times X[t{-}1]_n \text{ , and} \qquad (7)$$

$$\frac{\Delta X[t]_n}{\Delta[t]} = a_x \times X[t{-}1]_n + b_x \times S_{xn'} + c_x \times Y[t{-}1]_{n'} \text{ ,} \qquad (8)$$

where the change in one variable is a function of both itself and the other variable.

This kind of model can be expressed in terms of a set of predictions about the score changes from one point to another in a statistical vector field plot (for details, see Boker & McArdle, 1995; McArdle & Hamagami, 1995, 1998). Perhaps more important, these time-dependent dynamic equations for the group also include all previous individual differences in the dynamic components. We expect to see more LGMs like this one in the future.

Analysis of Causes (Determinants) of Interindividual Differences in Intraindividual Change

These kinds of dynamic LGMs can be extended using all the ways defined earlier: (a) calculating individual differences in parameters representing slopes and functions, (b) examining which parameters of the dynamic models are predictable from extension variables, (c) separating the data into subgroups and examining the invariance of the dynamic process, and (d) separating the data into time groups and examining stationarity of the dynamic process.

There is no doubt that a most informative aspect of future LGM analyses will be based on differences between groups in the fundamental dynamic processes. For example, McArdle and Hamagami (1995) showed how a dynamic process among intellectual growth variables seemed to differ over different educational groups (college versus no-college education). Thus, progress on the first four goals will certainly lead to progress on this last issue as well.

Final Comments

These LGM concepts obviously represent only one kind of formal model for intraindividual and interindividual change. The LGM analyses presented here do not apply to different kinds of situations or answer all questions of interest. These illustrations do show how the current LGM and SEM computer analyses have led to several theoretical and practical advantages for current and future developmental research.

On a theoretical basis, there are several statistical advantages in using SEM that are important. In line with this thinking, the SEM approach encourages a more formal considerations of individual change models. This will be especially valuable when more complex measurement issues are introduced. Historians of developmental psychology and behavioral science will be pleased to find that there are some improved formal ways to deal with the kinds of questions that are routinely asked but rarely answered (e.g., Featherman, Lerner, & Perlmutter, 1994; Wohwill, 1973). In future work, investigators may even begin an analysis by asking, "What is the model for $\Delta Y[t]/\Delta B[t]$?" It will be intriguing to find if future modeling analyses will have the accuracy and power to let researchers know when they are wrong.

On a practical basis, the SEM approach may be seen by some as a tool for every problem—much like the hammer we carry while we look for nails. Nevertheless, this approach can be used to provide some appealing answers to longitudinal questions raised many decades ago (e.g., Bell, 1954). Also, the flexibility of the SEM approach continues to permit novel but practical solutions for the area of research termed "dynamic but structural equation models" (e.g., McArdle, 1988). There is no doubt that future SEM programs, whatever they will be called, will benefit those developmental researchers who themselves remain flexible.

TECHNICAL NOTES

Note [1]: These NLSY data were selected by Dr. Patrick Curran (Duke University) for a presentation on comparative longitudinal analyses at the Meeting of the Society for Research on Child Development (SRCD, April, 1997). All NLSY data used here are publicly available, and the computer program scripts used here are available (from the first author), so all analyses to follow should be relatively easy to reproduce from the available files or from the original data.

Note [2]: In any longitudinal analysis, one typically assumes some subjects ($n = 1$ to N) have been independently sampled with observed scores ($Y[t]_n$) at some occasion (time t). The scores Y are usually assumed to have been repeatedly measured under the same conditions and measured in the same units at all times. From such measurements, one should be able to create a variety of statistical indicators describing the time series, including means ($M[t]$), standard deviations ($S[t]$), and time-to-time correlations ($R[t, t+j]$).

Note [3]: The *augmented moments matrix* (such as the one in Table 5.1, section d) is a sample corrected sums-of-squares and cross products matrix (SSCP) conveniently formed from the means and covariances ($\mathbf{W} = \mathbf{MM'} + \mathbf{C}$) or directly from the raw data ($\mathbf{W} = \mathbf{YY'} \ \mathbf{N^{-1}}$). A unit constant ($K = 1$) is usually added in place of a variable—this is an unusual variable because it always has a mean of 1, a variance of 0, and undefined correlations with other variables (in path diagrams, a triangle is used to isolate this constant). This constant is added to easily separate the mean vector (in the first column) from the rest of the covariances and mean squares in the other parts of this matrix (for proof, see McArdle, 1988). In some of the more complex models, this approach cannot be used and the models are fit to raw data (as in McArdle & Hamagami, 1996).

Note [4]: To obtain this expression we first remove the unique component ($Y^*[t]_n$ = $Y[t]_n - U[t]_n$). We can write the first difference between two consecutive periods of time as

$$\Delta Y[t]_n = Y^*[t]_n - Y^*[t-1]_n \tag{8}$$
$$= \{L_n + (S_n \times B[t])\} - \{L_n + (S_n \times B[t-1])\}$$
$$= \{L_n - L_n\} + \{(S_n \times B[t]) - (S_n \times B[t-1])\}$$
$$= S_n \times \{(B[t] - B[t-1]\}$$
$$= S_n \times \Delta B[t] \text{ , so}$$
$$\Delta Y[t]_n / \Delta B[t] = S_n \text{ ,}$$

where changes in the score (ΔY_n) as a function of changes in time ($\Delta B[t]$) are constant S_n for each person.

Note [5]: In the general LGM form, the expected means over time are written as

$$E\{M_y[t]\} = M_l + B[t] \times M_s \tag{9}$$

where the M_l is the mean of the level scores, the M_s is the mean of the slope scores, and the $B[t]$ is the weight or basis coefficient associated with time point t. The expected covariances between adjacent time points can be written as a sum of additive components as

$$E\{C_y[t,t-k]\} = V_l + (B[t] \times V_s \times B[t-k]) + (B[t] \times C_{ls}) + (B[t-k] \times C_{ls}) \text{ ,} \tag{10}$$

where the V_l is the variance of the level scores, the V_s is the mean of the slope scores, and the C_{ls} is the covariance of the level and slope scores.

Note [6]: The LISREL computer program series is well known and may be the most widely used computer program for SEM, LISREL input scripts are now available in many published sources (e.g., Jöreskog & Sörbom, 1993; McArdle & Hamagami, 1992; Neale & Cardon, 1992). The Mx program (Neale, 1993) uses a much newer approach, but it accomplishes many of the same tasks in the same way as LISREL, includes advanced provisions for "raw scores" and "unbalanced data," and it is still in the public domain (i.e., free to use). All LISREL and Mx scripts used here can be obtained from the FTP site of the first author (McArdle at the University of Virginia) under the subdirectory labeled BERLIN97.

Note [7]: RAM notation (McArdle & Boker, 1990; McArdle & McDonald, 1984) allows the user to describe any linear system of equations using only three parameter matrices (**A**, **S**, and **F**). Although these three model matrices are not intended to have any substantive meaning, they are each directly related to the graphic elements in a path diagram: (a) All one-headed arrows representing regression or deviation coefficients are included in matrix **A**, (b) all two-headed arrows representing variance, covariance, or correlations are included in matrix **S**, and (c) the separation of the squares from the circles is included in matrix **F**. This notation is used in all path diagrams here, and also in the computer input scripts.

Note [8]: These SEM programs provide estimates for model parameters by itera-tively minimizing a fitting function (f_{ml}) based on weighted differences between the observations and the expectations. At some final solution point where the parameters do not change from one iteration to another (i.e., convergence), one obtains the final model parameters and their standard errors, and a substantive interpretation may fol-low. At some final solution point, the numerical results are used to form an approxi-mate likelihood ratio test statistic ($LRT = [N - 1]*f_{ml}$) as an index of lack-of-fit, with the degrees of freedom ($df = [v*[v + 1]/2] - p$) based on the number of v observed variables and the p unknown parameters estimated. Under assumptions of the multi-variate normality of the residual error terms, these LRT indices and their differences ($dLRT$) may be compared to a chi-square (χ^2) distribution for a probability interpre-tation of the adequacy of specific models. The associated chi-square test of fit exam-ines a very rigid hypothesis of "perfect fit," so we often employ another index of "close fit" (the $RMSEA < .05$) proposed by Browne and Cudeck (1993).

Note [9]: The fourth LGM result has a few useful properties: (a) All model param-eters now refer to change over the full 8-year period (i.e., $M_s = 39.6$ points change over the 8 years); (b) the rescaling of the basis in the seemingly arbitrary range 0–1 permits an interpretation of growth in terms of percentages—the growth between time 1 and 2 was 47% of all growth in this 8-year time period, and the growth between 1 and 3 was 76% of all growth (Of course, this is only true if all coefficients are in the 0–1 range); and (c) as in any factor analysis model, the ratio of any pair of basis loadings (i.e., $Q[t,t+j] = B[t]/B[t+j]$) remains the same (i.e., invariant) under any arbitrary scaling. This latter result is important because it means that the growth and change interpretations based on these LGM ratios are nonarbitrary, and a plot with the same shape would be drawn from the growth estimates obtained under any rescaling.

Note [10]: These raw data age-based results (Model 1 of Table 5.8) are very similar to the previous time-based model (Model 2 of Table 5.3) except for the poor fit. The poor fit may be due to an increase in statistical power obtained by stretching the age scale from 6 to 16, and this is a benefit. But we also obtain an unusually high latent correlation, and this is a limitation. The lack of separation of level and slope scores is likely to occur when the data are sparsely spread over age. This result is also partially a result of placing the central part of the basis at the early ages (i.e., $B[6] = 0$). That is, a smaller correlation will result from centering the age basis (e.g., $B[10] = 0$).

CHAPTER SIX

Modeling True Intraindividual Change in Structural Equation Models: The Case of Poverty and Children's Psychosocial Adjustment

Rolf Steyer
University of Jena, Germany

Ivailo Partchev
University of Sofia, Bulgaria

Michael J. Shanahan
Pennsylvania State University

Across the behavioral sciences it is often observed that some people change more than others. For example, some individuals learn faster than others in their youth; some lose their cognitive capacities more quickly than others in old age. Why do individuals differ in their patterns of change? What variables predict differences in growth and decline? Questions such as these require models of change. Yet observed change may be due to fluctuations of measurement error, which necessitates models of growth that depict the true change experienced by individuals across occasions of measurement.

How can we conclude that there is true differential intraindividual change? A simple rule of thumb is to compare the retest correlations of the observed variables to their reliability estimates. If there were no true differential intraindividual change, the retest correlations and the reliability estimates should be about the same. If, however, the retest correlations are considerably smaller than the reliability estimates, the underlying true score variables are correlated less than one, and a correlation less than one between true score variables pertaining to a test and retest means that some individuals change more than others with respect to the attribute considered; otherwise, this correlation would be equal to one. Hence, in such a situation the question: "Why do some individuals change more than others?" is meaningful.

Structural equation models (SEMs) (see e.g., Arbuckle, 1997; Bentler, 1995; Bollen, 1989; Bollen & Long, 1993; Hayduk, 1987; Hoyle, 1995; Jöreskog & Sörbom, 1993; Marcoulides & Schumacker, 1996) have been developed to decompose observed values into true components and measurement error components and to directly interrelate the true components to each other. Within SEMs, *latent growth curve* models have proven useful in the study of development (see e.g., McArdle & Anderson, 1990; McArdle & Epstein, 1987; Meredith & Tisak, 1990; Muthén, 1991; Raykov, 1992, 1996; Tisak & Meredith, 1990; Willet & Sayer, 1994, 1996). The basic idea of a standard latent growth curve model is to decompose individual growth curves into latent variables that represent an intercept (a level) and a linear (the slope) or higher order component of change. These latent variables are then interrelated to other variables that might explain the interindividual differences in levels and slopes.

Steyer, Eid, and Schwenkmezger (1997) presented a more direct approach to modeling interindividual differences in intraindividual change: the *true intraindividual change* models. According to this approach, the true intraindividual change scores (i.e., the difference between two true score variables) between two occasions of measurement are the values of the latent variables. However, Steyer et al. (1997) consider neither (a) models with different factor loadings for each observed variable (i.e., models with congeneric variables) nor (b) models with non-zero expectations of the latent variables. In the present chapter, we generalize the approach of Steyer et al. (1997) with respect to these two points and illustrate this more general model with an application involving children's psychosocial adjustment and poverty.

The chapter is organized as follows: We first specify the *multistate model (for multiple occasions of measurement) with invariant parameters* (MSIP). We then rewrite this model so that the true intraindividual change scores between two occasions of measurement are the values of the latent variables. Because the models with true intraindividual change scores are just reparameterizations of the MSIP model, we call them the *change versions of the MSIP* model, as opposed to its *state version*. Next, we study issues of identification. Finally, we illustrate the model in its two versions by examining poverty and change in children's psychosocial adjustment.

MULTISTATE MODEL WITH INVARIANT PARAMETERS

The model on which the rest of this chapter is based assumes that there are at least two observed variables measuring the same latent variable within each of at least two occasions of measurement. Additionally, it is assumed that the measurement model (i.e., the coefficients of the regressions of the observed values on the latent variables) is invariant across occasions. Hence, we call this model the *multistate model* (for multiple occasions of measurement) *with invariant parameters* (MSIP).

Figure 6.1 illustrates this assumption: Each Y_{ik} measures the same η_k, although the effects of η_k on the observable Y_{ik} may be different for each measurement instrument, i. However, it is important to notice that the coefficients of the regressions of the observed values on the latent variables are invariant across occasions. Hence, in Figure 6.1, there are only three different loadings for nine observables because three measurement instruments are repeatedly applied at three time points. In the next two subsections, we first treat the state version and then the two change versions of this model.

The State Version

Suppose that within each of n occasions of measurement there are m observables Y_{ik} measuring the same latent variable η_k such that

$$Y_{ik} = \lambda_{i0} + \lambda_{i1}\,\eta_k + \varepsilon_{ik}, \quad \lambda_{i0}\,\lambda_{i1} \in \mathrm{IR}, \quad \lambda_{i1} > 0, \tag{1}$$

and
$$Cov(\eta_k, \varepsilon_{ik}) = E(\varepsilon_{ik}) = 0 \tag{2}$$

hold for each $i = 1, \ldots, m$ and each occasion $k = 1, \ldots, n$. This will be called the *multistate model* (for multiple occasions of measurement) *with invariant parameters* (MSIP). Furthermore, we assume that the measurement errors, ε_{ik}, are uncorrelated, that is,

$$Cov(\varepsilon_{ik}, \varepsilon_{jl}) = 0, \quad \text{for } (i, k) \neq (j, l). \tag{3}$$

FIGURE 6.1
The State Version of the Multistate Model for Multiple Occasions With Invariant Parameters

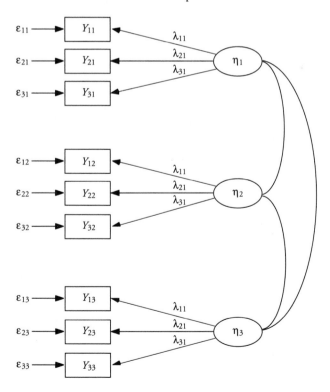

Note that variations of these assumptions may be formulated allowing some measurement error variables ε_{ik} to be correlated (see e.g., Marsh, Byrne, & Craven, 1992). Alternatively, it is possible to introduce method factors in order to account for a certain covariance structure of the variables, ε_{ik}. In fact, in the application section, we present an example with method factors. The only limitations to the MSIP are the invariant regression coefficients λ_{i0} and λ_{i1} in Equation 1 and the general limitations of identifiability. This state version of the MSIP is illustrated by Figure 6.1 for three occasions of measurement for each of which there are three observables.

The Change Versions

For simplicity, let us consider three occasions of measurement. Then Equation 1 may more explicitly be rewritten and reparameterized as follows:

$$Y_{i1} = \lambda_{i0} + \lambda_{i1} \eta_1 + \varepsilon_{i1} \tag{4}$$

$$Y_{i2} = \lambda_{i0} + \lambda_{i1} \eta_2 + \varepsilon_{i2} = \lambda_{i0} + \lambda_{i1} \eta_1 + \lambda_{i1} (\eta_2 - \eta_1) + \varepsilon_{i2} \tag{5}$$

$$Y_{i3} = \lambda_{i0} + \lambda_{i1} \eta_3 + \varepsilon_{i3} = \lambda_{i0} + \lambda_{i1} \eta_1 + \lambda_{i1} (\eta_3 - \eta_1) + \varepsilon_{i3} \tag{6}$$

$i = 1, \ldots, m$. These three equations capture the basic idea of the class of models presented in this chapter. Hence, note that the right-hand sides of Equations 4 to 6 are equivalent to Equation 1. However, some of the latent variables, namely $\eta_2 - \eta_1$ and $\eta_3 - \eta_1$, are now latent difference variables. The values of these variables are the true intraindividual change scores between occasions 2 versus 1 and 3 versus 1. This set of equations is called the *baseline version* of the MSIP (see Figure 6.2): Occasion 1 serves as a baseline against which change at subsequent occasions is to be analyzed.

Equation 1 can also be rewritten so that true intraindividual change always refers to the neighbored occasions of measurement:

$$Y_{i1} = \lambda_{i0} + \lambda_{i1}\eta_1 + \varepsilon_{i1} \tag{7}$$

$$Y_{i2} = \lambda_{i0} + \lambda_{i1}\eta_2 + \varepsilon_{i2} = \lambda_{i0} + \lambda_{i1}\eta_1 + \lambda_{i1} (\eta_2 - \eta_1) + \varepsilon_{i2} \tag{8}$$

$$Y_{i3} = \lambda_{i0} + \lambda_{i1}\eta_3 + \varepsilon_{i3} = \lambda_{i0} + \lambda_{i1}\eta_1 + \lambda_{i1} (\eta_2 - \eta_1) + \lambda_{i1} (\eta_3 - \eta_2) + \varepsilon_{i3} \tag{9}$$

(see Figure 6.3). Hence, we call such a set of equations the *neighbor version* of the MSIP model.

Extensions to more than three measurement occasions are straightforward. The basic principle is to preserve the equalities between the equation $Y_{ik} = \lambda_{i0} + \lambda_{i1}\eta_k + \varepsilon_{ik}$ and its reformulation involving latent difference variables. Hence, for a fourth occasion, we would add

$$Y_{i4} = \lambda_{i0} + \lambda_{i1}\eta_4 + \varepsilon_{i4} = \lambda_{i0} + \lambda_{i1}\eta_1 + \lambda_{i1} (\eta_4 - \eta_1) + \varepsilon_{i4} \tag{10}$$

FIGURE 6.2
The Baseline Version of the Multistate Model for Multiple Occasions
With Invariant Parameters

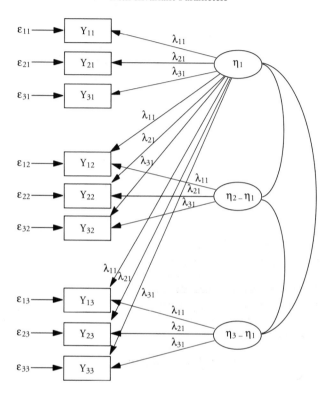

in the baseline model and, in the neighbor model:

$$Y_{i4} = \lambda_{i0} + \lambda_{i1}\eta_4 + \varepsilon_{i4} \tag{11}$$
$$= \lambda_{i0} + \lambda_{i1}\eta_1 + \lambda_{i1}(\eta_2 - \eta_1) + \lambda_{i1}(\eta_3 - \eta_2) + \lambda_{i1}(\eta_4 - \eta_3) + \varepsilon_{i4}$$

To summarize: Every multistate model with invariant parameters (MSIP model; Equations 1–3) may be transformed into a baseline version and/or a neighbor version. In these versions of the MSIP model, latent variables occur, the values of which are the true intraindividual change scores. In the baseline version, these latent variables represent the true change between occasions 1 and k, whereas in the neighbor version they represent the true change between occasions k and $k + 1$.

After a model involving latent difference variables is formulated, it is easy to treat the latent difference variables as ordinary latent variables in structural equation models. Equations 4 to 11 may be translated into path diagrams using the usual conven-

FIGURE 6.3
The Neighbor Version of the Multistate Model for Multiple Occasions
With Invariant Parameters

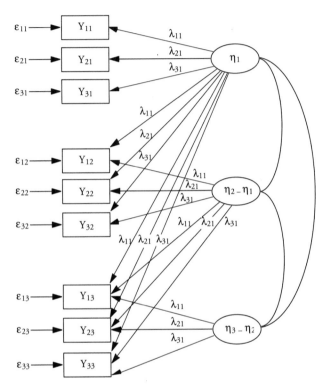

tions, and the latent difference variables can serve as endogenous variables to be explained by other latent variables or as exogenous variables explaining other variables. Both ways of using latent difference variables open up interesting possibilities. Using them as endogenous variables is tantamount to explaining interindividual differences in intraindividual change, one of the key interests of developmental science. However, using latent difference variables as exogenous variables may also be of interest in many applications, because it is often change, and not necessarily the actual state, that is the important causal agent (e.g., Wu, 1996).

IDENTIFICATION

If there is one latent variable η_k for each occasion k of measurement such that Equations 1 to 3 hold, then there is an infinite number of such variables fulfilling these equations. This can be seen from

$$
\begin{aligned}
Y_{ik} &= \lambda_{i0} + \lambda_{i1}\eta_k + \varepsilon_{ik} \\
&= (\lambda_{i0} - \alpha\lambda_{i1}/\beta) + (\lambda_{i1}/\beta)(\alpha + \beta\eta_k) + \varepsilon_{ik} = \lambda_{i0}^* + \lambda_{i1}^*\eta_k^* + \varepsilon_{ik},
\end{aligned} \tag{12}
$$

where $\lambda_{i0}^* = \lambda_{i0} - \alpha\,\lambda_{i1}/\beta$, $\lambda_{i1}^* = \lambda_{i1}/\beta$, $\eta_k^* = \alpha + \beta\,\eta_k$, and $\alpha, \beta \in \mathbb{R}$, $\beta > 0$.

A uniquely defined latent variable η_k is obtained only if its expectation and variance are fixed in one way or another. There are two ways to fix the expectations and variances—and in this sense, the scales—of the latent variables η_k: a direct and an indirect way.

Fixing the Expectation and the Variance

A direct way is to set

$$
E(\eta_1) = 0 \quad \text{and} \quad Var(\eta_1) = 1, \tag{13}
$$

for instance. That is, fix the expectation and the variance of the latent variable for the first measurement occasion. This has two consequences. First, this identifies (i.e., uniquely determines) the regression constants λ_{i0} and the regression slopes (loadings) λ_{i1}. Second, it identifies the expectations and variances of the latent variables η_k at other occasions of measurement. Table 6.1 summarizes the identification formulas that can be derived from the MSIP model (i.e., from Equations 1–3) and scale fixing via Equation 13.

According to Equation 14 in Table 6.1, the regression constants λ_{i0} are equal to the expectations, $E(Y_{i1})$, of the observables, Y_{i1}, assessed on occasion 1, provided that the scales of the latent variables are fixed via Equation 13. According to Equation 15 in Table 6.1, two observables at each of two occasions of measurement are sufficient to compute the loadings λ_{i1} from the covariances of the observables. Note that, in Equation 13, we only fix the expectation and variance of η_1. The expectations and variances of the latent variables η_k at other occasions $k > 1$ can be determined from the expectations, variances, and covariances of the observables (see Equations 16 and 17 in Table 6.1). Thus, it is meaningful to test hypotheses about expectations and variances of the latent variables η_k, $k > 1$.[1] Furthermore, the covariances of the latent variables η_k are identified (see Equation 18 in Table 6.1), as well as the variances of the measurement error variables (see Equation 19 in Table 6.1).

---

[1] Note that the possibility to test hypotheses about expectations and variances of latent variables η_k is a consequence of presuming a measurement model that is invariant across time.

TABLE 6.1
Identification Formulas for Setting $E(\eta_1) = 0$ and $Var(\eta_1) = 1$

$$\lambda_{i0} = E(Y_{i1}) \tag{14}$$

$$\lambda_{i1} = \sqrt{\frac{Cov(Y_{i1}, Y_{j1})}{\sqrt{\dfrac{Cov(Y_{jk}, Y_{jk})}{Cov(Y_{ik}, Y_{il})}}}} \quad , \quad i \neq j, \quad k \neq l \tag{15}$$

$$E(\eta_k) = \frac{E(Y_{ik}) - E(Y_{i1})}{\lambda_{i1}} \quad , \quad k > 1 \tag{16}$$

$$Var(\eta_k) = \frac{Cov(Y_{ik}, Y_{jl})}{\lambda_{i1}\lambda_{j1}} \quad , \quad k > 1 \tag{17}$$

$$Cov(\eta_k, \eta_l) = Cov(Y_{ik}, Y_{jl}) / (\lambda_{i1}\,\lambda_{j1}) \tag{18}$$

$$Var(\varepsilon_{ik}) = Var(Y_{ik}) - [\,\lambda^2_{i1}\,Var(\eta_k)\,] \tag{19}$$

Fixing the Intercept and the Slope

An indirect way to fix the expectations and variances of the latent variables η_k is setting

$$\lambda_{10} = 0 \quad \text{and} \quad \lambda_{11} = 1, \tag{20}$$

for instance. With these equations, fix the intercept and the slope of the regression of the first observable Y_{1k} on the latent variable η_k on each occasion k of measurement. Again, this has two consequences. First, this identifies (uniquely determines) the expectations and variances of the latent variables η_k and second, it identifies the other regression constants λ_{i0} and the other regression slopes (loadings) λ_{i1}, $i > 1$. Table 6.2 shows the identification formulas for the theoretical parameters in the case of fixing the intercept and slope for the first observable.

Compare the formulas displayed in Table 6.2 to those displayed in Table 6.1. Note that the different way of fixing the scales of the latent variables affects all identification formulas. Even in those cases in which the formulas look alike, the numerical values might be different, because the parameters that go into the right-hand sides of the equations change their numerical values. This is the case, for instance, for the covariances $Cov(\eta_k, \eta_l)$ of the latent variable, whereas the error variances $Var(\varepsilon_{ik})$ are not affected at all by the different ways of fixing the scales of the latent variables.

TABLE 6.2
Identification Formulas for Setting $\lambda_{10} = 0$ and $\lambda_{11} = 1$

$$\lambda_{i0} = E(Y_{ik}) - \lambda_{ik}E(Y_{1k}), \quad i > 1 \tag{21}$$

$$\lambda_{i1} = \frac{Cov(Y_{ik}, Y_{1k})}{Var(\eta_k)}, \quad i > 1 \tag{22}$$

$$E(\eta_k) = E(Y_{1k}) \tag{23}$$

$$Var(\eta_k) = \frac{Cov(Y_{1k}, Y_{ik})}{\sqrt{\dfrac{Cov(Y_{ik}, Y_{il})}{Cov(Y_{1k}, Y_{1l})}}}, \quad i > 1, \quad k \neq 1 \tag{24}$$

$$Cov(\eta_k, \eta_l) = Cov(Y_{ik}, Y_{jl}) \, / \, (\lambda_{i1} \lambda_{j1}) \tag{25}$$

$$Var(\varepsilon_{ik}) = Var(Y_{ik}) - [\lambda^2_{i1} Var(\eta_k)] \tag{26}$$

Thus far, we have examined identification for the state version of the model. However, if the state version is identified, the change versions are also identified because the expectations, variances, and covariances of difference variables can be computed from the expectations, variances, and covariances of the components of the difference:

$$E(\eta_k - \eta_l) = E(\eta_k) - E(\eta_l), \tag{27}$$

$$Var(\eta_k - \eta_l) = Var(\eta_k) + Var(\eta_l) - 2\, Cov(\eta_k, \eta_l), \tag{28}$$

and

$$Cov(\eta_k - \eta_l, \eta_{k'} - \eta_{l'}) = Cov(\eta_k, \eta_k) - Cov(\eta_k, \eta_l) - Cov(\eta_l, \eta_k) + Cov(\eta_l, \eta_l). \tag{29}$$

Because the terms on the right-hand sides of Equations 27, 28, and 29 are identified, the terms on the left-hand sides are likewise identified.

To summarize, we have shown that in the MSIP model it is sufficient to fix the expectation and the variance of the latent variable at a single occasion of measurement. If there are at least two observables measuring a common latent variable on each of at least two occasions of measurement, then the expectations, variances, and covariances of the latent variables and the measurement error variances are identified for the other occasions of measurement. This is true not only for the state version but also for the change versions of the MSIP model. Hence, we may estimate the expectations, variances, and covariances of the latent change variables.

The identification status will be slightly different if method factors are introduced. In this case, identification of all parameters involved might be possible only if some loadings are fixed or if there are at least three observables for each occasion.

APPLICATION: POVERTY AND CHILDREN'S PSYCHOSOCIAL ADJUSTMENT

Our approach can be illustrated by examining the true change in children's psychosocial adjustment as well as how poverty experiences predict interindividual differences in these patterns of change. Many studies provide evidence that poverty is related to the well-being of children (Hill & Sandfort, 1995). Previous research suggests links between economic deprivation and behavior problems (Erickson, Sroufe, & Egeland, 1985; Verhulst, Akkerhuis, & Althaus, 1985; Werner, 1985), depression (Gibbs, 1986), and troubled relationships with peers (Parker & Asher, 1987). However, virtually all previous research is based on cross-sectional comparisons between impoverished and nonimpoverished children (Goldstein, 1990; Walker, 1994). Thus, our current understanding of children in poverty largely fails to acknowledge the developmental patterns of children's well-being.

A few studies using latent growth curve models (McArdle, 1986) indicate that poverty experiences predict both the level and shape of children's growth curves. Drawing on repeated assessments of children between 1986 and 1990 in the National Longitudinal Survey of Youth (NLSY), McLeod and Shanahan (1996) showed that the number of years children are in poverty correlates significantly and positively with the latent slope of their antisocial behavior (see also Bolger, Patterson, Thompson, & Kupersmidt, 1995; Shanahan, Brooks, & Davey, 1997). That is, poverty experiences are related to the way in which children develop, not merely to their score at one measurement occasion. These results underscore the value of examining children's well-being in terms of both change and stability through the early life course. Yet, these models say little about true intraindividual change between two measurement occasions, because they depict change across all of the waves of data. In contrast, the neighbor version of the proposed true intraindividual change models, for instance, offers an approach to growth that decomposes change into a series of true change difference scores between consecutive sets of two measurement occasions. This allows for a more finely grained analysis of development.

Data and Measures

The data come from three waves of the National Longitudinal Survey of Youth and cover a cohort of young women who had been interviewed annually since 1979, at which time they were between 14 and 21 years of age (Center for Human Resources Research, 1988). In 1986, when the women were between the ages of 21 and 28, the first of a series of assessments of their children was conducted to track their develop-

TABLE 6.3
Items Constituting the Two Psychosocial Adjustment Scales

Scale 1	Internalizing	• Feels or complains that nobody loves him/her • Feels worthless or inferior • Cries too much • Is too dependent on others
	Externalizing	• Cheats, tells lies • Does not seem to feel sorry after he/she misbehaves • Argues too much • Is stubborn, sullen, or irritable
Scale 2	Internalizing	• Has sudden changes in mood or feeling • Is too fearful or anxious • Is unhappy, sad, or depressed • Demands a lot of attention
	Externalizing	• Bullies or is cruel to others • Is rather high-strung, tense, and nervous • Is disobedient at home • Has a very strong temper and loses it easily

mental progress. Child assessments were repeated in 1988, 1990, and 1992 (for further information, see McLeod & Shanahan, 1993).

We use data from the 1986, 1988, and 1990 waves, namely, a selection of items completed by the mothers and covering four types of behavior exhibited by their children ages 4 or older: depression, dependency, antisocial behavior, and headstrong behavior. The rating scale is a modification of the Achenbach Behavior Problems Checklist (Achenbach & Edelbrock, 1981) created by Zill and Peterson (Baker, Keck, Mott, & Quinlan, 1993). All indicators share the rating categories *often true, sometimes true, not true,* coded as 3, 2, and 1, respectively.

Out of a larger pool of items, we constructed two new "parallel" scales of psychosocial adjustment, Y_1 and Y_2, taking care that each represented internalizing problems (depression, dependency), and externalizing problems (antisocial or headstrong behavior) in a balanced way. When selecting the items for each scale, we were guided mainly by substantive considerations, but also tried to avoid items with overly skewed distributions. The items used for the two scales are shown in Table 6.3.

The values of the two scales were calculated as simple averages across the scores for the corresponding eight items, subject to the condition that there were nonmissing data for at least four items per scale. In spite of this procedure, the percentage of missing data of the scales is considerable. Computing the covariance matrix of the six measures showed that some covariances were computed from 93%, others from only 60% of the cases (median 75%, interquartile range 71% through 81%). Hence, an alternative way of treating the missing data problem was chosen: the Amos full information maximum likelihood approach (Wothke, chap. 12, this volume). This method seemed optimal in face of the large amount of missing data.

The reliabilities of the resulting six measures (the two scales at three measurement occasions), as estimated by Cronbach's α, were between .66 and .77, with a median of .72. These values seem acceptable for scales that are short and heterogeneous in nature. We used a measure of poverty, expressed as the proportion of time the family lived in poverty during the survey, as a predictor of level and change in psychosocial adjustment (for details, see McLeod & Shanahan, 1996).

Models and Results

We present all three versions of the MSIP model: the state version, the baseline version, and the neighbor version. In all versions we used the indirect way of fixing the scales of the latent variables, and all versions include intercepts of the structural regressions and the expectations of the latent variables involved. Note, however, that, according to Equation 1, the intercepts and loadings of the measurement models are fixed across time. To achieve good fit, we included one method factor that is uncorrelated with the latent state/change variables and loads on one of the two scales for each occasion of measurement. Including a method factor was necessary because the two scales are not perfectly parallel in the sense of classical test theory (see Lord & Novick, 1968; or Steyer & Eid, 1993). (Eid, 1998, provides the theoretical background for this kind of modeling method factors with one method factor less than the number of methods.) We also allowed the residuals of the latent state variables to correlate because we cannot expect the poverty variable to explain all the correlation between the latent psychosocial adjustment state variables. In fact, most of that covariance can be explained by a latent psychosocial adjustment trait variable (see Steyer, Ferring, & Schmitt, 1992, for an introduction to latent state-trait theory). Figures 6.4 to 6.6 show the models fitted. For simplicity, the intercepts and means are not displayed in the figures. However, they are reported in Tables 6.5 to 6.7.

TABLE 6.4
Means, Standard Deviations, and Correlations of Poverty Duration and the Psychosocial Adjustment Scales (Implied Moments Under Saturated Model, Amos Estimates)

	Y_{11}	Y_{21}	Y_{12}	Y_{22}	Y_{13}	Y_{23}	Poverty
Means	1.448	1.501	1.457	1.505	1.438	1.495	0.310
SD	0.311	0.330	0.330	0.355	0.336	0.371	0.358
Y_{11}	1.000						
Y_{21}	0.724	1.000					
Y_{12}	0.431	0.456	1.000				
Y_{22}	0.408	0.502	0.758	1.000			
Y_{13}	0.416	0.435	0.532	0.472	1.000		
Y_{23}	0.379	0.457	0.491	0.552	0.779	1.000	
Poverty	0.127	0.115	0.147	0.131	0.128	0.111	1.000

Table 6.4 shows the means, standard deviations, and correlations of the poverty measure and the two psychosocial adjustment scales at each of three occasions of measurement. These quantities have been estimated by Amos and are actually the moments implied by the saturated model. However, they are not sufficient statistics and fitting our model with them only approximately reproduces our results.

The saturated model had a log-likelihood function of –13753.33 with 35 estimated parameters, and our model had a log-likelihood of –13741.89 with 24 estimated parameters. The difference in the two log-likelihood functions is a chi-squared statistic of 11.44, which, at 11 degrees of freedom, indicates a very good fit (p = .406; RMSEA = 0.005).

The State Version

The unstandardized solution of the state version of the MSIP model is depicted in Figure 6.4. Additional information on the model is given in Table 6.5. Figure 6.4 reveals that the loadings of the two psychosocial adjustment scales are almost equal. However, they are not fixed to be equal, in order to demonstrate that, in true intraindividual change models, one may have different loadings for the observables.

According to Table 6.5, the means of the latent state psychosocial adjustment variables are stable over time. Their estimates range between 1.440 and 1.454.[2] This indicates that there is no general trend in the sample toward an increase or a decrease in psychosocial adjustment.

Nevertheless, there is differential intraindividual change over time with respect to psychosocial adjustment because the retest correlations are between .54 and .63, whereas the reliability estimates (the squared multiple correlations for the observables

TABLE 6.5
Means, Variances, Correlations, and Regressions for the State Model
(Full Information ML Estimates)

	η_1	η_2	η_3
Means	1.448	1.454	1.440
Variances	0.073	0.087	0.096
η_1	1.000		
η_2	0.583	1.000	
η_3	0.541	0.630	1.000
Correlations with poverty	0.143	0.162	0.137
Regression on poverty: slopes	0.108	0.133	0.118
Intercepts	1.415	1.413	1.403

---

[2] A model comparison between the two models with and without equality restrictions on these three means yields a χ^2-difference of 3.00 with two degrees of freedom. This comparison was made excluding the poverty variable from the model with the effect that we have direct access to the means of the three latent psychosocial adjustment variables.

FIGURE 6.4
The Final Model in Its State Version, With Amos Estimates of the Free Parameters
$(\chi^2 = 11.444, df = 11, p > 0.406, \text{RMSEA} = 0.005)$

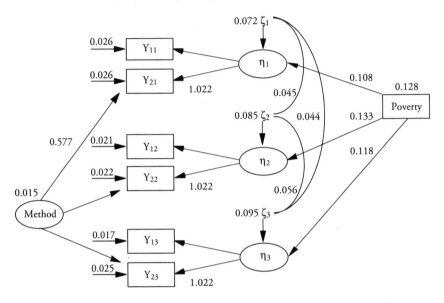

in Figure 6.4) range between .74 and .85. If there were no differential intraindividual change, the retest correlations and the reliability estimates should be about the same. Hence, the question: "Why do some children change more than others?" is meaningful in this context, although there is no change in the mean of the psychosocial adjustment variables.

According to Table 6.5, there are small but significant positive correlations between poverty duration and the latent state psychosocial adjustment variables ranging between .14 and .16. Hence, poverty duration could predict psychosocial adjustment. Figure 6.4 shows the corresponding unstandardized path coefficients for the regressions of the three psychosocial adjustment statevariables on poverty.

The Baseline Model

How is true intraindividual change in psychosocial adjustment related to poverty duration? Looking at the correlations between the two latent change variables $\eta_2 - \eta_1$ or $\eta_3 - \eta_1$ and poverty duration (see Table 6.6 and Figure 6.5) reveals that true intraindividual change in psychosocial adjustment is not related to poverty duration in this study. The estimates of the two correlations are 0.034 and 0.013, which are not significantly different from zero. (The corresponding test yields a nonsignificant χ^2-

difference of 0.87 with two degrees of freedom.) Note that the negative correlation between η_1 and $\eta_2 - \eta_1$ is because η_1 is a component of the difference $\eta_2 - \eta_1$, because $Cov(\eta_1, \eta_2 - \eta_1) = Cov(\eta_1, \eta_2) - Var(\eta_1)$. Hence, if the variances of two latent variables are equal and their correlation is smaller than one, the covariance (and therefore the correlation) between η_1 and $\eta_2 - \eta_1$ will be negative. A similar argument holds

FIGURE 6.5

The Final Model in Its Baseline Version, With Amos Estimates of the Free Parameters

$(\chi^2 = 11.444, df = 11, p > 0.406, RMSEA = 0.005)$

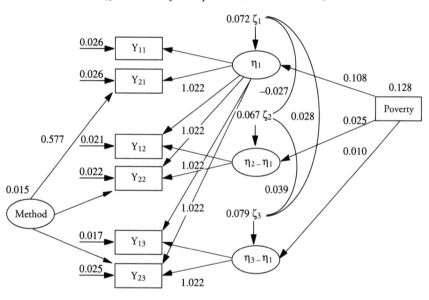

TABLE 6.6

Means, Variances, and Correlations for the Baseline Model (Full Information ML Estimates)

	η_1	$\eta_2 - \eta_1$	$\eta_3 - \eta_1$
Means	1.448	0.006	−0.009
Variances	0.073	0.067	0.079
η_1	1.000		
$\eta_2 - \eta_1$	−0.380	1.000	
$\eta_3 - \eta_1$	−0.364	0.536	1.000
Correlations with poverty	0.143	0.034	0.013
Regression on poverty: slopes	0.108	0.025	0.010
Intercepts	1.415	−0.002	−0.012

for the negative correlation between the two latent change variables $\eta_2 - \eta_1$ and $\eta_3 - \eta_1$. In this version of the MSIP model, the means of the latent change variables are close to zero, reflecting the finding that the means of the latent psychosocial adjustment variables do not change over time.

The Neighbor Model

A similar story is told by the neighbor model. Figure 6.6 displays the neighbor version of the MSIP model. Looking at the correlations between the two latent change variables $\eta_2 - \eta_1$ or $\eta_3 - \eta_2$ and poverty duration (see Table 6.7) again reveals that true intraindividual change in psychosocial adjustment between the neighbored occasions (two vs. one and three vs. two) is not related to poverty duration. The empirical estimates of the correlations are .034 and −.020 (see Table 6.7) and a test of significance yields again a nonsignificant χ^2-difference of 0.87 with two degrees of freedom. In this version of the model, too, the negative correlations between η_1, $\eta_2 - \eta_1$ and $\eta_3 - \eta_2$ are due to the fact that η_1 is a component of both latent difference variables.

The means of the latent change variables are close to zero, which again reflects the finding from the state version of the MSIP model that the means of the latent psychosocial adjustment variables are invariant over time.

FIGURE 6.6

The Final Model in Its Neighbor Version, With Amos Estimates of the Free Parameters
($\chi^2 = 11.444$, $df = 11$, $p > 0.406$, RMSEA = 0.005)

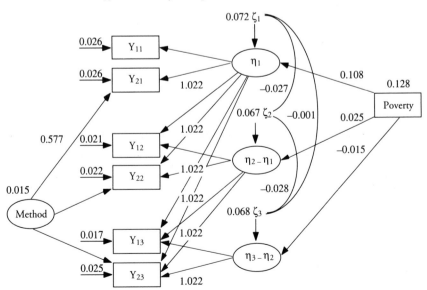

TABLE 6.7
Means, Variances, and Correlations for the Neighbor Model (Full Information ML Estimates)

	η_1	$\eta_2-\eta_1$	$\eta_3-\eta_1$
Means	1.448	0.006	−0.015
Variances	0.073	0.067	0.068
η_1	1.000		
$\eta_2 - \eta_1$	−0.380	1.000	
$\eta_3 - \eta_2$	−0.014	−0.418	1.000
Correlations with poverty	0.143	0.034	−0.020
Regression on poverty: slopes	0.108	0.025	−0.015
Intercepts	1.415	−0.002	−0.010

Discussion

We have shown how to specify a structural equation model such that the true intra-individual change scores between two occasions of measurement are the values of the endogenous latent variables in the model. Whereas the presentation of Steyer et al. (1997) was restricted to the model of essential τ-equivalent variables, we generalized the true intraindividual change approach to the case with different factor loadings for each observed variable (i.e., models with congeneric variables). This was possible only under the assumption of invariant loadings over time. If this restriction holds, one can specify the loading matrix in such a way that certain latent variables can be interpreted as true intraindividual change variables and can examine the predictors of interindividual differences in true intraindividual change. The models presented include mean structures and intercepts of the regressions of the latent psychosocial adjustment (state and change) variables on poverty duration. Within these models it is possible to test hypotheses about the expectations of the latent state (and change) variables and about the effects of explanatory variables on the true intraindividual state (and change) variables.

What are the differences between the true intraindividual change approach and the latent growth curve approach to modeling change? As already noted by Steyer et al. (1997), in latent growth curve models, certain components (such as the linear component) of intraindividual change may be correlated or explained by linear regressions. In contrast, in true intraindividual change models, the true intraindividual change itself, not a particular component of it, may be correlated with other variables, or, alternatively explained through linear regressions on other variables.

In the baseline model, one may study how the true intraindividual changes (in psychosocial adjustment) between the first and the second as well as between the first and the third time points are related to one or more explanatory variables (such as poverty). In the neighbor model, one may study true intraindividual changes between the first and the second as well as between the second and third time points. In contrast, in traditional growth curve models, one may study the linear and/or the quadratic trend in true change across all three time points. Hence, in our mind, true intraindividual change models offer a more direct approach to modeling true change.

In both classes of models, that is, true intraindividual change models and growth curve models, individual growth curves could be estimated via factor score estimation. However, this would be meaningful only for diagnoses of individual change.

According to our example, poverty duration was significantly correlated with the latent psychosocial adjustment state variables but not with the latent intraindividual change variables. Analyzing the data with a growth curve model, we found no significant effect of the poverty variable on the latent slope component or on the latent quadratic component. This finding is not surprising. If poverty is neither related to change between occasions one and two nor to change between occasions two and three, then it will not be related to either the linear or the quadratic trend of change across all three occasions of measurement.

Our empirical findings should not be generalized to say that poverty duration does not have a destructive effect on children's psychosocial adjustment. There are many studies that show a strong, negative effect of poverty on children's development (Duncan & Brooks-Gunn, 1997). In the present case, it may be that the effects of poverty can only be detected when subscales of the Behavioral Problems Index (BPI) are used. Our example uses the entire BPI, although other studies show both that this scale is comprised of multiple factors and that subscales of the BPI (such as antisocial behavior and anxiety/depression) are indeed related to developmental patterns of children's well-being (e.g., Shanahan et al., 1997). The example illustrates our approach to change, but also alerts the analyst that these models require the careful measurement and selection of the change variable, with special attention devoted to securing multiple, relatively parallel indicators.

The neighbor model is especially well-suited to the study of developmental phenomena characterized by discontinuous and rapid change. In such instances, the analyst can test whether exogenous variables differentially predict the $\eta_3 - \eta_2$ change score versus the $\eta_2 - \eta_1$ change score. Thus, one can examine how and why phenomena change before, during, and after transitions. Such an approach has a wide range of applications, including the ability to study in detail the effects of an experimental manipulation or an intervention. In a quasi-experimental framework, data can be organized around naturally occurring transitions. What is the typical pattern of depression before and after retirement and why do some adults get more depressed? What causes some children to be more anxious with the transition to school or some adolescents to suffer losses in self-efficacy with the transition to a new school setting? What predicts changes in marital relationships both before and after the birth of a child? With its focus on true change between measurement occasions, the neighbor model represents a potentially powerful and flexible tool to address questions such as these.

The true intraindividual change versions make explicit in a very convenient way the relationships of the true latent change variables with other variables included in the model. This specification can serve as a useful tool for detailed examinations of intraindividual patterns of developmental change and their interindividual predictors.

CHAPTER SEVEN

Modeling Simultaneously Individual and Group Patterns of Ability Growth or Decline

Tenko Raykov
Fordham University

Since the 1970s, the interest in studying change processes in the behavioral and educational sciences has rapidly increased. As a consequence, the number of utilized models of growth or decline has risen substantially as well. Among them, models based on the popular methodology of covariance structure analysis occupy a prominent place. Their wider application in social science research was initiated by pioneering articles by McArdle and colleagues in the 1980s and early 1990s (e.g., McArdle, 1988; McArdle & Aber, 1990; McArdle & Anderson, 1990; McArdle & Epstein, 1987). These and related models have received a comprehensive coverage in the latent curve analysis advanced by Meredith and Tisak (1990). Subsequently, dynamic models for change, developed within the covariance structure analysis methodology, have been proposed by Browne and DuToit (1991, 1992), Browne (1993), Muthén (1991, 1993), and Willett and Sayer (1994), to name a few.

A common feature of these models is that they are fitted to matrices of interrelationship indices between observed variables and their means. Most of them can be considered special cases of latent curve analysis. A major advantage of these models is that they permit the researcher to include fallible explanatory variables and thus take explicit account of measurement error that is nearly ubiquitous in the behavioral and educational sciences. Further, the models allow estimation and testing of general error structures (correlated errors), as long as they are identified (e.g., Cole, Maxwell, Arvey, & Salas, 1993). Moreover, these models do not need to make special assumptions—such as sphericity, covariance matrix homogeneity, or regression homogeneity—of conventional (M)ANOVA or (M)ANCOVA applications, for example, in repeated measure analyses.

The present chapter utilizes latent curve analysis for examining processes of growth or decline. In the center of interest is a comprehensive method for studying simultaneously individual and group latent change patterns along several longitudinally assessed dimensions. A general covariance structure model is outlined that is concerned with (a) the exploration of patterns of change on certain repeatedly measured variables in a given group considered as a whole and (b) subjects' developmental profiles along other longitudinally assessed dimensions. As with most mentioned approaches to change measurement, this model is a special case of latent curve analysis. It is particularly useful for modeling data from longitudinal designs where assumptions of repeated measure analysis of variance are violated (e.g., Maxwell & Delaney, 1990).

AN INTRODUCTION TO LATENT CURVE ANALYSIS

The latent curve analysis by Meredith and Tisak (1990) represents an approach to modeling repeated measurements using covariance structure analysis. It has its origins in the pioneering works in factor analysis of repeated measurements by Rao (1958), Tucker (1958), Scher, Young, and Meredith (1960), and Jöreskog (1970). It also bears close connections to change models by Rogosa and associates (Rogosa, 1987, 1996; Rogosa, Brandt, & Zimowski, 1982; Rogosa & Willett, 1985a, 1985b; see also Raykov, in press).

The remainder of this chapter assumes that a sample of N individuals from a prespecified population has been assessed at times $t_1, t_2, \ldots, t_q$ on m distinct dimensions ($m \geq 1$, $q \geq 2$). These dimensions can be studied abilities, personal characteristics, or behavioral constructs. (For its introductory purposes, this section draws substantially upon Meredith & Tisak, 1990.) The observed scores are denoted by Y_{pij}, for $p = 1, \ldots, N$ (designating individual), $i = 1, 2, \ldots, m$ (denoting characteristic), and $j = 1, \ldots, q$ (symbolizing assessment occasion). For example, the data used in a later section stem from $N = 248$ subjects assessed on $q = 4$ successive measurement occasions with a battery of $m = 2$ intelligence tests.

Idea

The general latent curve analysis model assumes the existence of a number of basis curves that represent group patterns of change over time. One can conceptualize the curves as indicative of underlying tendencies of growth or decline in the studied group considered as a whole. Their utility lies in the fact that, after appropriate weighting specific to an individual under consideration, they approximate his or her time-path. The latter represents his or her developmental profile, that is, the ordered set of his or her values on a longitudinally studied dimension, which is also called *individual growth/decline curve*. Every curve has its own characteristics, for example, initial position, linear tendency to increase/decrease with time, and possibly some curvature. These features naturally differ across subjects. A major goal of latent curve analysis is to capture their whole spectrum (variance). The expression of a given individual's developmental profile as an explicit function of time is typically unknown in the general empirical context of repeated assessments in behavioral and educational research. What is observed and recorded, however, are the values of this continuous function at the consecutive measurement occasions. Across subjects and repeatedly followed dimensions, these values build (part of) the longitudinal data set to be analyzed. The special utility of latent curve analysis for purposes of change measurement derives from the fact that its general model (a) expresses group-specific patterns of change in the basis curves and (b) simultaneously allows explicit description of the individual time-paths that can be considered the basis of a longitudinal data analysis (e.g., Rogosa & Willett, 1985a). This is achieved by permitting every subject to attach individual-specific weights (also called *saliences*) to each basis curve in approximating his or her own developmental profile, as described next.

The General Latent Curve Analysis Model

Let $\gamma_{ik}(t)$ be the kth basis curve reflecting an underlying pattern of change in a given group, considered as a whole, on the ith repeatedly assessed characteristic ($i = 1, ...,$ $m; k = 1, ..., d_i; d_i \geq 1$; 't' denotes time). Let $Y_{pi}(t)$ symbolize the developmental profile (growth/decline curve, time-path) of the pth subject. The assumption of the general latent curve analysis model is:

$$Y_{pi}(t) = w_{ip1}\gamma_{i1}(t) + w_{ip2}\gamma_{i2}(t) + ... + w_{ipd_i}\gamma_{id_i}(t) + E_{pi}(t) \ (p = 1, ..., N; i = 1, ..., m). \ (1)$$

In Equation 1, w_{ipk} are the earlier mentioned weights (saliences) characterizing the pth individual with regard to the kth basis curve $\gamma_{ik}(t)$ of relevance to the ith repeatedly followed dimension. Depending on their magnitude and/or sign, these saliences amplify, suppress, or possibly even invert (if they are negative) a particular shape feature of a basis curve in producing a subject's time-path.[1] The weights w_{ipk}, being individual-specific, can be considered realizations of corresponding random variables W_{ik} ($i = 1, ..., m; k = 1, ..., d_i$). Their means, variances, and covariances with other variables obtain main importance in the study of change. These statistics are especially informative in multigroup studies when one can compare them across groups in order to examine population differences in repeatedly followed dimensions. The residual $E_i(t)$ in Equation 1 represents the compound effect of error of approximation (model error) and measurement error in $Y_i(t)$. As usual, for each t, $E_i(t)$ is assumed to

---

[1] For example, the curve $y(t) = 2.5t$ has a steeper slope than the curve $y(t) = 1.25t$. Similarly, the curve $y(t) = 2t^2$ has a more pronounced curvature than the curve $y(t) = .5t^2$; thus the curve $y(t) = -.40t^2$ decreases more quickly than $y(t) = -.25t^2$ after they reach their maximum at $t = 0$. Whereas the curve $y(t) = 1.5t$ indicates increase with time, $y(t) = -1.5t$ describes decline. Relatedly, whereas the curve $y(t) = 3t^2$ is convex (i.e., reaches a minimum at $t = 0$ and then increases indefinitely), $y(t) = -3t^2$ is concave (i.e., reaches a maximum at $t = 0$ and then decreases indefinitely).

have vanishing mean and to be uncorrelated with all individual weight variables W_{ik}. From Equation 1, it follows that observed means are functions only of the means of the weight variables:

$$\mu_i(t) = v_{i1}\gamma_{i1}(t) + v_{i2}\gamma_{i2}(t) + \dots + v_{id_i}\gamma_{id_i}(t), \tag{2}$$

with $\mu_i(t)$ being the mean of $Y_i(t)$ and v_{ik} the mean of W_{ik}. Hence, manifest means are parameterized only in terms of latent means and basis curve values at successive assessment occasions, and have no intercept terms.

Thus, the general latent curve analysis model reflects (a) patterns of group change over time in the basis curves $\gamma_{ik}(t)$, and (b) aspects of individual change in the weights w_{pik}, $p = 1, \dots, N$; $i = 1, \dots, m$; $k = 1, \dots, d_i$. If one wishes to focus on patterns of change in a variable of interest for a given group considered as a whole, one needs to concentrate on the corresponding basis curves $\gamma_{ik}(t)$ and particularly their features that address the research question; in this sense, a basis curve is considered a group change curve. Thus, comparison across groups of basis curves makes it possible to study further aspects of population differences in addition to those captured by the individual weight variables. Alternatively, if one is concerned with aspects of individual growth curves one needs to concentrate on the weights, w_{ipk}, particularly the means, variances, and covariances of the pertinent random variables W_{ik} ($i = 1, \dots, m$; $k = 1, \dots, d_i$). A property of this general model, which is of special benefit in empirical applications, is the possibility of studying relationships among weight variables associated with different basis curves. Similarly, main interest in applications may be the weight variable relationships across or within repeatedly assessed characteristics, and/or across several studied groups. These possibilities are pursued by estimating and testing hypotheses about latent correlations among the W variables, as described in detail in the following sections.

Estimation and Fitting of the Latent Curve Analysis Model

At the occasions of discrete assessment, $t_1, t_2, \dots, t_q$, which is typical for educational and behavioral research, the continuous-time Equation 1 obtains the following form:

$$Y_{pi}(t_j) = w_{ip1}\gamma_{i1}(t_j) + w_{ip2}\gamma_{i2}(t_j) + \dots + w_{ipd_i}\gamma_{id_i}(t_j) + E_{pi}(t_j) \tag{3}$$
$$(p = 1, \dots, N; i = 1, \dots, m; j = 1, \dots, q)$$

(cf. Meredith & Tisak, 1990). Then, the general latent curve analysis model, extended to encompass all longitudinally followed dimensions, obtains the compact form

$$Y = \Delta W + E. \tag{4}$$

In Equation 4, Y is the vector of all assessments across measurement points and repeatedly followed dimensions, and E is the associated vector of corresponding error terms. Thereby, Δ denotes the appropriately constructed matrix containing the values of all postulated basis curves at the consecutive measurement occasions, and W is the total vector of weight variables. By appropriately extending Equation 4 by adding background variables—such as age, education, gender, or socioeconomic status—one is in a position to study correlates and predictors of change. This is accomplished by examining the correlations between the W variables and those external/background characteristics (e.g., Willett & Sayer, 1994; see also Meredith & Tisak, 1990).

Equation 4 is easily recognized as a confirmatory factor analysis model. Indeed, it is a special case of Submodel 3 of the comprehensive LISREL model (Jöreskog & Sörbom, 1993, chap. 3), with Δ being the factor loadings matrix and W the vector of factors. As with any confirmatory factor analysis model, the parameters of an identified latent curve analysis model are therefore (a) the variances, covariances, and means of the weight variables, W; (b) the unknown basis curve values (if any) at assessment occasions, and (c) the measurement error variances and covariances (if any), (e.g., Bentler, 1995, chap. 2). Thus, a latent curve analysis model, with appropriate identifying restrictions (see later section), can be fitted and tested using widely available covariance structure modeling algorithms and software, such as LISREL, EQS, or Amos. Restrictions on some of its parameters—that is, group identity in particular weight variable statistics or on basis curve values at measurement occasions—can be tested by examining the change in goodness of fit relative to the difference in degrees of freedom of the two nested models involved: the one before and the one after the restrictions are imposed (e.g., Jöreskog & Sörbom, 1993).

Three Simple Examples of Latent Curve Analysis Models

As a first example (cf. Meredith & Tisak, 1990), the case of no change, or strict stability over time for a single repeatedly studied dimension, is directly obtained from Equation 4. To this end, take $d = 1$ basis curve, namely $\gamma_1(t) = 1$ (the unity curve), and $w_{p1} = a_p$ being an individual-specific, time-average level. The resulting model is

$$
\begin{aligned}
Y_p(t) &= 1 \times w_{p1} + E_p(t) \\
&= a_p + E_p(t) \ (p = 1, \ldots, N).
\end{aligned}
\tag{5}
$$

Similarly, linear development represents another special case of Equation 4. To obtain it, take $d = 2$ basis curves $\gamma_1(t) = 1$ and $\gamma_2(t) = t$, and individual weights $\kappa_p = w_{p1}$ and $\lambda_p = w_{p2}$ in the role of individual-specific intercept and slope coefficients (Meredith & Tisak, 1990):

$$
Y_p(t) = 1 \times \kappa_p + t \times \lambda_p + E_p(t) = \kappa_p + \lambda_p t + E_p(t) \ (p = 1, \ldots, N).
\tag{6}
$$

This model has been utilized, for example, by Willett and Sayer (1994).

Furthermore, the quadratic model of individual change is also obtained straightforwardly from Equation 3. To this end, first take $d = 3$ basis curves $\gamma_1(t) = 1$, $\gamma_2(t) = t$, and $\gamma_3(t) = t^2$. Then use as individual weights $\kappa_p = w_{p1}$, $\lambda_p = w_{p2}$, and $\omega_p = w_{p3}$ in the role of individual-specific intercept, slope, and curvature coefficients, respectively. The model resulting then from Equation 3 is:

$$Y_p(t) = 1 \times \kappa_p + t \times \lambda_p \, t + t^2 \times \omega_p + E_p(t) = \kappa_p + \lambda_p t + \omega_p t^2 + E_p(t) \qquad (7)$$

$$(p = 1, \ldots, N).$$

In this equation, $\kappa_p = Y_p(0)$ denotes the recorded value on the studied dimension at time origin (i.e., at $t = 0$), and λ_p reflects the linear growth/decline tendency (trend) across the study period (called "linear slope" later). In addition, ω_p is a coefficient expressing the extent of curvature (i.e., bending) of the individual developmental profile: Larger ω's go together with stronger curvature, whereas smaller w's are associated with less discernible curving ($p = 1, \ldots, N$; see Footnote 1). This quadratic model has been employed by Muthén (1993) and Raykov (1996, 1997d).

More complex latent curve analysis models have been described, for example, in McArdle and Aber (1990), McArdle and Anderson (1990), McArdle and Epstein (1987), Meredith and Tisak (1990), Muthén (1991, 1993), Raykov (1995, 1996, 1997a, 1997c, 1997d, in press), Tisak and Meredith (1990), and Willett and Sayer (1994).

Two Types of Basis Curves and Their Implications for Latent Curve Modeling

A common feature of the models in the three preceding examples is that their basis curves are completely known. That is, their values at each repeated assessment occasion, $t_1, \ldots,$ and t_q, are fixed (given in advance) because the curves represent a priori specified functions of time only. For the practical purposes of behavioral and educational research using latent curve analysis, however, it is not necessary to know the values of each basis curve at all assessment points, although this knowledge may be available in some settings and models. The form or shape of each basis curve may be uniquely estimable when at least one value of it at an assessment occasion is prespecified. More specifically, given this knowledge, the curve's values at the remaining measurement occasions may be identified. In general, because a considered latent curve analysis model is a confirmatory factor analysis model, as indicated, it is identified after appropriate parameter restrictions are imposed that are specific for it. These restrictions are discussed in detail by Meredith and Tisak (1990, p. 110), and primarily amount to fixing an element within each column of the matrix Δ with basis curve values in Equation 4 (e.g., Browne & Arminger, 1995).

The distinction between completely known basis curves and those that are not completely known is of special relevance for the rest of this chapter. This is because the group patterns of change on the ith repeatedly followed characteristic are directly reflected in the basis curve values at consecutive assessment occasions, namely, in the quantities $\gamma_{ik}(t_j)$ ($i = 1, \ldots, m; k = 1, \ldots, d_i; j = 1, \ldots, q$). Given that all remaining quantities on the right-hand side of Equation 3 (apart from error term) reflect individual change aspects, it follows that if the basis curves pertaining to the ith repeatedly followed dimension are completely known—that is, if all $\gamma_{ik}(t_j)$ are known ($i = 1, \ldots, m; k = 1, \ldots, d_i; j = 1, \ldots, q$)—there will be no remaining aspects of group change along that dimension that are reflected in its basis curves and estimable from the data.

In that case, fitting and testing the model will focus only on individual growth curve aspects as reflected in the weight variables W_{ik} ($i = 1, \ldots, m; k = 1, \ldots, d_i$). Then, individual patterns of longitudinal change will be reflected in the statistics associated with the salience variables, W_{ik}; these statistics are their means, variances, and covariances as mentioned earlier. Conversely, in cases where basis curves pertaining to one or more repeatedly followed characteristics are not completely known (fixed) in advance, in the unknown quantities, $\gamma_{ik}(t_j)$, one will estimate aspects of the group patterns of longitudinal change with regard to the corresponding repeatedly assessed dimension.

Thus, one could distinguish between latent curve analysis models focusing on individual change patterns and such models focusing on group change patterns. The former models, called *individual change models*, are characterized by two features: (a) their basis curves are completely known, that is, all $\gamma_{ik}(t_j)$ are known/fixed in advance, and (b) aspects of individual change patterns are reflected in the statistics associated with the salience variables W_{ik} ($i = 1, \ldots, m; j = 1, \ldots, q; k = 1, \ldots, d_i$). Examples of such models are given by Muthén (1991, 1993), Raykov (1996), and Willett and Sayer (1994). The second type of models, called *group change models*, share two properties. First, their basis curves are not completely known, that is, not all $\gamma_{ik}(t_j)$ are known/fixed a priori. Second, aspects of group change patterns are reflected in the unknown values of these curves, namely in the model parameters $\gamma_{ik}(t_j)$ ($i = 1, \ldots, m; j = 1, \ldots, q; k = 1, \ldots, d_i$). Examples of group change models are found in McArdle and Aber (1990), McArdle and Anderson (1990), McArdle and Epstein (1987), and Raykov (1995).[2]

The concern of the present chapter is with a hybrid type of latent curve analysis models. Their utility for change measurement lies in the combination of features of group change models and individual change models. Thus, they provide for simultaneous study of group change patterns and individual change patterns. This combinatorial property may be of special interest in longitudinal settings in behavioral and educational research. In particular, the models permit focusing on the interrelationships among the patterns of individual and group change over time. These relations are reflected in the correlations between the weight variables pertaining to their basis curves and hence are routinely estimated when fitting the models. Because of this feature, these hybrid models can be considered extensions of individual change models or, alternatively, extensions of group change models. The remainder of this chapter deals with a class of combinatorial models that, along with the earlier mentioned ones, represent special cases of the comprehensive latent curve analysis method of Meredith and Tisak (1990). They are particularly useful for purposes

---

[2] In statistical terms the group and individual change models, as confirmatory factor analysis models, differ only in whether all factor loadings are known, that is, fixed at prespecified constants that may be zero or other numbers. If this is the case, one can consider the model an individual change model for the purposes of this chapter; if it is not the case, the model can be viewed as a group change model.

of studying change in empirical settings with repeated assessments on multiple dimensions.

A COVARIANCE STRUCTURE MODELING APPROACH TO THE SIMULTANEOUS STUDY OF INDIVIDUAL AND GROUP PATTERNS OF LATENT LONGITUDINAL CHANGE

This approach exhibits features of group change models with regard to some repeatedly followed latent dimensions and properties of individual change models with respect to other longitudinally assessed dimensions. Because it combines examination of individual change patterns with investigation of group change patterns, it requires at least $m = 2$ longitudinally followed dimensions.

Definition

Suppose one is interested in studying group change patterns with regard to the first u of m repeatedly assessed characteristics ($0 < u < m$). The present method postulates Equation 3 for each of these u characteristics, with some of the discrete-time values of the pertinent basis curves being unknown. That is, some $\gamma_{ik}(t_j)$ ($i = 1, \ldots, u; k = 1, \ldots, d_i; j = 1, \ldots, q$) are assumed model parameters to be estimated from data. Because they represent values of the corresponding basis curves, according to the preceding discussion, they reflect patterns of group change reflected in these curves. With regard to the remaining $m - u$ longitudinally followed characteristics, this approach assumes that one is interested in examining individual change patterns. Thus, all basis curve values for them are presumed fixed in advance. That is, all quantities $\gamma_{ik}(t_j)$ ($i = u + 1, \ldots, m; k = 1, \ldots, d_i; j = 1, \ldots, q$) are known. For all of these $m - u$ characteristics, each individual's growth curve is approximated by appropriately weighted sums of these known basis curve values, as seen from Equation 3.

Hence, the present method is a special case of the general latent curve analysis model, because for every repeatedly followed dimension, a special form of Equation 3 of the general latent curve analysis model is (a) postulated and then (b) augmented across dimensions. Thus, with standard restrictions (e.g., Meredith & Tisak, 1990, p. 110) the present approach leads to identified models. Therefore, as any latent curve analysis model, the resulting models can be fitted and tested using widely circulated covariance structure modeling algorithms and software, such as LISREL, EQS, or Amos.

A Special Case

To demonstrate the applicability of the presently considered general approach to the study of relationships among patterns of longitudinal change requires specialization to a particular modeling setting, which is considered next and exemplified in a later section. In this special model, a particular choice is made with regard to the group change dimensions. This is the decomposition of the latent ability score into a "level" and "shape" component for each of the first u repeatedly assessed characteristics, as originally utilized by McArdle and Anderson (1990; see also McArdle & Aber, 1990). For each of the remaining $m - u$ longitudinally followed variables on which individual change patterns are of interest, every individual's growth or decline profile is modeled by a quadratic-in-time curve of the form $Y^* = \kappa + \lambda t + \omega t^2$, where κ is the individual intercept, λ quantifies the linear tendency of change over time, and ω expresses the curvature of the individual developmental profile (e.g., Muthén, 1993; Raykov, 1996; see also Willett & Sayer, 1994). More complex modeling of individual development is also possible with this approach by using a higher order polynomial, rather than a quadratic one as employed here, as long as the overall model is identified. (The latter will generally not be ensured if the order of the polynomial is higher than the number of repeated assessments.) When deciding on this order, previous research in the particular substantive domain is beneficial. In addition, for reasons of model parsimony, recommend ordering the smallest possible number that provides satisfactory fit. To find it, one can choose randomly a number of individuals from the available sample or, even better, from an independent one, and determine which is the lowest order curve type—for example, linear, quadratic, cubic, or higher—that provides a reasonably good fit to most individual profiles from the subsample. That order can be used as the one of the assumed curve for the individual change dimensions in the model under consideration.

To make this discussion more explicit, borrowing concepts and notation from the classical test theory (e.g., Lord & Novick, 1968) is useful. Denoting by T_{pij} and E_{pij} the true and error scores of the jth successive measurement of the pth individual on the ith repeatedly followed dimension, the definition equations of the presently considered model are as follows ($p = 1, \ldots, N; j = 1, \ldots, q$):

$$
\begin{aligned}
Y_{p11} &= T_{p11} + E_{p11} \\
Y_{p12} &= T_{p11} + (T_{p12} - T_{p11}) + E_{p12} \\
Y_{p13} &= T_{p11} + f_{13}(T_{p12} - T_{p11}) + E_{p13} \\
&\quad \cdots \\
Y_{p1,q-1} &= T_{p11} + f_{1,q-1}(T_{p12} - T_{p11}) + E_{p1,q-1} \\
Y_{p1q} &= T_{p1q} + f_{1q}(T_{p12} - T_{p11}) + E_{p1q}, \\
&\quad \cdots \\
Y_{pu1} &= T_{pu1} + E_{pu1} \\
Y_{pu2} &= T_{pu1} + (T_{pu2} - T_{pu1}) + E_{pu2} \\
Y_{pu3} &= T_{pu1} + f_{u3}(T_{pu2} - T_{pu1}) + E_{pu3} \\
&\quad \cdots \\
Y_{pu,q-1} &= T_{pu1} + f_{u,q-1}(T_{pu2} - T_{pu1}) + E_{pu,q-1} \\
Y_{puq} &= T_{puq} + f_{uq}(T_{pu2} - T_{pu1}) + E_{puq},
\end{aligned}
$$

(8)

$$Y_{p,u+1,j} = 1 \times \kappa_{p,u+1} + t_j \times \lambda_{p,u+1} + t_j^2 \times \omega_{p,u+1} + E_{p,u+1,j}$$
$$Y_{p,u+2,j} = 1 \times \kappa_{p,u+2} + t_j \times \lambda_{p,u+2} + t_j^2 \times \omega_{p,u+2} + E_{p,u+2,j}$$
$$\ldots$$
$$Y_{pmj} = 1 \times \kappa_{pm} + t_j \times \lambda_{pm} + t_j^2 \times \omega_{pm} + E_{pmj}$$

In Equation 8, for each of the first u repeatedly followed characteristics, the symbols f_{ij} ($i = 1, \ldots, u; j = 3, \ldots, q$) denote model parameters that equal the unknown values of corresponding basis curves at third, fourth, ..., and qth assessment occasions ($q > 2$). (For a particular interpretation of them in an empirical context, see next section.) Each of the last $m - u$ lines of Equation 8 represents a quadratic-in-time curve assumed to approximate every individual's developmental profile. (Note the subject indexing attached to each of the unknown, individual-specific coefficients κ, λ, and ω.) For each of these longitudinally assessed characteristics, the model takes into account information about the time points of repeated assessment—which need not be equally spaced—and hence, also information about the time elapsed between successive measurement occasions.

Relationship to Latent Curve Analysis Revisited

Comparing Equation 3 and 8, one sees that the currently considered model is obtained from the general latent curve analysis model in two steps. First, one takes in Equation 3 $w_{pi1} = T_{pi1}$ and $w_{pi2} = T_{pi2} - T_{pi1}$, $p = 1, \ldots, N$, for the first u repeatedly followed dimensions ($i = 1, \ldots, u$). Then one uses $w_{pi1} = \kappa_{pi}$, $w_{pi2} = \lambda_{pi}$, and $w_{pi3} = \omega_{pi}$, $p = 1, \ldots, N$, for the last $m - u$ longitudinally assessed variables ($i = u + 1, \ldots, m$). The discrete-time representations of this model's basis curves are as follows: The curves pertaining to each of the first u repeatedly followed dimensions are

$$\gamma_1(t_1) = 1, \gamma_1(t_2) = 1, \ldots, \gamma_1(t_q) = 1, \qquad (9)$$

and $\qquad \gamma_2(t_1) = 0, \gamma_2(t_2) = 1, \ldots, \gamma_2(t_{q-1}) = f_{q-1}, \gamma_2(t_q) = f_q. \qquad (10)$

For each of the last $m - u$ longitudinally assessed characteristics, the triple of basis curves is

$$\gamma_1(t) = 1, \gamma_2(t) = t, \text{ and } \gamma_3(t) = t^2. \qquad (11)$$

Hence, the present model defined by Equations 8 to 11 is a special case of the general latent curve analysis model, with altogether $2u + 3(m - u)$ basis curves defined in Equations 9 to 11.

Parameter Interpretation

The basis curve values denoted by f_{ij} in Equation 8 ($i = 1, \ldots, u; j = 3, \ldots, q$) represent the ratio of change occurring between first and jth successive measurement ($1 \leq j \leq u$) of the ith repeatedly followed ability, to this change happening between first and second assessments (e.g., McArdle & Anderson, 1990). For example, in the case of steady growth, these parameters are all in excess of 1 and increase with time (i.e., with j increasing from 1 to q). In the case of initial growth followed by decline, these parameters initially increase (possibly beyond unity) and then decline. The statistics associated with the weight variables pertaining to these not completely known basis curves also have substantively interesting interpretations. In particular, $W_{i1} = T_{i1}$ is initial ability status, whereas $W_{i2} = T_{p2} - T_{p1}$ is ability change occurring between first and second assessment occasions, for each of the first u repeatedly assessed dimensions ($i = 1, \ldots, u;$ e.g., Raykov, 1995). The latter change is of special empirical interest in longitudinal investigations with a single pretest and several posttests, for example, in intervention studies (see previous section). In these cases, the second weight variables W_{i2} ($i = 1, \ldots, m$) contain information about intervention effects occurring immediately after training. The variances of these weight variables W_{ij} ($i = 1, \ldots, m$; $j = 1, 2$) reflect the extent of interindividual variability in initial status and first-to-second assessment change, respectively, in the abilities on which group change patterns are studied. The correlations among these weight variables reflect the consistency of individual ranking at the ability level across them, that is, the degree of linear interrelationship between these latent entities.

A special benefit of this model is that beyond the simultaneous parameterization of group and individual time-path aspects for a set of longitudinally followed characteristics, the interrelationships between two types of latent variables are also parameterized. On the one hand, these are the initial ability status and pretest-to-posttest ability change (the latter reference is used as shorthand for "ability change occurring between first and second assessments") for the characteristics on which group change patterns are focused. The other type of latent variables are the individual intercept, linear slope, and quadratic-bend parameters with regard to the remaining longitudinal dimensions. These "crossing" correlations provide information on the relationships among aspects of individual time-paths on the last $m - u$ repeatedly followed characteristics, with starting position and pretest-to-posttest change on the first u abilities. Specifically, depending on research question(s), one could consider the group-modeled dimensions $Y_1, \ldots, Y_u$ in Equation 8 as repeatedly followed covariates of aspects of the subjects' time-paths on the individual-modeled variables $Y_{u+1}, \ldots,$ Y_m in Equation 8. These aspects are position at time origin, linear slope, and quadratic-curvature coefficients for each subject. Conversely, one could consider the individual-modeled characteristics $Y_{u+1}, \ldots, Y_m$ as repeatedly assessed covariates of change along the group-modeled dimensions $Y_1, \ldots, Y_u$, particularly of initial ability status and true change. In multigroup contexts, therefore, the present model permits the study of group differences and invariance in these crossing correlations as well as in the remaining model parameters.

Graphical Diagram

A special case of the model under consideration is depicted on the path diagram in Figure 7.1. It represents the case of a single characteristic for group and for individual change modeling. This is a special case of Equation 8, which is of concern in the next empirical section, and is obtained by setting $m = 2$, $u = 1$, and $q = 4$.

Figure 7.1 largely follows widely used notation for graphical presentation of covariance structure models (e.g., Jöreskog & Sörbom, 1993). In it, Y_{11}, ..., Y_{14}, and Y_{21}, ..., Y_{24} are the eight observed variables, four for each of two repeatedly assessed characteristics. The latent variables, apart from measurement errors, represent the weight variables W discussed in detail earlier in this section. The crossing correlations of the model are symbolized by two-way arrows connecting latent variables belonging to the two repeatedly followed characteristics. Designated in the same way are the within-dimension correlations between pertinent latent entities. The remaining notation is essentially identical to the one used throughout the preceding discussion in this chap-

FIGURE 7.1
A Covariance Structure Model for Studying Simultaneously Individual and Group Patterns of Latent Change on Several Longitudinally Assessed Dimensions

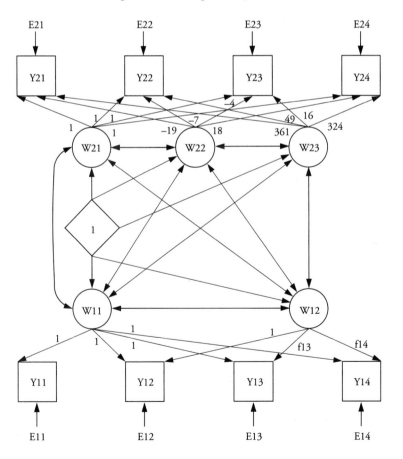

ter. The unit diamond in the middle signals that the mean structure rather than only the covariance matrix is analyzed (cf. Jöreskog & Sörbom, 1993; McArdle & Epstein, 1987).[3]

The numbers attached to the paths emanating from the latent variables W21, W22, and W23 reflect a special choice of the time origin (cf. Willett & Sayer, 1994). It is made in order to enhance the numerical stability during the minimization process underlying fitting the model to data. To this end, (approximately) one half of the total length of the empirical study dealt with in the next section is subtracted from each time point. To carry out this study, a total of 37 weeks were needed. Therefore, the time origin in the analyses reported next is chosen to be week 19, the (approximate) middle of the total study time. Because the four consecutive measurements of the study took place at pretest, 12 weeks after it, 3 weeks later, and then another 22 weeks later, in the new scale their times become equal to −19, −7, −4, and 18, respectively, in weeks. The remaining constants attached to the paths emanating from the latent variables W21 and W23 are the squares of these numbers, needed as coefficients of the curvature term ω in Equation 8, or simply unities that represent in Equation 8 the unitary coefficients of position at time origin, κ (cf., Raykov, 1996, 1997d; see Footnote 4). The numbers attached to the paths emanating from the remaining weight variables, W11 and W12, are identical to their corresponding coefficients in the pertinent first part of Equation 8.

The model defined by Equation 8, and whose special case is depicted in Figure 7.1, is particularly useful for purposes of simultaneous examination of group and individual patterns of latent longitudinal change. Its utilization is exemplified next on data from a cognitive training study of reserve capacity in fluid intelligence of older adults.

ILLUSTRATION ON DATA FROM A COGNITIVE TRAINING STUDY

This study was carried out by Baltes, Dittmann-Kohli, and Kliegl (1986) and had an experimental and a no-contact control group built via random assignment after pretest. At the latter and three subsequent posttests, an intelligence test-battery was administered to all participants. After the pretest, 10 sessions of cognitive training that targeted the fluid subabilities Induction and Figural Relations were conducted in the experimental group. The three posttests with the same test-battery were administered to both groups 12 weeks after pretest, then 3 weeks later, and finally 22 weeks thereafter, as mentioned in the preceding section. Further details about the study, training program, and measures used can be found in Baltes et al. (1986; see also Raykov, 1995, 1996). The remaining discussion in this section illustrates the model in

---

[3] This unit diamond has only symbolic nature if LISREL is used to fit the model (Jöreskog & Sörbom, 1993). If, alternatively, EQS is utilized, the diamond represents graphically the dummy variable V999 that can be thought of as having values of 1 for all subjects (Bentler, 1995).

TABLE 7.1

Covariances (Below Main Diagonal), Variances (Along Diagonal), and Means (Bottom Row)
for the ADEPT Induction and ADEPT Figural Relations Tests

AI1	AI2	AI3	AI4	AF1	AF2	AF3	AF4
Experimental group (N = 161)							
218.06							
219.38	328.11						
218.21	310.49	338.01					
225.19	305.80	312.18	345.96				
155.15	212.47	207.09	210.48	260.76			
136.15	200.05	200.81	197.07	159.40	199.24		
138.84	202.09	202.29	202.48	170.66	173.22	213.32	
155.56	219.36	220.43	224.30	180.44	187.92	197.85	251.71
30.83	49.08	51.66	48.58	49.48	71.42	73.37	70.78
Control group (N = 87)							
217.99							
221.82	313.09						
222.48	294.48	324.28					
214.60	298.15	302.42	328.86				
149.86	167.86	174.16	171.89	262.79			
146.69	188.83	178.22	179.61	195.64	252.79		
128.55	178.43	179.94	177.53	164.78	203.17	228.01	
134.39	178.33	180.60	183.74	171.48	206.13	183.05	209.66
30.09	41.51	44.68	43.79	51.97	62.04	66.15	65.77

Note. AIj: ADEPT Induction at *j*th Assessment; AFj: ADEPT Figural Relations at *j*th Assessment (j = 1, 2, 3, 4); *N* = Group size. Adapted from Baltes, Dittmann-Kohli, and R. Kliegl, 1986.

Figure 7.1 on the so-called ADEPT Induction and ADEPT Figural Relations tests. They consisted of letter sets, number sets, and figure series, and showed training sensitivity in the originally reported analyses (Baltes et al., 1986). Preliminary data exploration suggested no marked departures from normality and no outlying cases to be taken out of the following analyses (e.g., Raykov, 1995). The covariances, variances, and means of the eight variables focused on here, following transformation to percentage correct, are presented in Table 7.1.

Use of the model in Figure 7.1 makes it possible to conduct analyses that are complementary to the original ones reported by Baltes et al. (1986). Those authors used 204 of the studied subjects in order to achieve group-size equality via random exclusion of subjects. This was done in order to render the results of their ANOVA-based approach robust against violations of the underlying assumption of covariance matrix homogeneity (e.g., Hays, 1994). The following alternative analyses capitalize instead on the data from all 248 subjects with no missing value and are not affected by the degree of violation of sphericity or covariance homogeneity. In addition, this approach allows one to address the issue of differences and resemblance of the experimental and control groups with regard to latent correlations (cf. Raykov, 1995). This issue was not dealt with in the original analyses by Baltes et al. (1986) because their ANOVA approach focused primarily on mean profiles and group differences in them. In applying the present model, the fluid subability Induction is considered a repeatedly followed dimension along which individual change patterns are of interest. Alternatively, Figural Relations is considered a dimension along which group patterns of change are of concern. In Figure 7.1, therefore, W11 and W12 represent the initial ability status and pretest-to-posttest ability change with regard to the ADEPT Figural Relations test. The latent variables W21, W22, and W23 symbolize, respectively, the individual ability score at time origin—that is, at week 19 of the study (see earlier)—the linear trend across the total study period, and the curvature coefficient with regard to the ADEPT Induction test.[4]

The model in Figure 7.1 is next fitted to the data in Table 7.1 without any cross-group constraints. The resulting goodness of fit indices are (where appropriate, 90% confidence intervals follow index): $\chi^2 = 54.99$, $df = 40$, $p = .06$; noncentrality parameter (NCP) = 14.99 (0.0; 38.56); root mean squared error of approximation (RMSEA) = .039 (0.0; .06); and p-value of close fit = .75 (e.g., Browne & Cudeck, 1993). These indices point to an acceptable fit of this initial version of the model as a baseline for the following model nesting (e.g., Jöreskog & Sörbom, 1993). Its goal is (a) to test substantively meaningful cross-group constraints on the model parameters and, at the same time, (b) to find the most tenable restricted model version whose parameters and standard errors will be the subsequent focus. To achieve this goal, group restrictions that do not increase significantly the chi-square value are retained in subsequently fitted nested models. This leads to more parsimonious model versions that can be expected to have on average smaller standard errors associated with their parameter estimates.

Because the two groups were randomly formed after pretest, no group differences could be expected at initial assessment. Indeed, the cross-group equality on initial ability mean and variance associated with the Figural Relations test (i.e., the mean and variance of the latent variable W11) does not significantly increase the chi-square value, only bringing it up to $\chi^2 = 56.30$, for $df = 42$ (the difference in chi-squares is therefore $\Delta\chi^2 = 1.31$ and associated difference in degrees of freedom is $\Delta df = 2$, $p > .5$). Adding the cross-group equality constraints on the variances and covariances of position at time 0, linear slope, and curvature parameters associated with the ADEPT Induction test (i.e., the variances and covariances of W21, W22, and W23) does not

---

[4] The latent variable W21 in Figure 7.1 represents the individual intercepts $\kappa_{p,u+1}$ in the last four (for the currently considered special case with $u = 1$ and $m = 2$) of Equation 8. Because these intercepts are multiplied by 1 there, the paths emanating from W21 are fixed at 1. Similarly, the latent variable W22 in Figure 7.1 denotes the individual profile linear slopes, $\lambda_{p,u+1}$, in the same of Equation 8. Because their coefficients there represent the times of assessment, which with the new scale origin choice become −19, −7, −4, and 18, the four paths emanating from W22 are set equal to these four numbers, respectively. Their squares—361, 49, 16 and 324, respectively—are similarly the fixing constants for the four paths emanating from the latent variable W23 that according to the model represents the quadratic curvature coefficients $\omega_{p,u+1}$ (see Equation 8).

increase significantly the chi-square value either: $\chi^2 = 65.45$, $df = 48$ ($\Delta\chi^2 = 9.15$, $\Delta df = 6$, $p > .25$). Thus, it is suggested that these variances and covariances are identical in the experimental and control groups. Constraining additionally for group identity, the remaining variance and covariance of initial ability status and pretest-to-posttest ability change with respect to ADEPT Figural Relations test (i.e., the variance of W11 and its covariance with W12) in the next nested model does not increase significantly the chi-square: $\chi^2 = 66.72$, $df = 50$ ($\Delta\chi^2 = 1.18$, $\Delta df = 2$, $p > .5$). This finding points to group identity in this variance and covariance. Adding then in the final nested model the group-invariance restriction in the remaining parameters of the latent variable covariance matrix leads, however, to a significant increase in the chi-square: $\chi^2 = 80.98$, $df = 56$, $p = .02$ ($\Delta\chi^2 = 14.26$, $\Delta df = 6$, $.02 < p < .03$). It is concluded that there is moderately strong evidence of some differences in the correlations between the latent variables pertaining to one of the repeated tests and those pertaining to the other (see later). The additional goodness of fit indices of the immediately preceding model variant fitted are all acceptable: NCP = 16.72 (0.0; 42.10), RMSEA = .037 (0.0; .06), with p-value for the test of close fit being .82. Based on all reported fit indices and an

TABLE 7.2
Most Restrictive Tenable Version of the Model in Figure 7.1:
Parameter Estimates and Standard Errors (Behind/Beneath)

Experimental group					Factor loadings			
Test	MO	LV: AI_I	AI_L	AI_Q	AF_IS	AF_PPC	UNIQ
AI	1st	1	−19	361	0	0	24.51 (2.48)
	2nd	1	−7	49	0	0	24.51 (2.48)
	3rd	1	−4	16	0	0	24.51 (2.48)
	4th	1	18	364	0	0	24.51 (2.48)
AF	1st	0	0	0	1	0	36.20 (2.81)
	2nd	0	0	0	1	1	36.20 (2.81)
	3rd	0	0	0	1	1.08 (.03)	36.20 (2.81)
	4th	0	0	0	1	.98 (.03)	36.20 (2.81)
Means		54.84 (1.35)	.44 (.02)	−.0418 (.0017)	50.32 (1.03)	21.67 (.86)	
Variances		344.59= (32.14)	.044= (.007)	.00025= (.00005)	227.74= (23.42)	58.69= (9.52)	

			Latent correlations		
	LV: AI_I	AI_L	AI_Q	AF_IS	AF_PPC
AI_I	1				
AI_L	.64=	1			
AI_Q	−.66=	−.81=	1		
AF_IS	.80	.42	−.45	1	
AF_PPC	−.03°	.13°	−.13°	−.43=	1

TABLE 7.2 (continued)
Most Restrictive Tenable Version of the Model in Figure 7.1:
Parameter Estimates and Standard Errors (Behind/Beneath)

Control group			Factor loadings					
Test	MO	LV: AI_I	AI_L	AI_Q	AF_IS	AF_PPC		UNIQ
AI	1st	1	−19	361	0	0		21.71 (2.83)
	2nd	1	−7	49	0	0		21.71 (2.83)
	3rd	1	−4	16	0	0		21.71 (2.83)
	4th	1	18	364	0	0		21.71 (2.83)
AF	1st	0	0	0	1	0		32.19 (3.43)
	2nd	0	0	0	1	1		32.19 (3.43)
	3rd	0	0	0	1	1.34	(.08)	32.19 (3.43)
	4th	0	0	0	1	1.26	(.07)	32.19 (3.43)
Means		44.86	.34	−.0254	50.32	11.13		
		(1.83)	(.03)	(.0023)	(1.03)	(1.05)		
Variances		344.59=	.044=	.00025=	227.74=	58.69=		
		(32.14)	(.007)	(.00005)	(23.42)	(9.52)		

	Latent correlations				
LV:	AI_I	AI_L	AI_Q	AF_IS	AF_PPC
AI_I	1				
AI_L	.64=	1			
AI_Q	−.66=	−.81=	1		
AF_IS	.60	.18°	−.12°	1	
AF_PPC	.14	.33	−.49	−.43=	1

$\chi^2 = 66.72$, $df = 50$, $p = .06$, RMSEA = .037 (0.0; .06).

Note. AI: ADEPT Induction test; AF: ADEPT Figural Relations test; MO: Measurement Occasion (vertical); LV: Latent Variable (horizontal); UNIQ: Measurement Error Variance; AI_I: Intercept on ADEPT Induction test (first salience variable for AI, i.e., W21 in Figure 7.1); AI_L: Linear Slope on ADEPT Induction test (second salience variable for AI, i.e., W22 in Figure 7.1); AI_Q: Quadratic-Bend on ADEPT Induction test (third salience variable for AI, i.e., W23 in Figure 7.1); AF_IS: Initial Ability Status on ADEPT Figural Relations test (first salience variable for AF, i.e., W11 in Figure 7.1); AF_PPC: Pretest-to-Posttest Ability Change on ADEPT Figural Relations test (second salience variable for AF, i.e., W12 in Figure 7.1); °: Corresponding Covariance *t*-Value Within the Interval (-1.96; +1.96); =: Constrained for Equality Across Groups.

inspection of the model residuals that do not suggest considerable misfit, this model version is viewed as a most restrictive, tenable variant of the model under consideration. Its parameter estimates and standard errors are presented in Table 7.2 and are interpreted next.

First, the means parts of Table 7.2 in each group suggest that within both groups there is an improvement at the latent ability level on the Figural Relations test from first to second assessment. Indeed, the mean of the pretest-to-posttest latent variable, denoted by AF_PPC in Table 7.2, is significant in either group. Next, 95% confidence intervals are used to examine parameter relationships within and across groups. The intervals result by adding and subtracting to/from parameter estimate twice its standard error (e.g., Raykov, 1995). If two intervals are found not to overlap, the parameter whose interval is to the right can be considered larger in the population. This comparison of pertinent confidence intervals suggests that the intervention in the former group is associated with markedly better mean performance on the Figural Relations measure at first posttest relative to pretest, than are the retest effects at work in the control group. The factor loadings parts of Table 7.2 similarly reveal that on the Figural Relations test there is improved performance at all posttests relative to pretest in each group. Indeed, within either group the confidence intervals of the pertinent parameters, f_{13} and f_{14}, are found to be completely to the right of zero that corresponds to this parameter at pretest (see Equation 8). In the same way, one sees that at second posttest and at last posttest the control group was markedly higher on this measure relative to pretest. At the same time, the experimental group showed at last posttest on the Figural Relations measure about the same level of performance as at second assessment, and only slightly inferior performance to that at second posttest.

From the means part of Table 7.2 one finds in the same manner that the mean of individual intercepts associated with the Induction test is higher in the experimental group than in the control group. This suggests that on average the former group outperformed the latter at the middle of the study period on this test, that is, at week 19, where the time origin was set (see earlier). That is, at that time the intervention in the experimental group was still associated with markedly better mean performance on the Induction test relative to the practice effects at work in the control group. Similarly, it is found that the linear trend coefficients in the experimental group are on average considerably higher than those in the control group. This indicates steeper average improvement on this test in the former group across the whole study period (see Footnote 1). Also, the experimental group exhibits a more pronounced average drop in performance on this measure at the last posttest, as evinced by the markedly lower curvature coefficients' mean than in the control group.[5] In addition, the variances parts of Table 7.2 suggest marked, group-invariant interindividual differences with regard to each latent variable, as seen from their significant estimates. This finding is interpreted as evidence of considerable individual differences in (a) aspects of the individual developmental curves, such as intercept, slope and curvature coefficients, describing each subject's time-profile, and (b) initial Figural Relations status and pretest-to-posttest ability change with regard to the Figural Relations test.

The correlational parts of Table 7.2 suggest further revealing results. The upper 3 by 3 portions of the reported correlation matrices show that the two groups are iden-

---

[5] The average curvature coefficient in the experimental group (−.0418 with a standard error .0017) is first found to be significantly smaller than that in the control group (−.0254 with a standard error .0023), by observing that the 95% confidence interval (−0452, −0384) of the former average is completely to the left of that interval (−.0300, −.0208) of the latter average. Because we are dealing with negative average curvatures, from this follows that the performance decline in the experimental group is on average more pronounced than that in the control group (see Footnote 1).

tical in the indices of relationship between individual change patterns with regard to the Induction test, as evinced by the constrained for group equality correlations of .64, −.66, and −.81. There is a moderately strong relationship between individual position at week 19 of the study on this test and individual overall linear slope of improvement on it (correlation of .64). This indicates a group-invariant tendency of subjects high on the Induction test midway through the study to exhibit a steeper overall improvement trend. There is also a moderately strong, negative tendency in both groups for those high at the middle of the study to have more pronounced drops at its end (correlation of −.66; see Footnote 5). Similarly, the moderate-to-strong negative correlation of −.81 indicates a group-invariant tendency of subjects with steeper overall increases to show more pronounced drops in performance at delayed posttest. This may be explained by their forgetting of instruction elements and/or by the relatively long period between the last two assessments of the study. In simple terms, in both groups, those older people who gained more had then a higher chance of forgetting more, given their relatively advanced age—on average more than 70 (e.g., Baltes et al., 1986). The correlation of −.43 suggests a moderate-to-weak, group-invariant tendency (explaining only some 17% of pertinent latent variance) of those starting high on Figural Relations to gain more on the Figural Relations test from pretest to first posttest.

The "crossing" latent correlations suggest additional interesting findings. There is a positive tendency, of about the same strength in the experimental and in the control group (evinced by correlations of .80 and .60, respectively), of subjects high on initial status with regard to Figural Relations to be relatively high at the middle of the study on the Induction test. In the experimental group, there is essentially no relationship between ability change from first to second assessment on the Figural Relations test and any of the modeled aspects of individual change on the Induction measure. The picture in the control group, however, is the same only as regards the relationship between this change on Figural Relations and position on Induction in the middle of the study. There is some weak-to-moderate tendency, evinced by a correlation of .33 (thus capturing only some 10% of latent variability), of control subjects who gained more on Figural relations from pre- to first posttest to exhibit steeper overall trends on the Induction test. Also, there is some moderate negative tendency (explaining less than 25% of latent variance) of control subjects high on that gain on Figural Relations to be associated with more pronounced drops on the Induction measure at final posttest. In the same group, there is essentially no relationship between initial status on Figural Relations and (a) overall trend of increase on Induction, as well as (b) drop at delayed posttest on the latter measure. In the experimental group, however, there is a moderate-to-weak tendency, evinced by a correlation of .42 (explaining only some 17% of latent variance), of subjects initially high on Figural Relations to exhibit steeper overall improvement trends on the Induction test. There is a similar moderate-to-weak negative tendency of experimental subjects initially high on Figural Relations to be associated with more pronounced drops at delayed posttest on the Induction test, as evinced by a correlation of −.45 (explaining only some 20% of latent variability).

CONCLUSION

This chapter discussed a general covariance structure modeling approach to change measurement in the behavioral and educational sciences. It was developed within the comprehensive latent curve analysis framework and based on explicit modeling of intraindividual processes of growth or decline. The approach allowed the simultaneous study of individual and group patterns of longitudinal change as well as their interrelationships. Its main advantages were that it did not require the sphericity assumption of (univariate) repeated measures ANOVA, which is frequently violated in empirical practice in the social sciences, whereas corresponding corrections of degrees of freedom often lead to overly conservative statistical tests (e.g., Maxwell & Delaney, 1990). Furthermore, this combinatorial modeling approach did not assume identity of the covariance matrix across levels of the between-subject factors that is assumed, however, by corresponding (multivariate) analysis of variance applications. In addition, the model permitted a straightforward introduction, estimation, and testing of more general than diagonal error structure; the latter diagonal structure is frequently assumed in routine applications of ANOVA models. At the same time, the present approach permitted incorporation of fallible covariates and thus provided an analytic method of explicitly taking account of the nearly ubiquitous measurement error in the behavioral and educational sciences, rather than ignoring it. In addition, this method did not need the assumption of group homogeneity of regression slopes made in typical ANCOVA models. The modeling opportunity discussed will be of substantive interest also when one is concerned with studying correlates and predictors of group and/or individual change patterns, whereby the latter variables may have been perfectly measured or fallible, latent or observed, assessed once or repeatedly. In conclusion, the method of change measurement described represents a comprehensive modeling device that is particularly useful for purposes of studying the relationships between individual growth/decline patterns and group change patterns in empirical contexts characterized by repeated assessments on multiple dimensions in the behavioral and educational sciences.

Acknowledgments

I thank T. D. Little for valuable editorial comments and suggestions for improvement of this chapter. I am grateful to P. B. Baltes, F. Dittmann-Kohli, and R. Kliegl for permission to use data from their project "Aging and Plasticity in Fluid Intelligence;" and to R. Kliegl, D. Sowarka, and A. Rentz for informative details on the organization and conduct of that empirical study. I thank L. Erlbaum for the permission to reprint parts of Raykov (1997d) in this chapter.

CHAPTER EIGHT

Latent Transition Analysis as a Way of Testing Models of Stage-Sequential Change in Longitudinal Data

Linda M. Collins
Stephanie L. Hyatt
John W. Graham
Pennsylvania State University

INTRODUCTION TO LATENT CLASS THEORY

This book contains several excellent chapters on structural equation models for longitudinal data. For the most part, the approaches described in those chapters and elsewhere are based on an implicit assumption that any latent variables are continuous. By contrast, this chapter discusses a different point of view on latent variables. In the point of view described here, latent variables are discrete. Individuals are not arranged along a latent continuum, as they are in continuous latent variable models, but rather placed into latent categories. Just as in factor analysis, the latent variable must be measured by means of manifest or directly observed variables, often referred to as *indicators*. However, here the indicators are discrete categorical variables. This measurement model is known as latent class theory (e.g., Goodman, 1974).

Most statistical models involve quantities called parameters. In a traditional statistics framework (as opposed to a Bayesian framework), *parameters* are invariant quantities that describe a population. Because investigators work with samples rather than populations, they cannot know the values of parameters, but instead must estimate them based on the sample at hand. Latent class theory is a fairly simple measurement theory involving two different types of parameters. Suppose a group of individuals is to be given a test, the purpose of which is to determine what proportion of them can be considered masters of a particular skill and what proportion must be considered non-masters. The test consists of three practical tasks, each of which may be either passed or failed. The mathematical model for this situation can be described as follows:

Let us denote the three practical tasks as Task 1, Task 2, and Task 3. Each task has two response alternatives, pass or fail, which will be denoted $i = 1$, 2 for Task 1, $j = 1$, 2 for Task 2, and $k = 1$, 2 for Task 3. Let $Y = (i, j, k)$ denote a response pattern. A *response pattern* is a set of possible responses to all the items for an individual. For example, (pass, pass, fail) is one possible response pattern, corresponding to a situation where an individual passes the first two tasks and fails the third. In any data set, it is possible to count the frequency associated with each response pattern, in other words, how many individuals in a sample give each response pattern. These response pattern frequencies are the data analyzed in a latent class analysis. They are analogous to an input correlation or covariance matrix in factor analysis. In much the same way that a factor analysis model attempts to build a model that will reproduce an input correlation or covariance matrix, so a latent class analysis attempts to build a model that will reproduce the response pattern frequencies.

The latent class model is

$$P(Y) = \sum_{c=1}^{C} \gamma_c \rho_{i|c} \rho_{j|c} \rho_{k|c} \tag{1}$$

where

γ_c represents the probability of membership in latent class c;

$\rho_{i|c}$ represents the probability of response i to the first item, conditional on membership in latent class c.

The ρ parameters express the relationship between the latent variable and the manifest variables. Thus, they play the same conceptual role in latent class models that factor loadings play in factor analysis. However, their numerical values must be interpreted differently. In interpreting ρ parameters it is important to remember that they are probabilities, so they are bounded by zero and one, unlike factor loadings, which are standardized regression coefficients. Whereas a factor loading of zero means there is no relationship between an item and a factor, a ρ parameter of zero has a quite different meaning. It means that the response to a variable is completely determined by the latent class, in other words, that there is a very strong relation between the item and the latent class. The ρ parameters of zero and one represent the strongest possible relation between an item and a latent class.

Thus, the latent class model is conceptually a factor analysis model for categorical data and categorical "factors," with response pattern proportions playing the role of the correlation matrix and ρ parameters playing the role of factor loadings. As was traditional factor analysis, the latent class model was developed for static, cross-sectional data. However, it turns out that by extending the latent class model, it is possible to use this approach to estimate and test stage-sequential models (Collins, Graham, Long, & Hansen, 1994; Collins, Graham, Rousculp, et al., 1994; Collins, Graham, Rousculp, & Hansen, 1997; Collins & Wugalter, 1992; Graham, Collins, Wugalter, Chung, & Hansen, 1991; Velicer, Martin, & Collins, 1996). An advantage of this method is that it provides estimates of stage prevalence and the incidence of stage transitions adjusted for measurement error. In a later section, we introduce latent transition analysis (LTA), an extension of latent class theory to longitudinal data. In the next section, we give some background information on the empirical example we use to illustrate LTA.

The Empirical Example: Gender Differences in Adolescent Substance Use

Collins, Graham, Long, et al. (1994) examined gender differences in substance use onset in a sample of youth who were measured at age 12 and again at age 13. The sample was a subset of participants in the Adolescent Alcohol Prevention Trials (AAPT; Graham, Rohrbach, Hansen, Flay, & Johnson, 1989; Hansen & Graham, 1991). Information was obtained on whether the individuals had ever tried alcohol or tobacco, whether they had ever been drunk, and a composite item indicating whether the individual had engaged in any advanced use, defined as regular use of alcohol or tobacco or any use of marijuana. Collins et al. (1994) began by testing a series of models separately in males and females, to see whether the stages in the onset process differed across genders. They found that the same basic process operated across genders. After this was established, they performed a multiple-groups analysis for a direct comparison across gender. Collins et al. (1994) found that the rate of movement through the process was similar for the two genders. However, males appeared to be more advanced at the first observation, suggesting that they start the process earlier than females.

The data to be used in this empirical example are a partially overlapping sample taken from the same study. The subjects are 8,913 participants from the AAPT study. The sample is ethnically mixed, primarily White, Latino, and Asian. There were relatively few African Americans in this sample. (For analyses on ethnic differences in substance use onset, see Collins, Graham, Rousculp, et al., 1994.) These children are somewhat older than the children in the Collins et al. (1994) sample; they are approximately age 14 at the first measure and age 15 at the second. After the children reached this age, the experimenters were allowed to ask a question about cocaine use. This affords us the opportunity to model the onset of cocaine use, and to examine gender differences in the onset process. For purposes of this example, because the Collins et al. study indicated that the basic onset model is the same across genders, the Collins et al. model was estimated in the data in a multiple-groups approach.

The onset model to be estimated here and then compared across genders is shown in Figure 8.1. The circles in Figure 8.1 represent stages in the model, and the arrows represent possible transitions from one stage to another. (It is important to note the difference between what is represented by Figure 8.1 and what is represented by similar-appearing figures representing structural equation models. In Figure 8.1, the arrows represent a non-zero probability of a stage transition, whereas in a figure representing a structural equation model, the arrows would represent non-zero path coefficients.) Our analyses will estimate the prevalence of each stage in the model, and the

FIGURE 8.1
The Predicted Stage-Sequential Model of Substance Use Onset

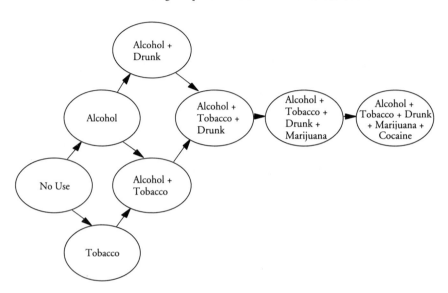

TABLE 8.1
Items Used in Sample Analysis

Gender indicator
1   Male
2   Female

Substance use measures
Lifetime alcohol use (Have you ever had a sip of alcohol?)
1   No (or only for religious service)
2   Yes
Lifetime tobacco use (Have you ever had even a puff of tobacco?)
1   No
2   Yes
Lifetime marijuana use (Have you ever tried marijuana?)
1   No
2   Yes
Lifetime cocaine use (Have you ever tried cocaine?)
1   No
2   Yes
Lifetime drunkenness (Have you ever been drunken?)
1   No
2   Yes
Number of alcoholic drinks on day when had most alcohol
1   2 or fewer
2   3 or more

probability of transitioning to one stage, conditional on membership in another stage, separately for males and females.

The variables used to measure the model shown in Figure 8.1 are listed in Table 8.1. Some of these variables were originally multicategory and were dichotomized for these analyses. In general, the variables asked about whether the individual had ever tried a substance, rather than about ongoing use of substances. They asked whether the individual had ever tried alcohol, ever tried tobacco, ever tried marijuana, ever tried cocaine, and ever been drunk. In addition, because drunkenness is a subjective state, we included a variable asking the largest number of drinks the individual had consumed in one day. This was dichotomized so that two drinks or fewer was coded as one, and three drinks or more was coded as two.

THE LATENT TRANSITION ANALYSIS MODEL

Suppose there are two times of measurement, Time t and Time $t + 1$. The model can incorporate more than two times. In our example, the times are ninth grade and tenth grade. Furthermore, suppose a stage-sequential process involving S stages. For technical reasons, in the LTA framework stages are referred to as *latent statuses*. Suppose $p, q = 1$, ..., S with p denoting a latent status at Time t and q denoting a latent status at Time $t + 1$. In our example, this is the substance use onset latent variable, with $S = 8$ latent statuses (see Figure 8.1). There is also an exogenous static latent variable dividing the population into latent classes $c = 1, ..., C$. In our example, this is gender, although technically gender is not a latent variable because we are assuming it is measured perfectly.

Suppose six manifest indicators (items or variables) of the dynamic latent variable at each occasion:

Item 1, with $i, i' = 1, ..., I$ response categories
Item 2, with $j, j' = 1, ..., J$ response categories
Item 3, with $k, k' = 1, ..., K$ response categories
Item 4, with $l, l' = 1, ..., L$ response categories
Item 5, with $m, m' = 1, ..., M$ response categories
Item 6, with $o, o' = 1, ..., O$ response categories

where i, j, k, l, m, and o refer to responses obtained at Time t, and i', j', k', l', m', and o' refer to responses obtained at Time $t + 1$. These correspond to the six substance use items listed in Table 8.1. Also suppose one manifest indicator of the static latent variable with $r = 1, ..., R$ response categories, corresponding to the gender indicator variable listed in Table 8.1.

Let $Y = \{r,i,j,k,l,m,o,i',j',k',l',m',o'\}$ represent a response pattern. The response pattern has the same meaning as was explained earlier with respect to latent class analysis. The only difference is that it is longer, because it includes responses taken at more than one time. Let $P(Y)$ represent the estimated proportion in response pattern Y.

Then
$$P(Y) = \sum_{c=1}^{C} \sum_{p=1}^{S} \sum_{q=1}^{S} \qquad (2)$$

$$\gamma_c \rho_{r|c} \delta_{p|c} \rho_{i|p,c} \rho_{j|p,c} \rho_{k|p,c} \rho_{l|p,c} \rho_{m|p,c} \rho_{o|p,c} \tau_{q|p,c} \rho_{i'|q,c} \rho_{j'|q,c} \rho_{k'|q,c} \rho_{l'|q,c} \rho_{m'|q,c} \rho_{o'|q,c}$$

where

γ_c = proportion in latent class c (e.g., *PROPORTION FEMALE*)

$\delta_{p|c}$ = proportion in latent status p at Time t conditional on membership in latent class c (e.g., *PROPORTION OF FEMALES WHO ARE IN THE NO USE LATENT STATUS IN NINTH GRADE*)

$\tau_{q|p,c}$ = probability of membership in latent status q at Time $t + 1$ conditional on membership in latent status p at Time t and membership in latent class c (i.e., an element of the latent transition probability matrix; e.g., *PROPORTION OF MALES IN THE NO USE LATENT STATUS IN NINTH GRADE WHO REMAIN THERE IN TENTH GRADE*)

$\rho_{i|p,c}$ = probability of response i to Item 1 at Time t, conditional on membership in latent status p at Time t and on membership in latent class c.

In summary, the LTA model is an extension of the latent class model to longitudinal data. Thus, as the latent class model, LTA is a latent variable model where both the indicators and the latent variable are categorical. LTA analyzes response pattern proportions and involves ρ parameters that play the same role as they play in latent class models, that is, a role conceptually similar to factor loadings. LTA allows the user to model change over time that occurs in the form of movement between stages. In order to model such phenomena, LTA adds some parameters to the latent class model. These parameters represent the distribution of stage memberships at each time point (δ) and the probability of moving into one stage conditional on prior membership in another (τ). In some LTA models, such as the example discussed here, these quantities are conditional on manifest or latent class membership, such as gender or an experimental condition.

Details of the Analysis

The analyses described here were done using WinLTA (Brunner & Schafer, 1997). Model fitting and parameter estimation in LTA are done in two phases, an Expectation Maximization (EM) algorithm phase and a data augmentation (DA) phase. The EM analysis provides maximum likelihood parameter estimates for the model being fit. Model selection is also done during this phase. The EM analysis provides a goodness of fit index, G^2. Although in theory this is distributed as a chi-square, for problems with very large degrees of freedom, as is typical in most LTA problems, it appears not to be distributed as a chi-square (Read & Cressie, 1988). Unfortunately, the exact distribution is not known, although it is known that the expectation is considerably less than the degrees of freedom (Collins, Fidler, Wugalter, & Long, 1993). If the sample size is sufficiently large, it is often better to use cross-validation for model selection, rather than to rely on the assumption that G^2 is distributed as a chi-square. Degrees of freedom are equal to the number of possible response patterns (which in general will be considerably larger than the number of observed response patterns) minus the number of independently estimated parameters minus 1.

After model selection and initial parameter estimation has taken place, the next step is to obtain standard errors and confidence intervals for each parameter. Unlike other estimation procedures, EM does not produce standard errors as a by-product. In LTA, standard errors are obtained in a separate step by means of data augmentation (Tanner & Wong, 1987). Data augmentation, a type of Markov chain Monte-Carlo procedure, is essentially a stochastic version of the EM procedure. The EM procedure alternates between an E (Expectation) step, where missing data (in this case, latent class membership) are predicted and an M (Maximization) step, where parameters are re-estimated based on the predicted missing data. Data augmentation alternates between an I (Imputation) step where missing data are simulated, and a P (Posterior) step where parameters are simulated. In other words, data augmentation simulates the data, treating the parameters as missing data and multiply imputing them. The procedure uses the EM algorithm parameter estimates as a starting point. The user specifies the desired number of imputations. The results of the multiple imputations are then combined using rules provided by Rubin (1987) to form a point estimate of each parameter and estimates of the standard errors. (For an excellent description of data augmentation and other Markov chain Monte-Carlo methods, see Schafer, 1997.)

RESULTS

Parameter Restrictions

Parameters in LTA may be either freely estimated or restricted in one of two ways. The restrictions involve (a) fixing a parameter estimate to a prespecified value, or (b) constraining a parameter estimate to be equal to one or more other parameter estimates. In general, every freely estimated parameter "costs" one degree of freedom. A fixed parameter involves no estimation, and thus is not deducted from the degrees of freedom. A set of parameters constrained to be equal to each other is equivalent to estimating a single parameter and thus costs one degree of freedom.

There are two reasons why parameter restrictions are employed. The first is to achieve identification. When a problem is identified, it means that there is enough information in the data to do all the estimation that is required. When a problem is underidentified, it means that there is not enough information to do all the estimation that the problem requires, and therefore fewer parameters must be estimated. Parameter restrictions provide a means to reduce the number of parameters estimated.

The second reason for using parameter restrictions is to specify various aspects of a model. For example, it is much easier to interpret change over time if the ρ parameters corresponding to the dynamic part of the model are constrained to be equal over time. This set of restrictions specifies that the meaning of the latent statuses is not changing over time. When making comparisons across groups, it is often desirable to constrain the ρ parameters to be equal across groups. Another example of the use of parameter restrictions to specify a model is when restrictions are applied to the τ matrix to specify what types of change are permissible. If a theory specifies that change occurs only in a forward direction, the user may wish to fix the elements of the lower triangle of the τ matrix to zero.

In the empirical example presented here, parameter restrictions were placed on the ρ parameters and the τ parameters. The ρ parameters corresponding to the static part of the model, that is, the ρ parameters associated with measurement of gender, were fixed to zero or one as appropriate. This was done because gender was measured without error. (This strategy can be employed under other circumstances, for example, when the grouping variable is experimental condition.) Some restrictions were placed on the ρ parameters corresponding to the dynamic part of the model. First, these parameters were constrained to be equal across times and across genders. Second, constraints were imposed so that two ρ parameters were estimated per item. Essentially, for each item the two parameters represented the probability of a "no" response when, according to the latent status, the response should have been "yes" (as, e.g., a response of "never tried alcohol" when the respondent is in the "tried alcohol" latent status) and the probability of a "yes" response when, according to the latent status, the response should have been "no" (as, e.g., a response of "tried marijuana" when the individual is in the "no use" latent status). Because these questions were worded "have you ever," it was not possible to revert to a previous latent status involving fewer substances tried. Thus, each element in the lower triangle of the τ matrix was fixed to zero. Furthermore, three other elements of the τ matrix representing logically impossible transitions were fixed to zero. These transitions are (a) from alcohol only to tobacco only; (b) from tobacco only to alcohol and drunkenness; and (c) from alcohol and tobacco to alcohol and drunkenness.

To sum up, parameter restrictions are an important tool in latent class and LTA models. By specifying that certain parameters are to be fixed to preset values or that groups of parameters are to be estimated at identical values, the user not only may achieve better parameter estimation overall in some circumstances by ensuring identification, but also may express conceptual aspects of the model to be tested.

Goodness of Fit

The G^2 for this model was 4,482.25 with 8,114 df. Because the distribution of the G^2 is not precisely known it is impossible to assign a probability value. However, the G^2 is so much smaller than the df that we conclude that the model fits reasonably well.

Parameter Values

There are five sets of parameters estimated in an LTA analysis. They are the ρs associated with the static part of the model (little ρ matrix), the γs, the ρs associated with the dynamic part of the model (big ρ matrix), the δs, and the τs. In the analyses reported here, no elements of the little ρ matrix were estimated; instead, all were fixed as described earlier. The γ parameters in this case are simply the proportion of the sample that are each gender, which is .48 males and .52 females.

Table 8.2 shows the ρ parameter estimates based on data augmentation. This table illustrates how the ρ parameters are used to interpret the latent statuses. For example, the first latent status is made up of individuals who have a very small probability of responding "yes" to any of the substance use items. Thus, this latent status is labeled *no use.* Another latent status, where individuals have a high probability of responding that they have tried alcohol and have been drunk, but a low probability of responding "yes" to any of the other items, is labeled *Alcohol and Drunk.* As discussed, the closer these are to the boundary values of zero and one, the stronger is the relationship between the latent status and the manifest variable. In general, an overall pattern of ρ parameters greater than about .75 and less than about .25 is a healthy sign, analogous to a well-saturated pattern of factor loadings in a factor analysis. In these data, we see this overall pattern, with one exception. The one exception is the ρ parameter corresponding to the probability of responding "yes" to the cocaine item, conditional on membership in the most advanced latent status.

Table 8.3 shows the δ parameter estimates based on data augmentation. These parameters represent the probability of membership in each latent status, conditional on gender, at the first occasion of measurement, ninth grade. The numbers in brack-

TABLE 8.2
ρ Parameter Estimates for the Dynamic Latent Variable

Latent Status	Alcohol	Tobacco	Drunk	3+	Marijuana	Cocaine
No use	.171	.061	.032	.050	.017	.005
Alcohol	.987	.061	.032	.050	.017	.005
Tobacco	.171	.959	.032	.050	.017	.005
Alcohol + tobacco	.987	.959	.032	.050	.017	.005
Alcohol + drunk	.987	.061	.860	.849	.017	.005
Alcohol + tobacco + drunk	.987	.959	.860	.849	.017	.005
Alcohol + tobacco + drunk + marijuana	.987	.959	.860	.849	.906	.005
Alcohol + tobacco + drunk + marijuana + cocaine	.987	.959	.860	.849	.906	.539

Note. These parameters were constrained to be equal across times and across genders. They were also constrained so that only two parameters per item were estimated.

TABLE 8.3
δ Parameter Estimates and Confidence Intervals

Latent status	Grade 9 males		Grade 9 females	
No use	.264	[.249, .280]***	.230	[.217, .243]
Alcohol	.193	[.180, .206]***	.241	[.225, .257]
Tobacco	.036	[.029, .044]	.024	[.018, .031]
Alcohol + tobacco	.185	[.172, .199]***	.148	[.131, .166]
Alcohol + drunk	.049	[.041, .058]	.050	[.042, .059]
Alcohol + tobacco + drunk	.126	[.112, .141]***	.179	[.164, .195]
Alcohol + tobacco + drunk + marijuana	.084	[.065, .106]	.088	[.075, .103]
Alhohol + tobacco + drunk + marijuana + cocaine	.065	[.048, .085]	.041	[.031, .054]

*** Confidence intervals do not overlap across genders.

ets are the 95% confidence intervals. Confidence intervals that do not overlap across genders are marked with three asterisks. Surprisingly, girls appear less likely than boys to be in the no use latent status at Time 1. They are more likely to be in the alcohol only and alcohol + tobacco + drunk latent statuses at Grade 9, whereas boys are more likely to be in the alcohol + tobacco latent status.

Based on the δ parameters, it is possible to compute prevalence rates for each substance. For example, the prevalence of having tried tobacco is computed by summing the δ parameters for all latent statuses involving tobacco. These prevalence rates appear in Table 8.4 for Grade 9. The majority of ninthgraders have at least tried alcohol, and about one-third report having been drunk at least once. Nearly one half have tried tobacco. In ninth grade, 15% of boys and 13% of girls have tried marijuana; as is also shown in Table 8.3, about 7% of boys and about 4% of girls have tried cocaine by ninth grade.

Table 8.5 shows the τ parameters and 95% confidence intervals based on data augmentation. The overall pattern looks similar across genders, with no 95% confidence intervals that do not overlap across genders. There are two instances where 90% con-

TABLE 8.4
Prevalence Rates

Substance	Grade 9 males	Grade 9 females
Alcohol	70%	75%
Tobacco	46%	48%
Drunkenness	32%	36%
Marijuana	15%	13%
Cocaine	7%	4%

TABLE 8.5
τ Parameter Estimates and Confidence Intervals

	1	2	3	4	5	6	7	8
Latent class 1: males, 9th to 10th grade								
1 None	.772 [.692, .837]	.069 [.030, .139]	.015 [.034, .077]	.051 [.034, .077]	.032 [.015, .064]	.028 [.016, .049]	.003 [.000, .038]	.031 [.017, .054]
2 A	–	.728 [.646, .799]	–	.044 [.015, .107]	.068 [.034, .123]	.106 [.070, .155]	.006 [.000, .070]	.048 [.029, .078]
3 T	–	–	.529 [.370, .683]	.227 [.119, .381]	–	.147 [.076, .258]	.009 [.000, .112]	.089 [.019, .279]
4 AT	–	–	–	.681 [.633, .725]	–	.186 [.134, .249]	.079 [.027, .193]	.054 [.014, .156]
5 AD	–	–	–	–	.655 [.555, .745]	.153 [.017, .573]	.126 [.042, .295]	.066 [.002, .488]
6ATD	–	–	–	–	–	.731 [.642, .806]	.181 [.102, .292]	.088 [.025, .230]
7ATDM	–	–	–	–	–	–	.967 [.483, 1.000]	.033 [.000, .517]
8 ATDMC	–	–	–	–	–	–	–	1.000
Latent class 2: females, 9th to 10th grade								
1 None	.772 [.699, .833]	.120 [.060, .217]	.011 [.000, .137]	.029 [.012, .062]	.025 [.008, .068]	.032 [.017, .058]	.006 [.000, .056]	.005 [.000, .058]
2 A	–	.744 [.695, .787]	–	.075 [.046, .118]	.106 [.078, .141]	.049 [.032, .073]	.022 [.011, .042]	.004 [.000, .051]
3 T	–	–	.430 [.284, .588]	.398 [.216, .607]	–	.151 [.060, .315]	.005 [.000, .076]	.016 [.001, .145]
4 AT	–	–	–	.642 [.571, .708]	–	.282 [.226, .345]	.039 [.013, .099]	.037 [.013, .088]
5 AD	–	–	–	–	.687 [.533, .812]	.171 [.067, .347]	.110 [.026, .318]	.033 [.000, .423]
6ATD	–	–	–	–	–	.715 [.664, .762]	.248 [.191, .314]	.037 [.007, .130]
7ATDM	–	–	–	–	–	–	.897 [.457, .995]	.104 [.005, .543]
8 ATDMC	–	–	–	–	–	–	–	1.000

fidence intervals do not overlap across genders. These are the probabilities of moving from alcohol only to alcohol, tobacco, and drunkenness, and from alcohol only to the most advanced latent status. Both of these probabilities are higher for boys. The latter probability is more than 10 times higher for boys, although the probabilities are small in absolute terms (.048 for boys, .004 for girls). Although the differences are not significant, the probability of boys moving into the most advanced latent status is higher as compared to girls for every starting point except the alcohol + tobacco + drunk + marijuana latent status. One finding, which replicates other findings with younger children in this data set, is that children who start their substance use onset experience with tobacco move out of this latent status relatively quickly. For females, the confidence interval for the probability of remaining in the tobacco-only latent status is non-overlapping with the confidence interval for the probability of remaining in the alcohol-only latent status, suggesting that females in the tobacco-only latent status are significantly more likely to move to a more advanced substance use latent status by tenth grade than are females in the alcohol-only latent status. In most cases, this more advanced latent status is the alcohol and tobacco latent status.

DISCUSSION

This chapter has demonstrated the use of LTA, an extension of latent class models to longitudinal data. LTA provides a means of estimating and testing stage-sequential developmental models. LTA is conceptually similar to Structural Equation Modeling (SEM), in that both LTA and SEM are latent variable models. An important difference is that in LTA, the latent variable is categorical, sorting individuals into stages across time.

Why a Latent Variable Model?

Latent variable models are not to everyone's taste. To some readers of this chapter, LTA may seem like a lot of trouble. Why bother with a latent variable model, when it is possible simply to cross-tabulate observed stage membership, examining Time 1 membership crossed with Time 2 membership, to obtain transition probabilities? There are two advantages to using LTA to examine transition probabilities. First, it is not as simple as it seems at first glance to cross-tabulate stage membership in an example such as the one used here. When an individual responds "no" to all the substance use items, it is pretty easy to decide what stage the individual is in—the no substance use stage. Similarly, an individual who responds "yes" to the tobacco question and "no" to all the others is easy to categorize. With other individuals, categorization is not so straightforward. For example, it is difficult to know what to make of an individual who responds "yes" to having tried cocaine but "no" to all the other use items. If there is a substantial number of individuals giving this response pattern, it might reflect a legitimate pattern of use. If there are only one or two instances of this

pattern, it is more likely that it is an error, caused by careless or mendacious responding. Cross-tabulating all the observed response patterns would make a huge contingency table, much of which would be difficult at best, and possibly meaningless,
to interpret. Implicit in LTA is an organizing philosophy that the latent variable consists of the latent statuses enumerated in the model and that response patterns such
as this one are provided by individuals who belong in one of the enumerated latent
statuses, but for whatever reasons erred (or lied) when responding to the questionnaire. Because LTA estimates an error structure by means of the ρ parameters, it
assigns troublesome response patterns such as this one to the appropriate latent statuses, making the resulting contingency table much more parsimonious and easier to
interpret.

Another advantage of taking a latent variable approach is that with transition
probability matrices in particular, measurement error tends to populate the off-diagonal elements at the expense of the diagonal. Just as random measurement error in
continuous variable models will cause an observation to be lower or higher than it
would be otherwise, random measurement error in categorical data causes an observation to be put in the wrong category. In any matrix larger than 3 by 3, the off-
diagonal elements outnumber the diagonal elements, with the difference growing
greater for larger matrices. Thus by chance alone, any element that is misclassified because of measurement error is more likely to be placed somewhere in the off-diagonal
than in the diagonal. Because in a transition probability matrix the off-diagonal elements represent movement over time and the diagonal elements usually represent stability, measurement error makes it appear that there is more movement over time, and
less stability than there really is. Because LTA adjusts for measurement error in
the transition probability matrix, it produces more realistic estimates of the amount
of stability and change.

Interpreting the ρ Parameters

Throughout the ρ matrix in this example (Table 8.2), the ρ parameters are close to
zero and one, indicating a strong relationship between the latent statuses and the observed variables. The one notable exception to this is the relationship between the
most advanced latent status and the cocaine item. The probability of responding
"yes" to the cocaine item for those in the most advanced latent class is .539, indicating
a relatively weak relation between the cocaine item and this latent status. There are
several ways to interpret this. One possibility is simply that there is a lot of random
error, in other words, latent status membership only weakly influences the response
to the cocaine item. Another possibility is that if everyone in the most advanced latent
status truly has tried cocaine, there is a tendency for cocaine users to underreport their
use. Note that there appears to be no corresponding tendency for nonusers of cocaine
to overreport their use; the probability of responding "yes" when in a latent status that
does not involve cocaine use is only .005. A third way of interpreting this is that in
the most advanced latent status, the probability of cocaine use is only .539, in other

words, not everyone in this latent status has tried cocaine, but the probability of having tried it is much higher in this group.

Hypothesis Testing and Type I Error Rate

WinLTA is the first version of the LTA software to provide confidence intervals for LTA parameter estimates. However, hypothesis testing in this context remains difficult in some ways. One reason is that the τ parameters tend to have large standard errors. A more stable method of estimating τ parameters is needed. More generally, there can be a large number of parameters in LTA models, raising the possibility of capitalizing on chance when making a long series of pairwise comparisons of parameter estimates. It is possible to use methods such as a Bonferonni correction, but, with as many comparisons as are possible in LTA, this would dramatically reduce statistical power. Statistical comparison of individual parameters in LTA is still very new. We recommend not using a Bonferonni correction, making theory-driven comparisons wherever possible, and using extreme caution in interpreting the results. Future research will explore these issues further.

Conclusions About Drug Use Onset

A surprising finding of this study is that ninth-grade girls appear to have slightly more substance use experience than boys. This runs counter to earlier findings with a different subset of these data at an earlier age (Collins et al., 1994), where seventh-grade boys appeared to have slightly more substance use experience than seventh-grade girls. It may be that by ninth grade, girls are more developmentally advanced than boys and thus more likely to be spending time with older peers who have access to drugs. It is interesting to note that this finding does not appear to be true for cocaine. Here, boys appear more advanced than girls, although this is not significant. There also was a non-significant tendency in the τ matrix for males to have a considerably higher probability of proceeding from the alcohol-only latent status all the way to the most advanced latent status, which involves having tried cocaine, in the one year between ninth and tenth grades. The corresponding τ parameter was almost zero for girls. In fact, the probability of moving into the most advanced latent status is larger, although not significantly larger, for males for all starting points except the alcohol + tobacco + drunk + marijuana latent status. Perhaps there is a small subset made up of males who are on an extremely accelerated onset trajectory. If so, research should be devoted to finding prospective predictors of this, with an eye toward intervention and, eventually, prevention.

Categorical Versus Continuous Approaches

When should a researcher consider taking a categorical approach to data analysis, such as LTA, as opposed to the more widely used continuous variable approaches? Of course, some theories are clearly either categorical or continuous and should be tested with corresponding methods. But a wide range of research questions can be framed in either categorical or continuous terms. Taking a categorical approach has costs and benefits. A cost is that in general, the models that can be tested in a categorical framework are more limited in size than their continuous counterparts. Every time a variable is added to a categorical analysis a dimension is added to the contingency table. This table can quickly become unwieldy, particularly if variables are measured at several points in time. Another cost is that sometimes categories of variables must be collapsed in order to simplify the analyses or to keep down the size of the contingency table, which can potentially result in a loss of information.

However, there are important benefits associated with a categorical variable approach such as LTA. LTA expresses change in the form of transition probabilities. These give a very detailed look at change. Anyone who has done an LTA has spent considerable time staring at transition probability matrices, trying to take in the rich information about change contained there. These matrices express not only the amount of change, but who ended up where. Because of the categorical nature of the model, LTA conditions these transition probabilities on previous stage membership. This feature addresses an important concern in longitudinal research: the effect that the starting point has on change. Taking a categorical approach, it is easy to see whether individuals in certain stages at an initial time point are moving faster or more slowly through a stage sequence. Another advantage of the categorical approach is that it can deal with subgroups who may be undergoing qualitatively different change. A model such as LTA can incorporate the possibility of individuals taking different paths through a stage sequence. For example, in the substance use data discussed in this chapter, some individuals began their substance use experience with alcohol, whereas others began it with tobacco. It is difficult to handle such qualitative differences between subgroups using continuous variable methods. Both continuous and categorical approaches are extremely useful in social science research. Which one to choose depends upon the nature of the underlying process being studied, the data at hand, and the questions of interest to the investigators.

CHAPTER NINE

Testing Cross-Group and Cross-Time Constraints on Parameters Using the General Linear Model

Keith F. Widaman
University of California at Riverside

The methodology for framing and testing theoretical predictions—subsuming tasks often identified as data analysis or hypothesis testing—has been a topic of intense concern throughout the 20th century. Following earlier insights (e.g., Student, 1907), Fisher (1935) systematized procedures that came to be known as experimental design and the analysis of variance. At the same time, parallel developments—designed to answer questions in genetics and biological inheritance—were being made in correlational methods and regression analysis. Since the 1970s, the underlying similarity of these approaches has been amply noted. Indeed, both the analysis of variance and regression analysis use variants of the general linear model, a very flexible representation of data that underlies many of the most commonly used statistical tests employed in psychology and the social sciences. The ways in which t tests, linear correlations, the analysis of variance, and multiple regression analysis can be formulated through the general linear model are well known, due to expositions by Cohen (1968; Cohen & Cohen, 1983) and others (e.g., Darlington, 1968).

The typical application of the general linear model involves the use of what has become known as null hypothesis significance testing. Throughout most of their training, graduate students are taught to formulate null hypotheses of some form, such as the hypothesis that treatment group means do not differ or that a regression weight does not differ from zero. Such null hypotheses are more properly termed nil hypotheses by Cohen (1990, 1994), because they represent a test of no (i.e., nil) difference of a sample value from a population value or no (i.e., nil) difference between multiple sample values. Then, using an appropriate adaptation of the general linear model, a significance test is formed. If a significant test statistic is obtained, the nil hypothesis may be rejected in favor of an alternative hypothesis that the parameter in question differs significantly from zero. Despite considerable dissatisfaction since the 1970s (e.g., Greenwald, 1975; Morrison & Henkel, 1970; Schmidt, 1996), nil hypothesis significance testing remains the staple in undergraduate and graduate courses on statistics in the behavioral sciences.

However, exciting advances in statistical methodology have occurred since the 1980s, particularly with the advent of structural equation modeling. Using structural equation modeling, the researcher formulates a statistical model to be tested. After fitting the structural model to the obtained data, a significant test statistic supports rejection of the hypothesized model in favor of a model with one or more additional parameters. Researchers using structural modeling have become used to fixing, freeing, and constraining parameters in models, leading to the specification and testing of competing nested structural models. The key aspect of a model tested using this approach is that the model is not a nil model; instead, the model tested is a non-nil model. The use of statistical tests in structural equation modeling has thus been characterized as "standing hypothesis testing on its head." That is, under standard null hypothesis testing, a researcher hopes to reject the null hypothesis of no difference in favor of the alternative hypothesis of a non-nil difference, as this latter hypothesis is consistent with the scientific hypothesis of interest. In contrast, under structural equation modeling, the specified structural model represents the researcher's scientific hypothesis. Because of this, the researcher hopes not to reject this structural model, as rejecting the structural model in favor of a model with additional parameter estimates means that the researcher must reject his or her scientific hypothesis in favor of a model that is more complex in some fashion.

TYPICAL APPROACHES TO HYPOTHESIS TESTING: PROBLEMS AND PROSPECTS

Problems With Null Hypothesis Testing

The methods of testing nil hypotheses are so well accepted that many researchers do not readily comprehend the problems associated with this approach to hypothesis testing. Given several reviews of problems with the typical approach (e.g., Schmidt, 1996) and limitations of space, only a few crucial issues are discussed here. One problem with the typical approach to testing hypotheses is the meager information provided by such a test. That is, a typical nil hypothesis test merely documents that a parameter estimate differs from zero, thus providing only evidence of the direction of the difference. For example, a significant test statistic merely shows that the mean of one group is larger than that of a second group or that a correlation is larger (or smaller) than zero. The test statistic does not provide any evidence of the strength or importance of the relationship. Indeed, if sample size were large enough, virtually any difference between empirical values would be statistically significant, and the likelihood of a significant difference in the predicted direction would near .50, the same as predicting "heads" on the flip of a coin.

A second problem with the use of significance tests is the tendency of researchers to deal with results in a "black or white" fashion. That is, investigators typically act as if a significant test statistic bestows some special status on a mean difference or correlation, signifying that the parameter of interest differs from zero. Moreover, if the test statistic is nonsignificant, researchers often act as if the parameter of interest is essentially zero. But, this approach completely neglects the issue of statistical power. If a correlation of a given magnitude is significant at the .06 level, this correlation should not be treated as if it were zero. If sample size had been somewhat larger, the correlation would now be statistically significant even though its value was unchanged. Clearly, nonsignificant correlations should not be treated as essentially zero unless they are very close to zero.

A third problem with the use of significance tests is that their use often seems to obstruct progress in many areas of psychology (Meehl, 1978). In any area of research, findings accumulate and reviews of research tend to use the "box score" approach to evaluating the state of findings. Using the box score approach, the researcher lists studies and then notes whether each study did or did not reject the nil hypothesis of interest. In some areas of psychology, 70% of the studies led to rejection of the nil hypothesis, but reviewers conclude that the presence of 30% of nonrejections represents a problem. Schmidt (1996), in touting the use of meta-analysis, argued that researchers may routinely fail to reject the nil hypothesis but that a quantitative review might show that the population parameter of interest differs significantly from zero when results are pooled across studies. These arguments converge on a position that the result of an individual test of a nil hypothesis is rarely conclusive for testing a theoretical prediction.

Solutions to the Problem of Significance Testing

One way of attempting to solve the problem with nil hypothesis tests of significance is the use of indices of variance explained, such as η^2, ω^2, or r^2. Regardless of the significance level of a test statistic, the magnitude of an index of variance explained provides an indicator of the strength of effect or the strength of relationship between two variables. For example, the correlation between two variables may be statistically significant. But, if sample size were 10,000, then one should not be surprised that the correlation differed significantly from zero. An index of the magnitude of variance shared is a far more useful index in such a case. If the squared correlation were .01, one might be relatively uninterested in the correlation, whereas a squared correlation of .50 would definitely attract attention.

The use of indices of variance explained is not without its problems. Central among these is the dependence of such indices on aspects of the sample. That is, indices of variance explained are affected by restriction of range, just as standardized beta weights are. If one obtains an unrestricted, representative sample from a population, then indices of variance explained may be accurate indicators of population parameters. However, if the sample is a restricted subset of the population, then indices of variance explained will be affected. Clearly, other alternatives to nil hypothesis testing are desirable.

A second alternative—and the one explored in more detail in this chapter—is the hypothesizing and testing of non-nil hypotheses. As argued, hypothesis testing in psychology and the behavioral sciences usually takes the form of the testing of nil hypotheses. However, nil hypotheses are not the only hypotheses that may be maintained; they simply are the hypotheses we, in the social sciences, have been taught to entertain. In the physical sciences, theory and prior research are used to predict the value of one or more parameters, such as the form of a function or the precise value of a constant in an equation. Experiments are then conducted to determine whether empirical results are consistent with the predicted parameters. Under such an approach, the researcher must provide much more explicit hypotheses about the form of the general linear model for particular phenomena of interest, and then test this more explicit model. If this model is rejected, the investigator must reject his or her scientific hypothesis in favor of a statistical model that is more complex in some fashion. In essence, this second way of circumventing problems associated with nil hypothesis testing amounts to importing the logic of significance testing employed by structural equation modeling into analyses using the general linear model.

BASIC ISSUES

The General Linear Model

Notation. Prior to a more detailed discussion of the general linear model, I first introduce a series of notational conventions to enable simple distinctions among various denotations of regression weights. One set of conventions is the use of (a) the letter 'B' to represent regression weights; (b) uppercase letters to represent raw score regression weights and lowercase letters to represent standard score weights; and (c) a subscript for each regression weight to designate its associated predictor variable.

A second set of conventions concerns the designation of population parameters and estimates of these parameters based on empirical data. Considering first a raw score regression equation, this set of conventions is (a) the hypothetical, unknown population parameter in the raw score equation is designated using a capital Greek beta, or B; (b) the typical unconstrained (e.g., least squares) and unbiased estimate of the regression parameter from an empirical data set is designated using an italic capital Roman B with a caret (^), or $\hat{B}$; (c) an optimal estimate, or "best guess," of a regression parameter based on theory or, more probably, prior research is designated using an italic capital Roman B with a tilde (~) over it, or $\tilde{B}$; and (d) a constrained estimate of the regression parameter will be designated using an italic capital Roman B with a circle (°) over it, or $\overset{\circ}{B}$. Thus, B_1 is the population value for the raw score regression weight for predictor X_1, $\hat{B}_1$ is the typical unconstrained and unbiased estimate of the raw score regression weight for variable X_1 based on analysis of a given set of data, $\tilde{B}_1$ is the best estimate of the corresponding population value available based on theory or prior research (e.g., meta-analysis), and $\overset{\circ}{B}_1$ is a constrained estimate of the raw score regression weight.

Similar conventions are used for standard score regression weights. Thus, β_1 is the population value of a regression slope parameter for the first predictor, $\hat{b}_1$ is the unconstrained estimate of the regression weight for variable X_1 based on analysis of a given set of data, $\tilde{b}_1$ is the best estimate of the corresponding population value available based on theory or prior research (e.g., meta-analysis), and $\overset{\circ}{b}_1$ is a constrained estimate of the regression weight.

A final convention relates to regression weights estimated in more than a single group. When analyses are performed on a single sample, no special notation is needed. However, when analyses are performed on two or more samples, then a parenthesized superscript designates group membership. Thus, $\hat{B}_1^{(1)}$ is the unconstrained estimate of the raw score regression weight for variable X_1 in sample 1.

General Form of the Linear Model. Given the foregoing, the raw score form for the general linear model, with population parameters, may be written for a single group as:

$$Y_i = B_0 X_{i0} + B_1 X_{i1} + B_2 X_{i2} + \ldots + B_v X_{iv} + E_i \tag{1}$$

where Y_i is the score on the dependent variable Y for observation i ($i = 1, \ldots, N$), variable X_{i0} is the unit constant (having a value of 1 for each subject), variable X_{ij} represents the score of the ith observation on the jth independent variable ($j = 1, \ldots, v$), B_0 is the intercept, or additive constant, in the model, weight B_j is the raw score regression weight, or regression slope, for the associated predictor variable X_{ij}, and E_i is the error in representing the observed Y value for observation i with the weighted combination of predictor variables reflected by Equation 1.

The corresponding raw score regression equation, with regression weights estimated using typical, unconstrained ordinary least squares (OLS) estimation, would be written as:

$$Y_i = \hat{B}_0 X_{i0} + \hat{B}_1 X_{i1} + \hat{B}_2 X_{i2} + \ldots + \hat{B}_v X_{iv} + \hat{E}_i \tag{2}$$

in which unconstrained sample estimates of the regression parameters have been substituted for the population estimates in Equation 1, and all other symbols are as defined earlier.

But, Equation 2 is not the only form of general linear model that may be entertained. For example, if an investigator had explicit hypotheses about certain regression weights, then the hypothesized form of the general linear model might be:

$$Y_i = \hat{B}_0 X_{i0} + \bar{B}_1 X_{i1} + \overset{\circ}{B}_2 X_{i2} + \hat{B}_3 X_{i3} + E_i \tag{3}$$

In this case, unconstrained versions of the intercept, $\hat{B}_0$, and the third regression weight, $\hat{B}_3$, were hypothesized, along with a *best guess* population value for the first regression weight, $\bar{B}_1$, and a constrained value of the second regression weight, $\overset{\circ}{B}_2$. As should be obvious, the provision of fixed, free, and constrained regression weights opens up a very wide array of hypotheses that may be proposed and tested, hypotheses bounded only by the knowledge and ingenuity of the investigator.

Typical Steps in Regression Analysis

The analysis of data using the general linear model typically proceeds by way of a series of steps. In the present chapter, I distinguish these steps with the acronym SEEK, which connotes the search by the investigator for models that represent phenomena in a given domain. The term *SEEK* stands for the steps of *s*pecification of a model, *e*stimation of parameters, *e*valuation of the resulting equation, and *k*ommensuration[1] of models and data.

Specification. Specification comprises the translation of theoretical propositions or hypotheses into statistical hypotheses, leading to a particular form of the general linear model. The usual way of specifying an equation is simply to place certain predictor variables in an equation in order to get the nil hypothesis machinery going. In effect, the specification stage is a routine process, and many researchers pay little attention to the specification of equations. At times, attention is paid to certain aspects of model specification, although these are only the rather surface aspects of which variables are in a particular equation and which have been excluded. Furthermore, when researchers use stepwise regression, the specification of the final equation is left to the discretion of a computer program, which determines the entry of variables into the regression equation.

However, the specification step is an extremely important one—often too little emphasized in discussions of the analysis and modeling of data. Indeed, this step should encompass a good deal of hard work to determine the precise form of the properly specified equation for a given set of data. Each parameter in the general lin-

---

[1] The term *kommensuration* was deliberately misspelled because no word beginning with "K" was available that conveyed the meaning of readjustment, and I wished to complete the compelling acronym (SEEK). The misspelling also connotes the fact that attempts to make models commensurate with data often require the researcher to invoke what are, in essence, post hoc auxiliary hypotheses (Lakatos, 1970; Meehl, 1967, 1978). Just as language was manipulated to complete the acronym, so are regression equations manipulated, at times, to describe patterns in empirical data.

ear model represents a hypothesis—that the particular predictor has a linear relation to the outcome variable and that the regression weight provides the slope of this function. In many areas of psychology, the hypothesis of a linear relation between predictor and criterion is open to question. Many types of human capability seem to be described by relationships that are nonlinear, at least with regard to the manner in which variables are typically measured. Thus, it is not surprising to find that variables must be transformed in some fashion, such as taking logarithms, in order to linearize the relation between variables.

In addition to the assumption of linearity, another key assumption is that all important predictors of the criterion variable of interest are included in the general linear model. This basic assumption is likely one that will never be satisfied in any empirical investigation. Moreover, the implications of the failure to meet this assumption are difficult to test. However, researchers would be well served by keeping this assumption in their conscious awareness, as science progresses most swiftly as more accurate models of phenomena are developed.

Estimation. Typically, the estimation step is also rather routinized, with the vast majority of analyses utilizing the general linear model using ordinary least squares (OLS) estimation. Using OLS estimation, we commonly read that the total mean corrected sums of squares are broken down into two parts, one linearly related to the predictor variables and the other linearly unrelated to the predictor variables. This is written as:

$$\sum(Y_i - \overline{Y})^2 = \sum(Y_i - \hat{Y}_i)^2 + \sum(\hat{Y}_i - \overline{Y})^2 \tag{4}$$

where all terms are defined above.

But, with the ability to develop constrained or fixed estimates of regression weights, Equation 4 may be altered in certain particulars. For example, if constrained estimates of all regression weights are obtained, then one would be using constrained least squares estimation, and the preceding equation should be written as:

$$\sum(Y_i - \overline{Y})^2 = \sum(Y_i - \mathring{Y}_i)^2 + \sum(\mathring{Y}_i - \overline{Y})^2 \tag{5}$$

with $\mathring{Y}_i$ substituted for $\hat{Y}_i$ to denote the use of constrained regression estimates in order to provide estimated values of the criterion variable.

Evaluation. Evaluation of a regression model usually takes at least two forms, testing the overall equation and evaluating the individual regression weights. Both of these tests may be effected through the use of special cases of a general purpose F test that may be written as:

$$F = \frac{(R^2_{M2} - R^2_{M1})/(k_{M2} - k_{M1})}{(1 - R^2_{M2})/(N - k_{M2})} \text{, with } df = (k_{M2} - k_{M1}), (N - k_{M2}) \tag{6}$$

where R^2_{M2} and R^2_{M1} represent the squared multiple correlations for regression models M2 and M1, respectively; k_{M2} and k_{M1} represent the number of estimates in regression models M2 and M1, respectively; and N represents sample size. This F test has $(k_{M2} - k_{M1})$ numerator and $(N - k_{M2})$ denominator degrees of freedom, as shown. Please note that k_{M2} and k_{M1} were defined as the number of estimates in regression models M2 and M1, respectively, not the number of predictors in each of these models. In any regression model, if one estimates an intercept parameter, this is a parameter estimate that must be included in the value of k for the equation.

The preceding F test (Equation 6) may be used to test an overall equation, in which case the test of significance is simultaneously a test of two nil hypotheses: the nil hypothesis that the R^2 for the model is zero, and the nil hypothesis that all regression weights are simultaneously zero. This may be accomplished in the following way. First, define regression model M1 as a model with only an intercept term and no predictor variables, so the R^2 for model M1 is zero. Next, define regression model M2 as a model with all v predictors in the model. If unconstrained OLS estimation were used, then the resulting F ratio would have numerator degrees of freedom equal to $(k_{M2} - k_{M1}) = [(v + 1) - 1] = v$, and denominator degrees of freedom equal to $(N - k_{M2}) = [N - (v + 1)] = (N - v - 1)$, where v is the number of predictors in the equation.

To test an individual regression weight, one need merely redefine the nature of regression model M1. If one wished to test whether the first regression weight, $\hat{B}_1$, differs significantly from zero, then regression model M1 would be identical to regression model M2 except for the deletion of the first predictor variable. Given this specification, the difference between squared multiple correlations for the two regression models provides the unique predictive power of the first predictor, over and above the influence of the remaining $(v - 1)$ predictors. With this change in the specification of model M1, the resulting F ratio would have 1 and $(N - v - 1)$ degrees of freedom. A similar approach would be taken to test the significance of each of the v predictors. A still better way of evaluating individual regression weights is to consider each weight along with its associated standard error. The standard error of a regression weight may be used to construct a confidence interval around the regression weight, such as a 95% confidence interval, which provides a better notion of the range of potential alternative values of the parameter estimate.

Kommensuration. The kommensuration stage is often called the readjustment stage and involves modifying a model to make it commensurate with the data. In many applications of regression analysis, researchers never execute this stage. Instead, a fully specified regression model, with all possible predictors, is fit to data, and the researcher simply interprets the significance of the overall regression model as well as the significance of the individual regression weights.

But, a far more informative way of using the general linear model is to hypothesize that certain variables will be significant and that, after these key variables are entered into the regression model, one or more sets of additional variables will not be significant. For example, when predicting grades in college, one might hypothesize that high school grades and SAT scores would be significant predictors, but that additional potential predictors, such as ethnicity and socioeconomic status, are no longer directly related to college grades. If this nil hypothesis is tested and rejected, then ethnicity and/or socioeconomic status must be added to the model, requiring the investigator to alter his or her theoretical conjecture.

In the preceding example, making the regression model commensurate with the data involved including or deleting variables to a regression model. As succeeding sections show, the ability to fix, free, and constrain regression parameters allows a wider variety of modifications to models to determine whether models are commensurate with data.

HIERARCHICALLY NESTED REGRESSION MODELS

In the foregoing section, two regression models, identified as models M2 and M1, were discussed, along with ways in which one may test the significance of both the overall squared multiple correlation as well as individual regression weights. This presentation presumed that model M1 was hierarchically nested within model M2. In the present section, the notion of nested models is discussed in more detail, including determining how models are nested within one another, the logic of testing nested models, and defining competing nested models in terms of the invariance of parameters.

Nested Regression Models: Continuum and Tree Structures

The notion of nested regression models is usually a fairly simple matter and is so widely discussed that the preceding discussion was justified. In typical applications of the general linear model in which unconstrained OLS estimation is used, one may identify whether one model is nested within the other in the following fashion: If model M1 is obtained only by deleting one or more predictors from model M2, and no new predictors are introduced into model M1, then model M1 is nested within model M2. Equivalently, if model M2 is obtained by adding one or more new predictors to model M1, and no predictors in model M1 are deleted, then model M1 is nested within model M2.

One way of thinking about nested models is as a continuum of models. As shown in Figure 9.1, section A, a continuum of models may be laid out with a null model, M0, at the left, a saturated model, Ms, at the right, and alternative models falling between these two shown as models Mp and Mq. On the continuum in Figure 9.1, section A, a model is nested within a second model if the first model falls to the left of the second model on the continuum. The null model, M0, has only a single parameter, B_0, the intercept, and no predictor variables. Because model M0 is to the left of all other models, model M0 is nested within all other models on the continuum. The model at the other end of the continuum is the saturated model Ms. Model Ms has all v predictor variables and therefore has the maximum number of predictors. Be-

FIGURE 9.1
Continua of Regression Models

A: A Unidimensional Continuum of Models

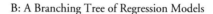

MO ──────────── Mp ──────────── Mq ──────────── Ms

B: A Branching Tree of Regression Models

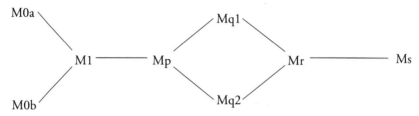

cause model Ms falls at the right end of the continuum, all other models on the continuum are nested within model Ms. The models that fall between the two extremes—models Mp and Mq—have eliminated certain predictor variables that appeared in model Ms. Given the appearance of Figure 9.1, section A, Mp has more variables excluded than does model Mq, so Mp is nested within Mq.

In some applications, the continuum depicted in Figure 9.1, section A may suffice to portray a series of regression models. For example, if one begins with a stripped down regression model and then adds successive sets of variables, this may be viewed as starting at the left end of the continuum in Figure 9.1, section A and moving to the right. Or, if one begins with a regression model with all possible predictors included in the model and then excludes sets of variables in some systematic fashion, one might begin at the right end of the continuum in Figure 9.1, section A and move toward the left.

However, most interesting research applications will appear more like the tree structure shown in Figure 9.1, section B. At the left of the figure are models M0a and M0b, which are two different null models. These null models may make one estimate from the data. Perhaps model M0a is a standard null model, with the one estimate being an intercept estimate that equals the mean of the dependent variable. The other null model, M0b, might make a single estimate from the data, but this estimate may be a regression slope, and the intercept might be fixed at zero. This is sometimes identified as regression through the origin and has applications in certain circumstances. What is shown graphically in Figure 9.1, section B is the fact that both of these models—models M0a and M0b—make a single estimate from the data and that neither model is nested within the other. Or, consider models Mp, Mq1, Mq2, and Mr. Model Mp is a model with a given set of predictors; adding a second set leads to model Mq1; separately adding a third set would result in model Mq2; and adding both the second and third sets to model Mp leads to model Mr. In such a situation, models Mp, Mq1, and Mq2 are all nested within model Mr, and model Mp is nested within both models Mq1 and Mq2. But, models Mq1 and Mq2 have no simple nesting relation with one another.

The Logic of Testing Nested Models

The most general way of determining whether models are nested is to start with a regression model with a given number of parameters. If a second model can be developed by placing constraints on parameters in the first model, then the second model is nested within the first. Now, in typical applications, the constraints imposed are constraints that one or more parameters are zero. But, this is only one of many types of constraints that may be entertained. For example, one might argue that certain regression parameters should be equal or have some specifiable relation to one another. For example, when predicting college grade point average from scores on the Scholastic Aptitude Test I Verbal and Quantitative scales, one might wish to estimate a model in which the regression weights for the Verbal and Quantitative scales were equal to one another. Or, assuming the presence of prior research that supported another constraint, perhaps the regression weight for the Verbal scale should be constrained to be twice as large as the weight for the Quantitative scale. Either of these two models with constrained parameter estimates would be nested within one in which the regression weights for the Verbal and Quantitative scales are separately and freely estimated, because one could move from the latter model to either of the constrained models by placing constraints on the freely estimated regression weights.

Given the presence of nested models, the constraints placed on parameters invoked to arrive at the nested model may be tested using the general incremental F test described in a preceding section. Because of the manner in which the F test was described, any of a variety of constraints on regression weights may be tested easily. The numerator degrees of freedom of the resulting F ratio represents the number of constraints placed on the more inclusive model to arrive at the nested model. If three constraints are placed on regression weights, even if these are complex constraints that each affect more than one regression parameter, then the F ratio would have three as its numerator degrees of freedom.

Competing Models Defined in Terms of Parameter Invariance

In standard applications of the general linear model, parameters of the model are freely estimated. Because of this, little regard is given to the precise values of the regression weights, with primary concern for their statistical significance. But, with the ability to fix or constrain parameter estimates, new ways of thinking about regression models become possible. These new ways of thinking involve the degree to which parameter estimates from a new study approximate those from prior research. In this section, terms developed in the context of factor analysis—specifically the factorial invariance across samples—are used to portray different levels of parameter invariance.

Configural Invariance of Regression Parameters. The first and most basic form of parameter invariance may be called *configural invariance.* Under configural invariance, the same pattern of significant and nonsignificant predictors are found across samples. For example, in each of two or more samples, a particular set of two predictors may be significant predictors of a given outcome variable. After these two significant predictors are included in a regression model, no additional predictors add significantly to the equation. If this pattern holds, then configural invariance of regression parameters holds, as the same variables are significant predictors and the same variables are nonsignificant predictors in each sample. Thus, the outcome variable is best represented as a linear combination of the same predictor variables in each sample, even though the linear combination may be rather different across samples. This difference in the linear combinations across samples would be reflected in the regression parameters, which are free to vary across samples and may indeed vary widely.

Scalar Invariance of Regression Parameters. A more constrained version of configural invariance may be termed *scalar invariance* of regression parameters. Under scalar invariance, we begin by assuming that configural invariance holds, but add another stipulation: The regression parameters in one sample are a multiplicative function of regression parameters in another sample.

Perhaps an equation would help convey the nature of scalar invariance. Consider the following equation:

$$Y_i = \hat{B}_0 X_{i0} + \hat{B}_1 X_{i1} + \hat{B}_2 X_{i2} + \hat{E}_i \tag{7}$$

Let us assume that the three regression parameters— $\hat{B}_0$, $\hat{B}_1$, and $\hat{B}_2$— were estimated in one sample and that one would like to impose scalar invariance on these parameters in a second sample. The simplest way of doing this would be to write the following equation:

$$Y_i = \hat{c}_1 (\bar{B}_0 X_{i0} + \bar{B}_1 X_{i1} + \bar{B}_2 X_{i2}) + \hat{E}_i \tag{8}$$

where $\hat{c}_1$ is a new regression weight estimated in the second sample and the three regression weights, $\bar{B}_0$, $\bar{B}_1$, and $\bar{B}_2$, are fixed equal to the values of the corresponding estimated regression weights, $\hat{B}_0$, $\hat{B}_1$, and $\hat{B}_2$, respectively, from the preceding equation.

To perform this analysis, one would simply compute the linear combination of variables within the parentheses of Equation 8, use this new combination as the sole predictor of the dependent variable in a new sample, and specify that no intercept parameter should be estimated. Under this model, the following constraints are imposed:

$$\overset{\circ}{B_0} = \hat{c}_1 \bar{B}_0, \quad \overset{\circ}{B_1} = \hat{c}_1 \bar{B}_1, \quad \text{and} \quad \overset{\circ}{B_2} = \hat{c}_1 \bar{B}_2 \tag{9}$$

In a sense, two constraints have been imposed in the second sample. Instead of three regression parameters being estimated, only a single regression parameter, $\hat{c}_1$, is estimated. One way of thinking about the two constraints imposed is this: The parameter $\hat{c}_1$ is estimated to represent the multiplicative difference between the intercept terms in the two equations, and this same multiplicative relationship is also imposed on the two additional regression weights. With the same constraint holding on the two regression weights, two constraints have been imposed. In fact, the new constant $\hat{c}_1$ is estimated to improve the fit of the entire equation, so it simultaneously optimizes the fit for all three regression parameters.

The fit of the regression model with scalar invariance of parameters may be tested against a model in which all three regression parameters are estimated separately and anew in the second sample. The resulting F test would have two degrees of freedom in the numerator, corresponding to the two constraints on parameters in the nested regression model. If the F test were significant, this would be statistical evidence that the constraint on parameters led to a significant drop in the ability of the model to represent the data. Note, however, that one could also evaluate a practical index of drop in fit—the magnitude of the drop in the R^2. If sample size were large, the F test might be significant, but the drop in R^2 could be sufficiently small that one might opt to accept the constrained equation as an appropriate representation of the data. Of course, if the F test and the change in R^2 are both small and nonsignificant, then the scalar constraint on the regression weights leads to a model that adequately represents the relations between predictors and the criterion in the new sample.

Given adequate fit of the model under scalar constraints, the value of the new constant $\hat{c}_1$ and its standard error are of importance. If the new constant $\hat{c}_1$ were 1, then the constrained parameters in the new sample would be identical to those in the old sample. If the new constant $\hat{c}_1$ were smaller (or larger) than 1, then the regression parameters in the new sample would be multiplicatively smaller (or larger) than the parameters in the first sample. For example, if $\hat{c}_1$ were 2, then the regression parameters in the second sample would be exactly twice the size of the corresponding regression parameters in the first sample. Turning to the standard error of the constant, if the standard error shows that the new constant $\hat{c}_1$ does not differ significantly from 1, then the parameters in the second sample differ nonsignificantly from the parameters in the first equation. Even in such a case, something has been bought by the constraining process—the regression weights in the second sample are constrained to have the same pattern of values as in the first sample rather than letting the regression parameters vary freely in the second sample.

Metric Invariance of Regression Parameters. Metric invariance of regression parameters is only one more step from scalar invariance. In addition to assuming that regression weights exhibit the same configuration of significant and nonsignificant regression parameters in a new sample as well as scalar constraints on these parameters, one might consider a still more strict constraint, which is that the regression parameters in a new sample are numerically identical to those in a prior sample. This constraint—that regression parameters are numerically identical to those in a prior sample—may be termed *metric invariance.*

One way of thinking about metric invariance is to consider the regression model under scalar invariance, which was:

$$Y_i = \hat{c_1}\,(\bar{B_0}X_{i0} + \bar{B_1}X_{i1} + \bar{B_2}X_{i2}) + \hat{E_i} \tag{10}$$

If one imposed the further constraint that $\hat{c_1}$ equals 1, then one would move from scalar invariance to metric invariance.

One interesting aspect of a regression model with metric invariance of parameters is the fact that a non-zero R^2 is obtained, even though no estimates are made from the data in the new sample. In traditional approaches to regression analysis, one makes at least one estimate from the data, an intercept term, when specifying a model. If this is the only estimate in the equation, then the R^2 is equal to zero. But, under metric invariance, one makes no estimates from the data, but, because non-zero values of regression weights are provided, some variability about the mean of the dependent variable is represented in the model. This regression model—with metric constraints on regression parameters based on previous research—is probably a more appropriate baseline model against which alternative models are judged than the typical baseline model, having an R^2 of zero. Especially in research areas in which much is known about which predictor variables should be included when modeling a well-researched dependent variable, investigators should capitalize on prior research by representing the dependent variable as well as possible with their best guesses as to population regression weights. Only after doing so should they proceed to inquire whether aspects of the current sample or additional predictors can improve on their accumulated knowledge in the given domain.

APPLICATIONS OF NESTED REGRESSION MODEL TESTING OF KEY THEORETICAL HYPOTHESES

A One-Group Application

To illustrate how the preceding ideas may be applied in a research situation, I consider how data from the Sternberg memory scanning paradigm could be modeled. The Sternberg short-term memory scanning paradigm consists of a set of simple experimental trials, usually presented via microcomputer. On each trial, between one and five digits or letters are presented on the computer screen to the participant; these stimuli constitute the memory set for the trial, and the person studies the digits or letters for verification. After a given amount of study time, the screen goes blank. After the requisite interval, a single probe digit or letter is presented, and the subject must indicate as quickly as possible whether the probe digit was or was not in the memory set by pushing one or another of two response keys. In addition, the probe digit or letter may be presented in its usual complete form (i.e., nondegraded) or in a degraded form, in which a certain percentage of pixels of the digit or letter are removed.

The general findings are (a) that reaction time (RT) increases linearly with the number of items in the memory set (S), (b) that RT is somewhat slower for trials in which the probe digit was not in the memory set (T, for "truth" or correctness of the trial, coded 0 = correct, or "in" the memory set, and 1 = incorrect, or "not in" the memory set), (c) that the linear slopes for correct and incorrect problems are approximately equal, so that set size and correctness do not interact, and (d) that degraded probe digits or letters require more time to encode than do complete versions. Thus, it should be possible to represent RT on the memory scanning paradigm as:

$$Y_i = \hat{B}_0 X_{i0} + \hat{B}_S X_{iS} + \hat{B}_E X_{iE} + \hat{B}_T X_{iT} + \hat{E}_i \tag{11}$$

where Y_i is RT for trial i,
X_{i0} is the unit constant,
X_{iS} is the size of the memory set (1–5) for trial i,
X_{iE} is the encoding value for trial i, coded 0 for a trial with a standard, undegraded probe digit, and 1 for a trial with a degraded probe digit,
X_{iT} is the truth value for trial i, coded 0 for "in" the memory set, and 1 representing "not in" the memory set,
each regression parameter estimate— $\hat{B}_0$, $\hat{B}_S$, $\hat{B}_E$, and $\hat{B}_T$—has a subscript identifying the predictor variable to which it is associated,
and other symbols are as defined earlier.

Previous research has found that, across many studies, the regression weights for the predictors in Equation 11 are approximately an intercept of 400 ms, a slope of 40 ms for every unit increase in set size (S), and a 100 ms additional increment in RT for problems in which the probe digit is "not in" the memory set. In addition, although less extensively studied, we assume that presenting probe digits in a degraded form takes an additional 600 ms of processing time. Thus, our best guess of population estimates would be:

$$Y_i = 400\, X_{i0} + 40\, X_S + 600\, X_{iE} + 100\, X_{iT} + \bar{E}_i \tag{12}$$

where all symbols are as defined earlier.

The typical way of analyzing data from the memory scanning paradigm is to perform a 5 (set size) × 2 (regular vs. degraded digits) × 2 (in vs. not in memory set) analysis of variance, or ANOVA. This 5 × 2 × 2 design implicitly involves 20 parameter estimates, if one considers all nonlinear trends of memory set size and all interactions among the linear and nonlinear main effects. We could term the typical ANOVA model an unconstrained, exploratory model, in which all potential parameters are implicitly estimated and no constraints based on previous data are invoked.

However, given the considerable amount of prior research on the memory scanning paradigm and the population estimates provided, many alternative models exist that are more restricted than the unconstrained ANOVA model and that allow the researcher to benefit from prior research. For example, one could specify a configural invariance model, which would look like this:

$$Y_i = \hat{B}_0 X_{i0} + \hat{B}_S X_{iS} + \hat{B}_E X_{iE} + \hat{B}_T X_{iT} + \hat{E}_i \tag{13}$$

Under this model, all four regression parameters would be estimated anew in the present sample. However, the fit of this model could be tested statistically by comparing the fit of this model to that of the unconstrained ANOVA model. The resulting F ratio would have numerator degrees of freedom of 16, because the unconstrained ANOVA model has 20 estimates, whereas the nested configural invariance model has only 4 estimates. If the configural invariance model differed nonsignificantly statistically and/or practically from the ANOVA model, then much would have been tested. Specifically, the nonlinear trends of memory set size and all interactions among main effects would have been tested and rejected as aspects of the current data, consistent with prior research on this paradigm.

But, one need not stop here, as still more constrained versions of the model in Equation 13 could be tested. For example, one could specify a scalar invariance model, which would have the following form:

$$Y_i = \hat{c}_1 (400\ X_{i0} + 40\ X_{iS} + 600\ X_{iE} + 100\ X_{iT}) + \bar{E}_i \tag{14}$$

where all symbols have been defined earlier.

The scalar invariance model in Equation 14 is of considerable interest for at least three reasons. First, only a single estimate, $\hat{c}_1$, is made from the data, three fewer than the freely estimated model in Equation 13. Thus, the model in Equation 14 is nested within the model in Equation 13. Given this nesting relationship, the fit of the restricted model in Equation 14 may be tested against the less constrained model in Equation 13, using the F test described earlier. The resulting F ratio would have three numerator degrees of freedom, given the difference between four parameter estimates in the model in Equation 13 and the single estimate in the model in Equation 14.

Second, the model in Equation 14 retains the same ratio relations among regression weights as holds in our best guess of the population parameters, which were shown in Equation 12, but does not require that the parameter estimates are precisely equal to the population weights. For example, if $\hat{c}_1$ were 2, then all parameter estimates in the current sample would be exactly twice as large as the "best guess" population parameters. Such an outcome would suggest that persons in the present sample tend to process the problems in the same fashion as do typical samples, but take a longer time to complete each step of the process. This slowing of processing should have some theoretical interpretation, such as the age of the participants or the average intelligence of persons in the sample.

Third, the value of the single estimate, $\hat{c}_1$, and its standard error are of considerable theoretical importance. This estimate is a "slowing" or "speeding" coefficient. If $\hat{c}_1$ were less than 1, the present sample would perform all mental operations faster than the population; conversely, if $\hat{c}_1$ were greater than 1, then the sample performs operations slower than the population. But, regardless of whether the value of $\hat{c}_1$ were less than or greater than 1, the standard error of this estimate must be examined. Let us say that $\hat{c}_1$ was 1.5, implying moderate slowing of processing. However, if the standard error of $\hat{c}_1$ was .30, then the 95% confidence interval around the estimate would extend from about .90 to 2.10, basing this confidence interval on the mean plus and minus twice the standard error. Because 1 falls within the 95% confidence interval, the estimate of 1.5 does not differ significantly from 1; hence, the parameter estimates from the present sample do not differ significantly from the "best guess" population parameters.

Extension to Multiple Groups or Multiple Times of Measurement

To show the flexibility of this approach when applied to multiple groups or multiple times of measurement, I briefly consider a three-group model. In Table 9.1, a typical design matrix and its associated vector of regression weights are shown. These matrices represent coding of variables for the Sternberg memory scanning experiment for three groups. I assume that the three groups are groups of young adults, middle-aged adults, and older adults, respectively. The first 12 rows of the design matrix represent coded variables for the first group (young adults); the second 12 rows, coded variables for the second group (middle-aged adults); and the final 12 rows, coded variables for the third group (older adults).

The first column of the design matrix is a unit constant for all subjects, the second column a vector representing the number of items in the memory set (set size, or S, which varies between 1 and 5), the third column is an effects-coded variable indicating whether additional encoding is required due to the presence of a degraded stimulus (encoding, or E, with codes of 1 and –1), and the fourth column is an effects-coded variable indicating whether the probe digit was "in" or "not in" the memory set (truth, or T). Columns 5 and 6 are effects-coded pseudovariates indicating group membership, with codes of 1, 0, or –1. Columns 7, 8, and 9 consist of the element-by-element product of the first-group membership variable, Column 5, by Columns 2, 3, and 4, respectively. Likewise, Columns 10, 11, and 12 consist of the product of the second-group membership variable, Column 6, by Columns 2, 3, and 4, respectively. As should be clear, Columns 7 through 12 represent interactions of group membership and the main effects of S, E, and T.

Given this method of coding, the regression weights shown in the accompanying vector in Table 9.1 have the following interpretation. The first four regression weights are, respectively, the average intercept, $\bar{B}_0$, the average slope of the set size, $\bar{B}_S$, the average deviation in RT due to encoding of a degraded stimulus, $\bar{B}_E$, and the average deviation in RT due to whether the probe digit was "in" or "not in" the memory

TABLE 9.1

Typical Design Matrix With Its Associated Vector of Regression Weights

1	1	1	1	1	0	1	1	1	0	0	0
1	3	1	1	1	0	3	1	1	0	0	0
1	5	1	1	1	0	5	1	1	0	0	0
1	1	1	-1	1	0	1	1	-1	0	0	0
1	3	1	-1	1	0	3	1	-1	0	0	0
1	5	1	-1	1	0	5	1	-1	0	0	0
1	1	-1	1	1	0	1	-1	1	0	0	0
1	3	-1	1	1	0	3	-1	1	0	0	0
1	5	-1	1	1	0	5	-1	1	0	0	0
1	1	-1	-1	1	0	1	-1	-1	0	0	0
1	3	-1	-1	1	0	3	-1	-1	0	0	0
1	5	-1	-1	1	0	5	-1	-1	0	0	0
1	1	1	1	0	1	0	0	0	1	1	1
1	3	1	1	0	1	0	0	0	3	1	1
1	5	1	1	0	1	0	0	0	5	1	1
1	1	1	-1	0	1	0	0	0	1	1	-1
1	3	1	-1	0	1	0	0	0	3	1	-1
1	5	1	-1	0	1	0	0	0	5	1	-1
1	1	-1	1	0	1	0	0	0	1	-1	1
1	3	-1	1	0	1	0	0	0	3	-1	1
1	5	-1	1	0	1	0	0	0	5	-1	1
1	1	-1	-1	0	1	0	0	0	1	-1	-1
1	3	-1	-1	0	1	0	0	0	3	-1	-1
1	5	-1	-1	0	1	0	0	0	5	-1	-1
1	1	1	1	-1	-1	-1	-1	-1	-1	-1	-1
1	3	1	1	-1	-1	-3	-1	-1	-3	-1	-1
1	5	1	1	-1	-1	-5	-1	-1	-5	-1	-1
1	1	1	-1	-1	-1	-1	-1	1	-1	-1	1
1	3	1	-1	-1	-1	-3	-1	1	-3	-1	1
1	5	1	-1	-1	-1	-5	-1	1	-5	-1	1
1	1	-1	1	-1	-1	-1	1	-1	-1	1	-1
1	3	-1	1	-1	-1	-3	1	-1	-3	1	-1
1	5	-1	1	-1	-1	-5	1	-1	-5	1	-1
1	1	-1	-1	-1	-1	-1	1	1	-1	1	1
1	3	-1	-1	-1	-1	-3	1	1	-3	1	1
1	5	-1	-1	-1	-1	-5	1	1	-5	1	1

Associated vector of regression weights:
$\bar{B}_0$, $\bar{B}_S$, $\bar{B}_E$, $\bar{B}_T$, $\Delta B_0^{(1)}$, $\Delta B_0^{(2)}$, $\Delta B_S^{(1)}$, $\Delta B_E^{(1)}$, $\Delta B_T^{(1)}$, $\Delta B_S^{(2)}$, $\Delta B_E^{(2)}$, $\Delta B_T^{(2)}$

set, $\bar{B}_T$, where these averages are mean values of each parameter estimate across the three groups. The fifth and sixth regression weights, $\Delta B_0^{(1)}$ and $\Delta B_0^{(2)}$, represent the deviation of intercept values for Groups 1 and 2 from the average intercept. The seventh, eighth, and ninth regression weights—$\Delta B_S^{(1)}$, $\Delta B_E^{(1)}$, and $\Delta B_T^{(1)}$—represent the deviation of slope values for Group 1 from the average slopes across all groups for S, E, and T, respectively. Finally, the tenth, eleventh, and twelfth regression weights—$\Delta B_S^{(2)}$, $\Delta B_E^{(2)}$, and $\Delta B_T^{(2)}$—represent the deviation of slope values for Group 2 from the average slopes across all groups for S, E, and T, respectively.

The design matrix in Table 9.1 is able to represent precisely each of the four parameter estimates—the intercept and the slopes for S, E, and T—in each of the three groups. But, the regression parameter vector reveals that these are represented as combinations of parameter estimates. For example, the intercept for Group 1 may be calculated as ($\bar{B}_0 + \Delta B_0^{(1)}$), the intercept for Group 2 as ($\bar{B}_0 + \Delta B_0^{(2)}$), and the intercept for Group 3 as ($\bar{B}_0 - \Delta B_0^{(1)} - \Delta B_0^{(2)}$). Similar calculations are required to estimate the slope values for each predictor for each group. For example, the slope for set size, S, for each group would be ($\bar{B}_S + \Delta B_S^{(1)}$) for Group 1, ($\bar{B}_S + \Delta B_S^{(2)}$) for Group 2, and ($\bar{B}_S - \Delta B_S^{(1)} - \Delta B_S^{(2)}$) for Group 3.

One may test several restricted hypotheses using the design matrix in Table 9.1. For example, one could test whether slopes for set size S differed across groups by dropping the seventh and tenth predictors from the design matrix. With these predictors deleted, only a single column, Column 2, would estimate the single, common slope estimate for S across groups. If deletion of the seventh and tenth columns of the design matrix led to nonsignificant or small change in the R^2 for the equation, then one could conclude that the slope for S varied little across samples or, equivalently, that there was no significant group × set size interaction. Conversely, if deletion of the seventh and tenth columns led to a statistically significant and large change in R^2, one would conclude that slope values for S differed in important ways across samples or, equivalently, that there was a group × set size interaction. The types of constraints that may be tested using the design matrix in Table 9.1 are, however, fairly restricted. Moreover, constraints across parameter sets, such as constraining relations between S and E parameters, would be difficult or impossible.

To circumvent these problems, consider the design matrix and associated regression parameter vector shown in Table 9.2. As with the design matrix in Table 9.1, the rows of the design matrix in Table 9.2 consist of 12 rows of codes for Group 1, then 12 rows of codes for Group 2, and then 12 rows of codes for Group 3.

Next, inspect the 12 columns of the design matrix. Note that, for ease of reference, I refer to these 12 columns using superscripts and subscripts similar to those used for regression weights. For example, the first four columns of the design matrix consist of coded variates for Group 1. Specifically, these four columns represent for Group 1 the unit constant, the size of the memory set (S), the absence (0) or presence (1) of a degraded stimulus requiring additional encoding (E), and presence of a probe digit that was "in" (0) or "not in" (1) the memory set. Therefore, these four columns will be referred to as $X_0^{(1)}$, $X_S^{(1)}$, $X_E^{(1)}$, and $X_T^{(1)}$, respectively. Columns 5 through 8, or $X_0^{(2)}$ through $X_T^{(2)}$, represent corresponding coded variables for Group 2, and Columns 9 through 12, or $X_0^{(3)}$ through $X_T^{(3)}$, corresponding coded variables for Group 3.

Given the design matrix in Table 9.2, the first four regression parameter estimates have the following interpretation: $B_0^{(1)}$ is the intercept for young adults (Group 1), representing a basic amount of time to respond to a nondegraded probe digit that is "in" the memory set; $B_S^{(1)}$ is the additional time taken by young adults (Group 1) to make each comparison to elements in the memory set; $B_E^{(1)}$ is the additional time taken by young adults to process or resolve a degraded stimulus; and $B_T^{(1)}$ is the additional time taken by young adults to decide and respond that a probe digit was "not in" the memory set. The fifth through eighth regression weights have comparable interpretations with regard to middle-aged adults (Group 2), and the ninth through

Table 9.2
Revised Design Matrix With Its Associated
Vector of Regression Weights

1	1	0	0	0	0	0	0	0	0	0	0	
1	3	0	0	0	0	0	0	0	0	0	0	
1	5	0	0	0	0	0	0	0	0	0	0	
1	1	0	1	0	0	0	0	0	0	0	0	
1	3	0	1	0	0	0	0	0	0	0	0	
1	5	0	1	0	0	0	0	0	0	0	0	
1	1	1	0	0	0	0	0	0	0	0	0	
1	3	1	0	0	0	0	0	0	0	0	0	
1	5	1	0	0	0	0	0	0	0	0	0	
1	1	1	1	0	0	0	0	0	0	0	0	
1	3	1	1	0	0	0	0	0	0	0	0	
1	5	1	1	0	0	0	0	0	0	0	0	
0	0	0	0	1	1	0	0	0	0	0	0	$B_0^{(1)}$
0	0	0	0	1	3	0	0	0	0	0	0	$B_S^{(1)}$
0	0	0	0	1	5	0	0	0	0	0	0	$B_E^{(1)}$
0	0	0	0	1	1	0	1	0	0	0	0	$B_T^{(1)}$
0	0	0	0	1	3	0	1	0	0	0	0	$B_0^{(2)}$
0	0	0	0	1	5	0	1	0	0	0	0	$B_S^{(2)}$
0	0	0	0	1	1	1	0	0	0	0	0	$B_E^{(2)}$
0	0	0	0	1	3	1	0	0	0	0	0	$B_T^{(2)}$
0	0	0	0	1	5	1	0	0	0	0	0	$B_0^{(3)}$
0	0	0	0	1	1	1	1	0	0	0	0	$B_S^{(3)}$
0	0	0	0	1	3	1	1	0	0	0	0	$B_E^{(3)}$
0	0	0	0	1	5	1	1	0	0	0	0	$B_T^{(3)}$
0	0	0	0	0	0	0	0	1	1	0	0	
0	0	0	0	0	0	0	0	1	3	0	0	
0	0	0	0	0	0	0	0	1	5	0	0	
0	0	0	0	0	0	0	0	1	1	0	1	
0	0	0	0	0	0	0	0	1	3	0	1	
0	0	0	0	0	0	0	0	1	5	0	1	
0	0	0	0	0	0	0	0	1	1	1	0	
0	0	0	0	0	0	0	0	1	3	1	0	
0	0	0	0	0	0	0	0	1	5	1	0	
0	0	0	0	0	0	0	0	1	1	1	1	
0	0	0	0	0	0	0	0	1	3	1	1	
0	0	0	0	0	0	0	0	1	5	1	1	

twelfth regression weights have comparable interpretations with regard to older adults (Group 3). The identity and interpretation of each regression weight is preserved using a superscript to indicate group membership and subscript to reflect the mental processes involved.

Three important observations may be made concerning the design matrix and parameter estimates shown in Table 9.2. First, the R^2 resulting from application of the design matrix in Table 9.2 would be precisely equal to the R^2 obtained using the typically formatted design matrix in Table 9.1. Both of these design matrices have 12 columns, the 12 columns are linearly independent within each design matrix, and all four parameter estimates within each group are represented among the estimates. Although it seems at first surprising that the R^2 values would be identical, upon further consideration this seems straightforward (cf. Cohen, 1968).

Second, the parameter estimates obtained on the vector of parameter estimates in Table 9.2 for each group are identical to those obtained if only the data for that group were analyzed. For example, assume that data for young adults (Group 1) were selected and that an analysis were performed on data for this group alone. Four estimates would be obtained in this analysis—an intercept and slope values for S, E, and T; these four estimates would be identical to those in the parameter vector in Table 9.2 for Group 1. The identical outcome would hold for parameter estimates for Groups 2 and 3.

Third, and perhaps most important, because the parameter estimates are obtained directly for each group, an extremely wide variety of constraints on parameter estimates may be invoked and tested. For example, a researcher may wish to test whether the parameter estimates within each group are scalar invariant with the population parameters discussed earlier in this chapter. To do this, the researcher could form linear combinations of the predictors for each group, using the "best guess" population estimates as weights. Then, these three linear combinations would be used as predictors in a multiple regression, specifying that no separate intercept should be estimated. The resulting equation could be represented as:

$$RT = \hat{c}_1^{(1)}(400 \times X_0^{(1)} + 40 \times X_S^{(1)} + 600 \times X_E^{(1)} + 100 \times X_T^{(1)}) + \quad (15)$$

$$\hat{c}_1^{(2)}(400 \times X_0^{(2)} + 40 \times X_S^{(2)} + 600 \times X_E^{(2)} + 100 \times X_T^{(2)}) +$$

$$\hat{c}_1^{(3)}(400 \times X_0^{(3)} + 40 \times X_S^{(3)} + 600 \times X_E^{(3)} + 100 \times X_T^{(3)}) + \overset{\circ}{E}$$

where RT is the dependent variable of reaction time, the elements within parentheses are the weighted combinations of predictors for each group, three estimates are made from the data ($\hat{c}_1^{(1)}$, $\hat{c}_1^{(2)}$, and $\hat{c}_1^{(3)}$), the error term is listed as $\overset{\circ}{E}$ to denote the fact that constrained regression estimates are obtained, and other symbols were defined previously.

The estimated parameters $\hat{c}_1^{(1)}$, $\hat{c}_1^{(2)}$, and $\hat{c}_1^{(3)}$ are multipliers of the population parameters for each group. Thus, within Group 1, the following constraints are invoked :

$$\overset{\circ}{B}_0^{(1)} = \hat{c}_1^{(1)} \bar{B}_0 = \hat{c}_1^{(1)} \times 400 \quad (16)$$

$$\overset{\circ}{B}_S^{(1)} = \hat{c}_1^{(1)} \bar{B}_S = \hat{c}_1^{(1)} \times 40 \quad (17)$$

$$\overset{\circ}{B}_E^{(1)} = \hat{c}_1^{(1)} \bar{B}_E = \hat{c}_1^{(1)} \times 600 \quad (18)$$

$$\overset{\circ}{B}_T^{(1)} = \hat{c}_1^{(1)} \bar{B}_T = \hat{c}_1^{(1)} \times 100 \quad (19)$$

and similar constraints are invoked in Groups 2 and 3 through the estimates $\hat{c}_1^{(2)}$ and $\hat{c}_1^{(3)}$, respectively. Because only three parameter estimates were made in this model, the viability of the constraints may be evaluated statistically by comparing the fit of this model against the freely estimated model shown in Table 9.2. Given the difference in number of parameter estimates, the resulting F ratio would have 9 numerator degrees of freedom. The effects of invoking these constraints may also be evaluated practically, by noting the difference in the variance accounted for by each model. If the highly constrained model in Equation 15, with only three parameter estimates, fit virtually as well as the less constrained model, in Table 9.2, with 12 estimates, then the former model would clearly be preferred.

In addition to the issue of parsimony of the three-estimate model in Equation 15, a more important benefit of this model is the theoretical interpretation of the three estimates, $\hat{c}_1^{(1)}$, $\hat{c}_1^{(2)}$, and $\hat{c}_1^{(3)}$. These coefficients represent the slowing constants for young adult, middle-aged adult, and older adult groups, respectively. Under a basic interpretation of the general slowing hypothesis, young adults process information at an optimal speed. With aging, slowing of mental processes should occur, particularly in older adults. Given this, if the sample of young adults were a random and representative sample from its population, then one would expect the estimate of $\hat{c}_1^{(1)}$ to be near 1, indicating that the regression weights for the young adult sample are approximately equal to the population parameters that have been based on samples of young adults (i.e., college students). The prediction with regard to the coefficient $\hat{c}_1^{(2)}$ for the middle-aged adult sample is less clear. Perhaps persons in this sample have not yet begun to exhibit cognitive slowing; if so, the parameter estimate for this coefficient would be near 1. However, if some cognitive slowing were apparent, then the parameter estimate would be expected to be above 1. Finally, for the older adult sample, cognitive slowing would be expected, so the coefficient $\hat{c}_1^{(3)}$ should fall above 1. Given sufficient power, the 95% confidence interval for $\hat{c}_1^{(3)}$ should not include 1. If this coefficient were 1.5 times larger than that for the young adult sample, this would indicate that the older adult sample took, on average, 50% more time to execute each mental process.

The restricted model in Equation 15 is only one of a host of alternative restricted models that could be entertained; limitations of space in the present chapter prevent consideration of these additional models. Moreover, I note that the design matrix in Table 9.2 is appropriate for three independent groups, but would require modification if the three groups represented a single sample measured at three times of measurement. One would still wish to format the design matrix as shown in Table 9.2, as this would enable the direct estimation of the model parameters at each time of measurement. But, the design matrix must be augmented to reflect the dependence of observations across time. This could be accomplished by the addition of effects-coded variates for each subject or by criterion scaling (Pedhazur, 1977). Because these results are well known, little need be said here about the implementation of these methods.

CONCLUDING REMARKS

The time has come to alter our approaches to the modeling of data in the behavioral and psychological sciences. From the very start of training in the use of statistical methods, undergraduate and graduate students should be taught methods that embody the testing of theoretical conjectures based on prior research, subjecting these conjectures to danger of refutation. Null hypothesis testing does not accomplish this goal; most commentators on null hypothesis testing argue that null hypothesis testing is a dead end, impeding progress in psychological science, rather than abetting it. The approach to model specification, estimation, and testing outlined in this chapter is one attempt to design a hypothesis testing machinery that yields predictions based on prior research and then determines whether these conjectures based on prior research must be amended in light of current data. Only by employing such methods will we achieve our scientific goals of rejecting our theoretical models when they do not fit the data. Only then will we be forced to develop better theoretical accounts of the psychological phenomena under study.

CHAPTER TEN

Selectivity and Generalizability in Longitudinal Research: On the Effects of Continuers and Dropouts

Todd D. Little
Yale University

Ulman Lindenberger
Heiner Maier
Max Planck Institute for Human Development, Berlin

Perhaps the quintessential goal in science is to ensure the accuracy of a study's results. When this goal is met, a study's conclusions can be generalized to a larger space of potential measurements and ultimately to an intended spectrum of generalization instead of being restricted to just the observed events and the sample in question. This goal is encapsulated in concepts such as *measurement representativeness,* which refers to the degree to which observations can stand for other nonmeasured events (McArdle, 1994), and *validity,* which refers to the degree of veridicality of conclusions that are drawn from empirical findings.

A common but often neglected threat to generalizability in longitudinal research is sample selectivity, or nonrandom participation. In this context, selectivity refers to the potential for systematic differences between continuers and dropouts. Although selective participation is only one possible factor endangering a study's validity, in our view, it is also one of the least considered threats to the representativeness and generalizability of longitudinal investigations. Few empirical studies have examined selectivity effects fully or attempted to quantify their influences on variables measured at later time points (cf. Lindenberger et al., 1999; McArdle & Hamagami, 1991; McArdle, Hamagami, Elias, & Robbins, 1991). In this chapter, our primary goal is to emphasize the importance of examining selectivity and to review general procedures to analyze their effects (see also Lindenberger et al., 1999).

Overview of the Problem

Sample attrition occurs when not all persons who have been asked to participate in a longitudinal study partake in all assessments. Attrition can lead to selectivity (or bias) if the persons who continue to participate (i.e., *continuers*) differ from those who do not (e.g., *dropouts*) on any characteristics that are relevant to a study (Kessler, Little, & Groves, 1995; Little & Rubin, 1987). Selectivity stemming from sample attrition is a unique threat to validity that is quite distinct from other sources of possible bias such as those related to sampling procedures (i.e., selective sampling vs. selective dropout; Baltes, Reese, & Nesselroade, 1988) or measurement and analytic procedures (T. D. Little, Lindenberger, & Nesselroade, in press). For example, bias related to nonrepresentative sampling of persons is well understood. Here, as is commonly acknowledged, random sampling procedures (i.e., whereby each person in a population has an equal chance of being selected) provide sound ways of minimizing systematic sampling-related biases (Kruskal & Mosteller, 1979a, 1979b, 1979c). Generally speaking, random sampling is advantageous because systematic sources of bias are much less likely to occur than with nonrandom sampling, thereby guarding against selectivity, or invalidity, due to sampling.

In typical longitudinal studies, however, researchers have little control over who drops out and who does not, and this process may or may not occur randomly. If (non)participation is random (i.e., unsystematic) then, all other things being equal, the integrity of a study would be maintained. If (non)participation is nonrandom, then, independent of the degree of generalizability associated with other aspects of a study, the effects of sample attrition would lead to some degree of bias. Under such conditions, conclusions based on selective samples are no longer fully accurate reflections of the original parent sample or the intended population. When sample attrition has lead to some degree of sample selectivity, all conclusions would need to be qualified accordingly (i.e., acknowledging and/or accounting for the estimated degree of observed selectivity).

A related problem in longitudinal designs is the effect that continuers have on the outcomes of a study. Those who continue may engender characteristics that also bias the study's results. For example, continuers have more exposure to various aspects of the testing situation. Repeated exposure can lead to a number of unwanted influences, from practice and memory effects to reactivity and boredom. Although these influences are not strictly related to selectivity influences, they are associated with the selective status of being a continuing participant. Therefore, not only do the characteristics of dropouts affect the outcomes of a study, the characteristics of the continuers do as well.

In what follows, we describe procedures for assessing the degree of selectivity and thereby the degree of representativeness and generalizability in longitudinal studies. Some of these procedures are exemplified using a fictitious example based on data from the Action Control and Child Development Project (T. D. Little, Oettingen, & Baltes, 1995), and more detailed examples can be found on the resource web page of this volume (http://www.mpib-berlin.mpg.de/research_resources/index.html). However, before we present our overview of the types of selectivity questions and review methodologies that can be applied to examine them, we first define concepts related to selectivity.

On Examining Participation Selectivity

In any study, values on variables are assigned to persons or groups of persons. Depending on the topic of study and the type of variable, these measurements are typically summarized as frequencies (prevalence rates), means, variances, and correlations. These mathematical summaries of the distributions of scores are used to characterize a sample and to address substantively meaningful questions. For example, (a) what proportion of adolescents smoke or drink alcohol (prevalence), (b) how large is the social network of rejected children versus popular children (mean), (c) how large are individual differences in intellectual abilities among 70- to 80-year-olds (variance), and (d) how closely linked are agency beliefs and school performance (correlation)?

Without further information, the validity of such statements is limited to those participants who were actually measured on the relevant variables. In other words, a study's conclusions are initially restricted to only those individuals who actually complete the measurement process. Because not all persons selected for a longitudinal study share the same participation profile and because each participation profile may have selective influences that are related to it, the question arises whether examining the full original sample (i.e., the parent sample) would have yielded different results—are the results based on continuers also true for the parent sample and, by implication, the population to which one wishes to generalize?

For instance, adolescents from disadvantaged households or with motivational difficulties may be less likely to continue in a longitudinal study of agency and school achievement. Conversely, adolescents who are quite conscientious or have high achievement motivation may be more likely to continue in a study. In scenarios such as these, statements about the links between agency beliefs and performance may, for example, misrepresent the true relations in the original sample and the population. Generally speaking then, validity is limited to the extent that observed (as well as non-observed) characteristics predicting participation or nonparticipation are correlated with variables of interest. Biased results would emerge, of necessity, if variables predicting those who drop out versus those who continue are systematically related to the variables under scrutiny (Graham & Hofer, chap. 11, this volume; Little & Rubin, 1987).

Quite too commonly, selectivity is addressed only in terms of mean-level differences between dropouts and continuers. Such an approach, as we emphasize in our discussion, is deficient because a greater wealth of information must also be examined in order to determine the full effects of selectivity. For example, even though questions about frequency or mean-level differences are often posed, information about the variances and covariances is often neglected and, in addition, estimates of the effects of such differences on later relations among variables are nearly non-existent.

In our view, at least two types of selectivity-related questions can be examined (these questions are described in more detail next). The first question looks at systematic differences between participants and nonparticipants on variables that are measured in common to the subgroups. The second type of question looks at the influence that any systematic differences may have had on the core outcomes of a longitudinal study. Although both questions address similar aspects of selectivity, examining each type of question provides a full and informative picture of the degree of selectivity and allows any biasing effects in a longitudinal sample to be considered.

Selectivity Analyses: Goals and a Paradox

Selectivity analyses of longitudinal data represent a methodological precaution to reduce the likelihood of false conclusions and misleading generalizations (Lindenberger et al., 1999). Assessing the degree of selectivity helps to address basic validity questions, such as, are educational levels overestimated because fewer people of lower education agree to participate in a study than do those with higher education (or underestimated for some similar reason), or is the variance of intelligence underestimated because both good performers and low performers are more likely to drop out than individuals of average intelligence (or overestimated for some similar reason)?

Unfortunately, in trying to answer such questions, selectivity analyses are confronted with a fundamental paradox: In order to optimally document the degree and nature of selectivity, precisely the information that is missing must be known. The "Catch-22" then, is that to truly know the characteristics of the nonparticipants, they would have had to have been participants. On the other hand, even with only limited information on dropouts, selectivity analyses can still yield useful information regarding the representativeness and generalizability of the obtained results.

A minimum precondition of selectivity analyses, therefore, is that at least some basic pieces of information are gathered on all persons, including early dropouts (Dalenius, 1988; von Eye, 1989; Herzog & Rodgers, 1988; Oh & Scheuren, 1983; Panel on Incomplete Data, 1983). At the most sparse level, external sources of information such as basic census data can be used. At the other extreme, longitudinal studies that utilize large batteries at each wave have a wealth of information available regarding the possible selectivity of dropouts versus continuers.

In relation to this paradox, however, we must emphasize that selectivity analyses are limited in that they can only show the extent of observed selectivity and not the extent of selectivity that is possible in principle. Selectivity analyses try to relate available data to each other and to make optimal use of the inherent information, but obviously they cannot deal with issues for which additional information is necessary. This necessary deficit is especially relevant for nonparticipants for whom only a few variables can be used to document any observable selectivity (e.g., early dropouts).

Whether more information would have identified greater or more selectivity effects, however, cannot be answered conclusively.

Selectivity Subgroupings

We have described selectivity subgroupings, thus far, in the general terms of participants and nonparticipants. As mentioned in our general introduction, one common form of attrition is to end participation at some point after a study has begun (i.e., dropouts). Although the concept of a dropout is well understood, one type of dropout is often overlooked. Namely, those who dropout at the beginning of a study, before the first measurement is taken. Even with a truly representative sample of possible participants, dropouts at this very early stage of a study, for various reasons (unwilling, unable, unreachable), reflect possible sources of selective attrition. Early dropouts may lead to selectivity because, for example, they may be more likely to be married, come from single-parent families, be of higher socioeconomic status, and so on. Clearly, such differential characteristics can lead to fundamental bias in the results of an investigation (Baltes et al., 1988). In fact, even if a study is not longitudinal, the effect of early dropouts can lead to selectivity in the sample. In this regard, many of the selectivity analyses that we describe are also relevant to nonlongitudinal research designs.

In addition to the basic groupings (continuers and dropouts), other groupings can be introduced. For example, *returners* would be individuals who participated in earlier assessments, dropped out, but then returned for later assessments. In many cases, alternative methodologies for treating missing data can be utilized to condition the data set such that the information on the returners is reflected in the data (see Graham & Hofer, chap. 11, this volume; Wothke, chap. 12, this volume). In terms of our general discussion of selectivity, such groups can also be examined for the degree to which they influence the patterns of results inherent in the data. That is, the procedures we review are generalizable to other types of selective influence.

Finally, a related feature of some longitudinal studies is to include *new participants* at later time points. As with returners, new participants can also be used to examine for selectivity effects. For example, the new participants can be compared to both the continuers and the dropouts to determine the robustness of possible selectivity effects, and effects of early dropouts in both the original sample and the newly added sample can be compared for similarities and differences, and so on. Although such design features can complicate the picture, the generality of the methods that we describe is sufficient to accommodate these various forms of comparisons in order to examine the degree of representativeness and generalizability of a study's results.

In any longitudinal investigation, the general classifications between dropouts and continuers will be relevant for examining the degree of bias that is inherent in the sample under scrutiny. However, for studies stretching over a longer period of time, we augment these dichotomies with the graded concept of *participation levels* or participation depth (Lindenberger et al., 1999). For selectivity analyses, this distinction has the important advantage that, at each wave (i.e., from one participation level to the next), the continuers can be compared with early, midway, and late dropouts on all previously measured variables. In this way, one can identify (a) variables that initially distinguish the two groups (early dropouts vs. continuers) and (b) variables that progressively differ or progressively converge in characterizing the nature of the continuing subsample in relation to the different levels of participation.

Another advantage of a levels approach to selectivity analyses is that estimates for constructs that are assessed at later time points can be calculated, given certain assumptions, such that they take into account the observed selectivity at previous time points. In other words, the later estimates can be adjusted given the degree of selectivity implicated by the early subsample of dropouts. These adjusted estimates can then be compared to the observed (i.e., unadjusted) estimates to index the degree of selectivity that is present in the data and the degree to which statements or conclusions would then need to be cautioned.

THE TWO TYPES OF SELECTIVITY QUESTIONS

To clarify the relations between the types of selectivity questions and methods that can be used to examine them, we employ a formalized representation of a longitudinal data structure (Lindenberger et al., 1999). With V_{ti}, we refer to the variables (i.e., variable vectors) related to different participation levels or times of measurement (e.g., V_{t1} = Time 1 variables, V_{t2} = Time 2 variables, and so on). For example, for persons who participate in all times of measurement, we have observations (i.e., value assignments on variables) for the groups of variables measured at Time 1, V_{t1}, Time 2, V_{t2}, and so on, up to the final time of measurement, V_{tn}. For persons who drop out after the first measurement occasion, for example, only observations on the variables V_{t1} are available.

For each time of measurement, we define y_{ti} as an indicator of participation versus nonparticipation. For example, y_{t1} = 1 if a person participated at level 1 (i.e., Time 1). If a person was not assessed at level i, y_{ti} is set to zero. We refer to y_{ti} as the participation indicator for a given time of measurement. Each participation indicator can then be used to determine a participation profile. A participation profile, p, is defined as the sum of each y_{ti} where y_{ti} is multiplied by 10 for each participation level higher than y_{ti}. For example, if a study has three times of measurement, p = $(y_{t1} \times 10 \times 10)$ + $(y_{t2} \times 10)$ + y_{t3}. A participation profile provides a unique index of each observed pattern of participation in the longitudinal study. With three times of measurement, for example, seven unique profiles are possible (e.g., 111, 110, 011, 101, 100, 010, and 001).

The statistical methods that can be used to assess selectivity questions are based on the assumption that V_{ti} and p reflect samples from a "superpopulation" that is characterized by a probability distribution (Cassel, Särndal, & Wretman, 1977). The concept of a superpopulation is useful because it allows aspects of the subsamples to be expressed as parameters and allows use of standard statistical procedures to estimate them. In other words, given this assumption of a superpopulation, various statistical methods can be applied to address the two different types of questions that can be posed to clarify sample selectivity.

Selectivity Question Type I: Multivariate Differences Between Participation Subgroups

The first type of selectivity question focuses on the multivariate differences between the participation subgroups. From this viewpoint, the classifications of dropouts, returners, continuers, and so on would be used as an independent variable to compare differences in the multivariate relations among the measured variables and constructs that are common to the subgroups. This type of selectivity question focuses on whether a given participation profile has a different set of relations among the variables than another profile. For example, do continuers differ from dropouts in terms of the means, variances, or covariances on the previously observed variables?

In other words, for each observed participation profile (p):

$$E\ (V_{ti} \mid p_j, y_{ti} = 1) = E\ (V_{ti} \mid p_k, y_{ti} = 1), \text{ where } j \neq k, \tag{1}$$

and

$$cov\ (V_{ti} \mid p_j, y_{ti} = 1) = cov\ (V_{ti} \mid p_k, y_{ti} = 1), \text{ where } j \neq k. \tag{2}$$

Here, if continuers differ from dropouts, some aspects of the means, variances, and/ or covariances among the variables at Time i (V_{ti}) for the continuers are not the same as for the dropouts, for example. Under such conditions, some degree of selectivity is present that would compromise the integrity of any generalizations to the original population from which the sample was originally drawn.

In our view, the optimal method of analysis in this case would be a multiple-group comparison of the mean and covariance structures (MACS; T. D. Little, 1997; McArdle & Hamagami, 1991) among the variables and constructs, with a grouping defined for each participation profile, p, and where $y_{ti} = 1$. In comparison to other procedures such as ANOVA, MANOVA, or a Box-M test, a MACS approach allows one to examine all of the primary moments (i.e., means, variances, and covariances) and to conduct significance tests for single matrix elements as well as groups of elements. This flexibility allows one to pinpoint those elements that reflect selectivity effects and those that do not. In other words, MACS analyses are ideally suited to examine selectivity effects on the means, variances, and covariances or correlations of continuous and normally distributed variables. We note, however, that the techniques are not suited, for example, to determine logistic probabilities for frequency distributions (see Lindenberger et al., 1999) and may be problematic when the sample sizes of specific participation profiles become too small.

Selectivity Question Type II: Projected Effects of Sample Attrition on Later Measured Constructs

The second type of selectivity question focuses on the projected effects of differential participation profiles when two or more different levels of participation are examined. For example, had the dropouts been included in the completing sample, would the relations among the constructs be different? With this type of question, information from previous measurements that include dropouts, returners, and/or new participants is used to provide projected estimates of the relations among the variables. As mentioned, these projections, or adjusted estimates, can be compared with the observed relations to index the degree of selectivity effects. Stated more generally, what are the effects of the different participation profiles on the basic moments (i.e., means, variances, and covariances) of the variables at later points in time?

In other words, across each observed participation profile (p):

$$E\ (V_{tn} \mid p_j, y_{ti} = 1) = E\ (V_{tn} \mid V_{ti}, p_k, y_{ti} \neq 0),\ \text{where}\ j \neq k, \tag{3}$$

and

$$\text{cov}\ (V_{tn} \mid p_j, y_{ti} = 1) = \text{cov}\ (V_{tn} \mid V_{ti}, p_k, y_{ti} \neq 0),\ \text{where}\ j \neq k. \tag{4}$$

For this type of question, at least three approaches can be taken. A first approach is to use the selectivity formula developed by Pearson (1903), Aitkin (1934), and Lawley (1943). This general formula provides estimates of the means, variances, and covariances that take into account (adjust for) observed selectivity (Meredith, 1964, 1993; Muthén, Kaplan, & Hollis, 1987; Smith, Holt, & Smith, 1989). From this vantage point, variables assessed or estimated for previous points in time are referred to as *selection variables,* and these variables are distinguished from the *dependent variables* (e.g., variables on which only continuers have scores). Means, variances, and covariances of the continuing sample are estimated on the basis of (a) the linear relationships between the selection variables and the dependent variables and (b) the differences in means between the lower level samples and the continuing sample.

The Pearson-Aitkin-Lawley method uses information on the relationships between the means, variances, and covariances assuming that the regressions of the dependent variables on the selection variables are linear and that the conditional variances are constant (homoscedasticity; although Meredith, 1993, suggests that this assumption is unnecessary). Under these assumptions (which cannot be tested empirically), the method allows a direct estimation of selectivity effects on the persons who complete a study. Within the framework of the linear model, this projection makes optimal use of nearly all available information (Meredith, 1964).

Aitkin (1934) and Lawley (1943) also showed that their formula can be applied repeatedly. For selectivity analyses, the additivity of the successive use of the basic formulae means that the variables available at Time 1 can be used to estimate, or project, the original sample's effects on the Time 2 variables. Then, the variables at Time 1 and 2 (i.e., the observed values at Time 1 and the estimated values at Time 2) can serve as selection variables and the variables available at Time 3 become the dependent variables, and so on.

When interpreting the results obtained with this method, the following caveat, related to the basic paradox of selectivity analysis mentioned earlier, needs to be kept in mind: The more closely variables at lower participation levels (i.e., the selection variables) are associated with variables on the following level (i.e., the independent variables), the more meaningful the calculated estimates become (Lindenberger et al., 1999). Dependent variables that do not have variables that predict them to any degree at previous measurement occasions possess very little information that can be used to correct them and, by necessity, the dependent variables will maintain the values that were actually observed in the subsample. Another potential disadvantage of using the Pearson-Aitkin-Lawley formula is that standard errors of the reference values are not automatic outcomes of the procedure. Alternative approaches to estimating the standard errors, such as by bootstrapping the samples or systematically imputing the parameter estimates, would need to be applied.

A second approach to answer this second type of selectivity question is to use full information maximum likelihood estimation procedures to model the relations among all pieces of information that are present across the various participation profiles (see McArdle & Bell, chap. 5, this volume; Wothke, chap. 12, this volume). One advantage of this technique is that the maximum likelihood estimator provides information that is quite useful to examine the significance of selectivity; namely, standard errors of estimates. Another advantage is that the selectivity influences of all subgroupings are simultaneously estimated. With the Pearson-Aitkin-Lawley approach, one needs to employ the formula a number of times for each relevant comparison.

A third approach to answer this second type of question is to impute the missing information using the full information that is available in the data set. Although imputation techniques are powerful, guidelines on the limits of how much of a data set can be imputed reliably have yet to be established (see Graham & Hofer, chap. 11, this volume).

Summary

The two selectivity questions refer to (a) the differences between participation subgroups on the means, variances, and covariances of observed variables and constructs that the subgroups share in common; and (b) the relationships between variables at previous time points and variables assessed at later time points, which are used to project, or adjust, the estimates of the multivariate relations in the completing subsample.

If differences between the various subgroups (e.g., dropouts, continuers) on the analyzed variables become apparent using the various procedures, it indicates that characteristics of the participants and nonparticipants have influenced the obtained results and some selectivity is present. The extent of selectivity can be represented by the reference values that emerge from the analyses. Clearly, such information is useful to determine both the degree of selectivity and, by implication, the degree of generalizability. However, we must emphasize, again, that the reverse does not necessarily hold. Finding no differences does not indicate that sample selectivity has not occurred. For instance, some relevant variables that predict sample attrition may not have been assessed in the first place and therefore could not be analyzed. This problem is particularly important for analyses of sample loss at the earliest stages of participation (e.g., early dropouts vs. continuers). At this level, only rudimentary demographic variables might be all that is available. In addition, the procedures that we outline here do not capture all forms of possible sample selectivity. They are limited to frequency distributions, means, variances, and covariances and the linear relations among them. However, given that these basic statistics are the most common and robust summaries of distributions, they are still quite relevant for most longitudinal investigations.

BRIEF EMPIRICAL EXAMPLE

Details of the Samples and the Data

To demonstrate some of these techniques, we created two subsamples from a group of 425 boys and girls (approximately equally distributed across grades 2–6) with complete data at two times of measurement (see T. D. Little, Oettingen, & Baltes, 1995; T. D. Little, Oettingen, Stetsenko, & Baltes, 1995; Oettingen, Little, Lindenberger, & Baltes, 1994 for details of the sample). To mimic a selective process, we randomly (but with a systematic bias) assigned participants to be dropouts or continuers. The systematic bias was introduced by using the intellective skill scores (i.e., the Raven progressive matrices) of the participants. Specifically, we selected more participants with low Raven scores to be dropouts (approximately a 2:1 ratio). The dropout group ($n = 122$) thereby represents a subgroup that is selective with regard to Raven intelligence. In order to simplify our example, we selected three constructs to examine for selectivity: school performance, academic achievement, and personal agency.

For the school performance measure, we used the teacher-assigned grades in math and language. For academic achievement, we used the scores from the math and language subscale of the Begabungstestsystem (BTS), a German-language achievement test. For the personal agency measure, we used the agency beliefs for effort, ability, and luck from the Control, Agency, and Means-ends Interview (CAMI; T. D. Little, Oettingen, & Baltes, 1995). Agency beliefs, which are similar to self-efficacy beliefs (Bandura, 1997), reflect a child's personal perception of whether he or she can utilize such means as effort, ability, and luck to obtain good school grades.

Selectivity Question Type I

To exemplify this question we conducted a two-group MACS analysis comparing the continuers and dropouts on the constructs represented at the first time of measurement. We used the MACS framework detailed by T. D. Little (1997).

Assessing Measurement Equivalence

When fit as a combined multiple-group model with no cross-group equality constraints, the basic model showed acceptable fit, $\chi^2_{(22)}$ = 28.73, *NNFI* = .992, *IFI* = .9996, *RMSEA* = .0402, indicating that the general structure is tenable. To test for measurement equivalence, we first evaluated the loadings and then, because this model was tenable, subsequently added constraints to the intercepts. Specifically, when invariance of the loadings and intercepts was enforced, the overall model fit was again quite acceptable, $\chi^2_{(28)}$ = 37.28, *NNFI* = .991, *IFI* = .994, *RMSEA* = .0406.

Taken as a whole, all the fit indices showed quite minimal differences in the sequence of steps between the freely estimated model and the measurement-equivalent model. Therefore, on the basis of the minimal differences in fit between Model 1 and Model 2 (i.e., a modeling rationale; see T. D. Little, 1997), these results indicate that the constructs have equivalent measurement properties across the two groups (continuers vs. dropouts). If measurement equivalence were not tenable, the nature of the selectivity effects would be quite pronounced because it would have affected the underlying factorial composition among the indicators, yielding noncomparable constructs. As a result, selectivity would be qualitative in nature and the quantitative degree of selectivity could not be estimated. In other words, such a situation would be quite problematic and reflect a serious threat to the validity of any conclusions. On the other hand, with comparably measured constructs, the nature of selectivity can be quantified and evaluated in terms of the degree of possible bias.

Testing for Selectivity Differences

Because construct comparability was tenable, we tested the three sets of basic moments for differences across the participation subsamples; specifically, we examined (a) equality of the latent means, (b) equality of the latent standard deviations, and (c) equality of the latent correlations. Table 10.1 contains the nested-model comparisons used to test for possible differences on these parameters.

As seen in Table 10.1, two of the tests of equivalence on the latent parameters were significant, indicating some degree of selectivity across the different participation profiles. For the mean-level tests, all three constructs showed significant differences whereby the dropouts had lower school performance, lower academic achievement, and lower personal agency. However, the selective process did not influence the variances of the three constructs (see tests of the standard deviations in Table 10.1). Finally, the correlational structure among the constructs also showed some evidence of

TABLE 10.1
Multivariate Comparison of Continuers Versus Dropouts

Tested parameter	$\chi^2_{(31)}$	Difference test		
		$\Delta\chi^2$	Δdf	p
Means	43.8	8.0	3	<.05
Standard deviations	36.5	0.7	3	>.80
Correlations	42.4	6.6	3	<.10

Note. Comparison $\chi^2_{(28)}$ = 35.8; Δ = a difference between the comparison model and the tested models; χ^2 = the maximum likelihood chi-squared statistic; df = degrees of freedom; p = the probability level.

selectivity, although the effects were not as pronounced as the mean-level effects. Follow-up analyses revealed that the correlational manifold among the three constructs was higher in the continuing sample than in the dropout sample. Specifically, for continuers versus dropouts, respectively, the correlation between personal agency and school performance was .71 versus .57; between personal agency and academic achievement, .34 versus .03; and finally, between school performance and academic achievement, the correlation was .54 versus .38.

Given these differences, one would be compelled to conclude that the continuing sample was no longer representative of the original sample and that various sources of selective bias have influenced various aspects of and relations among the measured variables. One problem, however, is that analyses such as these still do not indicate the degree of bias that the selectivity effects have on the parameter estimates at later measurement occasions. To address questions such as this, one needs to utilize an analysis that explicitly examines the influence of selectivity on the later time points. We now turn to one such approach.

Selectivity Question Type II

Table 10.2 shows the results of our analyses addressing the second type of selectivity question. Here we used the full information maximum likelihood approach wherein the complete longitudinal model is fit to all 425 participants, but the 122 dropouts have no values on the variables at the second measurement occasion. In the first column of Table 10.2, as a point of comparison, we present the results of the analyses as performed only on the subsample of participants who were assessed at each measurement occasion. These values would be the information from which one would typically draw conclusions.

In comparison to these values, the second column in Table 10.2 presents the analysis that include the subsample of dropouts. Here, the information on the dropouts at Time 1 is explicitly represented in the analyses such that the parameter estimates at Time 2 include the influences of the dropout subsample.

TABLE 10.2
Selectivity Bias in Estimates of Time 2 Parameters

Focal parameter at occasion 2	Continuers	Continuers with dropouts	Population
Variance AGENCY	.942	.923	.984
Variance PERFORMANCE	1.037	1.041	1.038
Variance ACHIEVEMENT	.859	.862	.897
Corr (AGENCY, PERFORMANCE)	.732	.726	.713
Corr (AGENCY, ACHIEVEMENT)	.512	.488	.444
Corr (ACHIEVEMENT, ACHIEVEMENT)	.637	.618	.613
Mean AGENCY	.024	.035	−.019
Mean PERFORMANCE	−.039	−.033	−.039
Mean ACHIEVEMENT	.543	.577	.581

Note. Corr = correlation; AGENCY = agency beliefs for effort, ability, and luck; PERFOR-MANCE = teacher-assigned school marks; ACHIEVEMENT = scores on the BTS (see text). *Continuers* are the estimates based on the sample of 303 continuers without any selectivity corrections. *Continuers with dropouts* are the estimates based on the derived sample of 303 continuers with 122 dropouts estimated simultaneously using the Full-Information Maximum Likelihood approach. *Population* are the true estimates based on the full population of 425 participants.

Finally, in the third column we present the true population values for these participants (recall that the dropout classification was artificial and that the data set we used started as a complete data set for all participants). Here we see that the values are also quite different from those for the continuers but they are generally more similar to the values in the second column, which reflect the adjustments based on the information about the dropouts at the first measurement occasion only.

The difference between the estimates in column two and column three reflect the fact that the selection variable (Raven intelligence) is not perfectly correlated with the variables of interest. Therefore, the adjustments that result from the full information approach are only part adjustments and still contain some evidence of bias. However, the nature of the adjustments is clearly more accurate than the estimates based on the continuers alone. For example, consistent with the higher correlational manifold among the constructs at the first occasion, the constructs show a higher positive correlational manifold at the second occasion for the continuers than for the adjusted estimates which, in turn, were closer to the estimates found in the population.

We wish to emphasize that the significance of these selectivity effects in our example is small. Our example was meant to be a conservative one in that our selection variable was only moderately correlated with the measures we examined and, because of the graded selection process, the strength of the association between being a dropout and variables we examined was quite low ($r = 0.2$). Therefore, the degree of selectivity on the constructs at the second occasion that we identified was relatively small. Future Monte-Carlo work can be done to systematically vary the association between the selection variable and the primary constructs under scrutiny to determine thresholds and cutoffs for the nature and degree of resulting bias.

CONCLUSION

Our primary goal has been to re-emphasize the importance of examining selectivity in longitudinal research. We highlighted two fundamental types of questions that can be addressed when examining the impact of selectivity. Clearly further work is needed to examine which methods are most appropriate to assess the degree of bias that selectivity introduces. In addition, further work is needed to explore the boundaries of generalizability given various degrees of bias. However, it is also clear that the analytic machinery that is available to detect, estimate, and correct selectivity bias has made tremendous advances. Our parting admonition is for researchers to utilize these techniques, when possible, to fully explore the degree of selectivity bias that may be evident in their longitudinal data sets. Relying on less sophisticated traditional approaches (seemingly in the hopes that their simplicity will yield null results) runs tremendous risks. Because selectivity is an inevitability, researchers must be mindful that it is a matter of degree. A small degree of bias will likely not invalidate broader conclusions. A large degree of bias would necessarily temper the breadth of one's conclusions. Either way, acknowledging the existence of selectivity bias and exploring as fully as possible its influences are needed to render one's generalizations as veridical as the data, the design, and the analytic techniques allow.

ACKNOWLEDGMENT

This work was supported in part by the Berlin-Brandenburg Academy of Sciences, the Max Planck Society, the Max Planck Institute for Human Development in Berlin, the Max Planck Institute for Demography in Rostock, and Yale University. We are grateful to the many members of the Berlin Aging Study, the Institute, and to various visiting scholars for discussions on the issues presented in this work. We are particularly thankful to Paul Baltes and John Nesselroade for their invaluable advice and support.

CHAPTER ELEVEN

Multiple Imputation in Multivariate Research

John W. Graham
Scott M. Hofer
The Pennsylvania State University

Statistical analysis with missing data has always been a challenge. However, there have been tremendous advances in statistical theory related to analysis with missing data. Of equal importance for the applied researcher is the ready availability of these advances in a variety of software applications. This chapter outlines a general approach to analysis with missing data called multiple imputation (Rubin, 1987; Schafer, 1997). The chapter is divided into three parts. In the first part, we give a brief introduction to analysis with missing data. In the second part, we discuss the general principles of multiple imputation and its application, particularly with Schafer's (1997) Windows-based multiple imputation program, NORM. In the last section, we illustrate the use of NORM with an empirical example.

A BRIEF INTRODUCTION TO ANALYSIS WITH MISSING DATA

Before discussing details of how to perform analysis with missing data, it is important to emphasize a few fundamental points. Most important, users of these methods should realize that missing data procedures do not give something for nothing. Missing data procedures, such as multiple imputation, simply allow one to make use of all of the available data. That is, with the imputation procedures we describe, data do not have to be discarded simply because there is no convenient way to analyze the partial data available.

When we impute a value we should not think of the imputation as creating a value where one did not exist. Although, technically, imputation does replace the missing value with a plausible value, the focus should not be on the imputed value, per se.

Rather, the focus should be on the overall effect of imputation, especially on the fact that proper imputation (in terms of Rubin, 1987) has very desirable effects on the data set as a whole. Proper imputation preserves important characteristics of the data set. It yields unbiased parameter estimates (e.g., variances, covariances, and means) and allows estimation of standard errors and/or confidence intervals.

Causes of Missingness

In any analysis with missing data, an important question that must be asked is why the data are missing. We describe three general causes of missingness. First, the data can be missing completely at random (MCAR). Alternatively, the cause (or mechanism) of missingness can be accessible (Graham & Donaldson, 1993; also referred to by many, e.g., Little & Rubin, 1987, as "ignorable" or "missing at random [MAR]"), or inaccessible (also referred to as "nonignorable" or "informative"). In this section, we assume that likelihood-based estimation procedures (e.g., maximum likelihood estimation, multiple imputation) are used. Indeed, the choice of appropriate statistical methods is a critical one, which we discuss in the following section.

MCAR. Most people think of missing data as MCAR if the cause of missingness is a completely independent random process (e.g., the roll of a die). However, it is important to note that missing data also can be MCAR if the cause of missingness is quite systematic, but simply uncorrelated with the variable containing missingness. The good thing about missing data that are MCAR is that the cause of missingness need not be included in the missing data model (or the analysis model). However, even if MCAR holds, simply omitting data from the analysis often leads to loss of statistical power, at least for some analyses.

Accessible Causes. An accessible cause of missingness is systematic and is correlated with the variable containing the missingness. Thus, in order for the analysis procedures to yield unbiased parameter estimates in this case, the cause of missingness must be included in the missing data model. We call this cause of missingness *accessible* because it has been measured and is available for inclusion in the missing data and/or analysis model.

Inaccessible Causes. An inaccessible cause of missingness is also systematic and is correlated with the variable containing the missingness. In order to control for bias, this cause of missingness must be included in the missing data model. This cause of missing data is termed *inaccessible* because the cause has not been measured and is therefore not available for analysis. This often occurs when the cause of missingness is the value of the variable itself. In this instance, the fact that a variable is missing is informative about the value of that variable had it been obtained. For example, if a drug-using adolescent skips a measurement session because of his or her drug use, the cause of missingness would be inaccessible (however, see comments later). The problem is that there is no other way to obtain information regarding the variable than by obtaining information about the variable itself. No general method for dealing with missing data (including the recommended ones, which assume MCAR or accessible mechanisms) can provide reasonable inferences under such circumstances. In order to make unbiased inferences to the population, models incorporating information regarding missingness (e.g., resampling; Graham & Donaldson, 1993; Rubin, 1987) and/or assumptions regarding inaccessible causes of missing values (what the values might have been) must be employed.

On the other hand, it is almost always incorrect to suggest that the cause of missingness is inaccessible. We have described the use of a sensitivity analysis to determine the approximate effect of inaccessible missing data mechanisms on statistical conclusions in a particular study (Graham, Hofer, Donaldson, MacKinnon, & Schafer, 1997). We suggested making several assumptions about the factors that affect the impact of the inaccessible mechanism on ultimate statistical conclusions in a program evaluation study. Even with rather conservative assumptions, results from the sensitivity analysis suggested that the overall effects of inaccessible (or nonignorable) mechanisms would often be minimal. Although situations undoubtedly arise in which the effects would be more substantial, it is important to conduct some kind of sensitivity analysis in every research situation to determine the likelihood of this being a problem. If the conclusion is that the effects of inaccessible mechanisms (over a reasonable range of assumptions) may be nontrivial, it may be useful to explore the use of developing procedures for dealing with such problems.

Finally, it is important to say that even if the assumptions underlying the missing data procedures recommended here (and elsewhere in this volume) are not met fully, it would be a mistake to assume that they should not be used. Given all that is known about missing data problems (MCAR, accessible, and inaccessible mechanisms), it is always the case that the methods recommended in this volume are better (e.g., less biased and more efficient) than other, more traditional, methods such as listwise deletion, pairwise deletion, or mean substitution, which are often the default methods in statistical packages.

"Traditional" Procedures

In previous work, we have dealt in some detail with the relative merits of the new procedures and the limitations of the more traditional, ad hoc approaches to dealing with missing data (Graham & Donaldson, 1993; Graham, Hofer, & MacKinnon, 1996; Graham, Hofer, & Piccinin, 1994; Graham et al., 1997; Graham & Schafer, in press). We have shown with various simulations that the "traditional" procedures are never better than the recommended likelihood-based procedures and can sometimes yield results that are extremely biased. Furthermore, with two of the procedures that are often used (pairwise deletion and mean substitution), there is no basis for estimating standard errors. Because of the extensive discussion of the limitations of traditional approaches available elsewhere, we do not provide comparisons in the present chapter with the traditional methods. In this section we outline the traditional approaches and provide a summary of the limitations for applied use.

Analysis of Complete Cases (Listwise Deletion).   Perhaps the most common approach for dealing with missing data has been to ignore cases that have any missing data and analyze only those cases that have data for all relevant variables. There are two fundamental problems with this approach. First, it may produce biased parameter estimates, that is, parameter estimates that are systematically higher or lower than the population values (Wothke, chap. 12, this volume, presents an example of bias using this approach). Second, the statistical power using listwise deletion is always worse than using multiple imputation or other likelihood-based procedures because a substantial number of cases must often be eliminated. On the other hand, a good aspect of listwise deletion is that there is a solid basis for estimating standard errors of the estimates obtained because the sample size is known.

We would always use one of the recommended procedures regardless of the amount of missingness, but this is because we are extremely familiar with them and find them very easy to use. However, for other researchers who are less familiar with these procedures, the benefit of using the recommended procedures may not outweigh the costs of using an unfamiliar procedure, when, say, 5% or fewer of the cases are lost to listwise deletion. Because of the small chance of bias and the small loss of power when 5% or fewer of the cases are lost to listwise deletion, reviewers would be on weak ground to criticize the use of listwise deletion in this situation.

On the other hand, situations are common in which listwise deletion is not a reasonable option. We have previously described a planned missing data situation, which we referred to as the "3-form design," in which we had no complete cases for certain analyses (Graham et al., 1994, 1996, 1997). In other situations, involving planned or unplanned missingness, the pattern of missing data may be such that there are very few complete cases, even when the amount of overall missingness is relatively small. For example, consider a simple design involving four variables and five equal groups of subjects, representing different patterns of missing and nonmissing data. Suppose that 20% of the subjects have complete data and that each of the remaining four groups are missing one of the four variables. In such an example, only 20% of all data points are missing, and yet only 20% of the subjects have complete data. It simply does not seem reasonable to discard 80% of the cases when only 20% of the data values are missing. This, situation may seem unlikely, but two published studies had missing data patterns even more extreme than this (Graham et al., 1997; Hawkins et al., 1997). In these cases, loss of power using listwise deletion was substantial.

Pairwise Deletion.   Another traditional procedure involves the analysis of a correlation or covariance matrix using pairwise deletion. If the data are missing other than MCAR, this approach will produce biased parameter estimates. In addition, the correlation matrix produced with pairwise deletion may not be positive definite and thus may not be analyzable with many usual procedures. Finally, and most important, there is no basis for estimating standard errors when using pairwise deletion. Bootstrap procedures could be employed for this purpose, but the cost in time would be near that of using one of the recommended procedures. The conclusion is that pairwise deletion should never be used, not even for "quick and dirty" analyses. In such situations, it would always be better to analyze a covariance matrix produced by an Expectation Maximization (EM) algorithm, and make a guess at a plausible sample size (e.g., $1 - p(\text{missing}) \times N$, where $p(\text{missing})$ is the overall proportion of missing data points).

Mean Substitution. This procedure should never be used. Parameter estimates will usually be biased (Graham et al., 1994, 1996, 1997), even when the data are MCAR, and there is no basis for estimating standard errors. Some people ask whether it is okay to use this procedure if they have only a few missing data points. We argue that it is always preferable to use one of the recommended missing data procedures.

Regression-Based Single Imputation. Regression-based single imputation is definitely a step in the right direction (more conceptually than practically, however). This procedure involves estimating the regression equation for subjects having complete data and then using the predicted score (Y-hat) for the variable that is sometimes missing. The problems with this approach are that (a) it is statistically appropriate only with certain, relatively rare (e.g., monotone) missing data patterns, and (b) it produces biased variance estimates. This procedure should not be used because of the biased variance estimates and because there is no basis for estimating standard errors. However, the procedure has value in that it is at the heart of the more appropriate EM algorithm and multiple imputation approaches described later.

Recommended Procedures

Model-Based Procedures. A model-based procedure is one in which the missing data model and the substantive model are estimated simultaneously. This "single-step" procedure allows estimation of unbiased estimates and standard errors under conditions of accessible missingness. Three model-based procedures are described here only in passing. Other chapters in this volume (Wothke, chap. 12) describe two of these approaches more fully. The first approach, which we refer to as the Multiple-Group Structural Equation Modeling (MGSEM) approach has been described in detail elsewhere (e.g., Allison, 1987; Graham et al., 1994; Muthén, Kaplan, & Hollis, 1987). MGSEM requires that a different group for each pattern of missing data be modeled with equality constraints across groups for variables that are present. Other model-based approaches are to be preferred when there are many different patterns of missingness and when the sample size for each pattern is smaller than the number of variables.

A second class of model-based procedure is what we refer to as "raw data maximum-likelihood" (RDML). The RDML procedure is currently implemented in the structural equation modeling (SEM) programs Mx (Neale, 1991) and Amos (Arbuckle, 1995). Wothke (chap. 12, this volume, RDML referred to as full information maximum likelihood) describes in much more detail the missing data features of this approach as implemented in Amos. We will say only that this approach has much to recommend it. It is especially useful when SEM (or virtually anything relating to the general linear model) is the analysis of choice. The approach is especially good for dealing with missing data when the model is correct.

A third class of model-based missing data procedures is to be implemented in a future version of the Latent Transition Analysis model (LTA; Collins & Wugalter, 1992). With this new version of the LTA program, one would test stage-sequential models of growth and estimate missing data in a single analysis. As with the RDML approaches, the LTA approach is good if stage-sequential models are being tested and if the model is correct.

Expectation Maximization Algorithm.   The EM algorithm was suggested by Dempster, Laird, and Rubin (1977; also Little & Rubin, 1987) as a method for estimating missing data. The EM algorithm, as it applies to continuous data and covariance matrices (EM algorithms can be applied to many other situations), is based on the idea that one makes guesses about the missing data and then uses the guesses to estimate the sums, sums of squares, and cross products (the E step). One then uses these sufficient statistics to calculate the covariance matrix (the M step) and then uses the updated covariance matrix to estimate the missing values during the next E step. This process continues until the elements of the covariance matrix stop changing to a meaningful extent.

The EM algorithm for continuous data has been implemented in EMCOV (Graham & Donaldson, 1993; Graham & Hofer, 1991; Graham et al., 1994, 1996, 1997), NORM (Schafer, 1991, 1997), and SPSS. The procedure has the advantage of being very easy to use. The covariance matrix that results from the EM analysis may be read into other statistical programs (e.g., SEM programs) for further analysis. The parameter estimates based on analysis of the EM covariance matrix are excellent in that they are unbiased and efficient (e.g., see Graham et al., 1994, 1997). The major drawback with the EM algorithm is that there is no built-in basis for estimating standard errors. Ad hoc procedures, such as bootstrap procedures (Efron, 1982) must be used for such estimation. Guessing about the appropriate sample size (e.g., $1 - p(\text{missing}) \times N$, where $p(\text{missing})$ is the overall proportion of missing data points) may be useful for preliminary analyses but is not appropriate for published work.

There are two times when use of EM analyses may be useful. First, if the data being analyzed deviate substantially from multivariate normal distributions, use of a bootstrap may provide a degree of protection for calculating the standard errors. Second, in the SEM context with missing data, it may often be useful to estimate goodness of fit[1] and to do most model exploration using the EM covariance matrix and then to estimate the final model using multiple imputation (described in this chapter in some detail) or one of the RDML programs. This final analysis would be used primarily for obtaining an estimate of the standard errors.

Multiple Imputation. With this procedure, multiple data sets are created with a set of plausible values replacing the missing values. Standard statistical analysis is then performed on each of these "complete" data sets and the results appropriately summarized so that the uncertainty due to the missing data is accounted for. The strength of this method is that standard errors are routinely obtained for each parameter estimate. This method is particularly useful when several researchers are using the same data set because much of the missing data handling is performed prior to statistical analysis. In the next section, we describe multiple imputation in greater detail.

MULTIPLE IMPUTATION

In this introduction to multiple imputation, we describe the various parts of the procedure at the general level wherever possible. However, because Schafer's NORM program is arguably the most accessible implementation of multiple imputation available to analytic practitioners, we always note Schafer's solution as implemented in NORM.

Multiple imputation is related to the EM algorithm and to single imputation procedures already described. The problem with single imputation is that imputed values have too little variability. In order for the imputations to be "proper" as described by Rubin (1987), two kinds of variability must be restored. The first kind relates to error variability. When values are imputed using the regression procedure, the imputed values fall exactly on the regression line. However, we know that the data deviate from the predicted regression line by some amount because of error and other unique systematic sources of variance. This unique variance can be restored by sampling from the distribution of known errors (i.e., observed score minus predicted score based on observed data) or by sampling from the normal distribution (Graham and Hofer's EMCOV program makes use of the former method, whereas Schafer's NORM program employs the latter).

The second kind of variability relates to the fact that the covariance matrix producing the imputed values is itself just one estimate of the population covariance matrix. If one were able to obtain several random draws from the population, the covariance matrices from the different samples would vary. The slopes of the regression lines, which are based on those covariance matrices and which are used to predict the missing values, would be slightly steeper or shallower than the regression line based on the original data. An estimate of this source of variability could be obtained using a bootstrap procedure (Efron, 1982). EMCOV (Graham & Hofer, 1991) makes use of bootstrapping to restore this kind of variability.

---

[1] Note, however, that the goodness of fit tests will be conservative (e.g., the chi-square will be too large) to the extend that one has missing data.

Alternatively, the covariance matrices could be sampled from a simulated population of covariance matrices using data augmentation (Tanner & Wong, 1987; Schafer's NORM program uses this approach). Data augmentation is similar in many ways to the EM algorithm and might be thought of as a stochastic version of EM. The EM algorithm alternates between the E step, in which missing values are predicted, and the M step, in which the covariance parameters are estimated. Data augmentation alternates between the I (imputation) step, in which missing data are simulated given the current estimate of the covariance matrix, and the P (posterior) step, in which the covariance matrix parameters are simulated given the current values of the data.

An important feature of data augmentation is that it does not converge in the same way that EM does. When EM converges, the elements of the covariance matrix stop changing to a meaningful extent from iteration to iteration. When data augmentation converges, the distribution of covariance matrices stops changing to a meaningful extent.

Another important feature of data augmentation is that the covariance matrix at one step is very similar to the covariance matrix at the next step. In fact, if one were to calculate the autocorrelation between parameter estimates at one step and those at the next step, one would find them to be substantially correlated. This is not a desirable simulation of draws from the true population in that we would expect random draws from the true population to be uncorrelated with one another (within the limits of the random variation around the true parameter values). Thus, if these draws from the simulated population are to be acceptable, they should be relatively independent of one another.

In many cases, this autocorrelation between estimates of the covariance matrix parameters at different steps of data augmentation remains unacceptably high for several steps of data augmentation. Only when one has moved a number of steps away from the original (say t steps) does this autocorrelation drop to near zero. As we see next, estimating how many steps of data augmentation are required for the estimates of the covariance matrix to be essentially independent is an important aspect of the diagnostics procedure.

The three basic steps in multiple imputation are impute, analyze, and combine the results. We discuss these three basic steps with Schafer's (1997) Windows-based NORM program in mind, but to a large extent, our discussion applies as well to any multiple imputation software. Readers may request step-by-step instructions for conducting multiple imputation with the latest version of NORM from the first author.

Impute the Data

The first step is to impute the m data sets. For illustration, we describe multiple imputation with $m = 5$ data sets. However, in reality, one would impute 5, 10, and sometimes even 20 data sets.

Preparing the Data Set.   Any multiple imputation program will require that the data set be in a form that is readable by the program. Future implementations of multiple imputation software may be imbedded into statistical packages (e.g., SAS, SPSS, or Splus). However, in the late 1990s programs require that the user output an ASCII (text) data set from SAS or SPSS in a form that can be read by the multiple imputation software. The discussion in this section applies mainly to such stand-alone software packages. These stand-alone multiple imputation packages, such as NORM, require that all missing values throughout the data set be set to a single value (e.g., −9), which is outside the range of legitimate values for all variables. There may also be other requirements of the program (e.g., each data value separated by one or more spaces).

Data Preparation and Summary.   Next, the data should be read into the multiple imputation program, prepared, and summarized. It may be useful to transform data prior to imputation so that the data will conform better to assumptions underlying the regression procedure. It may also be useful to standardize all variables prior to performing the next step of analysis to improve the meaningfulness of convergence criteria. All data may be reverse standardized and back-transformed to the original scales after imputation.

Useful summary information about the data include (a) identifying all patterns of missingness, along with the number of cases with each pattern; (b) the number of cases with no missing data; and (c) the overall proportion of missing data points. Problems in the data (e.g., some cases with no data, some "variables" that are constant) may be identified in this step.

Run EM.   Most multiple imputation run the EM algorithm on the data set prior to doing multiple imputation. This is done for two reasons. First, the EM solution (a covariance matrix and vector of means) is conceptually the same as the average of an infinite number of imputed data sets. Thus, for some applications, the EM covariance matrix will be of great value in its own right. Second, the EM solution provides excellent starting values for data augmentation.

EM typically converges rather quickly in time, although the speed of convergence is a function of a number of factors, including speed of the computer, N, k, and the percentage of missing information. This latter factor is determined by the total amount of missing data and the correlations between variables containing missing values and other variables in the model (less missing information if variables are highly correlated).

If one would like to report means and standard deviations (and the correlation matrix) as part of the simple descriptive statistics of the sample, these estimates should come from this output with a clear statement that these are EM algorithm estimates. When using Schafer's NORM program, it is a good idea to note the number of iterations it took EM to converge.

Run Data Augmentation (for Diagnostics). Data augmentation with NORM begins with the EM estimates. The biggest concern for data augmentation is the appropriate number of steps of data augmentation required for parameter estimates to be reasonably uncorrelated. A simplistic approach, but one that may often be useful, is to calculate this number by doubling the number of iterations for EM convergence. For example, if EM converged in 36 iterations, one could request 72 steps of data augmentation for each imputed data set.

A better procedure, however, is to perform more systematic diagnostics by saving the covariance matrix and vector of means for every step of data augmentation. Although this can become very large it can provide very useful information.[2] The discussion assumes 1,000 steps of data augmentation for performing diagnostics.

Diagnostics. Two kinds of diagnostics are helpful in this context. Schafer's NORM program provides these two diagnostics. First, one should plot the value of each parameter estimate over the 1,000 steps of data augmentation. A desirable pattern would be one in which the plot has rather high amplitude and its high and low points appear to form a rectangle over the 1,000 steps of data augmentation. A pattern that might indicate a data problem is one in which the plot looks like a "snake" that weaves its way high and low over the 1,000 steps.

A second diagnostic is the plot of the autocorrelation for each parameter estimate over t steps of data augmentation, where t varies between 1 and 100 (or more). The purpose of this diagnostic is to determine how many steps of data augmentation are required for the autocorrelation to fall consistently below the level of statistical significance. One should view this autocorrelation plot for every parameter estimate. The number of steps of data augmentation required for imputation is determined by the parameter estimate taking the most steps for the autocorrelation to fall below the significance level. In most instances, this number will be less than twice the number of iterations for EM convergence.

Data Augmentation/Imputation. Based on the diagnostics, or on the "2 × EM iterations" rule, one then performs t steps of augmentation, after which a data set is imputed. This is repeated m (e.g., 5) times, producing m (e.g., 5) imputed data sets, each with a different set of plausible imputed values. Random error variance is added to each imputed value as described earlier.

Bootstrap as Alternative to Data Augmentation. As an alternative to data augmentation, one could perform a bootstrap on the original data set. This new bootstrapped data set is then analyzed with the EM algorithm. The covariance matrices based on m (e.g., 5) bootstrapped data sets provide an estimate of the degree of vari-

---

[2] With just 10 variables, 10 means, 10 variances, and $10 \times 9/2 = 45$ covariances are estimated at each step of data augmentation for each data set. If one performs 1,000 steps of data augmentation, one must save 65,000 elements.

ability that one might expect from m random draws from the population. Each of these covariance matrices is then applied to the original data set to produce m imputed data sets. Random error variance is added to each imputed value as described earlier. EMCOV (Graham & Hofer, 1991) has utilities for performing multiple imputation in this manner.

Analyze Each Imputed Data Set Using Usual Procedures

The next step is to do your usual data analysis (e.g., SAS PROC REG, SPSS Regression, LISREL, EQS) on the m (5) imputed data sets. For these analyses, set the sample size in your analysis program to be the total number of cases in the data set, as if there were no missing data. This aspect of the procedure is the same as if one had no missing data, except that the analysis is performed five times rather than just once.

Combine the Results for Statistical Inference

All parameter estimates of interest and the corresponding standard errors should be saved from the m analyses just performed. From this information, one can easily calculate the parameter estimates and standard errors (or confidence intervals) to be included in the description of the work.

The parameter estimate to be reported is simply the average of that parameter estimate over the m imputed data sets. The standard error to be reported is the weighted sum of two kinds of variance, within- and between-imputation variance. *Within-imputation variance* is the average of the squared standard errors (or the m data sets) for that particular parameter estimate as calculated by the analysis program. The *between-imputation variance* is the sample variance of the parameter estimate over the m data sets. The overall standard error is given by:

$$SE = sqrt\ [(U + (1 + 1 / m)] \times B, \qquad (1)$$

where U is the average of the squared standard errors, B is the sample variance of the parameter estimate, and m is the number of imputed data sets.[3] The t-value is the parameter estimate divided by its standard error; the degrees of freedom (df) is given by:

$$df = (m - 1)[1 + \overline{SE} / (1 + 1 / m)\ B]^\wedge 2. \qquad (2)$$

The df will always be at least as large as the number of imputations and can be very large. The value is dependent on the percentage of missing information, which is in part a function of the amount of missing data and in part a function of the degree of relatedness with other variables in the model. If the estimated df is just larger than m for important parameter estimates, this is a sign that m should be larger.

---

[3] The formulas for standard error and degrees of freedom are adapted from Schafer (1997).

Logistics of Combining Results of m Analyses.   Conceptually, it is a simple matter to perform multiple imputation and translate the output from the analysis of choice into a form from which the appropriate calculations can be made. However, the process can be extremely tedious and error producing, especially if one has a large number of parameter estimates and a large number of imputed data sets. Thus, we have developed several utilities to facilitate this process, which can be downloaded from our website: *http://methcenter.psu.edu.* Utilities for facilitation of analyses with Schafer's NORM program are available for: SAS PROC REG, SAS PROC LOGISTIC, and LISREL (single or multiple group). Similar utilities are easily adapted to facilitate the use of any multiple imputation program and other analysis procedures.

AN ILLUSTRATION OF MULTIPLE IMPUTATION WITH AN EMPIRICAL EXAMPLE

The Sample

The data for this example were taken from the Adolescent Alcohol Prevention Trial (AAPT; Hansen & Graham, 1991). The study participants were $N = 3,183$ seventh graders who were present when the program was delivered in the Fall 1987 or Spring 1988. The immediate posttest measures were taken in Fall or Spring immediately following the completion of the 2- to 3-week program. The posttest data reported here were from these same students as ninth graders.

The Variables and Model

The variables included in the analyses fell into four categories: program variables, covariates, immediate outcome variables, and longer term outcome variables.

Program Variables (3 Variables).   There were four program groups. The first, which served as our control group, was an information-only intervention: Information about Consequences of Use (ICU). The second was intended to provide students with skills for resisting alcohol offers: Resistance Training (RT). The RT condition also contained the ICU sessions. The third group received a Normative Education (NE) curriculum, which was designed primarily to correct misperceptions about the prevalence and acceptability of adolescent alcohol and other drug use. The NE curriculum also included the ICU sessions. Finally, a fourth group (Combined) received key sessions from RT, NE, and ICU curricula. We used three dummy variables to represent program group membership. The first, RTICU, represented the comparison between RT and ICU. The second, NEICU represented the comparison between NE and ICU. The third, CombICU, represented the comparison between the Combined and ICU groups.

Covariates Measured at Seventh Grade (3 Variables).   Three covariates were included in the model. Smoking at pretest (Smk7: composite of three individual items),

TABLE 11.1
Missing Values for Each Variable

	N missing	$\%$ missing
RTICU	0	0.00
NEICU	0	0.00
CombICU	0	0.00
Smk7	157	4.93
Alc7	162	5.09
Percept7	239	7.51
Skills	1,933	60.73
Percept	528	16.59
Alc9	1,494	46.94

alcohol use at pretest (Alc7: composite of four items), and perceptions at pretest (Percept7: composite of several measures relating to perceptions about the prevalence and acceptability of adolescent alcohol use).

Mediating Variables Measured Immediately Following Program Implementation (2 Variables). Two key mediating variables were included. A measure of resistance skills (Skill) was obtained from an approximate one-third random sample of subjects. A paper and pencil measure of perceptions relating to the prevalence and acceptability of adolescent alcohol use (Percept; this was the same set of measures obtained at the pretest).

Longer-Term (Ninth Grade) Outcomes (1 Variable). The longer term outcome measure was a measure of alcohol use taken at the ninth grade. This was a composite of the same four variables used for the pretest measure of alcohol use: lifetime use, use in the past 30 days, use in the past 7 days, and number of days that alcohol was used in the past 30 days.

Multiple Imputation With NORM

The $N = 3,183$ cases and $k = 9$ variables described were subjected to multiple imputation analysis with NORM. Tables 11.1 and 11.2 describe the missingness for this data set. Note that there is relatively little missingness except for the mediating variable, Skill, and the longer term outcome variable, Alc 9. To perform multiple imputation, we followed the steps described in the second part of this chapter. For the purposes of this demonstration, we created ten imputed data sets.

The analyses were performed on a 166 MHZ Pentium (Dell) Laptop. EM converged after 34 iterations in just under 4 seconds. If we used the "easy" approach to data augmentation, we could perhaps just double the number of EM iterations and

TABLE 11.2
Patterns of Missingness for All Variables

Count	Pattern								
627	1	1	1	1	1	1	1	1	1
12	1	1	1	1	1	0	1	1	1
14	1	1	1	0	0	0	1	1	1
747	1	1	1	1	1	1	0	1	1
1	1	1	1	1	0	1	0	1	1
11	1	1	1	1	1	0	0	1	1
24	1	1	1	0	0	0	0	1	1
3	1	1	1	1	1	1	1	0	1
2	1	1	1	0	0	0	1	0	1
237	1	1	1	1	1	1	0	0	1
3	1	1	1	1	0	1	0	0	1
7	1	1	1	1	1	0	0	0	1
1	1	1	1	0	0	0	0	0	1
521	1	1	1	1	1	1	1	1	0
1	1	1	1	0	1	1	1	1	0
23	1	1	1	1	1	0	1	1	0
26	1	1	1	0	0	0	1	1	0
554	1	1	1	1	1	1	0	1	0
20	1	1	1	1	1	0	0	1	0
1	1	1	1	1	0	0	0	1	0
73	1	1	1	0	0	0	0	1	0
5	1	1	1	1	1	1	1	0	0
16	1	1	1	0	0	0	1	0	0
245	1	1	1	1	1	1	0	0	0
8	1	1	1	1	1	0	0	0	0
1	1	1	1	1	0	0	0	0	0

Note. Matrix of missingness patterns (1 = observed, 0 = missing), Count = number of observations with the specified pattern.

use that number of steps of data augmentation between imputed data sets. With this approach, we would choose 680 total steps of data augmentation and would produce an imputed data set every 68 steps. For this illustration, we went ahead and performed 1,000 steps of data augmentation in order to perform the diagnostics.

The 1,000 steps of data augmentation took 84 seconds. As is usually the case, the mean parameters looked very good in that all of the plots of parameter estimates looked uniformly random across the 1,000 steps of data augmentation. That is, there was no evidence that the mean parameters were "wandering" or "snaking" around the parameter space. Also, for all mean parameters, it appeared as if the autocorrelation was near zero within about 10 steps of data augmentation.

For the most part, the diagnostics on the variance and covariance parameters were the same as just described for the means. The exceptions were the covariances involving the "Skill" variable, for which 61% of the cases were missing. For these parameters, there was no evidence of "snaking" of the plot, but the autocorrelations showed a somewhat less than ideal pattern, although one that is not uncommon. The autocorrelation typically dropped to near zero after 10 to 15 steps of data augmentation. However, the autocorrelation then became slightly (and marginally significantly) negative, and then cycled back and forth between slightly positive and slightly negative. We looked at autocorrelations as far apart as 500 steps of data augmentation, and this pattern persisted. Our current thinking is that this pattern, although less than ideal, is not a problem.

For all variables, choosing 50 to 60 steps of data augmentation appeared to be about as good as we could do. In order to be even more conservative, we elected to impute a data set every 100 steps of data augmentation. In practical terms, this choice is probably not different in a meaningful way from the choice we might have made based on doubling the number of iterations it took EM to converge (68). We then reran data augmentation, specifying 1,000 total steps and writing an imputed data set every 100 steps.

The 10 imputed data sets were then subjected to a LISREL analysis. We tested a rather simple, manifest-variable, mediation model in which the first seven variables were all intercorrelated, and we predicted (as regressions) the remaining three variables (two mediators and outcome). In addition, the residuals of the two mediators (Skill and Percept) were specified to be correlated and predicted (as regressions) the outcome (Alc9). The LISREL model was run 10 times, once with each imputed data set. After running each model, we ran the READLIS.EXE utility (see our website to obtain this utility) to create a results file that could be read easily into NORM. To

TABLE 11.3
Case 1 for All 10 Imputed Data Sets

0	0	0	−.35	−.52	−.59	1.586	−.70	−.48
0	0	0	−.35	−.52	−.59	−0.014	−.70	−.48
0	0	0	−.35	−.52	−.59	−0.060	−.70	−.48
0	0	0	−.35	−.52	−.59	0.072	−.70	−.48
0	0	0	−.35	−.52	−.59	−0.233	−.70	−.48
0	0	0	−.35	−.52	−.59	0.408	−.70	−.48
0	0	0	−.35	−.52	−.59	0.263	−.70	−.48
0	0	0	−.35	−.52	−.59	−0.040	−.70	−.48
0	0	0	−.35	−.52	−.59	0.456	−.70	−.48
0	0	0	−.35	−.52	−.59	0.270	−.70	−.48

illustrate the kind of variability that we see with multiple imputation, we present the first case for all t10 imputed data sets (see Table 11.3). Only the seventh variable (Skill) is missing for this subject, so that is the only one that varies over the 10 data sets.

Results

The final results from the LISREL analyses, based on multiple imputation, are presented in Table 11.4. The results shown are only those relating to the program effects (i.e., effects relating to the covariates are not included). The results show that the RT and Combined programs had an effect on acquisition of resistance skills and that the NE and Combined programs had an effect on the perceptions of the prevalence and acceptability of adolescent alcohol use. There was also a small effect of the NE program on skill acquisition.

The NE program had a significant direct (i.e., unexplained) effect on alcohol use at ninth grade. The RT program had a similar, but smaller effect on alcohol use at ninth grade. Perceptions measured at the immediate posttest had a significant effect on alcohol use at ninth grade. However, the hypothesized effect of skills on ninth grader alcohol use was not observed.

Were 10 Imputed Data Sets Enough?   The results shown in Table 11.4 show that the estimated *df* for several of the parameter estimates were relatively low—not much higher than the number of imputed data sets (one estimate was just 12, and several more were around 20). Most of these low *df* estimates related to parameter estimates involving the Skill variable, for which missingness was considerable. These low *df* estimates may be an indication that the multiple imputation solution has not fully sta-

TABLE 11.4
Multiple Imputation Statistical Inference

Parameter name	est	se	t	df	p
RTICU-Skill	.379	.0551	6.87	28.8	.0000
NEICU-Skill	.140	.0539	2.59	42.4	.0136
CombICU-Skill	.353	.0669	5.28	19.9	.0001
RTICU-Percept7	.013	.0316	0.42	738.8	.6784
NEICU-Percept7	−.124	.0340	3.65	856.2	.0003
CombICU-Percept7	−.277	.0336	8.25	437.7	.0000
RTICU-Alc9	−.149	.0619	2.40	21.7	.0279
NEICU-Alc9	−.195	.0531	3.68	45.1	.0006
CombICU-Alc9	−.005	.0596	0.09	27.2	.9295
Skill-Alc9	−.035	.0484	0.73	12.0	.5013
Percept7-Alc9	.171	.0358	4.77	22.7	.0001

bilized for these parameter estimates with 10 imputations and that 15 or even 20 imputed data sets should be produced and analyzed. Had these estimates been closer to the borderline of a statistical decision, analyzing more imputed data sets would have been an important step.

Substantive Conclusions

The Normative Education program appears to have had a significant effect on ninth grader alcohol use, which was substantially, but not totally mediated by changes in perceptions relating to the prevalence and acceptability of adolescent alcohol use. The program that combined resistance training and normative education also appears to have had an effect on ninth grader alcohol use that was completely mediated by changes in perceptions. However, the Resistance Training program appears to have had no "explainable" effect on ninth grader alcohol use.[4]

These results are consistent with other work relating to the AAPT programs. It should be noted, however, that the apparent failure of the RT program has been shown to be because not all students who receive the RT program actually want to use the new skills they acquire. When the data were analyzed separately for those who wanted to resist, the effect of skills on alcohol outcomes was significant (Donaldson, Graham, Piccinin, & Hansen, 1995). One other factor should be noted about these results. These data were analyzed at the individual level, despite the fact that the individuals in the study were nested within 120 classrooms and 12 schools. When we have analyzed these data with the multilevel analyses, the results relating to ninth grade outcomes are similar, but somewhat weaker (Palmer, Graham, White, & Hansen, in press).

CONCLUDING COMMENTS ABOUT MULTIPLE IMPUTATION

Usefulness of Multiple Imputation Based on the Normal Model with Non-Normal Data

One concern users might have about using a program that is based on the normal model is that empirical data seldom conform to the assumption of normality. However, recent work suggests that the imputation part of the process can be done using the normal model with good results even when the data are seriously non-normal (e.g., see Graham & Schafer, in press). There are two reasons why this works. First, even when there is a high percentage of missing data, much of the data are not missing and therefore are not changing from imputed data set to imputed data set. Thus, even though the imputed data are much more normal than the real data, this fact has rel-

---

[4] Note that these statements about mediation do not employ the newer rules for mediation suggested by Collins, Graham, and Flaherty (in press).

atively little impact on the results. Second, and perhaps more important, it is generally the case that non-normal data have a much greater effect on standard errors than on parameter estimates themselves. Imputation has little effect on computation of standard errors. The program one uses to analyze the data is really what determines the quality of the standard errors. Thus, if the program being used handles standard errors well when data are non-normal, multiple imputation will provide excellent standard errors. Of course, the converse is also true. If one's analysis program does not produce reasonable standard errors when the data are non-normal, the standard errors based on multiple imputation will be equally bad.

Availability of Schafer's Programs

Schafer's multiple imputation programs (as described in Schafer, 1997) can be downloaded free from our website: *http://methcenter.psu.edu.* Please check the website for the latest versions of these programs. The programs available are:

NORM   For continuous data, based on the normal model. Available as Windows 95/NT application, and as part of Splus package.

CAT   For categorical data. Currently available only with Splus, but Windows 95/NT version will be available soon.

MIX   For mixed continuous and categorical data. Currently available only with Splus, but Windows 95/NT version will be available soon.

PAN   For special longitudinal and cluster data situations. Currently available only with Splus, but Windows 95/NT version will be available soon.

CHAPTER TWELVE

Longitudinal and Multigroup Modeling with Missing Data

Werner Wothke
SmallWaters Corporation, Chicago

Missing data are almost always a problem in longitudinal research. Item non-response, differential attrition, failure to obtain measurements at equal time intervals, and unbalanced panel designs used to be difficult to analyze at best and remain a threat to the validity of a study. A related technical problem, customarily given little importance but nevertheless strongly related to validity threats, is that most multivariate methods require complete data.

Incomplete data are often dealt with by listwise or pairwise deletion methods, which omit entire records, or pairs of variables, with missing values. Sometimes a researcher will substitute sample means for the missing values. All three approaches aim to fix the data so that they can be analyzed by methods designed for complete data, but are ad hoc and have little theoretical justification.

The method of full information maximum likelihood (FIML), in contrast, has long been known as a theory-based approach to the treatment of missing data. FIML assumes multivariate normality and maximizes the likelihood of the model given the observed data. The theoretical advantages of this full information method are widely recognized and have been implemented in the Amos and Mx structural equation modeling programs.

Unfortunately, theory has not had much influence on practice in the treatment of missing data. In part, the underutilization of maximum likelihood estimation in the presence of missing data may be due to the unavailability of the method as a standard option in packaged data analysis programs. There may also exist a (mistaken) belief that the benefits of using maximum likelihood (ML) estimation rather than conventional missing data techniques will in practice be small.

This chapter presents several examples of time-structured and multigroup problems demonstrating the ease of FIML and its greater statistical efficiency when compared to mean imputation and listwise or pairwise deletion methods. Model specifications for these problems and Visual Basic code used in simulations are available on the World Wide Web at the locations:

http://www.mpib-berlin.mpg.de/research_resources/index.html and
http://www.smallwaters.com/books/mpi_ modeling_code.html.

COMMON PRACTICE IN THE TREATMENT OF MISSING DATA

The most commonly practiced methods for structural equation modeling (SEM) with missing data apply complete data ML estimation to covariance matrices that have been somehow corrected. Such corrections can be:

1. *listwise deletion* (LD), which excludes from the calculations all records with missing values on any of the variables,
2. *pairwise deletion* (PD), by which each sample covariance between two variables is computed from pairwise-complete data, excluding cases with missing values on one or both of the variables, or
3. *mean imputation* (MI), which replaces the missing values of a variable by the mean of its observed values.

Brown (1983) studied LD, PD, MI, and FIML methods by Monte-Carlo simulation in the factor analysis context, Brown (1994) studied the performance of LD, PD, and MI by Monte-Carlo simulation in the context of structural equation modeling, and Little and Rubin (1987) reviewed all four methods in the general multivariate case. All three studies are critical of mean imputation, listwise deletion, and pairwise deletion methods, citing biased and/or inefficient estimates as well as the increased risk of obtaining indefinite sample covariance matrices. Brown (1983) qualified his comments about LD, PD, and MI with respect to the frequency and type of the missing data.

Model-based imputation of missing values is well known in the statistical literature but rarely used in SEM (Kim & Curry, 1977; Roth, 1994). In particular, the expectation maximization (EM) algorithm (Dempster, Laird, & Rubin, 1977), which implements the FIML approach by repeated imputation-estimation cycles, has been discussed as a method for estimating means and covariance matrices from incomplete data (Graham & Hofer, chap. 11, this volume; Graham, Hofer, Donaldson, MacKinnon, & Schafer, 1997; Rovine, 1994; Verleye, 1996). However, the EM algorithm, to my knowledge, has not been incorporated in a generally available computer program for SEM.

MAXIMUM LIKELIHOOD ESTIMATION WITH INCOMPLETE DATA

The principles of ML estimation with incomplete data are well known (Dempster et al., 1977; Hartley & Hocking, 1971; Little & Rubin, 1987, 1989; Rubin, 1976; Wilks, 1932). Allison (1987) and Muthén, Kaplan, and Hollis (1987) showed how the method applies to SEM. Unfortunately, their approaches are only practical when the data have just a few distinct patterns of missing data. They also require an exceptionally high level of technical expertise in the use of particular SEM programs. At present, ML estimation with missing data is a standard option in at least two SEM programs, Amos (Arbuckle, 1995) and Mx (Neale, 1997). Both maximize the casewise likelihood of the observed data, computed by minimizing the function

$$C(\gamma) = \sum_{i=1}^{N} \log|\Sigma_{i,mm}| + \sum_{i=1}^{N} (y_{i,m} - \mu_{i,m})'\Sigma_{i,mm}^{-1}(y_{i,m} - \mu_{i,m}), \qquad (1)$$

where $y_{i,m}$ is the observed (or *measured*) portion of the data vector for case i, and $\mu_{i,m}$ and $\Sigma_{i,mm}$ are the mean vector and covariance matrix parameters, but with only the rows and columns corresponding to the observed portions of the data vector for case i. Thus, the Amos and Mx programs are not limited by the number of missing-data patterns and do not require the user to take elaborate steps to accommodate missing data.

Numeric Example

Consider the data set (see Table 12.1):

TABLE 12.1
Example Data Set

Case	V1	V2	V3
1	13	23	21
2	14	22	17
3	15	–	11
4	16	18	–
5	17	17	12
6	–	20	8
7	–	20	15

There are three variables (V1–V3) and seven cases (1–7). Four of the possible 21 observations are missing, as indicated by a dash (–) symbol. There are four different missingness patterns.

222   WOTHKE

There are four possible alternatives for estimating means, variances, and covariances from the incomplete data set.

Listwise Deletion. All cases with missing observations are dropped from the computations. The complete data formulae are then applied to the complete cases (in Table 12.2: cases 1, 2, and 5). The estimates are:

TABLE 12.2
Listwise Deletion Estimates

Covariance	V1	V2	V3
V1	4.33		
V2	−6.67	10.33	
V3	9.17	13.83	20.33
Means	14.67	20.67	16.67

In this example, the LD method discards the records of four of the seven cases from calculations. Obviously, LD does not make efficient use of the observed data.

Pairwise Deletion. For each variable (see Table 12.3), PD computes mean and variance estimates from the univariate complete data. For each pair of variables, PD calculates the covariance estimates from all cases with complete observations on both variables; for instance, the covariance estimate for variables V1 and V2 would be based on cases 1, 2, 4, and 5:

TABLE 12.3
Pairwise Deletion Estimates

Covariance	V1	V2	V3
V1	2.50		
V2	−5.33	5.20	
V3	−6.58	7.95	21.60
Means	15.00	20.00	14.00

PD apparently uses more information from the data and should thus be a more efficient method than LD. On the other hand, analysis of PD covariance matrices presents some known statistical problems that are often overlooked. For one, each entry of such a matrix can be based on a different sample size, and this possibility imposes considerable complications on deriving the joint statistical distribution of the entries of the covariance matrix. In particular, the joint distribution of the elements of a PD covariance matrix cannot usually be considered Wishart,[1] even when the matrix is computed from multinormal data. As a consequence, it is not clear how the fit of a model to a PD covariance matrix can be statistically evaluated. A second often more obvious issue is that the elements of the covariance matrix are estimated not just from different sample sizes but more generally from different portions of the data set, and this can lead to inconsistencies. For instance, the value of -5.33 for cov(V1,V2) corresponds to a correlation of $r = -1.48$, which is an inadmissible value. PD-based sample covariance matrices are a common source of indefiniteness problems in SEM (Wothke, 1993).

Mean Imputation.   Each missing value is replaced by the mean observed value of the same variable (see Table 12.4). In other words, MI is an attempt to make the raw data matrix complete. Afterwards, means and covariances can be calculated as if from complete data:

TABLE 12.4
Mean Imputation Estimates

Covariance	V1	V2	V3
V1	1.67		
V2	−2.67	4.33	
V3	−3.50	5.50	18.00
Means	15.00	20.00	14.00

MI yields the same sample means as PD. Because MI's missing data replacements happen to be the PD means, this should hardly be surprising. The variance estimates under MI are clearly smaller than those obtained under PD. This is a function of the MI algorithm: Brown (1994) and Little and Rubin (1987) pointed out that variance estimates under MI are generally negatively biased. The covariance estimates are also different from either LD or PD. Depending on the pattern of missing data, MI covariance estimates may be systematically larger or systematically smaller than those obtained by LD or PD.

On the positive side, MI does not share the indefiniteness problems encountered under PD: Covariance matrices computed under MI must be positive definite or semidefinite.

---

[1] When complete data vectors are sampled from a multivariate normal population, the joint distribution of the elements in the resulting sample covariance matrix follows a Wishart distribution (Johnson & Kotz, 1972).

Full Information Maximum Likelihood. The FIML (see Table 12.5) estimates of the means and covariances are obtained by maximizing Equation 1 with respect to first and second moments:

TABLE 12.5
Full Information Maximum Likelihood Estimates

Covariance	V1	V2	V3
V1	1.44		
V2	-2.29	3.73	
V3	-3.59	6.14	19.48
Means	14.98	19.98	13.31

This FIML estimate uses all the information of the observed data, including information about the mean and variance of missing portions of a variable, given the observed portion(s) of other variables. Even though the indefiniteness problem observed with the PD estimate may also occur with FIML estimation, it does not seem to be as frequent a problem. In the present case, the FIML covariance matrix estimate is positive definite.

Obviously, the four methods of computing means and covariance matrices from incomplete data can produce radically different solutions, even when the same data are used. These method differences depend on several factors, including the proportion of data missing and the type of process(es) causing the incompleteness of the data.

MISSING DATA MECHANISMS

In order to state the advantages of ML estimation over MI, PD, and LD, it is necessary to consider the mechanisms by which missing data can arise. Rubin (1976) and Little and Rubin (1987) distinguished the processes that generate the missing data with respect to the information they provide about the unobserved data. Missing values of a random variable Y can be missing completely at random (MCAR), missing at random (MAR), or nonignorable. Under an MCAR process, the fact that a variable's data are observed or missing is not thought to affect its distribution, that is, $P(Y|y$ missing) $= P(Y|y$ observed). In this chapter, MCAR is the most restrictive assumption considered for missing data processes. MCAR can sometimes be established in behavioral and social surveys by randomly assigning test booklets or blocks of survey questions to different respondents.

MAR is a more relaxed condition, assuming only that missing and observed distributions of Y are identical, conditional on a set of predictor or stratifying variables X, that is, $P(Y|y\text{ missing}, \mathbf{X}) = P(Y|y\text{ observed}, \mathbf{X})$. One way to establish MAR processes is to include completely observed variables $\mathbf{X}$ that are highly predictive of Y. For instance, inasmuch as past behavior is an effective predictor of future behavior, initial (complete) measurement(s) in longitudinal designs can be a good choice of $\mathbf{X}$.

The performance of the four methods under different types of missing data processes is summarized by Little and Schenker (1995). For data that are MCAR, PD and LD estimates are consistent, although not efficient. MI is consistent in the first moments, but yields biased variance and covariance estimates. If the data are only MAR, then PD and LD estimates may also yield biased results. ML estimates, on the other hand, are already both consistent and efficient when the data are only MAR. In addition, some authors have suggested that ML estimates will tend to show less bias than estimates based on MI, LD, or PD, even when the data deviate from MAR (Little & Rubin, 1989; Muthén et al., 1987). As final shortcomings, PD does not provide standard errors of parameter estimates or tests of model fit, whereas MI can produce standard error estimates and fit statistics that are far too optimistic.

APPLICATION: GROWTH CURVE MODELING

Simulation 1: MCAR Data

To demonstrate the efficiency of ML estimation relative to MI, LD, and PD for a single, fairly typical estimation problem with MCAR data, a small Monte-Carlo simulation was undertaken. The variable names and parameter values are taken from a reanalysis of STEP science data collected by Hilton and Beaton (1971, pp. 343–344). To keep things simple, the Monte-Carlo simulation uses a multivariate normal distribution, with structural parameters provided by the path model shown in Figure 12.1. Suppose that the STEP science test was administered to the same students on four occasions—in 1961, 1963, 1965, and 1967. The substantive interest is to gauge the growth of the science scores over the four test occasions. However, this task is somewhat complicated by the measurement error in the test scores.

The model of Figure 12.1 is essentially the MANOVA approach to growth-curve modeling (Bock, 1975). Each test score is composed of a constant term, a slope, and a residual. The constant and slope terms are modeled as correlated random components, summarizing the individual differences of both initial level and subsequent improvement of the students' science knowledge. The constant term, with mean 254.92 and variance 98.98, is connected to the observed variables with fixed weights of unity. In addition, the constant term makes the only systematic contribution to the 1961 science knowledge test scores. Thus, the mean (254.92) of the constant term gives the mean of the 1961 scores in science knowledge, whereas its variance (98.98) describes the systematic dispersion of 1961 science knowledge among the group of students. The residual variance of 46.71 provides an estimate of the measurement error of the STEP science test.

FIGURE 12.1
Parameters of a Linear Growth Model
(from STEP Science Test, students with high school educated fathers)

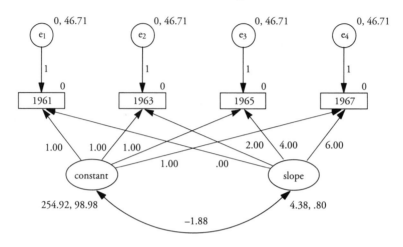

The four paths pointing from the slope term to the four observed variables have their coefficients fixed to a linear trend (0, 2, 4, 6). These fixed coefficients reflect the number of years since the first measurement (in 1961). Hence, the slope mean of 4.38 shows the average growth in science scores per year, and its variance of 0.80 quantifies the interindividual variation of the yearly slope. Constant and slope have somewhat of a negative correlation ($r = -0.21$), implying that students who start out with high 1961 scores have smaller subsequent gains than students with lower initial scores.

The Monte-Carlo simulation employed 400 random data sets of sample size 500, generated from a multivariate normal distribution with the parameters of Figure 12.1. The four variables had some of their values deleted completely at random. Missing data probabilities were 0% (none) for 1961, 10% for 1963, 20% for 1965, and 30% for 1967. Multivariate normal quasi-random numbers were generated by the RANLIB.C routines (Brown & Lovato, 1994) implementing the algorithms by L'Ecuyer and Côté (1991) and Ahrens and Dieter (1973).

Realized missing data rates varied somewhat within samples, because the MCAR process was executed independently on each individual observed value. The growth model of Figure 12.1 was fitted to each Monte-Carlo sample using MI, ML, LD, and PD methods. Altogether, the simulation comprised 1,600 attempts to fit the model.[2] This task was automated by calling the open programming AmosEngine interface from a Visual Basic routine.

---

[2] In 25% to 37% of these simulation runs, Amos indicated some convergence problems. However, this did not seem to make a difference in results. Solutions from "converged" and "non-converged" runs were statistically indistinguishable, thus all results from all simulations were included in the statistical reports.

FIGURE 12.2
Distribution of v (Constant) Estimates, MCAR With FIML (Var = 74.13)

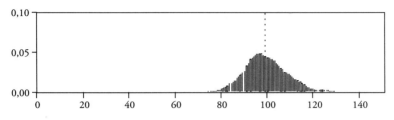

⊥   Gaussian kernel estimate.
· · ·   Parameter: 98.98.

FIGURE 12.3
Distribution of v (Constant) Estimates, MCAR With MI (Var = 73.62)

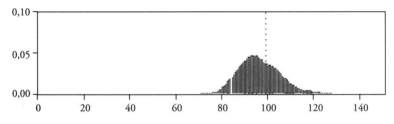

⊥   Gaussian kernel estimate.
· · ·   Parameter: 98.98.

The performance of a single estimation method (say, ML) was assessed in the following way. First, the method was applied to estimate the model for each of 400
Monte-Carlo samples, then the accuracy of the estimates was judged by comparing
them to the bootstrap population parameters in Figure 12.1. The question is which,
if any, of the four methods reproduces the parameter values most closely.

Figures 12.2 to 12.5 display the distributions of the variance estimates for the constant term, with the parameter value of 98.98 indicated by a vertical dotted line. With
the exception of the MI estimate, which is biased downward by 3%, the distributions
are centered on the parameter value within the margins of sampling error. Estimation
bias for this parameter thus appears to be negligible under the FIML, PD, and LD
methods, although the data indicate some difference in precision (or efficiency) of estimation. The relative sampling variance can be used to estimate relative gains in efficiency. Under asymptotic theory, the sampling variances of means, regression coefficients, and variances are inversely related to sample size (Kendall & Stuart, 1977,
p. 258). Thus, when estimating the variance of the constant term, switching from
FIML to LD nearly doubles its sampling variance ($1.80 = 133.17/74.13$). According
to this asymptotic rule, the sample size for LD would have to be increased by approx-

FIGURE 12.4
Distribution of v (Constant) Estimates, MCAR With PD (Var = 78.67)

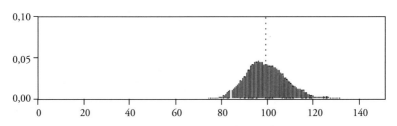

⊥ Gaussian kernel estimate.
... Parameter: 98.98.

FIGURE 12.5
Distribution of v (Constant) Estimates, MCAR With LD (Var = 133.17)

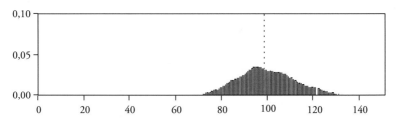

⊥ Gaussian kernel estimate.
... Parameter: 98.98.

imately 80% (i.e., to N = 900) in order to achieve the degree of precision provided by FIML at N = 500.

It has to be stressed that this relative figure of 80% is specific to a single parameter, a single sample size, and a particular choice of missing data rates. Table 12.6 shows means and empirical standard errors for all six parameters in the model. These statistics are affected by an undetermined amount of sampling error. Nevertheless, some broad trends are apparent. As expected with MCAR, the FIML, PD, and LD estimates are all unbiased. The MI method, although unbiased in means, produces notably biased variance and covariance estimates. Among the unbiased estimation methods, FIML yields the most efficient estimates—standard errors generally increase as one moves from FIML estimation to PD, and then to LD. The size of the overall change in precision is difficult to gauge, however, as it depends on characteristics of the model, complete-case population mean and covariance structure, sample size, and frequency of missing data. Simulation work by Arbuckle (1996), Graham et al. (1997), and Verleye (1996) suggests that the relative efficiency of FIML increases as the missing data rate increases.

TABLE 12.6
Model Estimates Under Simulated MCAR

Estimation type	Statistic	Constant			Slope		
		Mean	var	cov	Mean	var	ve
FIML	mean	254.95	98.99	−1.91	4.37	.80	46.56
	s.e.	.51	8.61	1.21	.09	.28	2.47
MI	mean	254.95	96.00	−5.74	4.37	.73	51.43
	s.e.	.51	8.58	1.26	.10	.24	2.36
PD	mean	254.95	99.24	−1.93	4.37	.80	46.71
	s.e.	.51	8.87	1.30	.10	.28	2.55
LD	mean	254.94	99.53	−2.00	4.37	.81	46.59
	s.e.	.76	11.54	1.54	.11	.32	2.90
Parameter value		254.92	98.98	−1.88	4.38	.80	46.71

Simulation 2: A Case of MAR Data

A second Monte-Carlo simulation[3] was performed to illustrate the benefits of ML with data that are MAR but not MCAR. The structural model of Figure 12.1 was used again for this simulation. The sample size was 500, except that the MAR process was set up to simulate a selective dropout mechanism in three stages. First, 80% of the cases with a 1961 knowledge score of less than 246 had their 1963–1967 measurements deleted. Second, of the remaining cases, 80% of those with a 1963 score of less than 255 had both their 1965 and 1967 scores set to missing. Finally, 80% of the remaining cases with 1965 scores of less than 263 had their 1967 values set to missing. The realized missing data rates were 0% in 1961, 16%–20% in 1963, 25%–33% in 1965, and 30%–40% in 1967, with differences in these proportions because of sampling variation.

This type of MAR process emulates the situation in which a person participates in a study for some time and then drops out after showing a low score and encountering other, presumably random, conditions. It is particularly easy to see how MI and LD would lead to biased estimates in this situation, as selectively removing records with low scores or substituting the means of the remaining higher scores would affect both means and covariances of the remaining sample. The effect of the missing data pattern on PD is not so clear-cut. We have already observed the superior efficiency of FIML estimates in the MCAR simulation where PD and LD estimates were known to be unbiased. By contrast, because the present data are only MAR, estimation bias is now of central concern with all estimates.

---

[3] Convergence problems were also indicated with MAR simulation, but again they did not appear to affect the overall results.

TABLE 12.7
Model Estimates Under Simulated MAR

Estimation type	Statistic	Constant			Slope		
		Mean	var	cov	Mean	var	ve
FIML	mean	254.95	98.53	−1.93	4.38	.80	46.53
	s.e.	.53	8.81	1.49	.11	.30	2.54
MI	mean	255.33	78.57	−8.62	5.13	1.59	51.24
	s.e.	.51	6.80	1.19	.11	.24	2.17
PD	mean	255.33	91.58	−5.87	5.13	1.22	50.75
	s.e.	.51	8.38	1.47	.11	.34	2.69
LD	mean	260.57	46.93	−.79	4.24	.80	42.02
	s.e.	.47	6.30	1.00	.09	.26	2.38
Parameter value		254.92	98.98	−1.88	4.38	.80	46.71

Examples of method-specific estimation bias with MAR data are shown in Figures 12.6 to 12.9. Although the FIML variance estimate of the constant is neatly centered at the parameter value—perhaps with a somewhat large sampling variance—the MI, PD, and LD estimates all show negative bias. PD estimates are biased downwards by a moderate degree (approximately 7.5%), but the sampling distributions of MI and LD estimates do not even appear to include the parameter value. Particularly, the LD estimates are all located below 70. Note that the sampling variance under MI and LD is at least 40% smaller than under FIML. One might summarize that MI and LD yield very precise estimates of exactly the wrong parameter.

Table 12.7 shows the means and standard errors of the six parameter estimates computed by the four estimation methods averaged across 400 samples of size 500. For almost every parameter, FIML provides the estimate with the least bias. Because the missing data process is MAR instead of MCAR, the MI, PD, and LD methods are not only biased in variances and covariances but also in the mean parameters of the constant and slope terms. For several parameters, estimation is dramatically better with FIML than with PD and LD.

Summary

It is impossible to put a single figure on the gain in accuracy of estimation to be had by abandoning MI, PD, and LD in favor of FIML. It is hard to imagine a situation, however, in which FIML would yield worse results than MI, PD, or LD. The advantage of FIML depends on the missing data rate, the covariance structure of the data, and the size of the sample, and it differs from one parameter to another. Nevertheless, the two simulations demonstrate that FIML can be superior to PD, and superior to MI and LD by a wide margin.

FIGURE 12.6
Distribution of v (Constant) Estimates, MCAR With FIML (Var = 77.62)

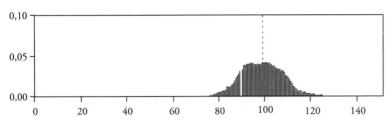

⊥ Gaussian kernel estimate.
... Parameter: 98.98.

FIGURE 12.7
Distribution of v (Constant) Estimates, MCAR With MI (Var = 46.24)

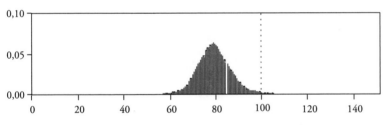

⊥ Gaussian kernel estimate.
... Parameter: 98.98.

FIGURE 12.8
Distribution of v (Constant) Estimates, MCAR With PD (Var = 70.22)

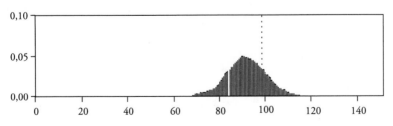

⊥ Gaussian kernel estimate.
... Parameter: 98.98.

231

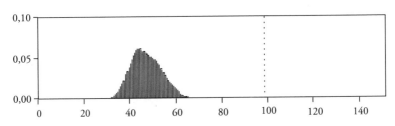

FIGURE 12.9
Distribution of v (Constant) Estimates, MCAR With LD (Var = 39.69)

⊥   Gaussian kernel estimate.
· · ·   Parameter: 98.98.

APPLICATION: AUTOREGRESSIVE PROCESS

A series of time-dependent autoregression and Markov models (Jöreskog, 1977a) demonstrates the ease of analyzing incomplete longitudinal data and of testing all models
simultaneously against an artificial sample. James Arbuckle first presented this example
at the 1996 Meeting of the American Educational Research Association. The Amos
Graphics specification of the most general model appears in Figure 12.10. There are
four time-dependent variables, Q1, Q2, Q3, and Q4, which can be thought of as four
consecutive measurements of the same variable or quantity. Each observed variable is
modeled as a linear function of the earlier variables, plus a random shock or residual
term.

The three-equation model is just-identified. It has zero degrees of freedom and
cannot be rejected by a global test of fit. Note that the path diagram shows nine parameters with the distinct labels b12, b13, b14, b23, b24, b34, v2, v3, and v4. These
labels may be used in constraints defining submodels that can be tested against the
data. Three submodels might be considered interesting in this type of longitudinal
application:

1. *Saturated model.* This is the model of Figure 12.10 without any constraints. It is a
   descriptive account of a four-occasion longitudinal design. The measurement at a
   given occasion is a linear function of the preceding measurements. Although the
   model itself cannot be tested, the parameter estimates and their approximate standard errors may be of exploratory value.
2. *Markov model.* In a Markov model, the values of a time-dependent variable are dependent only on the values of the previous occasion. In other words, there are neither lag-2 nor lag-3 effects. A (linear) Markov model can be defined by the three
   constraints: b13 = b14 = b24 = 0. Assuming normality, model fit can be assessed
   by a χ^2 test with three degrees of freedom.

FIGURE 12.10
Time-Dependent Process—Model Specification

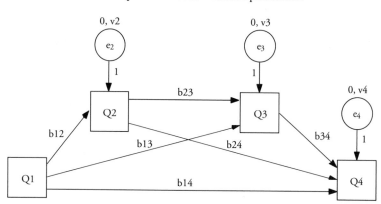

3. *Stationary Markov model.* A Markov model with time-invariant prediction equations is called stationary. Ignoring intercept terms, two equality constraints are required to make the regression weights stationary: b12 = b23 = b34. Two additional constraints are needed to render the residual variance terms stationary as well: v2 = v3 = v4. The stationary Markov model can be tested under normality by the χ^2 fit statistic with seven degrees of freedom. Incremental change of fit from the general Markov model can be assessed by the likelihood ratio χ^2 test with four degrees of freedom.

The input data for estimating the three models may look like the file fragment shown in Table 12.8. Amos handles several popular data formats with different conventions for coding missing values. In many spreadsheet-type data formats, missing data are simply coded as blank entries, as in Table 12.8. For instance, case 2 is missing the value of Q4; case 37 is missing Q1, Q3, and Q4; and case 39 is missing Q1.

When Amos encounters missing values among the modeled data, the program switches automatically from its default moment-based maximum likelihood algorithm to the casewise formula in Equation 1. The Amos user must request estimation of mean and intercept parameters because, with incomplete data, their contribution to the likelihood is no longer independent of variance and covariance terms. The most general model is specified as the input-path diagram of Figure 12.10. The three submodels are defined within the Amos 4 Model Manager.

Table 12.9 presents a short list of the more than twenty[4] fit statistics provided by Amos 4 with incomplete data. To evaluate the fit of a working model in the missing data case, Amos must fit both working and saturated models. Assuming both models

---

[4] Some fit indices, such as the GFI and RMR, are defined only for complete data. Other fit indices, including the BIC and CAIC, were devised only for single group analyses without mean structures. These statistics do not apply to incomplete data, at least not in their 1990s formulations.

converge to global solutions,[5] the χ^2 fit-statistic is obtained as the difference in function of the log likelihood (l) values between the working and saturated models. The (positive) difference in number of parameters between models gives the associated degrees of freedom. The χ^2 fit statistics appear in the CMIN column of Table 12.9. The first three lines display the fit of the specified Saturated, Markov, and Stationary Markov submodels. With our artificial data, the fit of the Markov model would appear quite reasonable (χ^2 = 3.8; df = 3; p = .28), whereas the large χ^2 of the Stationary Markov model (χ^2 = 31.4; df = 7; p = .00) would indicate misspecification of that model. The bottom panel of Table 12.9 shows the Markov model with the smallest AIC and BCC statistics—smaller even than the Saturated model. According to Akaike (1987), the model with the smallest AIC has the best fit. Akaike's rule would pick the Markov model over either Stationary Markov or Saturated models.

TABLE 12.8
Input Data for Autoregressive Process

Case	Q1	Q2	Q3	Q4
1	19	14	15	17
2	19	16	17	
3	18	20	18	17
... many more similar records ...				
37		7		
38	12	12	18	17
39		19	15	15

TABLE 12.9
Model Fit

Summary of models Model	NPAR	CMIN	df	p	CMIN/df	AIC	BCC
Saturated	14	0.000	0			28.000	32.242
Markov	11	3.822	3	0.281	1.274	25.822	29.155
Stationary Markov	7	31.364	7	0.000	4.481	45.364	47.485
Saturated model	14	0.000	0			28.000	32.242
Null model	8	424.405	6	0.000	70.734	440.405	442.829

---

[5] Unless the number of observed variables becomes large relative to number of cases and observed data rates, both working and saturated models usually converge to global maxima. This χ^2 statistic can usually be computed whenever the saturated model has a global solution.

TABLE 12.10
Incremental Fit Statistics

Model comparisons	df	CMIN	p	NFI δ–1	IFI δ–2	RFI ρ–1	TLI ρ–2
Assuming model saturated to be correct							
Markov	3	3.822	0.281	0.009	0.009		
Stationary Markov	7	31.364	0.000	0.074	0.074		
Assuming model Markov to be correct							
Stationary Markov	4	27.542	0.000	0.065	0.065	0.045	0.046

TABLE 12.11
Parameter Estimates of the Markov Model

		Estimate	S.E.	C.R.	Label
Regression weights					
	Q2<----Q1	0.857	0.137	6.261	b12
	Q3<----Q2	0.452	0.152	2.972	b23
	Q4<----Q3	0.167	0.072	2.311	b34
Means					
	Q1	15.059	0.636	23.692	
Intercepts					
	Q2	2.475	2.126	1.164	
	Q3	7.714	2.433	3.170	
	Q4	13.584	1.100	12.349	
Variances					
	Q1	14.576	3.478	4.191	
	e2	9.279	2.287	4.057	v2
	e3	14.128	3.632	3.890	v3
	e4	2.229	0.637	3.498	v4
Implied (for all variables) covariances					
		Q1	Q2	Q3	Q4
	Q1	14.576			
	Q2	12.490	19.982		
	Q3	5.639	9.022	18.202	
	Q4	0.941	1.505	3.037	2.736
Implied (for all variables) means					
		Q1	Q2	Q3	Q4
		15.059	15.380	14.658	16.030

Because the three models are hierarchically nested, their relative discrepancies can be tested by the likelihood ratio χ^2 statistic. Table 12.10 summarizes these incremental fit statistics. Comparing the Markov and Stationary Markov models is particularly interesting. The large χ^2 of 27.542 (df= 4) is a strong rejection of the stationarity assumption: The residual variances and lag-1 regression weights do vary over time.

Parameter estimates and approximate standard errors of the general Markov model appear in Table 12.11. The standard errors are an implicit and convenient by-product of the FIML algorithm employed by Amos. Their primary use is to gauge the likely ranges of the parameter estimates under replication. A common rule of thumb (based on the asymptotic normality of the estimates) assumes a 95% confidence interval at ± 2 standard errors from the estimate. According to this rule, the size of the lag-1 autoregression weights appears to decline over time. In addition, the residual variances at occasions 2, 3, and 4 come out heterogeneous. Both findings corroborate the earlier decision against the Stationary Markov model.

Note the implied covariance matrix and mean vector at the bottom of Table 12.11. These first and second moments derive from the estimated parameters of the Markov model and are thus a function of the observed data as well as the working model.

Summary

Model specification and estimation with missing data follow the same strategies as in the complete data scenario. Except for specifying a missing data code, the FIML implementation of the Amos and Mx programs does not complicate the model setup. In return, FIML delivers parameter estimates unbiased under MAR and standard errors estimates based on asymptotic normal theory. For model testing, fit χ^2 statistics are usually available whenever the Saturated model has a FIML solution. In addition, when competing models are hierarchically nested, the likelihood ratio chi-square test provides a powerful tool for detecting sources of misfit.

APPLICATION: MULTIPLE GROUPS WITH MISSING DATA

The first practical maximum likelihood implementation of incomplete data modeling in the SEM framework used a multiple-group approach (Allison, 1987). The example in this section is based on one presented in Allison's original paper, but has been modified to show how latent variables are conceptually the same as missing data (cf. Dempster et al., 1977).

Bielby, Hauser, and Featherman (1977) studied the relationship between indicators of occupational status and educational attainment in a sample of 2,020 African American fathers. Using a single indicator for each construct, Bielby et al. estimated the correlation between occupational status and educational attainment as r = 0.43 for the entire sample. Realizing that measurement error and temporal instability of

their single indicators would likely attenuate the correlation estimate, Bielby et al. re-interviewed a random subsample of 348 study participants approximately three weeks after the first interview. For this subgroup, they obtained a second set of occupational status and educational attainment indicators that can be used for estimating the size of the measurement error. The data were reported (Allison, 1987) as two subsamples:
(a) Bielby et al. (1977) complete data ($n = 348$; see Table 12.12):

TABLE 12.12
Bielby et al. Complete Data Subsample

Covariances	FAOC_t1	FAOC_t2	FAED_t1	FAED_t2
FAOC_t1	180.90			
FAOC_t2	126.77	217.56		
FAED_t1	23.96	30.20	16.24	
FAED_t2	22.86	30.47	14.36	15.13
Means	16.62	17.39	6.65	6.75

(b) Bielby et al. (1977) incomplete data ($N = 1,672$); unobserved means and (co-)variances indicated by dashes (see Table 12.13):

TABLE 12.13
Bielby et al. Incomplete Data Subsample

Covariances	FAOC_t1	FAOC_t2	FAED_t1	FAED_t2
FAOC_t1	217.27			
FAOC_t2	–	–		
FAED_t1	25.57	–	16.16	
FAED_t2	–	–	–	–
Means	16.98	–	6.83	–

The two-group factor model of Figures 12.11 and 12.12 proposes a simple way to separate stable (or systematic) measurement components from measurement error and to estimate the disattenuated correlation. Figure 12.11 shows the confirmatory factor model for the complete data subsample. Father's occupational status has two observed indicators, FAOC_t1 and FAOC_t2, with independent error terms e1 and e2. Father's educational attainment has two observed indicators, FAED_t1 and FAED_t2, again with independent error terms e3 and e4. The hypothetically error-free occupational status and educational attainment variables are correlated. The

FIGURE 12.11
Measurement Model for the Complete Subsample

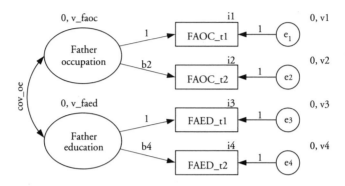

FIGURE 12.12
Measurement Model for the Incomplete Subsample

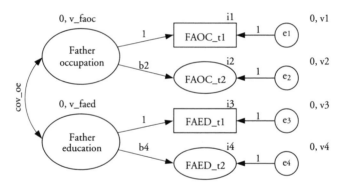

model has 13 free parameters, all labeled: one factor covariance (cov_oe), two factor variances (v_faoc and v_faed), two regression weights (b2 and b4), four intercepts (i1, i2, i3, and i4), and four specific variance terms (v1, v2, v3, and v4).

Figure 12.12 uses the same measurement model for the incomplete subsample, including parameter labels. In Amos's notation, two parameters that share the same label are automatically equal-valued. In other words, using the same label for a parameter throughout all groups makes that parameter group-invariant. All corresponding free parameters in panels of Figure 12.11 are shown with group-invariant labels, and all fixed parameters have the same value in both groups. This means the entire model is group-invariant and implies that the missing data process is MCAR. The only difference is that the model in Figure 12.12 accommodates the missing variables. Placing FAOC_t2 and FAED_t2 in ellipses in the second group declares these variables as latent or unobserved—in other words, missing.

The analysis estimates the disattenuated correlation between occupational status and educational attainment as $r = 0.623$ (s.e. $= 0.029$). The overall fit of the two-group model is quite acceptable ($\chi^2 = 7.8$, $df = 6$), supporting the implied assumption that the data are MCAR.[6] This estimate is quite different from the correlation of 0.43 between the observed variables FAOC_t1 and FAED_t1.

Summary

Allison's (1987) multigroup implementation can also be accommodated within Amos. The setup is similar to other contemporary SEM programs, except that Amos permits additional simplifications. The multigroup setup for missing data analysis involves these steps:

1. Draw a model for complete data and label all free parameters. Select mean-level analysis.
2. Turn the single group specification into a multigroup analysis, declaring one "group" for each pattern of missing data. Issue Amos' *Heterogeneous Groups* command. Connect each group with its data file. The *Heterogeneous Groups* command removes the necessity of having the same model and the same variables in all groups. It also allows different groups to use different numbers of variables.
3. In each group's path diagram, use the *Toggle Observed/Unobserved* tool to mark the missing variables as latent (or unobserved).

Allison's multigroup approach may be regarded as an alternative to Amos' casewise (default) FIML estimation with incomplete data. There are some obvious trade-offs to using Allison's multigroup setups. As mentioned previously, model specification by the multigroup approach is both more laborious and only feasible with a small number of missing data patterns. On the other hand, all fit statistics, modification indices, and residual analyses normally available with complete data are provided when the multigroup setup is employed. In addition, the group-specific means and variances of the exogenous variables are under the modeler's control, permitting detailed tests of MCAR, MAR and other assumptions.

DISCUSSION

Maximum likelihood (FIML) estimation with incomplete data is a feasible method, now available in the Amos and Mx SEM programs. FIML is more efficient and less biased than listwise and pairwise deletion and mean imputation methods. In the case of MAR data, FIML can be dramatically less biased than listwise deletion and mean

---

[6] The MAR assumption can be incorporated into multigroup missing data approach by letting means and covariances of the exogenous observed variables vary freely across groups. Such an MAR analysis is possible when missing data occur only among endogenous variables, but not exogenous ones.

imputation methods. This is why FIML should be the preferred method of treating missing data when the alternative is pairwise or listwise deletion or mean imputation.

Maximum likelihood's lack of reliance on the MCAR requirement is a feature that remains to be fully exploited. Unbiasedness under MAR and higher efficiency under MCAR make maximum likelihood the method of choice in situations with incomplete multinormal data.

Feasible alternatives to the FIML approach of Amos and Mx are the EMCOV and NORM approaches (Graham & Hofer, chap. 11, this volume), which use EM and data augmentation methods based on the saturated model for imputing values of the missing data. The completed data matrices would subsequently be analyzed by traditional SEM methods.

With the FIML approach of Amos and Mx, in contrast, it is not necessary either to impute values for missing data or to estimate the population moments as a prerequisite to model fitting by ML. These are optional steps, which—if performed at all—are best done after the model is fitted (see the Technical Appendix on http://www.mpib-berlin.de/research_resources/index.html), not before. Most structural modeling programs report estimates of population means, variances, and covariances, calculated from parameter estimates under the assumption of a correct model.

It should not be overlooked that structural modeling with the Amos program can also be used to solve missing data problems that arise in conventional analyses, such as regression with observed variables or the simple estimation of means and variances.

CHAPTER THIRTEEN

Customizing Longitudinal and Multiple-Group Structural Modeling Procedures

James L. Arbuckle
Temple University

If you use a structural modeling program, you probably use other statistical software as well. Solving a complex data analysis problem typically requires the use of a variety of tools. Unfortunately, the design of structural equation modeling (SEM) programs as stand-alone programs presents an obstacle to their integration with other software. It is customary to use SEM programs in only one way: First, use a mouse or a keyboard to enter a model specification. Then, run the SEM program. Finally, visually inspect the program's output or transfer the output manually into some other program such as a word processor. Many developments in SEM programs have been directed towards simplifying this process, making the programs more "user friendly." However, a computer program that is friendly to users is not necessarily friendly to other programs.

Occasional efforts have been made to create software that automates the use of SEM programs, for example in simulation studies in which it can be necessary to perform thousands of SEM analyses, and in the development of preprocessors and postprocessors for SEM programs. Such efforts demonstrate that it is possible, with difficulty, to execute stand-alone SEM programs under the control of other programs. However, this approach to automation of SEM requires a very high level of programming skill.

Beginning with Version 4, Amos supports OLE automation, a feature of the Microsoft Windows operating system that allows one computer program to directly use and extend the capabilities of another program. Through the mechanism of OLE automation, any Windows program can use Amos to perform a SEM analysis. This chapter explains how OLE automation is supported in Amos and outlines some of its

benefits. The chapter begins by describing the widespread practice of using preprocessors and postprocessors to extend the capabilities of SEM programs. The remainder
of the chapter introduces OLE automation as an alternative method for re-using and
extending the model-fitting capabilities embedded in SEM programs. Examples are
presented to show the benefits of OLE automation as applied to problems in longitudinal and multiple-group analyses. Although the chapter reports experiences with
OLE automation in Amos, similar benefits would be realized by the implementation
of this technique in connection with any SEM program.

PREPROCESSORS AND POSTPROCESSORS

Sometimes a preprocessor, or "front end," program is used to enhance the capabilities
of a SEM program or to make it easier to use. A preprocessor creates an input file for
a SEM program and then executes the SEM program. The PRELIS (Jöreskog &
Sörbom, 1996) program, for example, is a preprocessor that enhances the capabilities
of LISREL.

The STREAMS software is an especially ambitious and successful example of a preprocessor. STREAMS also employs a postprocessor that scans the output from a SEM
program, reformats the output, and performs additional calculations. The STREAMS
program demonstrates that a preprocessor/postprocessor combination can be used to
effectively put a new face on an old program. From the point of view of the STREAMS
user, the user interface of the original SEM program is discarded and the computational portion of the original program is reused with a new interface and additional
functionality.

The operation of a preprocessor/postprocessor combination is illustrated in
Figure 13.1. A preprocessor/postprocessor combination provides an effective means
of reusing the capabilities of an existing SEM program, but it is an effortful approach
to software reuse because it relies on an existing user interface that was designed for a
human user.

OLE AUTOMATION

Microsoft Windows provides a facility called *OLE automation,* or just *automation,*
that allows one computer program (the *automation controller*) to control the operation of another program (the *automation server*). The implementation of automation
in Amos is depicted in Figure 13.2.

The *SEM calculator* and the *user interface* in Figure 13.2 are separate programs that
run concurrently. Both programs can run on the same machine, or they can run on
different machines. The model-fitting algorithm is contained in the box labeled *SEM
calculator.* The *user interface* box interacts with the user to obtain a model specification and other information about how the analysis is to be performed, and it displays
the results of fitting the model.

FIGURE 13.1

Preprocessor/Postprocessor Interface for an Existing SEM Program

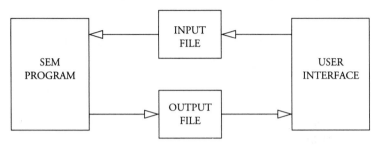

Amos comes with both a SEM calculator and a user interface. The user interface is an enhanced version of the general purpose graphical interface that was provided with earlier versions of Amos. The advantage of isolating the SEM calculator from the user interface is that alternative interfaces can be substituted without modifying the SEM calculator. Some alternative user interfaces, a few of which are described later in this chapter, are available at http://www.mpib-berlin.mpg.de/research_resources/index.html and at http://www.smallwaters.com/books/mpi_modeling_code.html. Researchers can also write their own user interface. A user interface is simply a computer program that gives instructions to the SEM calculator. A user interface can specify a model, give the location of data files, and select options such as which discrepancy function to use, whether to obtain bootstrap confidence intervals, and so on. It can interact with a user, preprocess the data, or construct a data set in the case of simulation studies. It can perform additional processing on the results of an analysis and display or save the results in a custom format. The user interface can carry out a single SEM analysis or multiple SEM analyses.

FIGURE 13.2

Use of Automation to Isolate SEM Calculations From the User Interface

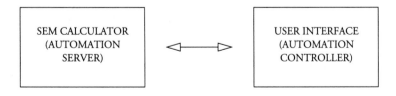

SIMPLE SEM PROGRAMMING

It is not necessary to be a proficient computer programmer in order to benefit from automation. If researchers wish to avoid programming entirely, they can be a consumer of user interfaces written by other people. Some alternative user interfaces are mentioned later, in the section, "Advanced SEM Programming."

If researchers choose not to use the graphical user interface that is supplied with Amos and cannot obtain a suitable interface elsewhere, then they can write their own. Writing a SEM program may sound like a lot of trouble, but it turns out that writing a short program to fit a specific model to a specific set of data is not that hard. Also, as a point of comparison, it should be remembered that preparing a text file for input to any SEM program is not that easy. The class of models that SEM encompasses is sufficiently large that specifying a particular model requires what numerous authors have referred to as a model specification language. Steiger (1989) spoke of the PATH1 language. Jöreskog (1997) referred to the LISREL language and the SIMPLIS language, and Bentler (1997) referred to the EQS language. Gustafsson and Stahl (1997) referred to the Amos language and to the Model Building language employed by STREAMS. Indeed, it is common to hear someone speak of writing a "LISREL program" or an "EQS program" for performing an SEM analysis.

Writing an Amos program for fitting a specific model to a specific set of data does not in fact differ much from preparing a text file for input to other SEM programs. The web sites mentioned earlier provide an example of a simple Amos program written in Visual Basic. Equivalent input files for some other SEM programs are also provided for comparison. The purpose of the comparison is not to point out any advantages to using a general purpose programming language for SEM, but to demonstrate that there are no substantial drawbacks. The benefits of using an existing general purpose programming language for SEM are realized only when one goes beyond the task of writing a program to fit a specific model to a specific set of data. Programming at a higher level of generality is addressed later. However, even from the perspective of a person who wants only a keyboard interface for model specification, piggybacking on an established general purpose programming language has substantial benefits. First, each investigator can choose his or her own programming language. Second, popular implementations of widely used general purpose programming languages come with exceptionally sophisticated parsing, error detection, text editing, and debugging capabilities—superior to any that could be economically provided for a language dedicated to SEM.

What Is Needed

Several programming environments and languages are available for creating automation controllers. These include Microsoft Visual Basic, Microsoft C++, Visual Fortran, Borland Delphi, SPSS, SAS, and Mathcad. As of the late 1990s, only Visual Basic (VB) and SPSS have been used to write automation controllers for Amos. The examples in this chapter employ Visual Basic as the programming language. The language is relatively easy to learn and is widely available in several versions. The Control Creation Edition of Visual Basic (VBCCE) has the advantage of being free. It can be downloaded from the Microsoft web site (www.microsoft.com). One shortcoming of VBCCE is that the programs written with it can only be used by persons who have their own copies of Visual Basic. For many purposes, this is not an important limitation. An investigator may also create an automation controller using Visual Basic for Applications (VBA), which is included with Microsoft Office 97. This version of VB provides an excellent environment for developing Amos programs, but it is slightly less convenient to use than other versions of VB. As with VBCCE, programs that are written using VBA can only be used by persons who have their own copies of Visual Basic. Finally, the Learning Edition, the Professional Edition, and the Enterprise Edition of Visual Basic can be used to create automation controllers that can be distributed in compiled form.

ADVANCED SEM PROGRAMMING

Programs that fit a specific model to a specific data set are easy to write, but do not fully exercise the capabilities of a general purpose programming language. An accomplished programmer can take fuller advantage of the SEM calculator in Figure 13.2 by writing user interfaces that solve a wider class of problems. For that matter, it is quite practical to write one's own general purpose SEM program with an entirely original user interface, extending the functionality of the calculating engine and tailoring input and output to personal requirements.

Model-Specific SEM Programs

One important opportunity for experts in structural modeling lies in the creation of model-specific SEM programs for others to use. Methodologists have proposed many SEM models that are intended not for the analysis of a single set of data but as prototypes that can be adapted by many researchers to their own data. Such prototypical models include growth curve models (McArdle, 1988), dynamic factor models (Molenaar, 1994), autoregressive models (Browne & DuToit, 1991), models for multiple-group factor analysis and analysis of covariance with latent variables (Sörbom, 1974, 1978), and models for change (Raykov, 1994a; Steyer, Partchev, & Shanahan, chap. 6, this volume), just to name a few. In fact, the exploitation of SEM for model fitting has become a significant source of new developments in methodology. A volume on methodology in the study of change (Collins & Horn, 1991) contains 18 chapters, of which 9 develop or discuss at least one model for change within the framework of structural modeling.

The implementation of these techniques as special cases of SEM is theoretically and computationally economical. It is easier to adapt a general purpose SEM program to a specific modeling problem than it is to write a special purpose modeling program from scratch. Innovations in the SEM algorithm, such as bootstrap procedures or new methods of treating missing data or ordinal data, are inherited by every technique that has been implemented through SEM. Finally, SEM provides a conceptual framework within which a wide variety of data analysis methods can be understood.

Unfortunately, general purpose SEM programs can be hard to use, especially for the specification of complex models. It is easy to make a mistake and get a wrong result because of human error. One well-known practitioner of SEM has remarked more than once (McArdle, 1991a; McArdle, 1994, p. 454) on his own difficulties in correctly specifying a complex model. What hope is there then for the rest of us?

The reason it is so hard to get a general purpose SEM program to do the right thing is that it can do so many things. Its very generality constitutes an obstacle to its use. If investigators use a program that can fit many kinds of models, they must make the effort to specify what model they want to fit. Moreover, they run the risk that they will make a mistake, and that the program will fit some model other than the one they had in mind.

Automation provides a way for an expert in the use of a particular type of model to create software that allows users with less expertise to use the model. By way of example, the file *GrowthCurve.vbp* contains a generic growth-modeling subroutine. An investigator wishing to fit a growth curve model to his or her own set of data need only supply three pieces of information to this subroutine: the name of the data file, a list of the names of the variables containing the measurements at successive time points, and the time measurements at the successive time points.

The user of the generic growth modeling subroutine does not need to know how to constrain the parameters of a growth curve model in order to make it identified. The creator of the subroutine has built in that knowledge. This is an example of how a model-specific SEM program can help the user in ways that a general purpose SEM program cannot. When it comes to particular models, rules for ensuring identification are often known and can be provided in a model-specific program. A model-specific program may also be able to choose especially good initial parameter values, to perform additional checks on assumptions, or to detect and flag unacceptable parameter estimates.

An improved growth curve subroutine might well produce output that is customized for growth curve models instead of relying on generic SEM output. The output could be made model specific and, perhaps, more easily understood, by displaying only results that are relevant to growth curve models and by labeling the output in language that is appropriate to growth curve modeling. An enhanced growth curve modeling interface that implements all these refinements as well as others can be downloaded from the web site referred to earlier. The enhanced interface is implemented as a type of program that has come to be called a *wizard*. The *GrowthCurve* wizard presents a sequence of simple forms that allow an investigator to specify (a) the name of the data file, (b) the names of the variables to be analyzed, and (c) the time points at which successive measurements were made. The wizard automatically fits a linear growth curve model, a quadratic growth curve model (when there are four or more time points), and a "level" (McArdle & Aber, 1990) baseline model. It also performs nested model comparisons of the three models.

Other wizards are available. The *FactorMeans* wizard implements Sörbom's (1974) method for estimating factor means when fitting a factor model to multiple samples. The user of the wizard needs to specify (a) the names of the data files, (b) the number of groups, (c) the number of factors, (d) the names of the factors, and (e) which observed variables depend on which factors. The wizard automatically constrains the model parameters in order to make the model identified and fits the hierarchy of models described by Sörbom.

The *Sorbom78* wizard implements Sörbom's (1978) alternative to analysis of covariance in which both the dependent variable and the covariate are latent variables. The wizard asks the user to (a) give the names of the data files, (b) name the (latent) dependent variable and the (latent) covariate, (c) specify the indicators of the two latent variables, and (d) specify whether the indicators of the dependent variable and those of the covariate constitute two repeated measurements on the same variables (for instance pretest and posttest measurements). The wizard then constrains the model parameters in order to make the model identified and fits the hierarchy of models that Sörbom recommends.

The development of model-specific SEM software can be a useful tool for promoting the use of new models by making them more accessible. When a new application of SEM is being presented, it is a common practice (e.g., Dolan & Molenaar, 1994; Little, 1997; McArdle & Prescott, 1992; Wothke, 1996) to provide an illustrative input file that shows how to implement the new method using some well-known SEM program. It is then left as a problem for the reader to adapt the example to the reader's own data. An alternative approach that places fewer burdens on the reader is to make available a parameterized subroutine or a stand-alone program for the new method.

SEM as a Component in Other Data Analysis Programs

The previous section suggested that model-specific SEM software can enable more researchers to use SEM while reducing the chance of incorrect use. The present section describes a way of incorporating SEM into other data analysis programs in such a way that the end user need not necessarily understand the principles of structural modeling at all.

Raykov (1997b) developed a method based on SEM for estimating the reliability of a composite of congeneric measures. This reliability estimate can be computed in the same circumstances in which Cronbach's coefficient α can be computed, but does not suffer from coefficient α's underestimation of reliability in the general case of congeneric measures (as opposed to essentially τ-equivalent measures). Estimating composite reliability requires fitting a structural equation model that Raykov calls the composite reliability for congeneric measures model (CRCMM).

It is possible that an investigator who is unacquainted with SEM would neverthe-less benefit from using the Raykov reliability measure. Such a need could be met by the Visual Basic function contained in the file *RaykovReliability.vbp*. The function ac-cepts a list of variable names and returns the Raykov reliability coefficient for the composite obtained by summing the variables. The function does not require any of the usual SEM input and does not generate any of the usual SEM output. In practice, this function might usefully be embedded in an item analysis program. A suitably in-formed user of the item analysis program could in this case obtain and interpret the reliability coefficient without being aware that an SEM analysis was performed in the course of calculating it. As an aside, the function in *RaykovReliability.vbp* returns the full information maximum likelihood estimate (Arbuckle, 1996) of composite reli-ability even when some measurements are missing. This is an additional benefit of us-ing the Raykov coefficient instead of coefficient α.

CHAPTER FOURTEEN

Individual Fit, Heterogeneity, and Missing Data in Multigroup Structural Equation Modeling

Michael C. Neale
Virginia Commonwealth University

For many years, structural equation models have been fitted to summary statistics, primarily covariances, but sometimes to the means as well. Beginning in the 1990s, programs such as Mx and Amos have shown the advantages of fitting models to raw data, and it is extensions of this method that form the main focus of this chapter. A frequently asked question is: "How does one fit structural equations models to the raw data by maximum likelihood?" In some ways, this is a strange question because it is a simpler question to answer than one that asks about the origin of the formula used for fitting models to covariance matrices. Therefore, this chapter begins with an elementary introduction to maximum likelihood (ML), including the concepts of individual fit and the multivariate normal distribution. The second section discusses various alternative measures of individual fit, suitable for use when some of the data are missing. The third section considers moderator variables as a potential source of non-normality. If these moderators have been measured, it is possible to explicitly model their effects. For the case of binary moderators, the model may be specified as a two-group structural equation model, but continuous moderators require an extension to ML analysis of raw data such that there is a different model for every subject in the sample. Finally, although individual-fit statistics can be useful for detecting outliers or mixture distributions and for judging the value of adding moderating variables, heterogeneity may not always be directly related to an observed moderator variable. Formal methods for detecting "latent" heterogeneity require the application of finite-mixture distributions, which are described in the fourth section.

FITTING MODELS BY MAXIMUM LIKELIHOOD

Basic Principles

Likelihood is a simple concept based in probability theory. The relationship of likelihood to probability is so close that it can be confusing for the novice. To take a trivial example, suppose a coin is tossed 100 times and that 53 times it shows heads. The
probability of this outcome, given that the coin has a probability $p = .5$ of heads, is
easy to calculate from the binomial distribution, which is:

$$\frac{(h + t!)}{h! \times t!} \times (p)^h \times (1 - p)^h .\tag{1}$$

When this formula is applied to our example, where $h = 53$, $t = 47$, and $p = .5$ we
obtain

$$\frac{100!}{53! \times 47!} \times .5^{53} \times (1 - .5)^{47} = .07 .\tag{2}$$

This probability statement is the usual way of viewing the outcome or results of an
experiment. If we ran a number of such experiments, we would obtain a series of
probabilities for the particular sequence of number of heads observed in the experiments. In contrast, with likelihood, we are interested in whether the coin is really unbiased, and we wish to examine one particular set of results as a function of p, which
would not be .5 for a biased coin. Figure 14.1 shows the likelihood of obtaining 53
heads plotted for values of p from zero to one. The original probability is calculated
under the assumption that $p = .5$ and appears as .07 in the figure; this is also the likelihood for $p = .5$. Notice that the curve has a maximum (the maximum likelihood estimate or MLE) at a value somewhat greater than .5; in fact this is at .53, corresponding to the 53/100. Elementary calculus can be used to show that the MLE of a proportion is the observed proportion, but this simple relation does not hold for all
maximum likelihood estimates. Often, the calculus and algebra involved is very complicated and may defy analytic solution, so that one resorts to using numerical optimization to find MLEs. This optimization approach is used in all the SEM programs
(e.g., Amos, EQS, CALIS, LISREL, and Mx).

Likelihood theory concerns itself with comparisons between the height of the
curve—the likelihood—at various values of parameters such as p. In Figure 14.1 the
likelihood at the maximum is $L_{p = .53} = .0797332$, which can be compared with the
likelihood under the hypothesis that the coin is unbiased, $L_{p = .5} = 0.0665905$, via a
likelihood ratio test. Twice the difference between the logarithm of these likelihoods
is asymptotically distributed as χ^2 with one degree of freedom. (Fixing p at the prior
chosen value of .5 instead of allowing it to vary as a free parameter gives one degree
of freedom.) In this case we have

FIGURE 14.1
Likelihood Curve Based on the Binomial Distribution for the Outcome of 53 Heads From
100 Tosses; the Likelihood Varies as a Function of the Parameter p, the Probability of
Obtaining Heads

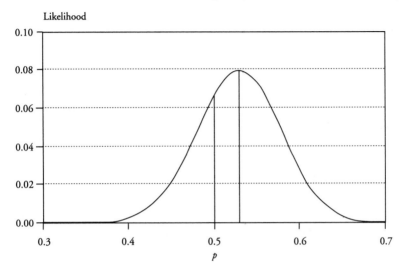

Likelihood

Twice the Log-Likelihood Showing the Difference (χ^2) Between the Maximum
Likelihood Estimate of .53 and the Population Value of Point Five

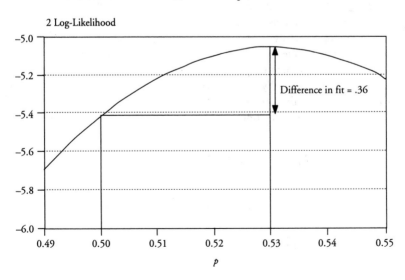

2 Log-Likelihood

$$2 \times (\log 0.0665905 - \log 0.0797332) = 0.360248, \qquad (3)$$

which is considerably below the value of 3.84 for the .05 level of significance. This difference in log-likelihoods is shown graphically in the lower part of Figure 14.1.

Individual Likelihoods

The binomial distribution formula in Equation 1 is probably familiar to most readers. If one thinks a minute about its origin, it is easy to see that it contains the likelihood for each individual coin toss. Heads occurs with probability p, and there are h outcomes of this type. Because the coin tosses are independent, their probabilities may be multiplied, that is, $p(A$ and $B) = p(A)p(B)$ for independent events A and B. Therefore, neglecting the constant term $\frac{(h + t!)}{(h! \times t!)}$, the contribution to the likelihood of each individual observation is either p or $(1 - p)$. It is this most basic, individual level of likelihood that is explored in this chapter.

Normal Theory Maximum Likelihood

Univariate Case.   The univariate normal distribution is characterized by two parameters, the mean, μ, and the variance, σ^2. The likelihood of a particular observed score, x_i, is simply the height of the normal curve at that point, as shown in Figure 14.2. Clearly, the likelihood of the observation x_i will change as the parameters μ and σ^2 change. When there is only one observation, the likelihood has a maximum where $\mu = x_i$ and $\sigma^2 = 0$, as the curve has infinite height under these conditions. A sample size of one will lead to problems for numerical estimation because infinity cannot be represented or manipulated by computers with finite precision. Although inconvenient, this result makes some sense because it is difficult to generalize from the particular. Typically, there is more than one observation in a sample, which is useful both scientifically and computationally. These obvious points should be born in mind later when we consider models that are different for each case in the sample.

For the univariate normal distribution, the likelihood of the individual observation i is:

$$L_{Ui} = \frac{1}{\sqrt{2\pi\sigma^2}} \exp[(-.5(x_i - \mu)^2] \qquad (4)$$

and the likelihood for a sample of N independent observations is simply:

$$L_U = \prod_{i=1}^{N} \left\{ \frac{1}{\sqrt{2\pi\sigma^2}} \exp[-.5(x_i - \mu)^2 / \sigma^2] \right\}. \qquad (5)$$

Computationally, this product is difficult to handle because each term is usually less than one in value. As the sample size increases, L_U gets so small that a computer with

FIGURE 14.2
Illustration of the Likelihood of an Observation x_i Under a Normal Distribution
With Mean μ and Variance σ^2; Height of the Curve is the Likelihood

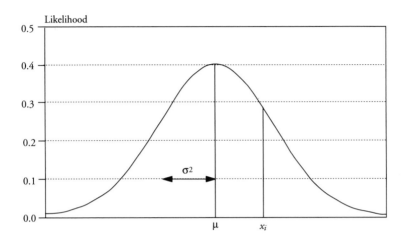

FIGURE 14.2
Illustration of the Likelihood of an Observation x_i Under a Normal Distribution
With Mean μ and Variance σ^2; Height of the Curve is the Likelihood

limited precision arithmetic cannot distinguish it from zero. Therefore, we take the logarithm of L_U, and recognizing that log $(A \times B) = \log A + \log B$, we obtain:

$$\log L_U = \sum_{i=1}^{N} \log \left\{ \frac{1}{\sqrt{2\pi\sigma^2}} \exp[-.5(x_i - \mu)^2 / \sigma^2] \right\} . \qquad (6)$$

This likelihood is made up of two terms: $1/\sqrt{2\pi\sigma^2}$, which does not depend on the data, and $\exp[-.5(x_i - \mu)^2 / \sigma^2]$, which does. The latter term is simply the square of the standardized distance, for each observation i, from the mean. There are therefore, two quantities that may be of use in assessing the individual fit of each score. First, the distance measure, known as a *Mahalanobis distance,* which is asymptotically distributed as χ^2 with one degree of freedom, because it is the square of a normal deviate when the model is correct. Second, there is the contribution of each data vector i to the χ^2 fit of the model of the individual data vector, as given by Equation 6. Both these quantities may be used to detect outliers or population heterogeneity; those observations with the largest deviations fit most poorly.

Multivariate Normal Distribution. To generalize to the multivariate normal distribution is very straightforward, although it gets difficult to visualize the Mahalanobis distance in more than three-dimensional space. The algebra is entirely equivalent, however, so there is no need to try to think about hyperspheres.

FIGURE 14.3
Illustration of the Mahalanobis Distance in Two-Dimensional Space

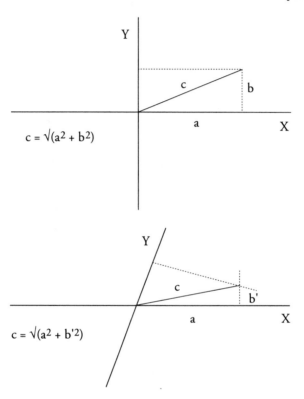

For two uncorelated dimensions (upper figure), the Mahalanobis distance is the sum of the squared deviations of the two variables from their respective means, or $c^2 = \sqrt{(a^2 + b^2)}$ in the diagram. This distance changes to $\sqrt{(a^2 + b'^2)}$ when the dimensions corelate, as shown with oblique axes in the lower figure.

For k observed variables, the multivariate normal probability density function of an observed vector of scores **x** is

$$L_M = |2\pi\Sigma|^{-n/2} \exp[-.5(\mathbf{x} - \mu)'\Sigma^{-1}(\mathbf{x} - \mu)] \tag{7}$$

where Σ is the covariance matrix and μ_j is the (column) vector of means of the variables, and $|\Sigma|$ and Σ^{-1} denote the determinant and inverse of the matrix Σ, respectively. This likelihood function has become more complex in several ways, but retains the basic form of Equation 6. There is still the simple product between a constant term $|2\pi\Sigma|^{-n/2}$ that does not depend on the data and a Mahalanobis distance. This time the distance measure takes into account not only the variances of the measures (on the diagonal of Σ) but also the fact that the measures may covary, which affects the distance between points (see Figure 14.3). It is here that the nonindependence of observations (several measures from a subject at one time, or repeated measures) is taken into consideration. Independent observations (different, unrelated subjects sampled from a population) each have their own likelihoods according to Equation 7, and the sum of the log of these likelihoods gives the log-likelihood for the whole sample:

$$\log L_M = N \log |2\pi\Sigma|^{-n/2} + \sum_i^N \exp[-.5(\mathbf{x}_i - \mu)'\Sigma^{-1}(\mathbf{x}_i - \mu)] \qquad (8)$$

It was Karl Jöreskog's brilliant work (Jöreskog, 1967, 1970) that reduced the above term for the log-likelihood of a set observations to the formulae used to fit models to covariance matrices (see Mardia, Kent, & Bibby, 1979, p. 98, for a succinct account). In the 1970s, computers were slow, so the great increase in computational speed from using summary statistics was essential to make structural equation modeling practical. In the late 1990s, even palm-top computers exceed the speed of the fastest machines available in the 1970s—machines that filled large rooms. This increase in computational power makes ML analysis of raw data very practical.

MISSING DATA

A remarkable property of the individual likelihood method is that it offers a simple but powerful treatment of missing data. The method that is implemented in Mx does not use any imputation, it merely calculates the likelihood of those observations that are present. That is, for any particular vector of observed scores the estimated covariance matrix Σ in Equation 7 is filtered to contain only those rows and columns corresponding to the variables that were observed. Likewise, μ, the column vector of estimated means, is filtered to contain only the means corresponding to the variables that have been observed. The overall likelihood of a set of data is then made up of the product of individual likelihoods that are based on different numbers of observed variables. The earliest description of this method to my knowledge is that given by Lange, Westlake, & Spence (1976), where the application was directed at unbalanced pedigrees; families differ in the number of children, which is a special form of missing data.

When the data are missing because of factors completely independent of any of the observed measures, they are said to be *missing completely at random* (MCAR; Little & Rubin, 1987). Correct maximum likelihood estimates will be obtained. It is relatively easy to see intuitively why this is so. Suppose either one or two measures on a sample were made, and subjects were randomly assigned to being measured on just X (group 1) or X and Y (group 2). One would not expect any difference between the mean and variance of X in the two groups. Formally, the conditional likelihood given the missingness status is unchanged from the original likelihood because of the independence of the missingness.

A more complicated situation is where random missingness of the MCAR variety is augmented by missingness that is entirely predicted by variables that are not missing. A practical example of this might be a study in which one measure, X, is either available for all subjects or missing completely at random. Those subjects with scores above a certain cutoff on X are selected for a further measurement Y. In this case, known as *missing at random* (MAR), maximum likelihood estimates will also be unbiased, but it is not very easy to see intuitively why this approach works. Indeed, the sample mean and variance of X will be quite different for the two groups, and fitting a two-group model with means and variances equated across the groups to the data would fail, given sufficient sample size. However, at the raw likelihood level there is no separation into different groups. The missingness of Y is completely predicted by a known, measured variable X, so the conditional distribution of Y given the value of X does not contain missingness due to Y itself. It is when the missingness is associated with a part of the variance not explained by other variables in the model (the "residual" variance) that one says the data are *not missing at random* (NMAR). NMAR data will give biased estimates with the basic raw data ML method, but it may be possible to model the missingness to control for its effects.

The consequence of missing data is that the individual fit statistics have different distributions according to the number of nonmissing data points for an individual case. This is because the distances of a set of vectors of k variables are asymptotically distributed as χ^2 with k degrees of freedom. On average, the larger the number of variables for which the likelihood Equation 7 is computed, the larger the value of the Mahalanobis distance and the larger the contribution to the fit function. Simply identifying the cases with the largest Mahalanobis distances or the largest contributions to the fit function would preferentially select the cases that contained the fewest variables missing. This problem was noted by Hopper and Mathews (1983), who describe two formulae provided by Johnson and Kotz (1970) that may be used to obtain an approximate z score for the individual fit statistic. These are:

$$Q_i^{(1)} = 2(Q_i)^{.5} - (2n_i - 1)^{.5} \qquad (9)$$

$$Q_i^{(2)} = [(Q_i/n_i)\,1/3 - 1 + 2/(9n_i)]\,(9n_i/2)^{.5} \qquad (10)$$

where $Q_i = (\mathbf{x} - \mu)'\Sigma^{-1}(\mathbf{x} - \mu)$ is the Mahalanobis distance for subject i. Early versions of Mx printed out $Q_i^{(1)}$ because it was simpler to compute. However, following a small simulation study indicated that $Q_i^{(2)}$ was superior. Admittedly the evidence is very flimsy, and a proper simulation study should be done using a variety of distributions of vector lengths. Possibly, a third, superior statistic could be developed that would be superior to both $Q_i^{(1)}$ and $Q_i^{(2)}$. The simulation study involved generating 1,000 pairs of scores from a bivariate normal distribution with correlation point five. A saturated model of three free covariance parameters and two free means was fitted to the data, and the two Q statistics were computed for each observation in the sample. Half normal probability plots for the two statistics are shown in Figure 14.4. As can be seen, the plot for $Q_i^{(2)}$ follows the normal distribution much more closely in the tails than does $Q_i^{(1)}$, although both are a good approximation in the middle of the range. For now at least, Mx writes $Q_i^{(2)}$ to a file when `Option Mx\%p=<filename>`

FIGURE 14.4

Half Normal Plots of $Q_i^{(1)}$ and $Q_i^{(2)}$ for Bivariate Standard Normal Data With Correlation .05; $Q_i^{(2)}$ is Closer to the Theoretical Distribution Described by the Straight Line

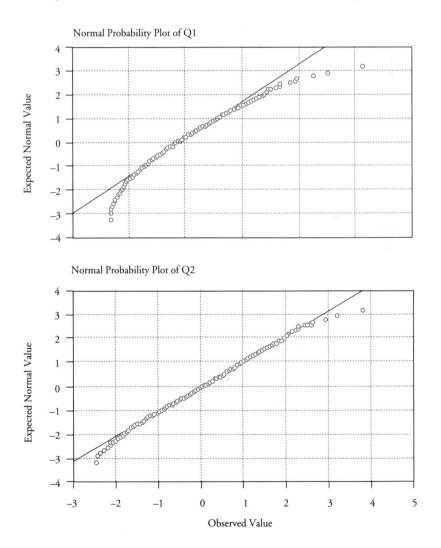

is specified and raw data are being analyzed. This file also contains other useful information, namely: (a) the contribution to the likelihood function for that vector of observations; (b) the unsigned square root of the Mahalanobis distance, Q_i; (c) the estimated z score $Q_i^{(2)}$; (d) the number of the observation in the active (i.e., post selection) dataset; (e) n_i the number of data points in the vector; (f) the number of times that the log-likelihood of this vector was found to be incalculable during optimization; (g) a flag coded 000 if the likelihood could be evaluated at the solution, or 999 otherwise; and (h) the model number if there are multiple models requested with the NModel argument for mixture distributions (see later). This information may be read into programs such as SAS for sorting and to help detect outliers with large χ^2 or z scores.

Implementation in Mx

Structural equation modeling of raw data with Mx is relatively straightforward, but there are some considerations that make it less simple than modeling summary statistics. First, it is necessary to model both the means and the covariances. The maximum likelihood function in Equation 7 has parameters for both the means, μ, and the covariances, Σ. Usually, researchers wish to parameterize Σ in terms of the parameters of a structural equation model, and sometimes the mean vector μ also will be modeled. In Mx, structural equation models for means and covariances may be modeled using the graphical user interface (GUI), which is available free of charge at the website http://www.vipbg.vcu.edu/mxgui. Preparation of the raw data for such a model is relatively straightforward, involving the creation of a ".dat" file that contains all the information concerning the data: the number of variables, their names, and the raw data or the location of the raw data file. For example, the following lines:

```
! Comment - example .dat file for raw data
Data Ninput=4 Nobservations=0
Labels Age Sex Verbal Performance
Rectangular File=verb.rec
```

would identify the source file for the raw data as verb.rec. By specifying rectangular, the program expects a file in which each case is on a single line, with variables separated by spaces. The default code for missing values is a dot "." but other codes may be selected with the Missing command. Example lines of the file verb.rec. might therefore read:

```
55 1 103.78 115.40
48 0 112.96 105.33
49 1 98.77 .
. 0 125.86 105.21.
```

The first two cases contain complete data, the third has missing data on the fourth (Performance) variable, and the fourth case has missing data on age. Having prepared the .dat file, it is a relatively simple matter to draw a diagram to fit the structural equation model for means and covariances with the Mx GUI. Complete instructions are given in the documentation available on the website.

One additional consideration with the modeling of raw data is the use of starting values. Mx, as all model-fitting programs, is sensitive to starting values and may not find the global minimum from bad initial estimates (although it seems better than most in this regard; Hamagami, 1997). This problem is exacerbated when raw data are used, because at bad starting values, especially for the predicted means, the likelihood may evaluate to zero because of the limited numerical precision of computers. Whenever Mx encounters such a case at the starting values, the user is informed of the problem, and the observed data vector, the predicted mean vector, and the standardized deviations of the observed scores from the predicted mean are tabulated. It is up to the user to find a set of starting values that reduces these distances to smallish quantities, perhaps less than two for all variables. Sometimes the deviations of the scores from the means are suitably small, but there is still a problem evaluating the likelihood, perhaps because the starting values predict high correlations between the variables, but the observed scores do not follow this correlated pattern of deviations from the means. To avoid this type of problem, it may be best to supply starting values that generate a predicted covariance matrix that is almost diagonal.

CONTINUOUS MODERATOR VARIABLES

The term *moderator* is usually applied when a variable changes the relationship between two other variables. For example, a difference in correlation between height and weight for men and women might be termed a moderating effect of sex on the height-weight correlation. These simple effects of binary variables are relatively straightforward to model using regular multiple-group SEM. For a comprehensive review of this area, see Schumaker and Marcoulides (1998). Here we focus our attention on continuous moderating variables.

As Muthén (1989) pointed out, the problem of moderators becomes more difficult when there are several binary variables to be considered. The group sizes diminish rapidly, and adequate sample sizes for stable parameter estimates become difficult to achieve. Muthén recommends the use of Multiple-Indicator-Multiple-Cause (MIMIC) models in this case, allowing the group membership variables to be causes of both latent variables and observed variables, thereby moderating the relationship between latent and observed variable as a function of group membership. The MIMIC method is indeed a valuable approach, especially in the context of simple factor models where the relationship between the factor and the observed measures is of interest. Especially useful in the context of analyzing summary statistics is the fact that the sample sizes are not reduced by partitioning into many different groups. Analysis of the raw data offers another way around this problem. In addition, it allows researchers to model moderating relationships directly into any part of a model.

To describe Mx's definition variable approach to continuous moderating variables, we use the simple example of bivariate regression with interaction, where the dependent variable, Y, is a function of two independent variables, X and Z, and their product, XZ. The model is written:

$$Y = b_1 X + b_2 Z + b_3 XZ + e \qquad (11)$$

where b_i are regression coefficients, and e is a residual error term. This unimaginative example may seem boring, and compared to interactions between latent variables and real-world examples, it certainly is, but it serves to illustrate the main statistical points very nicely. First, recognize that the interaction term, XZ, can be regarded as a form of moderation. The effect of Z on Y depends on the value of X. A simple rearrangement of Equation 11 yields:

$$Y = b_1 X + (b_2 + b_3 X) Z + e \qquad (12)$$

or equivalently, a moderating effect of the value of Z on the regression of Y on X might be described as:

$$Y = (b_1 + b_3 Z)X + b_2 Z + e. \qquad (13)$$

Although bivariate regression with interaction is a solved problem, its restatement as a structural equation model is not without difficulties. If the strategy of computing XZ and adding it to the data set is taken, the first problem would be that if X and Z were normally distributed, then the product variable, XZ, would not be. In addition, if b_3 were nonzero, the dependent variable Y would be non-normal. Goodness of fit tests and significance tests on the ML estimates of the parameters would be adversely affected by the non-normal distributions of the variables. Therefore, there is some advantage to recasting the model in the form of Equation 12 or 13 as the non-normal variable XZ is no longer a part of the data to be analyzed but simply a moderator of the relationship between X (or Z) and Y. Furthermore, for any particular value of Z, the distribution of Y is conditionally normal under this model. Because the raw maximum likelihood fitting function is used instead of summary statistics, the normality assumption (conditional on X) will be upheld. Better statistical properties of the model should result.

To some extent, interpretation of individual fit becomes more difficult with this approach, because each subject potentially has a different predicted covariance matrix. An outlier might arise because of extreme values of the observed data because of extreme values of the moderators, or because of an unusual combination thereof.

Implementation in Mx

It is possible to use either the diagram-drawing software or the script language to devise models with continuous moderator variables. For the bivariate regression example, an Mx diagram is shown in Figure 14.5. The diagram, script, and data may be downloaded from the Mx website http://griffin.vcu.edu/mx following the

FIGURE 14.5
Path Diagram of Moderating Effect of Z on X Such That Bivariate
Regression of Y on X, Z and the Product XZ is Modeled

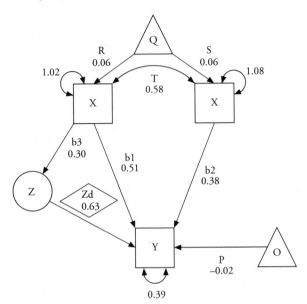

links to examples and moderated regression. There are several noteworthy features of the path diagram in Figure 14.5. First, there is the use of variance arrows—double-headed paths from a variable to itself. This is a graphical tool that makes a one to one relationship between the graphical and the algebraic representations of the model (McArdle & Boker, 1990). Second, the use of triangles may be unfamiliar. Triangles allow the modeling of means via simple tracing rules or simple matrix algebra, as described in the documentation for the Mx graphical interface available at http://www.vipbg.vcu.edu/mxgui. Third, the most unusual feature of the diagram is the presence of the variable Zd inside a diamond on a path. By mapping variables to paths, we are specifying a model for raw data such that the individual values of Zd change with each subject in the dataset. The diamond graphically flags the presence of this definition variable in the model. In this case, Zd and Z are identical, requiring two columns of identical data in the raw data file. Z is used to model the main effect of Z on Y and Zd is used to model the moderating effect that Z has on the regression of Y on X. A small amount of simulation indicates good recovery of parameter estimates using this method. More comprehensive testing of the method would be relatively simple to automate and should be done to establish whether the modeling of interaction effects this way has superior statistical properties.

FINITE MIXTURE DISTRIBUTIONS

A frequently challenged assumption of structural equation modeling is that it assumes the same model for all subjects in the sample. This assumption is indeed worth examining, because it seems highly unlikely that the same relationships between variables hold for all subjects unless the population is very homogeneous. As Muthén (1989) showed, parameter estimates may be substantially biased when the population contains a mixture of subpopulations, although the goodness of fit of the model may be perfectly satisfactory. One solution to this problem, to be considered in this section, is explicit modeling of mixture distributions via maximum likelihood.

When a population consists of a limited number of subpopulations, for example, two subpopulations with different means, the problem is known as a *finite mixture distribution*. Whole volumes have been written on the advantages, disadvantages, and practicalities of modeling mixture distributions (Everitt & Hand, 1981; Jedidi, Jagpal, & DeSarbo, 1997) and it would serve little purpose to reiterate these excellent works here. The present aims are simply to describe how Mx may be used to fit models of mixture distributions via maximum likelihood and to consider briefly some of the problems that may arise.

First, we consider standard methods for dealing with such mixtures. One extremely powerful method is multiple-group structural equation modeling. The usual way of handling heterogeneity in means or covariance structure between two groups is to subdivide the population and to fit models to both groups simultaneously. This approach has the advantage of being able to statistically test for heterogeneity. For example, Neale and Cardon (1992, chap. 11) tested for sex differences in the parameters of a simple model of genetic and environmental effects on Body Mass Index (BMI). Twin pairs were subdivided into male and female groups, and the fit of a model where the parameters were constrained to be equal across genders was compared with that of a model where the parameters were allowed to differ. A significant improvement in fit was observed when the parameters differed between the genders. Clearly, splitting the data into groups according to gender is important in the genetic analysis of Body Mass Index (Maes, Neale, & Eaves, 1997).

Wherever possible, tests of heterogeneity should be performed and data from potentially heterogeneous groups should not be combined without first testing for group differences. In the BMI example, such tests would be impossible to perform if the twins' gender had not been assessed. Although most studies of humans record the gender of the subjects, some do not. Furthermore, there may be other variables that have not been measured or that have not been measured accurately, that index population heterogeneity. It is in the treatment of this unmeasured or *latent* heterogeneity that mixture distributions can prove useful.

Normal Likelihood for Mixture Distributions

It is very simple to write the likelihood for a mixture of multivariate normal distributions. From Equation 7 we can write a weighted sum of likelihoods for r subpopulations as:

$$L_M = \sum_{d=1}^{r} w_d \left| 2\pi\Sigma_d \right|^{-n/2} \exp[-.5(\mathbf{x} - \mu_d)'\Sigma_d^{-1}(\mathbf{x} - \mu_d)]. \quad (14)$$

There are several things to note about this formulation. First, the data vector $\mathbf{x}$ remains invariant across the different models. Attention to starting values is very important here. In general, the best place to start is where the models differ slightly in their predicted covariances. No difference at all will impede optimization as the derivatives of the mixing proportion parameters cannot be estimated. Too large a difference may lead to incalculable likelihoods for some of the data points.

Second, the $d = 1, \ldots, r$ likelihoods of the mixture are weighted by w_d, often characterized as a mixing proportion, with $\sum w_d = 1$. These weights may be measured at the population level, for example, the weights may be fixed to be .25 and .75 in a two component mixture, or they may be estimated at the population level as free parameters. Perhaps more interesting is the possibility that the weights can be measured at the individual level, so that each subject has a different set of group membership probabilities. This formulation encompasses standard multiple-group structural-equation models as a special case; for the gender differences example, the two components would be the parameters to model the covariance matrices, Σ_d, and the mean vectors, μ_d. The weights would be the probabilities that each subject is male, p(male) and p(female), and expressed as a vector would be either $\mathbf{w}' = (1, 0)$ or $\mathbf{w}' = (0, 1)$. Subjects of unknown gender would be easy to add to this study, with weights $\mathbf{w}' = (.5, .5)$ or some other prior probabilities appropriate for the age and other characteristics of the sample.

Third, there are now several likelihoods being evaluated. If researchers wish to assess the individual fit, then the likelihoods for the component models must all be taken into consideration. Corresponding to the single distribution case, the contributions to the overall fit (the individual likelihood), the Mahalanobis distance, and the z score, $Q^{(2)}$, may be computed for each component distribution. That is, a particular subject may be an outlier in any or all of the subpopulations. With strong separation between subpopulations (imagine two univariate normal distributions with a mean difference of six standard units), almost all points would be outliers in one of the subpopulation distributions. Taken another way, these statistics may inform the investigator of the probability that a given subject belongs to a particular subpopulation. One simple function to compute the posterior probability of belonging to subpopulation k is

$$L_k / \left(\sum_{d=1}^{r} L_d \right). \quad (15)$$

Fourth, note that there are some statistical problems with comparing the likelihood of a mixture distribution with that of a submodel in which there is no mixture. There are two ways in which the submodel might be represented: (a) the parameters for the mean and covariance structures of the subpopulations are constrained to be equal and the mixing proportion is fixed at an arbitrary value; and (b) the mixing proportion parameter is fixed at 1 for one component and at 0 for the rest. This latter case is really a *boundary condition* because the mixing proportions are constrained to lie in the interval from 0 to 1. As a result, tests of the difference between a model with a mixture and one without a mixture are not asymptotically distributed as χ^2. This problem has been studied quite extensively by Dijkstra (1992), Self and Liang (1987), and Shapiro (1988), among others. All indicate the problem of the fit statistic having a distribution under the null hypothesis that takes the value zero some proportion of the time and is distributed as χ^2 otherwise. Some resolution to this problem may be afforded by resort to bootstrapping (Schork, Allison, & Thiel, 1996), although these procedures are not implemented in Mx as of 1998. Another problem is that with small sample sizes or poor separation between the components of the mixture, there is a chance that optimization will converge to a local rather than a global maximum likelihood (Hosmer, 1974). Exactly how sensitive the NPSOL optimization routines (Gill, Murray, Saunders, & Wright, 1986) used by Mx (Neale, 1997) are to starting values, sample sizes, and separation of components within mixture distributions is a matter for extensive simulation. Experience suggests that they are fairly robust, but this should be investigated thoroughly.

Implementation in Mx

Built into Mx is an extension of the maximum likelihood fitting function that allows specification of a finite mixture distribution model. In the single distribution case, the user is required to supply a matrix formula for the predicted covariances that yields a matrix of order $m \times m$ and a formula for the predicted means that yields a vector of order $1 \times m$. For a mixture of d distributions, it is first necessary to tell Mx that there will be more than one model, which is done with the parameter to the data line, for example, NModel=3 for the case of $d = 3$. Second, all d models must be supplied in a single matrix algebra formula for the covariances, stacked on top of each other in a vector of covariance matrices, being of order $md \times m$. Similarly, the predicted mean vectors must be stacked to create a matrix of means of order $d \times m$. Finally, it is necessary to supply a matrix formula for the weights that will evaluate to a $d \times 1$ vector corresponding to the d models. Because Mx has a general matrix algebra interpreter, it is easy to configure the covariance matrices and mean vectors in this way, using the vertical concatenation operator.

The general case in which the weights vary according to the individual subject may be implemented using the "definition variable" approach. A definition variable is used to define the model; after a variable is declared to be a definition variable, it is no longer part of the active set of variables to be analyzed. Here I briefly illustrate the

TABLE 14.1
Number of Alleles Shared Identical by
Descent in All Possible Pairs of Siblings

| | Sibling1 | | | |
Sibling 2	AC	AD	BC	BD
AC	2	1	1	0
AD	1	2	0	1
BC	1	0	2	1
BD	0	1	1	2

Note. Parental Genotypes are AB and CD,
Giving Siblings of Types AC, AD, BC, and BD.

use of mixture distribution methods in the context of data collected from studies of genetic linkage. The mixture distribution methods available in Mx were specifically developed to tackle this problem (Eaves, Neale, & Maes, 1996), but it is my hope that they will prove fuseful in a much broader context.

Example: Genetic Marker Data. There is growing interest in the linkage analysis of quantitative traits. This is not the place or a detailed description of the methods in this area, but for a clear exposition on genetic linkage and concepts such as identity by descent and identity by state, the reader should consult Sham (1997). Linkage studies use genetic markers to assess directly the genetic similarity of family members. Humans are diploid; they have pairs of chromosomes, one inherited from each parent. At any particular place on the genome or "locus," an individual's genotype may be expressed as the pair of alleles that they have at that locus. Supposing two parents with entirely different alleles at a particular locus (father = AB, mother = CD), it is possible to describe the genotypes of all the possible offspring that they might create, namely AC, AD, BC and BD. For any particular pair of siblings, simply count the number of alleles that they share in common. This type of allele-sharing is known as *identity by descent* (IBD), because it measures whether the alleles originated from the same parental strand of DNA. It is useful to find if any nearby genes are having an effect on sibling similarity for a trait of interest.

Table 14.1 shows the number of alleles shared IBD for all the possible configurations of two siblings in a family. For example, if sibling 1 inherits AC and sibling 2 inherits BC, they share one allele identical by descent. Clearly, a population of sibling pairs will consist of a mixture of three types: those sharing 2, 1 or 0 alleles IBD. If a locus has an effect on a trait, then siblings who share two alleles IBD are expected to be more similar than siblings who share one allele, who in turn would be more similar than siblings who share zero alleles, that is, $r(IBD2) > r(IBD1) > r(IBD0)$. Places on the genome that affect quantitative traits are usually called a *quantitative trait locus* or QTL.

Usually, identity by descent at the quantitative trait locus itself is not measured or has a limited number of alleles, so one cannot precisely distinguish sibling pairs into

FIGURE 14.6
Three Models for the Covariance of Siblings,
According to Whether They Share 2, 1, or 0 Alleles Identical by Descent at a Locus

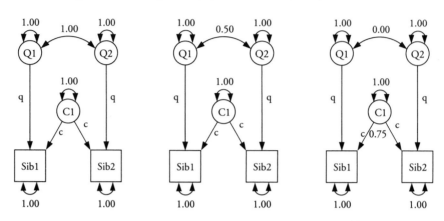

The likelihood of a pair of scores under these three models is weighted and summed by the probability that the pair is that particular type, as computed from the generic marker data.

the three types. Instead, one can compute the probability that a particular sibling pair belongs to each type. It is these probabilities, which may be computed by a program such as Mapmaker/sibs (Kruglyak & Lander, 1995), that form the weights for the different models. In practice, these weights may be different for each sibling pair in the sample.

If known with certainty whether each pair was IBD2, IBD1, or IBD0, it would be a relatively straightforward case of a three-group structural equation model, sometimes known as "Partitioned Twin Analysis" (Nance & Neale, 1989). However, because the genetic data are not fully informative, one can only assign probabilities that pairs are of each type, which is where the mixture model comes in.

The model for the resemblance of siblings while allowing for the effects of a QTL is quite simple and is shown in Figure 14.6. The latent variables are the QTL effect Q, residual shared (non-QTL genetic and environmental) factors C, and residual individual-specific factors E, which include measurement error. Key to the identification of this model is the fact that the correlations between the latent variables are fixed. In the model for siblings sharing zero genes IBD, at the QTL, the correlation between Q1 and Q2 is fixed at zero; for the models of one and two genes IBD, it is fixed at .5 and 1.0, respectively.

The test for linkage to a locus is simply a difference in fit (the likelihood ratio test described in Equation 14) between the model that includes versus excludes an effect of Q on the phenotypes. Typically, these tests are repeated many times across a region of interest or even the whole genome, which leads to potential statistical problems from multiple testing. Repeated testing leads to apparently improbable results even when there is no true effect. To account for this, tests of linkage usually involve a high significance level of p = .00074 that corresponds to a χ^2_1 difference of 13.82 (a logarithm of odds score of 3.0). This happens to correspond to a value based on a Bayesian argument that takes into account the number of chromosomes in man. Both these arguments are clearly described in Sham (1997).

Mx scripts to fit this model are available on the website `http://griffin.vcu.edu/mx` via the examples and QTL links. In 1999, it is not possible to use the graphical interface to generate models with mixture distributions. If the model is complex and facility with the Mx script language is not to hand, some part of the work could be done by generating an intermediate script using the graphical interface to build the models, changing the script to add a data group with the mixture, and using matrix equality constraints to obtain the predicted means and covariances from the previous groups. We hope to offer graphical modeling of mixture distributions in version 2.0 of the Mx GUI.

References

Achenbach, T. M., & Edelbrock, C. S. (1981). Behavioral problems and competencies reported by parents of normal and disturbed children aged four through sixteen. *Monographs of the Society for Research in Child Development, 46* (Serial No. 188).

Addelman, S. (1970). Variability of treatments and experimental units in the design and analysis of experiments. *Journal of the American Statistical Association, 65,* 1095–1109.

Ahrens, J. H., & Dieter, U. (1973). Extensions of Forsythe's method for random sampling from the normal distribution. *Mathematics of Computation, 27,* 927–937.

Aitkin, A. C. (1934). Note on selection from a multivariate normal population. *Proceedings of the Edinburgh Mathematical Society, 4,* 106–110.

Akaike, H. (1987). Factor analysis and AIC. *Psychometrika, 52*(3), 317–332.

Allison, P. D. (1987). Estimation of linear models with incomplete data. In C. C. Clogg (Ed.), *Sociological methodology* (pp. 71–103). San Francisco: Jossey-Bass.

Alwin, D. F. (1988). Structural equation models in research on human development and aging. In K. W. Schaie, R. T. Campbell, W. Meredith, & S. C. Rawlings (Eds.), *Methodological issues in aging research* (pp. 71–169). New York: Springer.

Arbuckle, J. L. (1995). *Amos for Windows. Analysis of moment structures. Version 3.5.* Chicago: SmallWaters Corporation.

Arbuckle, J. L. (1996). Full information estimation in the presence of incomplete data. In G. A. Marcoulides & R. E. Schumacker (Eds.), *Advanced structural equation modeling: Issues and techniques* (pp. 243–277). Mahwah, NJ: Lawrence Erlbaum Associates.

Arbuckle, J. L. (1997). *Amos users' guide. Version 3.6.* Chicago: SmallWaters Corporation.

Arminger, G. (1986). Linear stochastic differential equation models for panel data with unobserved variables. In N. B. Tuma (Ed.), *Sociological methodology* (Vol. 16, pp. 187–213). San Francisco: Jossey-Bass.

Baker, P. C., Keck, C. K., Mott, F. L., & Quinlan, S. V. (1993). *NLSY Child Handbook: A guide to the 1986–1990 National Longitudinal Survey of Youth Child Data* (rev. ed.). Columbus: The Ohio State University, Center for Human Resources Research.

Baltes, P. B., Dittmann-Kohli, F., & Kliegl, R. (1986). Reserve capacity of the elderly in aging-sensitive tasks of fluid intelligence: Replication and extension. *Psychology and Aging, 1,* 172–177.

Baltes, P. B., & Nesselroade, J. R. (1979). History and rationale of longitudinal research. In J. R. Nesselroade & P. B. Baltes (Eds.), *Longitudinal research in the study of behavior and development* (pp. 1–39). New York: Academic Press.

Baltes, P. B., Reese, H. W., & Nesselroade, J. R. (1988). *Life-span developmental psychology: Introduction to research methods.* Hillsdale, NJ: Lawrence Erlbaum Associates.

Bandura, A. (1997). *Self-efficacy: The exercise of control.* New York: Freeman.

Bayley, N. (1956). Individual patterns of development. *Child Development, 27,* 45–74.

Bell, R. Q. (1953). Convergence: An accelerated longitudinal approach. *Child Development, 24,* 145–152.

Bell, R. Q. (1954). An experimental test of the accelerated longitudinal approach. *Child Development, 25,* 281–286.

Bentler, P. M. (1995). *EQS structural equation program manual.* Encino, CA: Multivariate Software.

Bentler, P. M. (1997). EQS. *Behaviormetrika, 24,* 89–95.

Bentler, P. M., & Chou, C. P. (1987). Practical issues in structural modeling. *Sociological Methods & Research, 16,* 78–117.

Bentler, P. M., & Dudgeon, P. (1996). Covariance structure analysis: Statistical practice, theory, and directions. *Annual Review of Psychology, 47,* 563–592.

Bentler, P. M., & Weeks, D. G. (1980). Linear structural equations with latent variables. *Psychometrika, 45,* 289–308.

Bielby, W. T., Hauser, R. M., & Featherman, D. L. (1977). Response errors of black and nonblack males in models of the intergenerational transmission of socioeconomic status. *American Journal of Sociology, 82,* 1242–1288.

Blalock, H. M. (1979). The presidential address: Measurement and conceptualization problems. The major obstacle to integrating theory and research. *American Sociological Review, 44,* 881–894.

Bock, R. D. (1975). *Multivariate statistical methods in behavioral research.* New York: Wiley.

Boker, S. M., & McArdle, J. J. (1995). Statistical vector field analysis applied to mixed cross-sectional and longitudinal data. *Experimental Aging Research, 21,* 77–93.

Bolger, K. E., Patterson, C. J., Thompson, W. W., & Kupersmidt, J. B. (1995). Psychosocial adjustment among children experiencing persistent and intermittent family economic hardship. *Child Development, 66,* 1107–1129.

Bollen, K. A. (1989). *Structural equations with latent variables.* New York: Wiley.

Bollen, K. A., & Long, J. S. (1993). *Testing structural equation models.* Newbury Park, CA: Sage.

Brown, B. W., & Lovato, J. (1994.) *RANLIB.C: Library of C routines for random number generation.* Houston: The University of Texas, M.D. Anderson Cancer Center (available on the NETLIB internet archive).

Brown, C. H. (1983). Asymptotic comparison of missing data procedures for estimating factor loadings. *Psychometrika, 48*(2), 269–291.

Brown, R. L. (1994). Efficacy of the indirect approach for estimating structural equation model with missing data: A comparison of five methods. *Structural Equation Modeling: A Multidisciplinary Journal, 1,* 287–316.

Browne, M. W. (1984). Asymptotic distribution-free methods for the analysis of covariance structures. *British Journal of Mathematical and Statistical Psychology, 37,* 62–83.

Browne, M. W. (1993). Structured latent curve models. In C. M. Cuadras & C. R. Rao (Eds.), *Multivariate analysis: Future directions 2* (pp. 171–197). Amsterdam, The Netherlands: Elsevier-North Holland.

Browne, M. W., & Arminger, G. (1995). Specification and estimation of mean- and covariance structure models. In G. Arminger, C. C. Clogg, & M. E. Sobel (Eds.), *Handbook of statistical modeling for the social and behavioral sciences* (pp. 185–249). New York: Plenum.

Browne, M. W., & Cudeck, R. (1993). Alternative ways of assessing model fit. In K. A. Bollen & J. S. Long (Eds.), *Testing structural equation models* (pp. 132–162). Beverly Hills, CA: Sage.

Browne, M. W., & DuToit, S. H. C. (1991). Models for learning data. In L. M. Collins & J. L. Horn (Eds.), *Best methods for the analysis of change* (pp. 47–68). Washington, DC: American Psychological Association.

Browne, M. W., & DuToit, S. H. C. (1992). Automated fitting of nonstandard models. *Multivariate Behavioral Research, 27,* 269–300.

Brunner, R. M., & Schafer, J. L. (1997). *Inference for latent transition models* (Tech. Rep. No. 97-11). University Park: The Pennsylvania State University, The Methodology Center.

Bryk, A. S., & Raudenbush, S. W. (1987). Application of hierarchical linear models to assessing change. *Psychological Bulletin, 101,* 147–158.

Bryk, A. S., & Raudenbush, S. W. (1992). *Hierarchical linear models: Applications and data analysis methods.* Newbury Park, CA: Sage.

Bryk, A. S., Raudenbush, S. W., & Congdon, R. T. (1996). *Hierarchical linear modeling with the HLM/2L and HLM/3L programs.* Chicago: Scientific Software International.

Burstein, L. (1980). The analysis of multilevel data in educational research and evaluation. In D. Berliner (Ed.), *Review of research in education* (Vol. 8, pp. 158–233). Washington, DC: American Educational Research Association.

Burstein, L., Linn, R. L., & Cappel, F. J. (1978). Analyzing multilevel data in the presence of heterogeneous within-class regression. *Journal of Educational Statistics, 3,* 347–383.

Burstein, L., & Miller, M. D. (1981). Regression-based analysis of multilevel educational data. In R. F. Boruch, P. M. Wortman, & D. S. Cordray (Eds.), *Reanalyzing program evaluations* (pp. 194–211). San Francisco: Jossey-Bass.

Byrne, B. M. (1994). *Structural equation modeling with EQS and EQS/Windows.* Thousand Oaks, CA: Sage.

Cassel, C. M., Särndal, C. E., & Wretman, J. H. (1977). *Foundations of inference in survey sampling.* New York: Wiley.

Center for Human Resources Research. (1988). *NLS Handbook.* Columbus: Ohio State University.

Chase-Lansdale, P. L., Mott, F. M., Brooks-Gunn, J., & Phillips, D. A. (1991). Children of the National Longitudinal Study of Youth: A unique research opportunity. *Developmental Psychology, 27*(6), 919–931.

Chou, C. P., Bentler, P. M., & Pentz, M. A. (1998). Comparison of two statistical approaches to study growth curves: The multilevel model and latent curve analysis. *Structural Equation Modeling: A Multidisciplinary Journal, 5*(3), 247–266.

Cohen, J. (1968). Multiple regression as a general data-analytic system. *Psychological Bulletin, 70,* 426–443.

Cohen, J. (1990). Things I have learned (so far). *American Psychologist, 45,* 1304–1312.

Cohen, J. (1994). The earth is round (p < .05). *American Psychologist, 49,* 997–1003.

Cohen, J., & Cohen, P. (1983). *Applied multiple regression analysis for the behavioral sciences* (2nd ed.). Hillsdale, NJ: Lawrence Erlbaum Associates.

Cohen, P. A. (1996). *Enhancing the clarity of presentation of multivariate data.* Annual meeting of the Society of Multivariate Experimental Psychology, Bellingham, WA, October.

Cole, D. A., Maxwell, S. E., Arvey, R., & Salas, E. (1993). Multivariate group comparisons of variable systems: MANOVA and structural equation modeling. *Psychological Bulletin, 114,* 174–184.

Coleman, J. S. (1968). The mathematical study of change. In H. M. Blalock & A. B. Blalock (Eds.), *Methodology in social research* (pp. 428–478). New York: McGraw-Hill.

Collins, L. M., Fidler, P. L., Wugalter, S. E., & Long, J. L. (1993). Goodness-of-fit testing for latent class models. *Multivariate Behavioral Research, 28,* 375–389.

Collins, L. M., Graham, J. W., & Flaherty, B. P. (in press). An alternative framework for defining mediation. *Multivariate Behavioral Research.*

Collins, L. M., Graham, J. W., Long, J., & Hansen, W. B. (1994). Crossvalidation of latent class models of early substance use onset. *Multivariate Behavioral Research, 29,* 165–183.

Collins, L. M., Graham, J. W., Rousculp, S. S., Fidler, P. L., Pan, J., & Hansen, W. B. (1994). Latent transition analysis and how it can address prevention research questions. In L. M. Collins & L. Seitz (Eds.), *Advances in data analysis for prevention research* (pp. 81–111). Washington, DC: National Institute on Drug Abuse Research Monograph.

Collins, L. M., Graham, J. W., Rousculp, S. S., & Hansen, W. B. (1997). Heavy caffeine and the beginning of the substance use onset process: An illustration of latent transition analysis. In K. Bryant, M. Windle, & S. West (Eds.), *The science of prevention: Methodological advances from alcohol and substance abuse research* (pp. 79–99). Washington, DC: American Psychological Association.

Collins, L. M., & Horn, J. L. (Eds.). (1991). *Best methods for the analysis of change.* Washington, DC: American Psychological Association.

Collins, L. M., & Wugalter, S. E. (1992). Latent class models for stage-sequential dynamic latent variables. *Multivariate Behavioral Research, 27,* 131–157.

Cook, T. D., & Campbell, D. T. (1979). *Quasi-experimentation: Design & analysis issues for field settings.* Boston: Houghton Mifflin.

Cook, T. D., & Campbell, D. T. (1979). *Quasi-experimentation: Design and analysis issues for field settings.* Chicago: Rand McNally.

Cudeck, R. (1996). Mixed-effects models in the study of individual differences with repeated measures data. *Multivariate Behavioral Research, 31,* 371–403.

Curran, P. J., Harford, T., & Muthén, B. O. (1997). The relation between heavy alcohol use and bar patronage: A latent growth model. *Journal of Studies of Alcohol, 57,* 410–418.

Curran, P. J., Stice, E., & Chassin, L. (1997). The relation between adolescent alcohol use and peer alcohol use: A longitudinal random coefficients model. *Journal of Consulting and Clinical Psychology, 65,* 130–140.

Dalenius, T. (1988). A first course in survey sampling. In P. Krishnaiah & C. R. Rao (Eds.), *Handbook of statistics: Vol. 6. Sampling* (pp. 15–46). Oxford, UK: North-Holland.

Darlington, R. B. (1968). Multiple regression in psychological research and practice. *Psychological Bulletin, 69*(3), 161–182.

de Leeuw, J., & Kreft, I. (1986). Random coefficient models for multilevel analysis. *Journal of Education Statistics, 11,* 57–85.

Dempster, A. P., Laird, N. M., & Rubin, D. B. (1977). Maximum likelihood estimation from incomplete data via the EM algorithm. *Journal of the Royal Statistical Society, Series B39,* 1–38.

Diggle, P. J., Liang, K.-Y., & Zeger, S. L. (1994). *Analysis of longitudinal data.* New York: Oxford University Press.

Dijkstra, T. (1992). On statistical inference with parameter estimates on boundary of the parameter space. *British Journal of Mathematical and Statistical Psychology, 45,* 289–309.

Dolan, C. V., & Molenaar, P. C. M. (1994). Testing specific hypotheses concerning latent group differences in multi-group covariance structure analysis with structured means. *Multivariate Behavioral Research, 29,* 203–222.

Donaldson, S. I., Graham, J. W., Piccinin, A. M., & Hansen, W. B. (1995). Resistance skills training and onset of alcohol use: Evidence for beneficial and potentially harmful effects in public schools and in private Catholic schools. *Health Psychology, 14,* 291–300.

Duncan, G. J., & Brooks-Gunn, J. (1997). *Consequences of growing up poor.* New York: Russell Sage Foundation.

Duncan, S. C., & Duncan, T. E. (1995). Modeling the processes of development via latent variable growth curve methodology. *Structural Equation Modeling: A Multidisciplinary Journal, 2,* 187–213.

Dunn, G., Everitt, B., & Pickles, A. (1993). *Modelling covariances and latent variables using EQS.* London: Chapman & Hall.

Dwyer, J. H., Feinleib, M., Lippert, P., & Hoffmeister, H. (1992). *Statistical models for longitudinal studies of health.* New York: Oxford University Press.

Eaves, L. J., Neale, M. C., & Maes, H. H. (1996). Multivariate multipoint linkage analysis of quantitative trait loci. *Behavior Genetics, 26,* 519–526.

Efron, B. (1982). *The jackknife, the bootstrap, and other resampling plans.* Philadelphia: Society for Industrial and Applied Mathematics.

Eid, M. (1998). *A multitrait-multimethod model with minimal assumptions.* Manuscript submitted for publication.

Erickson, M. F., Sroufe, L. A., & Egeland, B. (1985). The relationship between quality of attachment and behavior problems in preschool in a high-risk sample. *Monographs of the Society for Research in Child Development, 50,* 147–166.

Everitt, B. S., & Hand, D. J. (1981). *Finite mixture distributions.* London: Chapman & Hall.

von Eye, A. (1989). Zero-missing non-existing data: Missing data problems in longitudinal research and categorical data solutions. In M. Brambring, F. Lösel, & H. Skowronek (Eds.), *Children at risk: Assessment, longitudinal research, and intervention* (pp. 336–355). Berlin, Germany: de Gruyter.

Featherman, D. L., Lerner, R. M., & Perlmutter, M. (1994). *Life-span development and behavior* (Vol. 12). Hillsdale, NJ: Lawrence Erlbaum Associates.

Fisher, R. A. (1935). *The design of experiments.* London: Oliver and Boyd.

Gibbons, R. D., Hedeker, D., Elkin, I., Waternaux, C., Kraemer, H. C., Greenhouse, J. B., Shea, M. T., Imber, S. D., Sotsky, S. M., & Watkins, J. T. (1993). Some conceptual and statistical issues in analysis of longitudinal psychiatric data. *Archives of General Psychiatry, 50,* 739–750.

Gibbs, J. T. (1986). Assessment of depression in urban adolescent females: Implications for early intervention strategies. *American Journal of Social Psychiatry, 6,* 50–56.

Gill, P. E., Murray, W., Saunders, M. A., & Wright, M. H. (1986). *User's guide for npsol (version 4.0): A FORTRAN package for nonlinear programming* (Tech. Rep. No. SOL 86-2). Stanford, CA: Stanford University, Department of Operations Research.

Goldstein, H. (1987). *Multilevel models in educational and social research.* London: Griffin.

Goldstein, H. (1995). *Multilevel statistical models* (2nd ed.). New York: Halsted.

Goldstein, H., & McDonald, R. P. (1988). A general model for the analysis of multilevel data. *Psychometrika, 53,* 435–467.

Goldstein, N. (1990). *Explaining socioeconomic differences in children's cognitive test scores.* Cambridge, MA: Harvard University, John F. Kennedy School of Government.

Gollob, H. F., & Reichardt, C. S. (1987). Taking account of time lags in causal models. *Child Development, 58,* 80–92.

Goodman, L. A. (1974). Exploratory latent structure analysis using both identifiable and unidentifiable models. *Biometrika, 61,* 215–231.

Graham, J. W., Collins, L. M., Wugalter, S. E., Chung, N. K., & Hansen, W. B. (1991). Modeling transitions in latent stage-sequential processes: A substance use prevention example. *Journal of Consulting and Clinical Psychology, 59,* 48–57.

Graham, J. W., & Donaldson, S. I. (1993). Evaluating interventions with differential attrition: The importance of nonresponse mechanisms and use of follow-up data. *Journal of Applied Psychology, 78,* 119–128.

Graham, J. W., & Hofer, S. M. (1991). *EMCOV.EXE users guide.* Unpublished manuscript, University of Southern California.

Graham, J. W., Hofer, S. M., Donaldson, S. I., MacKinnon, D. P., & Schafer, J. L. (1997). Analysis with missing data in prevention research. In K. Bryant, M. Windle, & S. West (Eds.), *The science of prevention: Methodological advances from alcohol and substance abuse research* (pp. 325–366). Washington, DC: American Psychological Association.

Graham, J. W., Hofer, S. M., & MacKinnon, D. P. (1996). Maximizing the usefulness of data obtained with planned missing value patterns: An application of maximum likelihood procedures. *Multivariate Behavioral Research, 31,* 197–218.

Graham, J. W., Hofer, S. M., & Piccinin, A. M. (1994). Analysis with missing data in drug prevention research. In L. M. Collins & L. Seitz (Eds.), *Advances in data analysis for prevention intervention research. National Institute on Drug Abuse Research Monograph Series* (pp. 325–366). Washington, DC: National Institute on Drug Abuse.

Graham, J. W., Rohrbach, L., Hansen, W. B., Flay, B. R., & Johnson, C. A. (1989). Convergent and discriminant validity for assessment of skill in resisting a role play alcohol offer. *Behavioral Assessment, 11,* 353–379.

Graham, J. W., & Schafer, J. L. (in press). On the performance of multiple imputation for multivariate data with small sample size. In R. Hoyle (Ed.), *Statistical strategies for small sample research.* Thousand Oaks, CA: Sage.

Greenwald, A. G. (1975). Consequences of prejudice against the null hypothesis. *Psychological Bulletin, 82,* 1–20.

Griffiths, D., & Sandland, R. (1984). Fitting generalized allometric models to multivariate growth data. *Biometrics, 40,* 139–150.

Gustafsson, J.-E., & Stahl, P. A. (1997). *STREAMS user's guide.* Mölndal, Sweden: MultivariateWare.

Hamagami, F. (1997). A review of the Mx computer program for structural equation modeling. *Structural Equation Modeling, 4*(2), 157–175.

Hansen, W. B., & Graham, J. W. (1991). Preventing alcohol, marijuana, and cigarette use among adolescents: Peer pressure resistance training versus establishing conservative norms. *Preventive Medicine, 20,* 414–430.

Harris, C. W. (1963). *Problems in measuring change.* Madison: University of Wisconsin Press.

Hartley, H. O., & Hocking, R. R. (1971). The analysis of incomplete data. *Biometrics, 27,* 783–823.

Harville, D. (1977). Maximum likelihood approaches to variance component estimation and related problems. *Journal of the American Statistical Association, 72,* 320–340.

Hawkins, J. D., Graham, J. W., Maguin, E., Abbott, R., Hill, K. G., & Catalano, R. F. (1997). Exploring the effects of age of alcohol use initiation and psychosocial risk factors on subsequent alcohol misuse. *Journal of Studies on Alcohol, 58,* 280–290.

Hayduck, L. A. (1987). *Structural equation modeling with LISREL. Essentials and advances.* Baltimore: Johns Hopkins University Press.

Hays, W. L. (1994). *Statistics.* Fort Worth, TX: Harcourt Brace Jovanovich.

Hedeker, D., & Gibbons, R. D. (1996). MIXREG: A computer program for mixed-effects regression analysis with autocorrelated errors. *Computer Methods and Programs in Biomedicine, 49,* 229–252.

Herzog, A. R., & Rodgers, W. L. (1988). Age and response rates to interview sample surveys. *Journal of Gerontology: Social Sciences, 43,* 200–205.

Hill, M. S., & Sandfort, J. R. (1995). Effects of childhood poverty on productivity later in life: Implications for public policy. *Children and Youth Services Review, 17*, 91–126.

Hilton, T. L., & Beaton, A. E. (1971). *Stability and instability in academic growth—A compilation of longitudinal data.* Washington, DC: U.S. Dept. of Health, Education and Welfare, Office of Education, Bureau of Research.

Hopkins, K. D. (1982). The unit of analysis: Group means versus individual observations. *American Education Research Journal, 19*, 5–18.

Hopper, J. L., & Mathews, J. D. (1983). *Extensions to multivariate normal models for pedigree analysis: II. Modeling the effect of shared environments in the analysis of variation in blood lead levels,* Vol. 117.

Horn, J. L. (1976). On extension analysis and its relation to correlations between variables and factor scores. *Multivariate Behavioral Research, 11*, 320–331.

Horn, J. L., & Little, K. B. (1966). Isolating change and invariance in patterns of behavior. *Multivariate Behavioral Research, 1*, 219–228.

Horn, J. L., & McArdle, J. J. (1980). Perspectives on mathematical and statistical model building (MASMOB) in research on aging. In L. Poon (Ed.), *Aging in the 1980's: Psychological issues* (pp. 503–541). Washington, DC: American Psychological Association.

Horn, J. L., & McArdle, J. J. (1992). A practical and theoretical guide to measurement invariance in aging research. *Experimental Aging Research, 18*(1), 117–144.

Horn, J. L., & Miller, W. C. (1966). Evidence of problems in estimating common factor scores. *Educational and Psychological Measurement, 26*, 617.

Hosmer, D. (1974). Maximum likelihood estimates of the parameters of a mixture of two regression lines. *Communications in Statistics, 3*, 995–1006.

Hox, J. J. (1993). Factor analysis of multilevel data. Gauging the Muthén model. In J. H. L. Oud & R. A. W. van Blokland-Vogelesang (Eds.), *Advances in longitudinal and multivariate analysis in the behavioural sciences.* Nijmegen, The Netherlands: Instituut vor Toegepaste Sociale Wetenschappen.

Hox, J. J. (1995). *Applied multilevel analysis.* Amsterdam, The Netherlands: TT-Publikaties.

Hox, J. J. (1998). Multilevel modeling: When and why. In I. Balderjahn, R. Mathar, & M. Schader (Eds.), *Classification, data analysis, and data highways* (pp. 147–154). Berlin, Germany: Springer.

Hoyle, R. (1995). *Structural equation modeling: Concepts, issues, and applications.* Thousand Oaks, CA: Sage.

Jedidi, K., Jagpal, H., & DeSarbo, W. (1997). Finite-mixture structural equation models for response-based segmentation and unobserved heterogeneity. *Marketing Science, 16*(1), 39–59.

Johnson, N. L., & Kotz, S. (1970). *Distributions in statistics: Continuous univariate distributions -1.* Boston: Houghton Mifflin.

Johnson, N. L., & Kotz, S. (1972). *Distributions in statistics: Continuous multivariate distributions.* New York: Wiley.

Jones, R. H. (1993). *Longitudinal data with serial correlation: A state-space approach.* London: Chapman & Hall.

Jöreskog, K. G. (1967). Some contributions to maximum likelihood factor analysis. *Psychometrika, 32*, 443–482.

Jöreskog, K. G. (1970). Estimation and testing of simplex models. *British Journal of Mathematical and Statistical Psychology, 23*, 121–145.

Jöreskog, K. G. (1970). A general method for analysis of covariance structures. *Biometrika, 57*, 239–251.

Jöreskog, K. G. (1971). Simultaneous factor analysis in several populations. *Psychometrika, 36*, 409–426.

Jöreskog, K. G. (1973). A general method for estimating a linear structural analysis of covariance matrices. In R. C. Atkinson, D. H. Krantz, R. D. Luce, & P. Suppes (Eds.), *Contemporary developments in mathematical psychology* (pp. 1–56). New York: Academic Press.

Jöreskog, K. G. (1977a). Statistical models and methods for analysis of longitudinal data. In D. V. Aigner & A. S. Goldberger (Eds.), *Latent variable models in the social sciences* (pp. 285–325). Amsterdam, The Netherlands: North-Holland.

Jöreskog, K. G. (1977b). Structural equation models in the social sciences: Specification, estimation and testing. In P. R. Krishnaiah (Ed.), *Applications of statistics* (pp. 265–287). Amsterdam, The Netherlands: North-Holland.

Jöreskog, K. G. (1997). LISREL. *Behaviormetrika, 24*, 95–102.

Jöreskog, K. G., & Sörbom, D. (1979). *Advances in factor analysis and structural equation models.* Cambridge, MA: Abt Associates.

Jöreskog, K. G., & Sörbom, D. (1993). *LISREL 8: Structural equation modeling with the SIMPLIS command language*. Hillsdale, NJ: Lawrence Erlbaum Associates.

Jöreskog, K. G., & Sörbom, D. (1993). *LISREL 8 user's reference guide*. Chicago: Scientific Software.

Jöreskog, K. G., & Sörbom, D. (1994). *LISREL 8 user's guide*. Chicago: Scientific Software.

Kaplan, D. (1996). An overview of concepts and issues in multilevel structural equation modeling. In H. Ernste (Ed.), *Multilevel analysis with structural equation models* (pp. 1–18). Zürich, Switzerland: Geographisches Institut ETH.

Kaplan, D., & Elliott, P. R. (1997). A didactic example of multilevel structural equation modeling applicable to the study of organizations. *Structural Equation Modeling, 4*(1), 1–24.

Kendall, M., & Stuart, A. (1977). *The advanced theory of statistics* (Vol. 3). London: Griffin.

Kennedy, P. (1992). *A guide to econometrics*. Cambridge, MA: MIT Press.

Kessler, R. C., Little, R. J., & Groves, R. M. (1995). Advances in strategies for minimizing and adjusting for survey nonresponse. *Epidemiologic Reviews, 17,* 192–204.

Kim, J.-O., & Curry, J. (1977). The treatment of missing data in multivariate analysis. *Sociological Methods and Research, 6,* 215–240.

Kreft, I. G. G., de Leeuw, J., & van der Leeden, R. (1994). Review of five analysis programs: BMDP-5V, GENMOD, HLM, ML3, VARCL. *The American Statistician, 48,* 324–335.

Kruglyak, L., & Lander, E. S. (1995). Complete multipoint sib-pair analysis of qualitative and quantitative traits. *American Journal of Human Genetics, 57,* 439–454.

Kruskal, W., & Mosteller, F. (1979a). Representative sampling: I. Non-scientific literature. *International Statistical Review, 47,* 13–24.

Kruskal, W., & Mosteller, F. (1979b). Representative sampling: II. Scientific literature, excluding statistics. *International Statistical Review, 47,* 111–127.

Kruskal, W., & Mosteller, F. (1979c). Representative sampling: III. The current statistical literature. *International Statistical Review, 47,* 245–265.

L'Ecuyer, P., & Côté, S. (1991). Implementing a random number package with splitting facilities. *ACM Transactions on Mathematical Software, 17*(1), 98–111.

Lakatos, I. (1970). Falsification and the methodology of scientific research programmes. In I. Lakatos & A. Musgrave (Eds.), *Criticism and the growth of knowledge* (pp. 91–195). Cambridge, UK: Cambridge University Press.

Lange, K., Westlake, J., & Spence, M. A. (1976). Extensions to pedigree analysis: III. Variance components by the scoring method. *Annals of Human Genetics, 39,* 485–491.

Lawley, D. N. (1943). A note on Karl Pearson's selection formulae. *Proceedings of the Royal Society of Edinburgh, 62,* 28–30.

Lee, S. Y., & Poon, W. Y. (1992). Two level analysis of covariance structures for unbalanced designs with small level one samples. *British Journal of Mathematical and Statistical Psychology, 45,* 109–123.

Lee, S. Y., & Poon, W. Y. (in press). Analysis of two-level structural equation models via EM type algorithms. *Statistica Sinica.*

Li, F., Duncan, T. E., Duncan, S. C., Harmer, P., & Acock, A. (1997). Latent variable modeling of multilevel intrinsic motivation data. *Measurement in Physical Education and Exercise Science, 1,* 223–244.

Lindenberger, U., Gilberg, R., Little, T. D., Pötter, U., Nuthmann, R., & Baltes, P. B. (1999). Sample selectivity and generalizability of the results of the Berlin Aging Study. In P. B. Baltes & K. U. Mayer (Eds.), *The Berlin Aging Study: Aging from 70 to 100* (pp. 56–82). New York: Cambridge University Press.

Lindsey, J. K. (1993). *Models for repeated measurements*. New York: Oxford University Press.

Little, R. J. A., & Rubin, D. B. (1987). *Statistical analysis with missing data*. New York: Wiley.

Little, R. J. A., & Rubin, D. B. (1989). The analysis of social science data with missing values. *Sociological Methods and Research, 18,* 292–326.

Little, R. J. A., & Schenker, N. (1995). Missing data. In G. Arminger, C. C. Clogg, & M. E. Sobel (Eds.), *Handbook of statistical modeling for the social and behavioral sciences* (pp. 39–75). New York: Plenum.

Little, T. D. (1997). Mean and covariance structures (MACS) analyses of cross-cultural data: Practical and theoretical issues. *Multivariate Behavioral Research, 32*(1), 53–76.

Little, T. D., Lindenberger, U., & Nesselroade, J. R. (in press). On selecting indicators for multivariate measurement and modeling with latent variables: When 'good' indicators are bad and 'bad' indicators are good. *Psychological Methods.*

Little, T. D., Oettingen, G., & Baltes, P. B. (1995). *The revised control, agency, and mean ends interview (CAMI): A multicultural valididty assessment using mean and covariance (MACS) analyses.* Berlin, Germany: Max Planck Institute for Human Development (Materialien aus der Bildungsforschung, 49).

Little, T. D., Oettingen, G., Stetsenko, A., & Baltes, P. B. (1995). Children's action-control beliefs and school performance: How do American children compare with German and Russian children? *Journal of Personality and Social Psychology, 69,* 686–700.

Loehlin, J. C. (1992). *Latent variable models: An introduction to factor, path, and structural analysis* (2nd ed.). Hillsdale, NJ: Lawrence Erlbaum Associates.

Lohmöller, J. B. (1989). *Latent variable path modeling with partial least squares.* Heidelberg, Germany: Physica-Verlag.

Longford, N. T. (1989). Fisher scoring algorithm for variance component analysis of data with multilevel structure. In R. D. Bock (Ed.), *Multilevel analysis of educational data.* San Diego, CA: Academic Press.

Longford, N. T. (1990). *VARCL. Software for variance component analysis of data with nested random effects (maximum likelihood).* Princeton, NJ: Educational Testing Service.

Longford, N. T. (1993). *Random coefficients models.* Oxford, UK: Clarendon.

Longford, N. T., & Muthén, B. (1992). Factor analysis for clustered populations. *Psychometrika, 57,* 581–597.

Lord, F. M., & Novick, M. R. (1968). *Statistical theories of mental test scores.* Reading, MA: Addison-Wesley.

Maas, C. J. M., & Snijders, T. A. B. (1997). *The multilevel approach to repeated measures with missing data.* Manuscript submitted for publication.

MacCallum, R. C., Kim, C., Malarkey, W. B., & Kiecolt-Glaser, J. K. (1997). Studying multivariate change using multilevel models and latent curve models. *Multivariate Behavioral Research, 32,* 215–253.

Maes, H., Neale, M., & Eaves, L. (1997). Genetic and environmental factors in relative body weight and human adiposity. *Behavior Genetics, 27,* 325–351.

Malarkey, W. B., Kiecolt-Glaser, J. K., Pearl, D., & Glaser, R. (1994). Hostile behavior during marital conflict alters pituitary and adrenal hormones. *Psychosomatic Medicine, 56,* 41–51.

Marcoulides, G. A., & Schumacker, R. E. (1996). *Advanced structural equation modeling: Issues and techniques.* Mahwah, NJ: Lawrence Erlbaum Associates.

Mardia, K. V., Kent, J. T., & Bibby, J. M. (1979). *Multivariate analysis.* New York: Academic Press.

Marsh, H. W., Byrne, B. M., & Craven, R. (1992). Overcoming problems in confirmatory factor analyses of MTMM data: The correlated uniqueness model and factorial invariance. *Multivariate Behavioral Research, 27,* 489–507.

Maxwell, S. E., & Delaney, H. D. (1990). *Designing experiments and analyzing data: A model comparison perspective.* Belmont, CA: Wadsworth.

McArdle, J. J. (1986). Latent variable growth within behavior genetic models. *Behavior Genetics, 16*(1), 163–200.

McArdle, J. J. (1988). Dynamic but structural equation modeling of repeated measures data. In J. R. Nesselroade & R. B. Cattell (Eds.), *Handbook of multivariate experimental psychology* (2nd ed., pp. 561–614). New York: Plenum.

McArdle, J. J. (1989). Structural modeling experiments using multiple growth functions. In P. Ackerman, R. Kanfer, & R. Cudeck (Eds.), *Learning and individual differences: Abilities, motivation, and methodology* (pp. 71–117). Hillsdale, NJ: Lawrence Erlbaum Associates.

McArdle, J. J. (1991a). Comments on "Latent variable models for studying differences and change." In L. M. Collins & J. L. Horn (Eds.), *Best methods for the analysis of change* (pp. 164–169). Washington, DC: American Psychological Association.

McArdle, J. J. (1991b). Structural models of developmental theory in psychology. In P. Van Geert & L. P. Mos (Eds.), *Annals of theoretical psychology* (Vol. 7, pp. 139–160). New York: Plenum.

McArdle, J. J. (1994). Structural factor analysis experiments with incomplete data. *Multivariate Behavioral Research, 29*(4), 409–454.

McArdle, J. J. (1998). Recent trends in modeling longitudinal data by latent growth curve models. In G. Marcoulides (Ed.), *New statistical models with business and economic applications* (pp. 359–406). Mahwah, NJ: Lawrence Erlbaum Associates.

McArdle, J. J., & Aber, M. S. (1990). Patterns of change within latent variable structural equation models. In A. von Eye (Ed.), *Statistical methods in longitudinal research: Principles and methods of structuring change* (pp. 151–224). New York: Academic Press.

McArdle, J. J., & Anderson, E. (1990). Latent variable growth models for research on aging. In J. E. Birren & K. W. Schaie (Eds.), *Handbook of the psychology of aging* (3rd ed., pp. 21–44). New York: Academic Press.

McArdle, J. J., & Boker, S. M. (1990). *RAMpath: A computer program for automatic path diagrams.* Hillsdale, NJ: Lawrence Erlbaum Associates.

McArdle, J. J., & Cattell, R. B. (1994). Structural equation models of factorial invariance applied to parallel proportional profiles and confactor problems. *Multivariate Behavioral Research, 29*(1), 63–113.

McArdle, J. J., & Epstein, D. (1987). Latent growth curves within developmental structural equation models. *Child Development, 58*(1), 110–133.

McArdle, J. J., & Hamagami, F. (1991). Modeling incomplete longitudinal and cross-sectional data using latent growth structural models. *Experimental Aging Research, 18*(1), 145–166.

McArdle, J. J., & Hamagami, F. (1992). Modeling incomplete longitudinal data using latent growth structural equation models. In L. Collins & J. L. Horn (Eds.), *Best methods for the analysis of change* (pp. 276–304). Washington, DC: American Psychological Association.

McArdle, J. J, & Hamagami, F. (1995, July). *A dynamic structural equation modeling analysis of the theory of fluid and crystallized intelligence.* Paper presented at the annual meeting of the American Psychological Society, New York, and the European Congress of Psychology, Athens, Greece.

McArdle, J. J., & Hamagami, F. (1996). Multilevel models from a multiple group structural equation perspective. In G. Marcoulides & R. Schumacker (Eds.), *Advanced structural equation modeling: Issues and techniques* (pp. 89–124). Mahwah, NJ: Lawrence Erlbaum Associates.

McArdle, J. J., & Hamagami, F. (1998). *Dynamic structural equation analysis of longitudinal data based on a latent difference score approach.* Manuscript submitted for publication.

McArdle, J. J., Hamagami, F., Elias, M. F., & Robbins, M. A. (1991). Structural modeling of mixed longitudinal and cross-sectional data. *Experimental Aging Research, 17,* 29–51.

McArdle, J. J., & McDonald, R. P. (1984). Some algebraic properties of the Reticular Action Model for moment structures. *The British Journal of Mathematical and Statistical Psychology, 37,* 234–251.

McArdle, J. J. & Nesselroade, J. R. (1993). Structuring data to study development and change. In S. H. Cohen & H. W. Reese (Eds.), *Life-span developmental psychology: Methodological innovations* (pp. 223–268). Hillsdale, NJ: Lawrence Erlbaum Associates.

McArdle, J. J., & Prescott, C. A. (1992). Age-based construct validation using structural equation modeling. *Experimental Aging Research, 18*(3), 87–115.

McArdle, J. J., Prescott, C. A., Hamagami, F., & Horn, J. L. (1998). A contemporary method for developmental-genetic analyses of age changes in intellectual abilities. *Developmental Neuropsychology, 14*(1), 69–114.

McArdle, J. J., & Woodcock, J. R. (1997). Expanding test-retest designs to include developmental time-lag components. *Psychological Methods, 2*(4), 403–435.

McDonald, R. P. (1978). A simple comprehensive model for the analysis of covariance structure. *British Journal of Mathematical and Statistical Psychology, 31,* 59–72.

McDonald, R. P. (1985). *Factor analysis and related methods.* Hillsdale, NJ: Lawrence Erlbaum Associates.

McDonald, R. P. (1994). The bilevel reticular action model for path analysis with latent variables. *Sociological Methods & Research, 22,* 399–413.

McDonald, R. P., & Goldstein, H. (1989). Balanced versus unbalanced designs for linear structural relations in two-level data. *British Journal of Mathematical and Statistical Psychology, 42,* 215–232.

McLeod, J. D., & Shanahan, M. J. (1993). Poverty, parenting, and children's mental health. *American Sociological Review, 58,* 351–366.

McLeod, J. D., & Shanahan, M. J. (1996). Trajectories of poverty and children's mental health. *Journal of Health and Social Behavior, 37,* 207–220.

Meehl, P. E. (1967). Theory testing in psychology and physics: A methodological paradox. *Philosophy of Science, 34,* 103–115.

Meehl, P. E. (1978). Theoretical risks and tabular asterisks: Sir Karl, Sir Ronald, and the slow progress of soft psychology. *Journal of Consulting and Clinical Psychology, 46,* 806–834.

Meehl, P. E. (1995). Bootstrap taxometrics: Solving the classification problem in psychopathology. *American Psychologist, 50*(4), 266–275.

Menard, S. (1991). *Longitudinal Research* (Vol. 76). Newbury Park, CA: Sage.

Meredith, W. (1964). Notes on factorial invariance. *Psychometrika, 29,* 177–185.

Meredith, W. (1993). Measurement invariance, factor analysis, and factorial invariance. *Psychometrika, 58,* 525–543.

Meredith, W., & Tisak, J. (1990). Latent curve analysis. *Psychometrika, 55,* 107–122.

Molenaar, P. C. M. (1994). Dynamic latent variable models in developmental psychology. In A. von Eye & C. C. Clogg (Eds.), *Latent variables analysis: Applications for developmental research* (pp. 155–180). Thousand Oaks, CA: Sage.

Morrison, D. E., & Henkel, R. E. (1970). *The significance test controversy.* Chicago: Aldine.

Mueller, R. O. (1996). *Basic principles of structural equation modeling.* New York: Springer.

Muthén, B. (1989). Latent variable modeling in heterogeneous populations. *Psychometrika, 54,* 557–585.

Muthén, B. (1991a). Analysis of longitudinal data using latent variable models with varying parameters. In L. M. Collins & J. L. Horn (Eds.), *Best methods for the analysis of change: Recent advances, unanswered questions, future directions* (pp. 1–17). Washington, DC: American Psychological Association.

Muthén, B. (1991b). Multilevel factor analysis of class and student achievement components. *Journal of Educational Measurement, 28*(4), 338–354.

Muthén, B. (1993, July). *Growth modeling within binary criteria: The case of psychiatric diagnoses with multiple criteria.* Paper presented at the Eighth European Meeting of the Psychometric Society, Barcelona, Spain.

Muthén, B. (1994). Multilevel covariance structure analysis. *Sociological Methods & Research, 22,* 376–398.

Muthén, B. O. (1997). Latent growth modeling with longitudinal and multilevel data. In A. Raftery (Ed.), *Sociological methodology* (pp. 453–480). Boston: Blackwell.

Muthén, B., Kaplan, D., & Hollis, M. (1987). On structural equation modeling with data that are not missing completely at random. *Psychometrika, 52,* 431–462.

Muthén, B., & Satorra, A. (1989). Multilevel aspects of varying parameters in structural models. In R. D. Bock (Ed.), *Multilevel analysis of educational data* (pp. 87–99). San Diego, CA: Academic Press.

Muthén, B., & Satorra, A. (1995). Complex sample data in structural equation modeling. In P. Marsden (Ed.), *Sociological methodology* (pp. 267–316). Cambridge, MA: Blackwell.

Nance, W. E., & Neale, M. C. (1989). Partitioned twin analysis: A power study. *Behavior Genetics, 19,* 143–150.

Neale, M. C. (1991). *Mx: Statistical modeling.* Richmond, VA: Department of Human Genetics.

Neale, M. C. (1993). *Mx: Statistical modeling* [program manual]. Richmond, VA: Virginia Commonwealth University, Medical College of Virginia.

Neale, M. C. (1997). *Mx: Statistical modeling.* Box 980126 MCV, Richmond, VA 23298, 4th ed.

Neale, M. C., & Cardon, L. R. (1992). *Methodology for genetic studies of twins and families.* London: Kluwer.

Nesselroade, J. R. (1983). Temporal selection and factor invariance in the study of development and change. In D. L. Featherman & R. M. Lerner (Eds.), *Life-span development and behavior* (Vol. 5, pp. 59–87). New York: Academic Press.

Nesselroade, J. R. (1991). Interindividual differences in intraindividual change. In L. M. Collins & J. L. Horn (Eds.), *Best methods for the analysis of change* (pp. 92–105). Washington, DC: American Psychological Association.

Nesselroade, J. R., & Baltes, P. B. (1979). *Longitudinal research in the study of behavior and development.* New York: Academic Press.

Oettingen, G., Little, T. D., Lindenberger, U., & Baltes, P. B. (1994). Causality, agency, and control beliefs in East and West Berlin children: A natural experiment on the role of context. *Journal of Personality and Social Psychology, 66,* 579–595.

Oh, H. L., & Scheuren, F. J. (1983). Weighting adjustment for unit non-response. In W. G. Madow, I. Olkin, & D. B. Rubin (Eds.), *Incomplete data in sample surveys: Vol. 2. Theory and bibliographies* (pp. 143–184). New York: Academic Press.

Palmer, R. F., Graham, J. W., White, E. L., & Hansen, W. B. (in press). Applying multilevel analytic strategies in adolescent substance use prevention research. *Preventive Medicine.*

Panel on Incomplete Data. (1983). Part I: Report. In W. G. Madow, I. Olkin, & D. B. Rubin (Eds.), *Incomplete data in sample surveys: Vol. 1. Report and case studies* (pp. 3–106). New York: Academic Press.

Pankratz, A. (1991). *Forecasting with dynamic regression models.* New York: Wiley.

Parker, J., & Asher, S. (1987). Peer acceptance and later personal adjustment. *Psychological Bulletin, 102,* 357–389.

Pearson, K. (1903). Mathematical contributions to the theory of evolution: XI. On the influence of natural selection on the variability and correlation of organs. *Philosophical Transactions of the Royal Society of London (Series A), 200,* 1–66.

Pedhazur, E. J. (1977). Coding subjects in repeated measures designs. *Psychological Bulletin, 84,* 298–305.

Pentz, M. A., Dwyer, J. H., MacKinnon, D. P., Flay, B. R., Hansen, W. B., Wang, E. J., & Johnson, C. A. (1989). A multicommunity trial for primary prevention of adolescent drug use. *Journal of American Medical Association, 261,* 3259–3266.

Rao, C. R. (1958). Some statistical methods for comparison of growth curves. *Biometrics, 14,* 1–17.

Rasbash, J., Yang, M., Woodhouse, G., & Goldstein, H. (1995). *Mln: Command reference guide.* London: Institute of Education.

Raudenbush, S. W., & Bryk, A. S. (1986). A hierarchical model for studying school effects. *Sociology of Education, 59,* 1–17.

Raykov, T. (1992). Structural models for studying correlates and predictors of change. *Australian Journal of Psychology, 44,* 101–112.

Raykov, T. (1995). Multivariate structural modeling of plasticity in fluid intelligence of aged adults. *Multivariate Behavioral Research, 30,* 255–287.

Raykov, T. (1996). Plasticity in fluid intelligence of older adults: An individual latent growth curve modeling application. *Structural Equation Modeling, 3,* 248–265.

Raykov, T. (1997a). Disentangling intervention and temporal effects in longitudinal designs using latent curve analysis. *Biometrical Journal, 39,* 239–259.

Raykov, T. (1997b). Estimation of composite reliability for congeneric measures. *Applied Psychological Measurement, 21,* 173–184.

Raykov, T. (1997c). Growth curve analysis of ability means and variances in measures of fluid intelligence of older adults. *Structural Equation Modeling, 4,* 283–319.

Raykov, T. (1997d). Simultaneous study of group and individual latent longitudinal change patterns using structural equation modeling. *Structural Equation Modeling, 4,* 212–236.

Raykov, T. (in press). "Satisfying a simplex structure is simpler than it should be": A latent curve analysis revisit. *Multivariate Behavioral Research.*

Read, T. R. C., & Cressie, N. A. C. (1988). *Goodness-of-fit statistics for discrete multivariate data.* New York: Springer.

Rogosa, D. R. (1987). Myths about longitudinal research. In K. W. Schaie, R. T. Campbell, W. M. Meredith, & S. C. Rawlings (Eds.), *Methodological issues in aging research* (pp. 171–209). New York: Springer.

Rogosa, D. R. (1996). Myths and methods: Myths about longitudinal research plus supplemental questions. In J. M. Gottman (Ed.), *The analysis of change* (pp. 3–66). Mahwah, NJ: Lawrence Erlbaum Associates.

Rogosa, D., Brandt, D., & Zimowski, M. (1982). A growth curve approach to the measurement of change. *Psychological Bulletin, 92,* 726–748.

Rogosa, D. R., & Saner, H. (1995). Longitudinal data analysis examples with random coefficient models. *Journal of Educational & Behavioral Statistics, 20*(2), 149–170.

Rogosa, D. R., & Willett, J. B. (1985a). Satisfying a simplex structure is simpler than it should be. *Journal of Educational Statistics, 10,* 99–107.

Rogosa, D. R., & Willett, J. B. (1985b). Understanding correlates of change by modeling individual differences in growth. *Psychometrika, 50,* 203–228.

Roth, P. L. (1994). Missing data: A conceptual view for applied psychologists. *Personnel Psychology, 47,* 537–560.

Rovine, M. J. (1994). Latent variable models and missing data analysis. In A. von Eye & C. C. Clogg (Eds.), *Latent variable analysis: Applications for developmental research.* Thousand Oaks, CA: Sage.

Rovine, M. J., & Delaney, M. (1991). Missing data estimation in developmental research. In A. von Eye (Ed.), *Statistical methods in longitudinal research* (pp. 35–79). Cambridge, MA: Academic Press.

Rubin, D. B. (1976). Inference and missing data. *Biometrika, 61,* 581–592.

Rubin, D. B. (1987). *Multiple imputation for nonresponse in surveys.* New York: Wiley.

Saris, W. E., de Pijper, W. M., & Mulder, J. (1978). Optimal procedures for the estimation of factor scores. *Sociological Methods and Research, 7,* 85–106.

Schafer, J. L. (1991). *Algorithms for multiple imputation and posterior simulation from incomplete multivariate data with ignorable nonresponse.* Unpublished doctoral dissertation, Harvard University.

Schafer, J. L. (1997). *Analysis of incomplete multivariate data.* London: Chapman & Hall.

280

Scher, A., Young, A. C., & Meredith, W. M. (1960). Factor analysis of the electrocardiograph. *Circulation Research, 8,* 519–526.

Schmidt, F. L. (1966). Statistical significance testing and cumulative knowledge in psychology: Implications for training of researchers. *Psychological Methods, 1,* 115–129.

Schnabel, K. (1996). Latent difference models as alternatives to modeling residuals of cross-lagged effects. In U. Engel & J. Reinecke (Eds.), *Analysis of change: Advanced techniques in panel data analysis* (pp. 253–278). Berlin, Germany: de Gruyter.

Schork, N., Allison, D., & Thiel, B. (1996). Mixture distributions in human genetics research. *Statistical Methods in Medical Research, 5,* 155–178.

Schumacker, R. E., & Lomax, R. G. (1996). *A beginner's guide to structural equation modeling.* Mahwah, NJ: Lawrence Erlbaum Associates.

Schumacker, R., & Marcoulides, G. (1998). *Interaction and nonlinear effects in structural equation modeling.* Mahwah, NJ: Lawrence Erlbaum Associates.

Self, S. G., & Liang, K.-Y. (1987). Asymptotic properties of maximum likelihood estimators and likelihood ratio tests under nonstandard conditions. *Journal of the American Statistical Association, 82,* 605–610.

Sham, P. (1997). *Statistics in human genetics.* New York: Wiley.

Shanahan, M. J., Brooks, J., & Davey, A. (1997). *Pathways of poverty and children's well-being in dynamic perspective: New findings.* Paper presented at the meeting of the American Sociological Association, Toronto.

Shapiro, A. (1988). Towards a unified theory of inequality constrained testing in multivariate analysis. *International Statistical Review, 56,* 49–62.

Smith, C. J., Holt, D., & Smith, T. M. F. (1989). *Analysis of complex surveys.* New York: Wiley.

Snijders, T. A. B. (1996). Analysis of longitudinal data using hierarchical linear model. *Quality and Quantity, 30,* 405–426.

Snijders, T. A. B., & Bosker, R. (1994). Modeled variance in two-level models. *Sociological Methods & Research, 22,* 342–363.

Sörbom, D. (1974). A general method for studying differences in factor means and factor structure between groups. *British Journal of Mathematical and Statistical Psychology, 27,* 229–239.

Sörbom, D. (1978). An alternative to the methodology for analysis of covariance. *Psychometrika, 43,* 381–396.

Steiger, J. H. (1989). *EzPATH: A supplementary module for SYSTAT and SYGRAPH.* Evanston, IL: Systat.

Steyer, R., & Eid, M. (1993). *Messen und Testen* [Measurement and testing]. Berlin, Germany: Springer.

Steyer, R., Eid, M., & Schwenkmezger, P. (1997). Modeling true intraindividual change: True change as a latent variable. *Methods of Psychological Research-Online, 2,* 21–33. Available at http://www.hsp.de/MPR/

Steyer, R., Ferring, D., & Schmitt, M. (1992). States and traits in psychological assessment. *European Journal of Psychological Assessment, 8,* 79–98.

Stoolmiller, M. (1994). Antisocial behavior, delinquent peer association, and unsupervised wandering for boys: Growth and change from childhood to early adolescence. *Multivariate Behavioral Research, 29,* 263–288.

"Student." (1907). The probable error of a mean. *Biometrika, 6,* 1–25.

Tanner, J. M. (1960). *Human growth.* New York: Pergamon.

Tanner, M. A., & Wong, W. H. (1987). The calculation of posterior distributions by data augmentation (with discussion). *Journal of the American Statistical Association, 82,* 528–550.

Tate, R. L., & Wongbundhit, Y. (1983). Random versus nonrandom coefficient models for multilevel analysis. *Journal of Educational Statistics, 8,* 103–120.

Tisak, J., & Meredith, W. (1990). Descriptive and associative developmental models. In A. von Eye (Ed.), *Statistical methods in longitudinal research* (pp. 387–406). New York: Academic Press.

Tucker, L. R. (1958). Determination of parameters of a functional relation by factor analysis. *Psychometrika, 23,* 19–23.

van Peet, A. A. J. (1992). *De potentieeltheorie van intelligentie* [The potentiality theory of intelligence]. Unpublished doctoral dissertation, University of Amsterdam.

Velicer, W. F., Martin, R. A., & Collins, L. M. (1996). Latent transition analysis for longitudinal data. *Addiction, 91*(Suppl.), S197–S209.

Verhulst, F. C., Akkerhuis, G. W., & Althaus, M. (1985). Mental health in Dutch children: I. Across-cultural comparison. *Acta Psychiatrica Scandinavica, 72*(323), 1–108.

Verleye, G. (1996). *Missing at random data problems in attitude measurement using maximum likelihood structural equation modeling.* Unpublished doctoral dissertation, Frije Universiteit Brussels, Belgium.

Wackwitz, J. H., & Horn, J. L. (1971). On obtaining the best estimates of factor scores. *Multivariate Behavioral Research, 6,* 389–408.

Walker, A. J., Acock, A. C., Bowman, S. R., & Li, F. (1996). Amount of care given and caregiving satisfaction: A latent growth curve analysis. *Journal of Gerontology: Psychological Sciences, 51B,* 130–142.

Walker, R. (1994). *Poverty dynamics: Issues and examples.* Brookfield, VT: Ashgate.

Werner, E. E. (1985). Stress and protective factors in children's lives. In A. R. Nicol (Ed.), *Longitudinal studies in child psychology and psychiatry* (pp. 335–355). New York: Wiley.

Wilks, S. S. (1932). Moments and distributions of estimates of population parameters from fragmentary samples. *Annals of Mathematical Statistics, 3,* 163–195.

Willet, J. B., & Sayer, A. G. (1994). Using covariance structure analysis to detect correlates and predictors of individual change over time. *Psychological Bulletin, 116,* 363–381.

Willet, J. B., & Sayer, A. G. (1996). Cross-domain analyses of change over time: Combining growth modeling and covariance structure analysis. In G. A. Marcoulides & R. E. Schumacker (Eds.), *Advanced structural equation modeling: Issues and techniques* (pp. 125–157). Mahwah, NJ: Lawrence Erlbaum Associates.

Wohwill, J. F. (1973). *The study of behavioral development.* New York: Academic Press.

Woodhouse, G. (1995). *A guide to MLn for new users.* London: University of London, Institute of Education.

Wothke, W. (1993). Nonpositive definite matrices in structural modeling. In K. A. Bollen & J. S. Long (Eds.), *Testing structural equation models* (pp. 256–293). Newbury Park, CA: Sage.

Wothke, W. (1996). Models for multitrait-multimethod matrix analysis. In G. A. Marcoulides & R. E. Schumacker (Eds.), *Advanced structural equation modeling: Issues and techniques* (pp. 7–56). Mahwah, NJ: Lawrence Erlbaum Associates.

Wu, L. (1996). Effects of family structure and income on risks of premarital birth. *American Sociological Review, 61,* 386–406.

Young, C. H., Savola, K. L., & Phelps, E. (1991). *Inventory of longitudinal studies in the social sciences.* Newbury Park, CA: Sage.

Yuan, K.-H., & Bentler, P. M. (1997). Mean and covariance structural analysis: Theoretical and practical improvements. *Journal of the American Statistical Association, 92,* 767–774.

Yung, Y.-F. (1997). Finite mixtures in confirmatory factor analysis models. *Psychometrika, 62,* 297–330.

Author Index

Subject Index

About the Authors

James L. Arbuckle is Associate Professor in the Psychology Department at Temple University. His research interests include the use of structural equation modeling with incomplete, ordinal, and censored data. He is a member of the editorial board of the journal, *Structural Equation Modeling*, and the author of the structural modeling program, Amos.

Jürgen Baumert is a codirector at the Max Planck Institute for Human Development and director of the Center for Educational Research. Noted research projects that he has guided include the Study Educational Processes and Psycho-Social Development in Childhood and Adolescence; the Third International Mathematics and Science Study, Populations 2 and 3; and the Program for International Student Assessment (a project of the Organization for Economic Cooperation and Development). He is a member of the Governing Board of the German Research Foundation.

Richard Q. Bell is Professor Emeritus in the Department of Psychology at the University of Virginia where he has worked since 1974. Bell's substantive research includes a book and a very frequently cited article on the "effects of children on adults and parents," which produced a fundamental change in the direction of research on socialization. Bell's methodological work includes seminal articles advocating the statistical reconstruction of long-lasting developmental phenomena from shorter observational segments, termed the convergence approach. This work inspired several topics in the present volume.

Peter M. Bentler is Professor of Psychology at the University of California, Los Angeles. He is past president of the Psychometric Society, the Society of Multivariate Experimental Psychology, and American Psychological Association's Division 5, and has received several awards for distinguished contributions on psychometrics, multivariate statistics, drug and alcohol abuse, and structural equation models. Bentler is also chief executive officer of Multivariate Software, Inc., distributors of the EQS Structural Equations Program (http://www.mvsoft.com).

Chih-Ping Chou is an Assistant Professor of Research in the Department of Preventive Medicine, University of Southern California. His research interests include the methodological and statistical issues in substance use prevention and treatment research. In 1995, he received the Research Scientist Development Award from the National Institute on Drug Abuse to investigate the applications of advanced statistical techniques for prevention research.

Linda M. Collins is Professor of Human Development and director of The Methodology Center, College of Health and Human Development, Pennsylvania State University. She is also director of the Center for the Study of Prevention through Innovative Methodology. She is a past president of the Society of Multivariate Experimental Psychology and has won the Cattell Award for outstanding contributions to multivariate psychology. Her research interests include prevention research, methodology for longitudinal research, measurement, and categorical latent variable models.

John W. Graham is Professor of Biobehavioral Health in the College of Health and Human Development at Penn State University. He is also associate director of the Center for the Study of Prevention through Innovative Methodology, funded by the United States National Institute on Drug Abuse. He is a member of the Society of Multivariate Experimental Psychology and the Society for Prevention Research. His research interests include social influence and health-related behavior in adolescents and adults and development and application of research methodology, including missing data analysis, structural equation modeling, and detection/correction of self-report biases.

Scott M. Hofer is a research associate at the Center for Developmental and Health Genetics at Pennsylvania State University. His research interests include individual differences in life-span development and aging, personality and cognitive abilities, and multivariate methodology.

Joop J. Hox is Professor of Social Sciences at Utrecht University and Professor of Methodology at the University of Amsterdam. He has taught extensively on topics in methodology and statistics, both domestically and internationally. A former Fulbright scholar, he is chair of the Netherlands Organization for Social-Methodological Research and coeditor of the Dutch *Journal of Educational Studies*. His research interests concern survey methodology, data quality, and complex data analysis with multilevel and structural equation techniques.

Stephanie L. Hyatt is a doctoral student in Human Development and Family Studies at Pennsylvania State University. Her Master's thesis examined the relationship between the onset of adolescent substance use and parental permissiveness toward alcohol use, and also introduced data augmentation as a method for getting standard errors of parameter estimates in latent transition analysis. Her main research interest is in longitudinal methods, including latent transition analysis and growth curve modeling. Hyatt's substantive interests include the onset of substance use and deviant behaviors in adolescence, change in academic motivation during adolescence, and the transition to adulthood.

Cheongtag Kim is an Assistant Professor of Psychology at Seoul National University, Korea. His main research interest is methodology in psychology, including the areas of covariance-structure modeling and multilevel modeling. In particular, his work has investigated methods of incorporating individual differences into models of cognitive processes.

Ulman Lindenberger is a research scientist at the Max Planck Institute for Human Development in Berlin, Germany. His main research interest is in life-span cognitive development, with a special emphasis on the structure, measurement, composition, and development of intellectual abilities across the life span, the relationship between sensory and cognitive development, and issues of cognitive control. He also has an interest in development methodology.

Todd D. Little is an Assistant Professor of Psychology at Yale University. Prior to joining the Faculty of Psychology at Yale, he was a research scientist for 7 years in the Center for Psychology and Human Development at the Max Planck Institute for Human Development in Berlin, Germany. In the Center, he was coprincipal investigator (with Paul Baltes and Gabriele Oettingen) on the Action Control and Child Development project and the Self-Regulation and Social Relations project (with Lothar Krappmann). In addition to his substantive work, he has conducted international workshops on structural equation modeling.

Robert C. MacCallum is a Professor of Psychology at Ohio State University, with joint appointments in the School of Public Health and the Institute for Behavior Medicine Research. He is Associate Editor of *Multivariate Behavioral Research* and Secretary-Treasurer of the Society of Multivariate Experimental Psychology. His research interests involve methods for studying the structure in correlational data and for modeling change over time, and the application of those methods in the study of effects of stress on physical and psychological well-being.

Heiner Maier is a research scientist at the Max Planck Institute for Demographic Research in Rostock, Germany. His research interests include social and psychological determinants of mortality and survival in old age, as well as research methods of life-span developmental psychology.

John J. McArdle is Professor of Quantitative Methods in the Department of Psychology at the University of Virginia. Most of his methodological research has dealt with the use of linear structural equation models for the analysis of growth and change, especially the use of dynamics and latent growth models. His substantive work has included long-term longitudinal studies of cognitive health across the life span, and longitudinal studies of student achievements in the college years. He has won the R. B. Cattell award for distinguished multivariate research (1987), served as president of the Society of Multivariate Experimental Psychology (1992–1993), and is the president of the Federation of Behavioral, Psychological, and Cognitive Sciences (1997–1999).

Michael C. Neale is an Associate Professor at Virginia Commonwealth University and the Virginia Institute of Psychiatric and Behavioral Genetics. He received his PhD in Psychology from the Institute of Psychiatry, London. In 1986, he joined the Department of Human Genetics at Virginia Commonwealth University; in 1992, he moved to the Department of Psychiatry. He is known as the developer of the structural equation modeling program, Mx (http://griffin.vcu.edu/mx). He has contributed extensively to methodology for the analysis of genetically informative data, and has authored numerous articles, chapters, and books.

Ivailo Partchev is an Associate Professor of Sociology and Statistics at the University of Sofia, where he teaches courses on modeling and statistics. His research interests focus on statistical modeling and analysis, especially multivariate and multilevel techniques, sampling and variance estimation, psychometrics, public opinion research, and electoral research. In addition, he has participated in numerous national and international research projects as a consultant and research fellow.

Mary Ann Pentz is Director of the Center for Prevention Policy Research and faculty in the Department of Preventive Medicine at the University of Southern California. Her research has focused on community and policy approaches to tobacco, alcohol, and drug abuse prevention in youths. She has published widely in psychology, public health, and medical journals on the use of multicomponent approaches to community-based prevention that include mass media. She serves on the ONDCP's Campaign Design Expert panel to design the new antidrug abuse media campaign.

Tenko Raykov is a Professor of Psychology at Fordham University. Previously, he taught at the universities of Melbourne and Sydney. His research interests are statistical modeling of behavioral phenomena, particularly structural equation modeling; longitudinal data analysis and multivariate statistics; and developmental psychology and cognitive aging.

Kai Uwe Schnabel is a research scientist in the Center for Educational Research at the Max Planck Institute for Human Development in Berlin, Germany. In 1998, he spent a year as Visiting Professor at the University of Michigan. Together with Jürgen Baumert and Olaf Köller, he is co-investigator on a large-scale longitudinal research project on German adolescents' development. Besides his work on motivational development in early adolescence and the transition from school to vocational training, he studies multilevel modeling and its use for latent growth curve analysis.

Michael J. Shanahan is an Assistant Professor of Human Development and Family Studies, Adjunct Professor of Sociology, and Research Affiliate of the Population Research Institute and Methodology Center at Pennsylvania State University. He has also served as Visiting Professor of Developmental Psychology at the Friedrich

Schiller University of Jena, Germany (1997), and as a Fellow at the Center for Advanced Study in the Behavioral Sciences (1998–99). Research interests include developmental models of children in poverty, adolescent work experiences and the transition to adulthood, and the role of adolescent planful competence in the life course. He is coeditor (with Jonathan Tudge and Jaan Valsiner) of *Comparisons in Human Development* (1997, Cambridge University Press).

Rolf Steyer is a Professor of Methodology and Evaluation Research with the Institute of Psychology at the University of Jena. He is Secretary General of the Executive Committee of the European Association of Psychological Assessment and is coeditor of the internet journal, *Methods of Psychological Research-Online*. His research interests include causality, measurement, latent state-trait models, mood states, assessing change, and evaluation research in health care and in teaching.

Keith F. Widaman is Professor of Psychology at the University of California, Riverside. He received his PhD degree in Developmental Psychology from Ohio State University in 1982. He has published extensively on cognitive processing models underlying mental abilities, the structure and development of adaptive behaviors by persons with mental retardation, and statistical topics in multivariate analysis, including factor analysis. He is a Fellow of the American Psychological Association and is a Past President of the Society of Multivariate Experimental Psychology. In 1992, he received the Raymond B. Cattell Award from the Society of Multivariate Experimental Psychology, for early career achievements in multivariate experimental psychology. In 1994, he received the Jeffrey S. Tanaka Award for the best article published in Multivariate Behavioral Research during the preceding year.

Werner Wothke is founder and president of SmallWaters Corporation, developer and publisher of Amos. He is an experienced structural equation modeler with both applied and methodological publications. He holds a PhD in Behavioral Sciences from the University of Chicago. His professional interests are in modern, computation intensive statistics and in how to make these new approaches easy enough to use to be of practical value.